A CELEBRATION OF POETS

ILLINOIS/INDIANA

GRADES 4-12

FALL 2011

creativeCOMMUNICATION
A CELEBRATION OF TODAY'S WRITERS

A CELEBRATION OF POETS
ILLINOIS/INDIANA
GRADES 4-12
FALL 2011

AN ANTHOLOGY COMPILED BY CREATIVE COMMUNICATION, INC.

Published by:

creativeCOMMUNICATION
A CELEBRATION OF TODAY'S WRITERS

PO BOX 303 · SMITHFIELD, UTAH 84335
TEL. 435-713-4411 · WWW.POETICPOWER.COM

Authors are responsible for the originality of the writing submitted.

ISBN: 978-1-60050-479-2

FOREWORD

In January of this year, I was watching the Miss America Pageant. I thought of all the accomplishments that culminate in this one ending competition. These outstanding women had decided what they wanted, paid the price and now were reaping the rewards of their hard work. While watching the pageant, the finalists were on stage and a few of their accomplishments were written across the screen. For Miss Arizona, Jennifer Sedler (who ended as 3rd runner-up), one of her accomplishments was having a poem published in 5th grade. In checking our records, it was our company, Creative Communication, that published her poem "Hawaiian Seas" in the Fall of 2002.

Jennifer wrote to us about the experience of being published:

> "I had a poem published by Creative Communication in 5th grade, and I will never forget how special and inspired it made me feel. I have since gone on to win numerous essay contests, many which earned me scholarship money for college, and I may have never believed in myself if it wasn't for Creative Communication. And as Miss Arizona, I write pages and pages of creatively-written updates for all of my followers. Now of course I still take time on my own to read, study, and write poetry. When you choose to be an active learner and writer, I think you will find, just as I did, that truly anything is possible."

When a poet enters our writing contest, they are students like everyone else. As they move on in life, talents are developed. A 5th grade student becomes Miss Arizona. Another student, novelist Angela Bishop, also wrote to me the following:

> "My name is Angela Bishop, and almost ten years ago you selected one of my poems to be published in the Southern edition of your book. I was 15 and it was the highlight of my young life. Although it has been nearly a decade, I just wanted to finally express the thanks I have felt all these years. I cannot thank you enough for accepting my work and publishing it. I have been writing since I was a child and have continued to write. I am currently working on my second novel. So, thank you, thank you, for the confidence you unknowingly gave me in 1999. I plan to keep writing for as long as I possibly can. Your poetry contest is a wonderful thing, and you open a window for tomorrow's great writers to find their way through and gain the confidence in their work. Keep it going, you are making dreams into realities."

To both Jennifer and Angela and the students in this anthology, I am glad that we are here for you. We helped you in creating an accomplishment that you can be proud of and add to your resume. When students wonder if they should enter a contest, I give a strong affirmative. You may not be accepted to be published, but if you don't enter, there isn't a chance of being published or being a Top Ten winner. Sometimes you have to take a risk and enter a contest. It may change your life. Just ask Jennifer and Angela.

I hope you enjoy the poems that are included in this anthology. We are pleased to help provide the spark that makes lifelong writers. Each of these students took a risk in entering and has the potential to achieve great things in their lives. Good luck.

Tom Worthen, Ph.D.
Editor

WRITING CONTESTS!

Enter our next POETRY contest!
Enter our next ESSAY contest!

Why should I enter?

Win prizes and get published! Each year thousands of dollars in prizes are awarded throughout North America. The top writers in each division receive a monetary award and a free book that includes their published poem or essay. Entries of merit are also selected to be published in our anthology.

Who may enter?

There are four divisions in the poetry contest. The poetry divisions are grades K-3, 4-6, 7-9, and 10-12. There are three divisions in the essay contest. The essay divisions are grades 3-6, 7-9, and 10-12.

What is needed to enter the contest?

To enter the poetry contest send in one original poem, 21 lines or less. To enter the essay contest send in one original non-fiction essay, 250 words or less, on any topic. Please submit each poem and essay with a title, and the following information clearly printed: the writer's name, current grade, home address (optional), school name, school address, teacher's name and teacher's email address (optional). Contact information will only be used to provide information about the contest. For complete contest information go to www.poeticpower.com.

How do I enter?

Enter a poem online at:
www.poeticpower.com
or
Mail your poem to:
    Poetry Contest
    PO Box 303
    Smithfield UT 84335

Enter an essay online at:
www.poeticpower.com
or
Mail your essay to:
    Essay Contest
    PO Box 303
    Smithfield UT 84335

When is the deadline?

Poetry contest deadlines are August 16th, December 6th and April 9th. Essay contest deadlines are July 19th, October 18th and February 19th. Students can enter one poem and one essay for each spring, summer, and fall contest deadline.

Are there benefits for my school?

Yes. We award $12,500 each year in grants to help with Language Arts programs. Schools qualify to apply for a grant by having 15 or more accepted entries.

Are there benefits for my teacher?

Yes. Teachers with five or more students published receive a free anthology that includes their students' writing.

For more information please go to our website at **www.poeticpower.com**, email us at editor@poeticpower.com or call 435-713-4411.

TABLE OF CONTENTS

Fall 2011
Poetic Achievement
Honor Schools

Teachers who had fifteen or more poets accepted to be published

The following schools are recognized as receiving a "Poetic Achievement Award." This award is given to schools who have a large number of entries of which over fifty percent are accepted for publication. With hundreds of schools entering our contest, only a small percent of these schools are honored with this award. The purpose of this award is to recognize schools with excellent Language Arts programs. This award qualifies these schools to receive a complimentary copy of this anthology. In addition, these schools are eligible to apply for a Creative Communication Language Arts Grant. Grants of two hundred and fifty dollars each are awarded to further develop writing in our schools.

Alexandria Monroe Intermediate School
Alexandria, IN
Mark Bartmas*

Benton Central Jr/Sr High School
Oxford, IN
Sandy Herre*

Bethel Lutheran School
Morton, IL
Renata Anderson*

Boylan Catholic High School
Rockford, IL
Sarah Scherer *

Carmi-White County High School
Carmi, IL
Erin Pennington*

Central Elementary School
Riverside, IL
Tara Kristoff*

Churubusco Elementary School
Churubusco, IN
Julie Mast*
Patricia Naragon
Mary Ray
Kileen Williams

Concordia Lutheran School
Fort Wayne, IN
Chris Murphy*

Copeland Manor Elementary School
Libertyville, IL
Ann Livermore*

Dee Mack Intermediate School
Deer Creek, IL
Meghan Frerichs
Doris Lee
Mrs. Nightingale
Fallan O'Neal

DeMotte Christian School
DeMotte, IN
Jayne Boer*

Divine Infant Jesus School
Westchester, IL
Renata Dargan
Colleen Doucet
Joanne Macpherson

Dunlap Valley Middle School
Dunlap, IL
Maureen Fandel
Katie Starnes*

Edison Elementary School
Stickney, IL
Karen Hybl*
Travis Olson*

Elverado High School
Elkville, IL
Jeanne Korando
Mr. Smith

Emmanuel-St Michael Lutheran School
Fort Wayne, IN
Connie Hoyer*

Florence Nightingale Elementary School
Chicago, IL
Brandon Barr*

Forreston Grade School
Forreston, IL
Sharon Winterhalter*

Frank H Hammond Elementary School
Munster, IN
Carol Schaap*

Galileo Scholastic Academy
Chicago, IL
Linda Deutsch*

Hannah Beardsley Middle School
Crystal Lake, IL
Lynette Fennell*

Hawthorne Elementary School
Elmhurst, IL
Geri Sorrentino*

Highland Hills Middle School
Georgetown, IN
Susan May*

Highlands Elementary School
Naperville, IL
Brian Horner*

Immaculate Conception School
Morris, IL
Loreen R. Vlk*

International School of Indiana
Indianapolis, IN
Emily Miller*

John Adams High School
South Bend, IN
Rebecca Folk*
Ann Raymer

Knox Community Middle School
Knox, IN
Kathleen Jerrell*

Liberty Jr High School
New Lenox, IL
Elise Fannin*

Lisle High School
Lisle, IL
Courtney Multhaupt*
David Sally

Manchester Intermediate School
Laketon, IN
Denny Craft*

Marion High School
Marion, IL
Melanie Poole*

North Knox West Intermediate/Elementary School
Bruceville, IN
Kathy Stephens*

Northern Heights Elementary School
Columbia City, IN
Amber Bretzman*
Todd Geiger
Michelle Simmons*

Northlawn Jr High School
Streator, IL
Nancy K. Hepner*

Our Lady of Peace School
Darien, IL
Mary Beth Calomino*

Our Shepherd Lutheran School
Avon, IN
Margo Martin*

Peck Elementary School
Chicago, IL
Kathe Myers*

Perry Central Elementary School
Leopold, IN
Darlene Davis
Rebecca Hubert*
Angela Shelby

Pierce Middle School
Merrillville, IN
Mrs. Shawn Johnson*
Danyale Kelly
Marcie Mathis

Ranch View Elementary School
Naperville, IL
Laura Atseff*

Red Bud Elementary School
Red Bud, IL
Kim Straub*

Rochester Jr High School
Rochester, IL
Suzanne Pettyjohn*

Sacred Heart School
Lombard, IL
Nancy O'Reilly*

Schaumburg High School
Schaumburg, IL
Kelly Lagioia
Darrell Robin
Nancy Sack

St Angela School
Chicago, IL
Sarah Miller*
Erica Sypek*

St Matthew School
Champaign, IL
Ann Case*
Mrs. Hoerner*
Kathleen Marietta
Jill Meade

St Michael School
Brookville, IN
Amy Cowen
Krista McKinney
Carey Weiler

Stanley Clark School
South Bend, IN
Gayla Vukcevich*
David Walsh*

Stratford Middle School
Bloomingdale, IL
Fotini Abou*

The Orchard School
Indianapolis, IN
Julie Berry*
Justin Burris
Mrs. Gelhausen
Terri Wallace

Thomas Middle School
Arlington Heights, IL
Jodi Cyr*
Karen Field
Susan Ward*

Tri-West Middle School
Lizton, IN
Patty Jensen*

Van Rensselaer Elementary School
Rensselaer, IN
Shannon Anderson*
Mrs. Bryant
Chastidy Chapman
Mrs. Cripe
Jessica Davis
Mrs. DelPrincipe
Mrs. Deno
Mrs. Dobson
Mrs. Hurd
Beth Korniak
Virginia Leichty
Miss Miller
Kelle Rowan
Mrs. Slade
Tim Taylor
Mrs. Wilder
Mrs. Wuethrich
Mr. Wynn
Denise Yentes

Walker Elementary School
Evanston, IL
Kelly Oldfield
Konstantina Panagiotidis*
Freda Wood-Livingston*

Washington Township Elementary School
Valparaiso, IN
Beverly Zborowski*

West Salem Grade School
West Salem, IL
LaVada Meeks*

Wethersfield Jr/Sr High School
Kewanee, IL
Joanne Imsland
Tammy Jackson*

William Fremd High School
Palatine, IL
Marilyn Berdick
Jaclyn DeRose
Gina Enk
Judy Klingner
Eric Schaefer

Zapata Academy
Chicago, IL
Stephanie Kleinfelder
Eliza Ramirez
Juan Sanchez
Mrs. Suarez Del Real

Language Arts Grant Recipients 2011-2012

After receiving a "Poetic Achievement Award" schools are encouraged to apply for a Creative Communication Language Arts Grant. The following is a list of schools who received a two hundred and fifty dollar grant for the 2011-2012 school year.

Annapolis Royal Regional Academy, Annapolis Royal, NS
Bear Creek Elementary School, Monument, CO
Bellarmine Preparatory School, Tacoma, WA
Birchwood School, Cleveland, OH
Bluffton Middle School, Bluffton, SC
Brookville Intermediate School, Brookville, OH
Butler High School, Augusta, GA
Carmi-White County High School, Carmi, IL
Classical Studies Academy, Bridgeport, CT
Coffee County Central High School, Manchester, TN
Country Hills Elementary School, Coral Springs, FL
Coyote Valley Elementary School, Middletown, CA
Emmanuel-St Michael Lutheran School, Fort Wayne, IN
Excelsior Academy, Tooele, UT
Great Meadows Middle School, Great Meadows, NJ
Holy Cross High School, Delran, NJ
Kootenay Christian Academy, Cranbrook, BC
LaBrae Middle School, Leavittsburg, OH
Ladoga Elementary School, Ladoga, IN
Mater Dei High School, Evansville, IN
Palmer Catholic Academy, Ponte Vedra Beach, FL
Pine View School, Osprey, FL
Plato High School, Plato, MO
Rivelon Elementary School, Orangeburg, SC
Round Lake High School, Round Lake, MN
Sacred Heart School, Oxford, PA
Shadowlawn Elementary School, Green Cove Springs, FL
Starmount High School, Boonville, NC
Stevensville Middle School, Stevensville, MD
Tadmore Elementary School, Gainesville, GA
Trask River High School, Tillamook, OR
Vacaville Christian Schools, Vacaville, CA
Wattsburg Area Middle School, Erie, PA
William Dunbar Public School, Pickering, ON
Woods Cross High School, Woods Cross, UT

Grades 10-11-12 Top Ten Winners

List of Top Ten Winners for Grades 10-12; listed alphabetically

Maria Capitano, Grade 11
Pittston Area High School, PA

Anna Daavettila, Grade 10
Houghton High School, MI

Anna Groeling, Grade 11
Arapahoe High School, CO

Arniecia Hinds, Grade 10
Germantown High School, TN

Sabrina Maus, Grade 10
Haynes Academy for Advanced Studies, LA

Erin McCune, Grade 10
Bellarmine Preparatory School, WA

Declan Routledge, Grade 12
Webber Academy, AB

Jacob Schriner-Briggs, Grade 12
Liberty High School, OH

Lianna Scott, Grade 11
Xavier College Preparatory School, AZ

Alexander Wimmer, Grade 10
Home School, GA

All Top Ten Poems can be read at www.poeticpower.com

Note: The Top Ten poems were finalized through an online voting system. Creative Communication's judges first picked out the top poems. These poems were then posted online. The final step involved thousands of students and teachers who registered as the online judges and voted for the Top Ten poems. We hope you enjoy these selections.

Love Is Like...

It's kind of like when you stick your finger in a light socket,
And a shock ripples through your body.
Then, everything is clear,
And you understand why your parents told you not to.
It's sort of like when you look at the sun,
And there's beauty and light in the first instant,
But then there are just black spots and pain,
And you understand why it's bad for your eyes.
It's almost like when you're falling,
And you feel weightless
Until you hit the pavement and cut your knee.
Then, you live in constant fear of falling,
But you meet that one guy,
And you can't help but take a chance.
You fall.
He shocks you;
He burns you,
But he doesn't catch you.

Emily Daluga, Grade 11
Libertyville High School, IL

Awaiting Winter

Outside the sky is dark there are no clouds
The snow is piled high upon the curbs
No cars pass by the silence is so loud
No wind blows through the trees, nothing's disturbed.

A snowman sits quietly in the snow
Alone, its scarf falls off onto the ground
It drifts down to the ground it doesn't blow
It lies there in the cold it makes no sound.

And then the sun comes up, morning is here
The snow frozen solid begins to thaw
The sky now bright with air that's cold and clear
A child comes out and looks and what he sees,

Is the snowman's scarf in the melting snow.
He puts it on and ties it in a bow.

Joanna Josten, Grade 10
William Fremd High School, IL

Wind

Wind blowing softly
Like a gesture of concern
To comfort me

Wind blowing softly
Like a warm greeting
To console me

Wind blowing softly
Like a gentle hug
To envelop me

Amanda Sau Yin Cheung, Grade 12
Schaumburg High School, IL

The Envision of War

War will come upon swift wings
It will be as a black angel, deadly and dark
Though it will not arrive for many springs
She comes, no one will escape without a mark

Her blade will be fast like lightning
The army she brings will be massive
These times will be frightening
Though you can't be passive

At the darkest hour light will come
Out of the night a hero will emerge
And the angel he will overcome
And the nations he will merge

Await the time and the hour
For the hero to come in glory and power

Amanda Dudich, Grade 12
Schlarman Academy, IL

You

You ask me as if you care what I say,
But in the end, I know you'll want it your way.
My thoughts and feelings mean nothing to you,
As society sees it, nothing important is true.
I starve, and I cry, but yet you walk by,
Unable to see that I'm dying inside.
Nothing I do ever seems enough
I can't fill the void; I'm a diamond in the rough.

My own body, I beat and I batter
So that to you I may finally matter.
The perfect picture, that's what you imagine,
The things that I do you can't even fathom.
To be the best, I take to my body
With tools of abuse to make me less gaudy,
For in the eyes of society, perfection is thin,
I work to become less in my own skin.

Dustin Dukes, Grade 12
Marion High School, IL

You

you think you know how to
CONTROL YOUR ANGER
you say you can
BITE YOUR TONGUE
you whisper when
YOU ARE VULNERABLE
you shout when
YOU ARE WRONG
you gloat when you are right
you fume AFTER
YOU MAKE HER CRY
but YOU don't CARE!

Jacob Buerger, Grade 11
Bolingbrook High School, IL

Left Behind

You left us behind a week ago
A week ago I held your hand
Held your hand and told you I loved you
Told you I loved you as you slipped away
As you slipped away, I kissed your cheek
I kissed your cheek as I said my goodbyes
My goodbyes which you could not hear
Could not hear, because you left us behind
Rachel Martie, Grade 12
Elverado High School, IL

Backpack

With my backpack full
It's hard to pull
But I'll grow to be very strong
Keep books and paper
Crayons for later
And an eraser to right my wrongs.
Niko Claudio, Grade 12
Bolingbrook High School, IL

Mind Games

Crazy out of mind
God made me special here on purpose
If something I did
Hurt just a little
Confronting the demons, yes
Succession, I win
Tony Schneider, Grade 11
Lisle Senior High School, IL

Forgiveness

Days pass
Years pass
The past is still within me
Trying to forgive and forget
I close my eyes and pray
I must learn to forgive and forget
Adri Tyrka, Grade 10
Schaumburg High School, IL

Rain

Rain falls peacefully,
From heaven to cleanse the Earth,
Of impurities.
Elizabeth Cribbs, Grade 10
Carmi-White County High School, IL

Trees

Unmoving pillars
Branches erupting in leaves
Homes for squirrels
Raymond Han, Grade 10
John Adams High School, IN

Ode to the Forbidden Fruit

In the high noon of the heavenly garden, where you loomed,
the color of your amber-brown gown danced in her head.
Your soft brown limbs wheeled her in—
temptation wove a dangerous net,
Paradise lost, you blossomed from her dust.

No! Prohibited you are, not a mere apple, but a forbidden fruit.
Euphoric bliss, your rough texture tainted her lips
Ah yes! Malum claimed you as their own centuries ago.

Many tales are told of the poisoned and red.
Your envied melody birthed the slash of blood to pure white snow.
Your sweet light flesh was imprisoned by topaz, golden and crimson coatings.
And then the rustic scent peeled away and unleashed a pale face.

But oh, your sweet ambrosia laughs and taunts me.
Don't you know I can resist it all?
Everything, if I am not tempted.
But oh! You are all too ripe
let me sink my teeth into you.

Natasha Reifenberg, Grade 10
John Adams High School, IN

Just Live

Life never goes how you want it, it never goes as planned.
Sometimes you're barely breathing, sometimes you can barely stand.
Your heart may sometimes break; your smile, at times, fade.
You'll think about the ones who left you more than the ones who stayed.
Sometimes you'll wonder why you're here and ponder the purpose of it all.
Sometimes you'll walk this world alone with no one to catch you when you fall.
You'll always have your doubts and dreams, you'll always have your fears.
Sometimes you'll look back in the past instead of shattering all the mirrors.
You'll want it all to be perfect, you'll always want to be right,
But sometimes it takes a fail or two to realize that everything's alright.
You can't predict the future; there's no way to change the past,
But you have to live in every moment and want it all to last.
For every smile that you've wasted, there's a happiness you can't take back.
For all those bitter tears you cry, there's a sadness holding you back.
You have to learn to love through the good times and the bad.
You'll learn to cherish what you have instead of regretting what you never had.
You'll sit back and take a few deep breaths and give this life all you can give.
You'll learn the greatest lesson in life, which is simple.
Just live.

Lauren Grimes, Grade 11
Zionsville Community High School, IN

I'll Always Remember…

I'll always remember…
    the way you looked at me,
    all the promises you made,
    the days we've spent together,
    our first fight,
    the first time you made me cry,
I'll always remember…the milestones in our relationship and all those to come.
Cassandra Mick, Grade 10
Carmi-White County High School, IL

To Be Human

If no one ever spoke,
the world would forever be in detention.
If no one ever jumped,
the world would forever be 2d.

If no one ever yelled,
the world would be full of robots.
If no one ever cried,
the world would be full of phonies.

If no one ever fell,
the world would have started lying down.
If no one ever needed help,
the world would forever be alone.

If you speak,
if you jump,
if you yell,
if you cry,

you might fall down; you might need help,
you might be human.

Ariana Pape, Grade 11
Metea Valley High School, IL

Why We Fight

I see the darkness in your eyes,
I see the fright, I see the lies.
But your beauty is among those,
That makes men, take up their bows.

Fighting on through time and space,
To this sacred, silent place.
The doors of fate will set free,
The end of all eternity.

But your body will stand strong,
To where it is where it belongs.
Still we fight, and we die,
But we never say goodbye.

David Galvin, Grade 11
Leo Jr/Sr High School, IN

The Pulse

The pulse drives through our veins
It consumes our blood
And enthralls our minds
It enriches everything within us,
And devours the fibers of our beings
Our silly human passions,
So vain, so real,
Driving innovation,
Driving creation,
The pulse grays our once-green world

Sara Maillacheruvu, Grade 10
Dunlap High School, IL

Thief

As I sit here in tears,
I am realizing all of my fears,
I was never good enough for you,
Even though you say that's not true,
I wish I could go back to the start,
To the moment you stole my heart.

Although I can admit,
I wouldn't change it one bit,
I would want to hold on tight,
Let you take away all of my fright,
Try not to think of what is ahead,
Because then it is my future that I dread,
All I want to do is show that I care,
That without you I have no air.

Just once, I want to lay my head down.
Knowing that I don't have to frown,
I want to know that you belong to me,
But I know that will never be,
I know that you will never defer,
Because now you are in love with her.

Shelbi Hyatt, Grade 11
New Castle High School, IN

I Swear They Are Raindrops

I swear they are raindrops
sliding off my cheek
it all blinks by
wet and sleek
it's all right in front of my eyes
and right behind me
just out of reach
the opportunities lost
and taken
leave me lost
and forsaken
screaming
while I'm dreaming
and dreaming
while I'm screaming
one by one
the raindrops fall
my heel to the wall
arms across my chest, there I pose
as a pale, red
rose

Isaiah Sanderman, Grade 10
William Fremd High School, IL

My Art

I love to do art
My deep expression of beauty
That comes from my heart

Sergio Amezquita, Grade 10
Schaumburg High School, IL

Life Is a Four Letter Word

Feel.
A four letter word.
Determine emotion to.
Nervous, crazy, content, overwhelmed.
Feel.
A normal way to sense.
A strange way to.
Confused, depleted, enthusiastic, horrible.
Feel.
A sensation on the skin.
Or an internal thought to.
Anxious, depressed, enraged, enthralled.
Feel.
A way to understand.
How do you.
Explain your emotion.

Feel is a four letter word.
To feel sets life in motion.
To feel is to live.
Life is a four letter word.

Brianna Lisak, Grade 12
Valparaiso High School, IN

Always

I wish I could be there
for the little things.
When you wake, when you sleep,
If I could take back moments missed,
I would be there, always.

To my dismay, I miss you.
Seasons change and we only speak.
Although time missed, the rarities remain.
Together we always love the same.

Our moments are great,
But then comes our good-byes.
Our love-hate relationship with secrecy,
The amazing relationship of you and me.
If we can get through this, we always say
That there will be a better day.
We laugh, we cry, we sing,
But there is always one unchanging thing.
Time passes; you are mine.
Always, all the time.

Olivia Schaefer, Grade 11
Newton Community High School, IL

In the Air

What if I could fly?
Sail through the clouds
Take you to the moon and stars
We could fly away together

Chanie Thompson, Grade 12
Lisle High School, IL

Of Wind and Fire

I was born a candle.
You were born the wind.
Not a thundercloud nor hurricane
Nor twister on the prairie,
But a flickering little breeze
Ever present
Dancing 'bout me like a faerie.
It causes me to flicker.
A flickering candle
That is to what you've reduced me.
But if I had one wish,
I'd never even for a moment
Wish to be a stone.
Hidden away in a shadow wood.
Never hearing animal nor man.
Never tasting wind nor fire.

Jade Strong, Grade 12
Huntley High School, IL

Lost

When the darkness surrounds me
and I take my flight,
would you be there for me?
Is my battle one you'd fight?
I'm getting so lonely
and I need you here now.
But I know I'll see you soon
somewhere, somehow.
For now I can only
dream of a place
where I won't be lost
and I can see your sweet face.
Forever and always
you promised me,
so forever and always
we shall be...

Melissa Feldmeyer, Grade 10
Salem High School, IN

Bird's-Eye

Ten thousand above ground —
Pines and oaks — like plants —
Houses — like building blocks —
Land Rovers — like ants —

Skyscraper towers — chopsticks —
Stuck in a bowl of soil —
Gray, like gunmetal, train tracks —
Exotic vipers — recoil —

Through mountains — of candy floss —
Volumeless turquoise seas —
The bird — of metal motion —
Floats on a scarf of the breeze.

Iryna Labazevych, Grade 12
Lincoln Park High School, IL

War

An evil idea
That sickens our minds

A savage fire
That destroys our environment

A merciless monster
That kills our people

A huge obstacle
That keeps us from progressing

A scary nightmare
That everyone fears

War

Fadi Rim, Grade 12
Schaumburg High School, IL

Virginia Bluebells

Hidden in the forest,
living a life of secret beauty.
Everyone ignores you
but I don't.
You paint the ground a sunset of colors
with hints of spring popping through.
Passersby tend to disregard you,
but I don't.
From shades of carnation to hues of celeste.
Touches of mauve contrast from the grass,
yet humans overlook you.
But I don't.
I observe your chartreuse leaves
and your graceful dance in the breeze.
Commoners forget to appreciate you,
but I do not.

Sara Simpson, Grade 10
Yorkville High School, IL

What if Words Just Fell from My Mouth

What if words fall from my mouth
Like rocks from a tumbling tower?
Cascading towards the floor
Like water from a wild waterfall
They pool at your feet
A puddle of emotions
Words meant never to be spoken

What if my words fell without restraint?
Words only for my mind
Could make a friendship unwind
You could laugh at these words
You could flee like a flock of scared birds
What if these words were "I love you?"

Erin Konicek, Grade 12
Boylan Catholic High School, IL

Languished Reveries

Olive drab droops to the earth and
A mind despairs of hopes long lost
In oblivion.

What once was, is no longer
As the vivacity once possessed in
Limp leaves vanishes.

Elapsed intervals of
Thought.
Encompassing latency and

Languished reveries that
Are no more
And shall never be.

Elizabeth Philipps, Grade 12
Marian Central Catholic High School, IL

Normal Simplicity

An accusation created by man
A word so simple and complex
What is expected of normal?

An image of the unknown
We all want to be unique
Yet different is just odd

An untold contradiction
To go with the crowd
Or to sparkle in the world

A glittering star among the blackened sky
All judgment fades
Like beauty to the blind

Allison Kelley, Grade 12
Harlem High School, IL

Bus Stop Nights

Standing under the bus shelter in the rain,
reading yesterday's Wall Street Journal,
the bell tower chimed in the distance,
a train whistle blew,
the sky opened up,
the clouds roared,
dogs barked,
the streetlight blinked,
the gutters flowed,
leaves gathered at my feet,
the wind screamed,
and my bus arrived.

I got on.
"Lovely night, isn't it?" said the driver.

Mike Gargrave, Grade 12
Oswego East High School, IL

A Voice

I had a voice.

A voice you did not know I had.
Or rather a voice you didn't choose
to hear, muffled by the doubts in your mind.

I had a voice.

A voice that became a cry.
A cry for life.
A cry unheard.

I had a voice.

A voice that people wanted to hear.
A voice that would be beautiful.
One that you missed out on.

I have a voice.

Paige Schultheis, Grade 11
Reitz Memorial High School, IN

A Forced Vibrato

I found my poem in the scattered remains
     of my broken cello
Music flowed from the instrument as you'd imagine
     a women's long hair cascades down her back
But now when I played the magnificent wooden instrument
No
I found my poem in a sound which seemed rigid and dark
     narrow and metallic
Sharp pangs would emerge from the strings
     Attacked with an unsuspecting desperation to sound good
Vibrato was a forced kind of death with smallest movement
     of the wrong finger in the wrong place
I found my poem in the hollow cry of a cello
     yearning to sound like the deep roars of a crashing wave
A deafening silence
     rather than the ringing of applause
filled the air with a sense of regret
     I found my poem scattered in the remains
     of my broken cello

Yasmin Mitchel, Grade 10
Elk Grove High School, IL

The Sea of Souls

Insides rotting to the point of nothing,
No longer believing in someone or something.
Dark thoughts and dreams consume his mind,
Not one clean memory in him will you find.
Nightmares of lines and blood and scars,
Daydreams filthier than that of Mars.
Every gesture of kindness is volleyed back,
Hitting you back in the face with a smack.
Coldness oozes from his heart,
His soul and mind are set apart.
All his hope, it fades away,
All his faith just seems to decay.
Laying his life in the hands of the reaper,
All goodness left sinks deeper and deeper.
The Sea of Green consumes him whole,
Too gone for too long has been his soul.

Kaitlin Gettinger, Grade 11
Streamwood High School, IL

Accomplished Nothing

She calls us in for yet another chat,
The sun blares in my eyes, and the track is burning.
We huddle together for safety and security,
Because we all know what is to come.
My stomach turns in worry,
Fearing that today it's me she chooses to belittle.
She yells about our latest imperfections,
And how we give her no respect.
She reverts to childish ways and sarcasm,
Is this her way to gain respect?
Oh, how the time just wastes away,
With the same spiel of irrelevant and belligerent criticism.
Yet another practice ends, and we have accomplished nothing.
For that, we will certainly hear about next time.

Mandy Marsh, Grade 12
Marion High School, IL

Yes, I Remember

Yes I remember, way back in December,
where all those lonely nights led to sorrow and tears —
And those times where you were never there hurt so bad —
My heart died a little more each night,
and I feared that it would shatter and break.
All those times where I trusted you because the bond,
were little white lies told then…
And even though I was strong,
my already wounded heart couldn't quite hold together;
only that December — yes, I remember.

Jennifer Tokarz, Grade 11
Lowell Sr High School, IN

Our Cup of Love

Tipping and spilling our cup of love,
Sharing words we no longer speak of,
What was once a perfect fire,
Got blown away by Providence Desire,
When we first got together I saw forever,
Best friends for worse or for better,
But I should have listened to my mama careful,
She always told me you weren't anything special,
Questioning what you would do,
If you had the chance to see my point of view,
Laid my trust among your affection,
Finding nowhere close, to any progression.

Chantele Weasel, Grade 11
Carmi-White County High School, IL

The Abyss

I stare into the room
Not knowing what to do
The suspense takes over
Then the darkness starts to creep upon me
As I lunge backward
The floor collapses
I scream for my life
Feeling as though I'm going to die

I see the ground
It is coming up quick
My life is over
Now I can't do anything about it
Warren McMillan, Grade 10
Prairie Heights Sr High School, IN

Time

Time is ongoing and instant
Things past are old and distant
Time is quick, fleeting
Faster than a heart beating
It is going, never stopping
Even when the world is dropping

Time is the true test
Nothing can beat its best
Time goes past all the ends
Nothing will make it around the bend
Time is final, it is all
It is the thing that will never fall
Ian La Fountain, Grade 10
John Adams High School, IN

A Winter's Night, City Street Lights

Sometimes at night
City street lights reflect the unreflected
Everybody that lives here
Should expect the unexpected
Many who enter this scene
Can think deeper than they ever did before
Forgotten memories
Laughter, embracing, honesty, and victory
Are brought back into mind
And newly restored
I long to be a reflecting light
Reminding the unreminded
Of their forgotten memories
Morgan Bramlett, Grade 10
John Adams High School, IN

Fall

Brown, Red, and Orange
Fall leaves rustling in the wind
Hay rides, Harvest, Fire
Katie Backs, Grade 11
Okawville Jr/Sr High School, IL

Pick-Up Plans

Cards full of money are handed to me.
I wait to count it and see how much bank I made.
Today, I turn 16.
I offer to take any unwanted money from anyone and everyone, with no takers.
Years ago, when I began to think about driving, I decided I wanted a truck.
Every time my mom purchased a paper, I would look for a cheap one,
With hopes of someday driving it to school.
As I got older, I began to learn persuasive tactics.
I began to use these newly acquired skills on my parents,
All in preparation for the big prize,
The truck that would become mine.
Visions of me driving it by myself gave hope every day,
Images of me jamming out to my favorite music,
Images of me just strait up ballin',
Rolling like a big shot.
The thoughts of me being able to go where I wanted when I wanted kept me awake at night.
Finally, I am of age, and the day has come to claim my V8 monster.
I anxiously count the money I have managed to save from years past.
I realize that, sadly, I do not have enough.
And then, my dad says that he'll pay for the rest, since I have saved the majority of it.
My anxiety passes, and I am filled with excitement
Brandon England, Grade 12
Marion High School, IL

Christmas Will Never Be the Same

It's supposed to be the happiest day of the year,
But this time it won't be the same.
I'll be wishing day and night, that this season will leave as quickly as it came.
I'd give up all the packages with the ribbons and the bows,
just to hear him say again that he could make it snow.
I'd give up ever gift I got
just to see on Christmas morn,
My whole family together —
unbroken and untorn.
I think about it every day — how lucky I used to be,
when I was with my daddy as we sat around the tree.
He never really asked for much,
and he gave everything he could,
to make my Christmas special,
the way he thought it should.
I would forget about the presents,
every package, every sack.
I'd give up every Christmas,
just to bring my daddy back.
Kate Runyon, Grade 12
Norwell High School, IN

The Sweater

I promise to be your soft cashmere sweater.
I will you warm when the nights are dark and cold.
I'll be your safe haven when the world becomes harsh and scary.
You can wear me until I'm faded and worn.
Just promise that you'll sew me back together when I start to unravel.
Sarah Birkla, Grade 12
Carmi-White County High School, IL

Secrets

Soft words, soft voices,
secrets kept in the night,
but all the mice stay away in the daylight.
Things happen behind closed doors,
behind shuttered windows,
things you wonder about,
everyone has their secrets…
but it's none of your business,
and no one knows.
After all, three may keep a secret,
if two of them are dead.

Jessica Steinhiser, Grade 10
John Adams High School, IN

Closure

You loved and lied,
I hurt and cried,
Thinking you'd come back.
Now I'm glad you're gone,
I'm moving on…
It's time to face the facts.
You're a liar and a cheater,
Hope she's still there when you need her.

Macy Pesavento, Grade 10
Carmi-White County High School, IL

scandal

gossip and trust
pain and fire
grasping the brush
of youth's desire
fancy as fake
case of riches
pay the meal
or do the dishes

Alexis Sorensen, Grade 12
Boylan Catholic High School, IL

I Miss…

I miss…
My puppy waiting for me at the door.
I miss…
My big bed.
I miss…
Taking my brother to his football games.
I miss…
Living at home with my family.

Stephanie Reuter, Grade 12
Carmi-White County High School, IL

What's Yours

The curls of your hair
That golden smile of yours
Your wondrous voice

Kylie Kendra, Grade 12
Lisle Senior High School, IL

Treasure

What I wish I could do, I hand it over to you
Hoping you will accept it
Praying to God Almighty. You will be careful and protect it.
I gently place it in your hands. And you curl your fingers around.
I tell you, you now own it. In me, it cannot be found.
You grip it firmly in your hand. And gaze into my eyes
You realize this treasure. And begin to cry
I am warmed at this and thankful
That this thing in your hand,
Is why I love you so?
A tear streaks upon your face
And I begin to kiss it away
You brush my hand aside
And tell me what you have to say
"I will carry this gift in a golden case"
I will never allow
Another tear to streak your face
I look into you, you into mine. I know that you don't lie
I trust you. I gave you this. You put it away. And blow a kiss
This is what I've been waiting for.
This is my brand new start. This gift I give so freely is only but my heart.

Aleesha Lieberenz, Grade 10
McQueen High School, IN

International Slave Trade

I saw so many deaths
N o one deserves this treatment
T oday another person jumped
E veryone is in pain
R ather not remember
N othing will go our way
A nother person died
T oday
I wish I can be set free
O nly God knows
N o one knows what to expect
A merica's shoreline is not far
L ay down and never wake up

S uch sadness
L eave me now
A t last we are here
V ery little joy
E very day I cry I'm coming home

T rade day is here
R un away fast,
A nd never look back
D ie slowly,
E very time you're reminded of home you weep slowly

Tia Crawford, Grade 12
Guilford High School, IL

I Haunt You

When I was hit by a car, I was given a second chance with you.
But when I got home, you had changed.
I see you, but you look right past me.
I say, "How has your day been," but you just keep watching TV.
I mow the lawn and do the dishes for you, but you do not even acknowledge it.

I'm beginning to feel like you don't love me anymore.
You don't know the pain it causes me when you don't say, "I love you."
Even though you may not feel the same way I do, I still love you.
And when I go to hug you, you just walk right through me.
It is like I'm not even there.
It is almost like I am a ghost that is haunting you.

Steven Woods, Grade 11
Bluffton Harrison High School, IN

Renewing of the Rose

The rose was once
a beautiful flower
that stood tall
in the midst of a meadow,
but a cold night came
the frost laid on the petals.
The softness became rough
and the leaves were burned
from the frost.
Slowly, the petals fell off
and the flower was left
to its stalk.
It took many months
of enduring rabid storms
and surviving the grip of winter
but the flower grew back
and the petals grew bigger
with each passing day;
until it became
a more beautiful rose than before.

Mikayla Wagner, Grade 10
Hononegah High School, IL

The Impact

Always the forgotten;
Always the left out.
Never the remembered;
Never the invited.

Always the mistreated;
Always the one in pain.
Never the respected;
Never the healed.

Always kind;
Always caring.
Never cruel;
Never destroying.

Hurting on the inside;
A past of pains and tears.
Wishing others happiness;
Hope they never feel this.

Amelia Reckelhoff, Grade 12
Mater Dei High School, IN

Space

Every night when I look up
I see a kingdom at the distant top
It holds tiny stars that always fly past
Its shiny planets spin round and fast
And oh I wonder how it feels
To be in the royalty of these.

Alina Pavlyuk, Grade 12
Lisle High School, IL

Dreams

In the depths of sleep, where improbable comes alive,
Where fantasies unfurl and our wildest reveries do strive,

No I'd never dreamed of you.

The eyes I'd dreamed were azure; vibrant drops, matching sapphires,
Framed like lovely rose bushes with long lashes like briers.
But yours are a deep earthen brown, pools of darkness yet they shine,
A synthesis of tenderness and humor by design,

But I'd never dreamed of you

I'd imagined locks of gold, corn silk glinting in the glow.
Flowing tresses without waves; straight as arrows from their bows.
But your tresses are russet, luscious curls like untamed vines,
Dancing in the summer breeze, begetting longing and repine.

Still I'd never dreamed of you.

I'd dreamed up arms to hold me, but they'd depart when I'd wake.
Dream hands could not swipe my tears; impart solace past daybreak.
You're not what I expected, envisioned or sought after,
But each day in your presence, sates me with blissful laughter.
Yes, dreams cannot construct one's life; cannot return one's love,

So though I'd never dreamed of you,
Your love was quite enough.

Lauren Myers, Grade 12
Fountain Central Jr/Sr High School, IN

Love, Desire, and the Beacon

I'm not sure at what point I will see again,
wherein from the sky the fog will fade,
whence the stirred mud subsides from the glassy surface of mine eye.

But love, the dirty fool, do you want it gone?
Already it has curdled bystander thoughts,
and devoured its way into the slime of your digestive tract, whilst you keep it yet.

In kind there is no real context for desire,
no understanding of handsome faces in our fate.
We're lost in these planes of never-ending ambiguity, life's faultless splendor
a splatter made of paint.

On milky frothed, tossing seas the ship sails on,
canvas catching wind, searching for meanings sought before
aided by a gilded hope's broken sextant core.

So dimly my truth's delusion calls, a crow upon cerebral eaves
"Beckon to the brethren in their dark ceremony garb,
pray tell them there's a bright light inside my head,
and it's brought the blind to God."

Alanna Davey, Grade 12
Jeffersonville High School, IN

Colors

The leaves change on an autumn day
Like invited guests that just couldn't stay.

As they change, their true colors are revealed
A change in the mix, their fates no longer sealed.

The reds and the yellows in the day shine bright
And the nacarat orange seems to glow in the night.

A multitude of colors just blowing in the breeze
No stress in their lives, just lives full of ease.

Their change seems natural, not forged or forced
Just feelings of freedom, not regret or remorse.

Their colors tell a story as they sit there and glisten
You can hear them tell their tale, you just have to listen.

Kevin Harold, Grade 12
Boylan Catholic High School, IL

Lighting Up the Night Sky

The sun is shining today,
As bright as a thousand stars in the night sky.
The day is dull and I feel alone.
Even while I'm in a crowd of people.
When I feel invisible, I see everything.
Like I see you now, in the middle of the crowd.
I'm waiting for the day you notice me,
Is today the day?
Yes it is; I will get you to notice me.
I will not be invisible anymore.
You said I was never invisible to you,
So I have one question.
Will you make my day shine…
Like a thousand stars lighting up the night sky?

Kim Jolliff, Grade 11
Bluffton Harrison High School, IN

Closure

All the things I have yet to do,
And all the things I am willing to prove.
It's coming soon, my life begins to move,
And I know I will have to see this through.
The winter is coming, the skies streaked blue.
Fates have looked up, I begin to improve,
Thoughts that leave my mind, stains to be removed.
Time speeds up, the sun is soon born anew.
Forward to the answer, get myself free.
Pieces put together, words understood.
Regain composure from overexposure.
Remember my melody, the sweet, soft song.
The large gaps I felt have been closed for good.
It has come, I can live with this closure.

Taylor Wells, Grade 10
Indian Creek Sr High School, IN

Swim Season

I don't want to come in last, so I try harder

You gave me the compliment, so I try harder
You gave her the compliment, so I try harder

I'm last in line, so I try harder
I'm first in line, so I try harder

It's so difficult, so I try harder
It's too easy, so I try harder

It hurts, so I try harder
I don't feel a thing, so I try harder

My muscles feel small, so I try harder
They feel like they're tearing, so I try harder

I win the race, so I try harder
I get second, so I try harder

I won because I tried my hardest

Samantha Barry, Grade 10
William Fremd High School, IL

Face Time

Act in haste
And please don't waste
A single chance to see my face
Because there are dragons
To be chased
And there are shoelaces
To be laced
In this endless race between time and space.
Just in case
You act in haste
My face will be waiting
Where the dragons are chased
By other knights
Wanting to take your place.
You can't compare with their pace
And they have already
Acted in haste.
Keep in mind, that there's no time to waste
In this endless race
Of time verses space,
That's the only thing standing between us and fate.

Lindsey Pape, Grade 10
Beecher High School, IL

Gone

Wondering where, not understanding why,
Gone for eternity, never lost temporarily.
Just one more chance, only one more goodbye.

Dominique Nadeau, Grade 12
Lisle High School, IL

Love

Love is like a fairy tale,
A journey wherever you go.
Occasionally you will fail
And your spirits will grow low.

But you'll have that deep sensation
To continue moving on,
Even if you have to travel across the nation
Your love will never be gone.

Don't worry you'll reach the time
Where you will arrive at your happy ending.
And your love will forever climb
Without any pending.

Your love is now a fire
Burning feverishly higher and higher.

Megan Perkins, Grade 10
William Fremd High School, IL

Joy in Life

The joy of life without thinking at all
Me without a brain that sounds insane
But thou does not see all of life's flaws
Highway of I myself in my own lane

Black thoughts that negative things brought
Me free relaxed mind off in another land
But why cry and sit on bad thoughts
Good and bad things always go hand in hand

Now a man because I can think clearly
Somewhat stronger because I thought longer
Life, money, joy, and God are all with me
My heart pounds at joy like a drummer

'Tis amazing what life gives you once you think
'Tis something I do first before I blink

Eliezer Davenport, Grade 12
Bolingbrook High School, IL

Who Would Have Thought?

A year ago from now, who would have thought?
That we'd be best friends?
That the simple sight of your brilliant smile
Could lighten up my day?
That every word you speak
Would mean a hundred times more to me?
That every time we'd be together
I couldn't help but be cheery?
That every thought I have would be consumed by you?
That I would never be able to let you go?
I would have never thought, one year ago, that
We would ever be this close.

Jacklyn Snider, Grade 10
Harlem High School, IL

Remembering

I zip away to get some Starbucks before school
I get my chocolaty chip Frappuccino and I'm off
Sipping the sweet creamy treat
But oh no there's a line for the zip line
I'm going to be late
I decide it would be best to walk
The lines above are a tangled mess
The people look caught like flies in a web wriggling to get out
The ground is deserted I have it all to myself
I take off my shoes and run through the grass
Feeling the dew on my naked feet
Everything feels more amazing down here than I remember
I pick flowers and weeds throwing them up everywhere
I walk on the concrete feeling the cold cement
I skip on South Avenue working the muscles of my legs
I race a bird to a large oak tree
Then I stop, realizing that 1st hour is already over
I sprint to school, vowing never to take the zip lines again

Courtney Boeding, Grade 11
Oswego East High School, IL

Piety

Of desserts, Pie bears greatest majesty
His soft meringue is as the clouds that line the heavens
His essence as different as the men of Earth
Apple, pumpkin, pecan, and lime,
Lemon, chocolate, and cherry delight
Each demanding a flavor of its own
And a crust of graham, nuts, or dough unwavering and true
Pie is brave and ever faithful,
Always assisting his brethren in the war on hunger
Facing a legion of Forks and Knives
Pie is at the forefront, leading his desserts into battle
Even as he is stricken down by the hand that formed him,
He accepts defeat humbly, and gladly enters the mouth of his maker
As his flavor pleases the one who smote him,
Corporeal and ethereal divide and his soul moves on
Long live the Pie!

Matthew Becker, Grade 11
Mater Dei High School, IN

Epidemic

It starts with a child giving an embrace
to a gentle peck upon the face.
Soon a world has turned around
and then the earth is upside down.
It sings with the wind and glides with the rain,
inhabits the streets and dwells in the pain.
It fuses the fabric and drives the wedge,
it begs the questions that seek our knowledge.
It puts us to sleep and keeps us awake,
it's always right and often a mistake.
It's as quiet as a prayer, a booming sound.
It's an unseen epidemic, yet visible all around.

Abigail Francisco, Grade 12
Boylan Catholic High School, IL

Baby Brother Birthday Blues*

I haven't seen you since you were two
We were inseparable but now we're apart that's why I'm blue
I remember you gurgling playfully in your crib
With so much saliva coming out later you had to wear a bib
I remember you laughing in your little alligator suit
Stepmom, Dad and I took that film, I look back at the pictures it's hard to believe that was me and you
Your laugh, the way you called my name
If I could go back to those times I'd give up even money and fame
Your smile, the big cheeks, the big brown eyes
If you could only see how much I miss you, how much your big brother cries
This year you turn three years old
I wonder dear brother if you still do what you're told?
In SIRYV I'm locked up wishing you were near
To hug you, kiss you, play you days on end without never having to shed a tear
I used to feed you, change you, burp you and more than the above
Little brothers Chago just know it's you forever that I love

Luis Castillo, Grade 12
Lakeview Jr/Sr High School, IN
*Dedicated to Chagito 11/11/11

A Broken Longing

Slowly, carefully, skimming
Beneath the surface. Hiding in the
Shadows of your soul lies an esoteric
Desire. Reaching, struggling, to pull Him
Closer to you. Longing with a deep hunger to
Feel the warmth, a fiercely burning flame, to surge
Through you as easily as water spreads across a level surface
Silently, you submit to the Spirit sweeping through your soul and
Suddenly
Like a brick wall, you push Him away with an intermittent fear that if you
Surrender the entirety of your simple life, you'll merely squander away into
Nothingness. Abruptly, a voice reaches out, speaking softly, yet still audible, to your
Spirit saying, "Do not fear, it is I. You have called, now I will answer. In Me, be faithful, and you shall be
Eternally safe."

Emily Hoffman, Grade 11
NorthWood High School, IN

Who Would I Be?

As I sit here listening to the wind blow past my ears, I think…
I think: where would I be, what would I be, or would I even exist, if my older sister had lived?
I wonder: Would I be dealing with the internal pain that I feel? Would I have what I have,
and who would I have if she hadn't rescued me from foster care as a baby?
Would I feel how I feel if I hadn't been rescued from that basement, from what happened there?
Would my memory be better if I didn't have to try and black out what happened?
Could I have stayed sane just a little longer if one of the most important people in my life,
the woman whose name is tattooed on my arm, my great-grandma, had lived a little while longer?
Would she even be gone if the doctors hadn't screwed up what they screwed up?
Would I have ever had real happiness again if I had never met him?
If I didn't get to know him for who he really is, would he still have my heart?
Thinking about my life and what could be, who I am, and who I could be.
I wonder: Am I crazy, am I strong, or what?
Trying to keep the tears from falling, I fight them; I hold them back.

Shyesha Rivers, Grade 11
MacArthur High School, IL

Ashes

Planes coming
Souls leaving
People falling
Ashes rising
A cloud of fire
A cloud of dust
Buildings fall
People crawl
Hearts are crushed
Tears are shed
Hatred is forged
Revenge is needed
Fathers, Mothers,
Sisters, Brothers
Lost
They tried to pull us apart
They only pushed us closer
Trying to erase our hope
But only made us stronger

Erika Lawrence, Grade 10
Oswego East High School, IL

Frozen Fire

Something so wild,
Should never be contained.
What you think is worth your while,
You should be so ashamed.
Magnificent, free, fearless, and grand,
Impossible to ignore.
Something so many yearn to understand,
Blinding, glorious, mysterious, and more.

I am the frozen fire,
Forced to live his preferred life.
Running and screaming,
Talking all around.
I cover my ears,
In attempt to block out his voice.
Telling me I am not worthy,
Enough to maintain my essence.
I am the frozen fire.

Sierra Ritchie, Grade 10
Prairie Heights Sr High School, IN

Sunrise

Morning's beauty caught the light
Bending, twisting away the night
Bluebirds sing their cadence song
Sing notes sweet, sing notes long
Dew melts away fears of old yesterdays
Sunrise washing down the drain
All the tears and all the pain
As I write with golden pen
I pray for Sunrise to come again

Olivia Gates, Grade 12
Griffith High School, IN

What Right?

What right do you have to criticize?
What right do you have to talk down about me?
You left and never looked back!
My life without you was just fine!
I was happy, without you!
Now, you walk into my life and criticize!?
You will let me talk!
She raised me, not you!
She gave me life and helped me keep it!
She came to my graduation and cried for me!
She helped me through the hard times of my life!
SHE was there, NOT YOU!
You have no right to criticize!
You had the chance to come back to raise me!
You took the easy way out and stayed away!
Do not walk into my life now and think you have some right!
Your rights were taken the day you decided to not come back for me!
Do me a favor and do what you're good at!
Leave!
And this time, stay away!

Jamilia Fair, Grade 12
Peoria High School, IL

Poids Lourd

For those that may read these words and the feelings that each one holds,
For the souls that have lost their way,
For the tragedy each person has to face,
For those that see meaning,
For those that see logic but do not follow upon it,
For the many that have fallen,
For the emptiness we hide within,
Deep inside fighting this blotchy life we have to live,
For those that may look upon this poem and acknowledge it,
For those who breath,
This is something for you to read.

Leyla Marin, Grade 11
Lawrence North High School, IN

Spring

Spring is a beautiful time of year,
with fresh flowers, green grass, budding trees, rain, and sun.
Spring devours the snow and frigid weather of winter.
Spring is like a newborn baby,
it is hope after a long winter, brings joy to the earth, and contains new life.
Sometimes spring is as harsh as a lion with bad, chilly weather.
Other times spring is a lamb that comes in peacefully with good, warm weather.
The crisp smell of spring dances in the air to the song of chirping birds.
Spring is a smile, it brightens everyone's day.
Spring can bring happiness to all.

Jacquelyn Luecke, Grade 10
Freeport High School, IL

The Frostiest Time of the Year

Winter — my favorite season;
As the snowflakes plummet from the sky,
Snow makes the trees and grass glisten in white.
Along with the glowing Christmas lights,
Icicles dangle from my house.
Breaking out my ice skates,
I stride down to my glossy pond.
Sliding my ice skates on,
I begin to glide across the ice.
Skating for a while,
Then ambling up to my house,
I rapidly take off my coat.
Reaching quickly for a cup of hot chocolate,
I consume the toasty, delicious hot cocoa,
Running down my throat.
I snatch a peppermint candy cane,
And eat the striped treat along with my warm chocolate delight.

Madison Dwenger, Grade 12
Benton Central Jr/Sr High School, IN

Holding Life

In the stillness of winter,
I dream of sunshine.
When snowflakes fall,
Imagine rays.
But when the spring arrives,
I get nostalgic
For the bitter frost
On chilly days.

When fall comes to pass
I don my jacket.
Hues of warm oranges, reds, browns.
The songbirds fly away
Habitats gone, as leaves litter the ground.

Summer comes again
Disguised as ice cream cones
And children playing at the pool
Memories of the past.

No one can stop the seasons.
As they come, they already go,
They rain and they snow,
But they are ever out of our grasp.

Kelly McAvoy, Grade 10
Norwell High School, IN

Allure

Clear as glass, flowing through
a valley filled with vibrant life.
Listen, for what it speaks is true,
its voice pierces, like a fife,
an alluring sight, that relieves our strife.

Isaac Shaw, Grade 10
John Adams High School, IN

Darkness Bound

Howling, churning, bashing, bouncing,
Cresting waves and mindless trouncing
Bearing down, denoting daunting
Juggling and juggernauting.

Darkness never seemed this evil;
Reprehensible, primeval
As the heavens caused upheaval
Lighting up a black festival.

And of the roaring, ceaseless weeping!
Thunder that seems never weakening,
And the lightning bouncing, leaping,
To the currents never sleeping.

Suddenly, as if commanded
And caught outrageously red-handed
Horizon lines are now expanded
And grayish black is now disbanded.

Children go outside to play,
While parents sit down by the bay
As they look to the sky and say,
"Perfect ending to the day."

Sammy Levey, Grade 10
William Fremd High School, IL

Limitless*

It consumes him like the darkness
Never letting him go.
Making him smarter, wiser,
Teaching him things he didn't know.
The drug lets him be in control,
Rise above everyone else.
It runs through his veins
Like fire growing, he's limitless.

When the effects wear off
And the knowledge he had leaves.
He realizes having that power's
Not worth it, not who he wants to be.
But as he tries to get off
This runaway train,
The reality sinks in that
This could be an everlasting pain.

So a cure is what he needs
To escape this nothingness.
Even if he's not on the drug
He's still him, still limitless.

Wilson Webel, Grade 11
New Berlin High School, IL
*Based on the movie "Limitless"

My Name

Kaitlyn is the name I hear people say
All day I shuffle various titles
Many labels I will receive today
But knowing my right name is so vital

There is only one title I will claim
I take the pure title of Kaitlyn Ann
It is a name that will never be tame
My name is not easy to understand

My name is something that tells a story
It tells of what I've done and where I've been
The things I've seen and what matters to me
A young life that is about to begin

Please don't give me any other label
For no other name is as capable

Kaitlyn Best, Grade 12
Norwell High School, IN

Forever and Always

The way you smile is incredible;
Your voice penetrates through the other sounds.
Your shining light is unforgettable.
Our hearts are beating fast, but time slows down.
Recall the night we both said forever?
With joyous tears, I slept thinking of you.
We've been through much — a lot of endeavors.
I kept my problems my own, but you knew;
You acknowledged my tears — happy or sad;
Smiling at me made it all vanish.
You are my treasure, and for that I'm glad.
Every moment with you I cherish.
When you hear these words, I pray you hold true —
Forever and always, I will love you.

Kelsey Gibson, Grade 10
Mississinewa High School, IN

Our Risk

We wake up into the world
A world full of fear and doubt
A world that gives us loneliness and betrayal
A world that causes us pain and grief
Yet, each day as the sun rises again, and again
We step out and become vulnerable
Become helpless, become weak
Why even go out into such a world?
Because through all the tribulations, there is triumph
Behind every obstacle, there is a goal
For every negative; two positives
Between our tears; laughter
In risking nothing we may be safe from the world
But the greatest of flaws in life is to risk nothing

Katelyn C. Genenbacher, Grade 12
Quincy Notre Dame High School, IL

Canada Means…

Warm maple syrup on a frosty morning
When the temperature reads -26°F outside, with seven feet of snow
And I am stuck at home

Canada means…
Walking through the mossy forest
Strolling along with the one I truly love
And we catch a glimpse of a moose

Canada means…
The feeling of being at home
500 miles away from the place
I am supposed to call "home"

Canada means…
A warm hug, the feeling of friendliness
When I am truly welcomed
Unlike I would be here

Canada means…
Seeing my love for the first time
The excited tackling
The titanic hugs
The zealous kissing…
Feeling like, finally, I belong somewhere

Quentin Harris, Grade 10
Benton Central Jr/Sr High School, IN

My Beatles Ballad

Hey John where's the revolution?
We've wanted this for so long.
Now Yoko lies alone in bed
and poor little Jude has no dad.
You're six feet under,
bullet in your chest.
I sometimes wonder how you were laid to rest.
My guitar will always weep,
John, I don't know how I sleep.
My heart beats like Ringo's drums
and Paul's voice resounds in my head
George's words have made me think
but now, good gracious, George is dead.
I imagine the world is sleeping
and dreaming of a mystery tour.
The people go on without listening
the broom has yet to hit the floor.
No matter how the people change
the music has always stayed the same.
Though John and George are too long gone,
I still find myself lost in the songs.

Rebekah Van Es, Grade 10
Greenwood Community High School, IN

Football

Yells and laughter
Fill my ears
As I listen to
The encouraging cheers.

This is it,
My final game.
Focus on winning
And ignore the pain.

Sweat running down my face
As I run the last yard in.
People screaming my name
As I try to get a win.

Catching the ball
As I fall to the ground.
There's not one noise
Except for…

Touchdown!
Trenton Murfin, Grade 12
Quincy Notre Dame High School, IL

Asylum

Padded but not inviting
Heated but eerily chill
Did I get put in for fighting
The fear that lies within me still?
Men in white strap me down
While I kick and scream
But my cries are being drowned
By the needles of their team
Every day I'm clothed and stripped
In here I have no dignity
Every day my switch gets flipped
From sane to insanity
I'm a suicidal child
I am very weak
I was raised to be mild
But wild is what I seek
That's why they put me on drugs
That make me quiet as a mouse
They treat us all like little bugs
In this crazy house
Paige Hatfield, Grade 11
Jefferson High School, IN

Moon

See her
So bright and fair
Radiant as her mate
Shining brighter than their children
Love her
Jackie Welch, Grade 11
Carmi-White County High School, IL

Time to Change

Spring
A time for fresh beginnings
The new warmth comforts the frozen land
The smell of daffodils waft through the air
The cry of a newborn baby echoes the cheer's of new life
Rain washes away the pains of yesterday
Summer
The sweat of summer sweetness rolls down a beet red cheek
Senses are heightened by the warm summer breeze
The spring of the diving board propels swimmers to an invigorating splash
The mystery of a summer romance is solved
For autumn has fallen into place
Fall
The crackle and spark of a kindling fire
The colors form a warm Sunday sky bursting with reds and oranges
The leaves descend like the imminent snowfall soon to come
Winter
The chill of frost nips bitterly at the nose
The jingle of Santa's sleigh rings of memories of Christmas's past
Icicles glisten in the sun as they wither away just as fast as the season arrived
Descending into hibernation until awakened by the chirping birds of the long awaited spring
Katherine Bender, Grade 11
Mater Dei High School, IN

Fifty-two…

Passed down from generation to generation soon becomes a family tradition
Finding the right one or waiting for the draw, each player embarks upon a mission
The nights are long and the name of the game changes
Too busy to leave the table, an abundant range of food patiently waits beside us
Participants modify the rules, leaving everyone confused
Arguments and fights will soon ensue
Round and round the cards we pass
Each person surpassed even more than before with excitement
One and all, we begin to stand
For this hand marks our ending
The final cards doled out
Leaving one person boasting about
The lone winner cheers
As the remainders begin to shed tears
Congratulations exchanged and expressed
Leaving behind fifty-two blessed cards on the table
Brooke Emilson, Grade 12
Benton Central Jr/Sr High School, IN

Chilled Heart

I stand, goose bumps cover my arms and legs: wondering will anything be warm again.
The numb feeling of the cold consumes me.
I wonder what being something other than cold feels like.
Darkness seems to be everywhere. I plunge into a black hole with darkness as my five senses.
Is it in my heart or just covering my eyes?
This icy feeling destroys every nerve ending in me.
How do I even think of warmth, when there is nothing to feel with?
I crumble into a cube of ice, just waiting and wanting to melt.
Sheridan Dove, Grade 11
Bluffton Harrison High School, IN

I Am From

I am from the church yard hillside,
from youth retreats to Ichthus weekends in the rain.
I am from playing corn hole
to cleaning toilets on Saturdays.
I am from getting the out at first
to four-wheeler rides in the field.
I am from photo albums
to Mamaw's chocolate pudding,
from hand baseball
to tractor and bus rides with Papaw.
I am from Skillet and Chris Tomlin
to Texas Chainsaw Massacre late at night.
I am from prayer groups and heart to hearts,
to running and jumping off the dock,
into to the mucky, brown water.
I am from late night phone calls with my best friend,
to wanting to be the best that I can.

Elizabeth Anderson, Grade 12
Southwestern Jr/Sr High School, IN

Stand Up

The grass isn't always greener
On the other side
And it never really helps
To run away and hide.
Face the world around you
With a smile on your face.
Stand up for what you want
Stand up and take your place.
Be who you want to be
Give up your fears and be free.
Even if it seems like it does nothing but rain
You must be strong and take the pain.
And always hold your chin up high
Even when you cry.

Jessica Clements, Grade 12
Northwestern High School, IL

Fool Me Once

They say that friends are forever.
With you I'm not so sure.
We're great when it's you
But when you are with him
It's just not the same.
It seems to happen more than once.

You lie, you become distant, manipulative,
Worst of all you aren't you.

I hate that when you get like this I feel alone.
I can't show how I feel because it "makes you look bad"
You know that old saying, "fool me once..."
To be honest, I don't think I want to stay.

Kiera Gephart, Grade 11
Bluffton Harrison High School, IN

Flashback

Tired of this fear
It's always there
Creeping up on me
At unexpected times
Last night I saw something
I'd hoped to never see again, yet I did
With the first punch it took me back
To when I was the victim of your attack
Lost in the past, I fell to pieces
Scared to death, I cried
I want to know: will I ever be okay?
Or will I always be blown away from my peace
Like a feather in the wind
And as I cried I heard your voice
Only inside my head, so cold
Just like the ice I held,
I'm stuck in a flashback

Tosha Gamble, Grade 11
Mahomet-Seymour High School, IL

Tortured and Tormented

He's dark and exciting like a black panther.
I opened my heart to him.
My tortured heart.
Emotions are just smoke and mirrors.
Emotions are a mask...completely false.
...eyes are the windows to the tormented soul.
What am I?
I'm not human, or animal, or monster, or thing.
I am nothing.
People ask me what condition my heart is in.
I'm emotionally broken and torn.
People ask me what condition my soul is in.
I'm tortured and tormented.
I have fallen.

Aliyah Harvey, Grade 10
MacArthur High School, IL

A Father's Love

A father Loves his daughter without thought,
A Love that carries on forevermore.
A Love that can't be found and can't be bought,
This Love is always like an open door.
A Love that always flows out constantly,
No man, no thing, no act to come between.
A Love that is so strong that you can see.
Not even death can try to come between.
A father Loves his daughter from above,
A Love that shines through heaven's pearly gates.
More time and power to send out his Love,
A daughter that will feel it and will wait
Until a day to see the father's eyes
With tears of joy as they both hug and cry.

Paige Clough, Grade 12
Boylan Catholic High School, IL

Curtain Call

I want to go back —
back to the long evenings of watching my world fall apart,
of allowing myself to be consumed by the stage
as every raw emotion melts into an art, without my knowing —
I want to go back.

Back to the lines —
the unpredictable pattern of a life that is not mine,
every word tangling into a web of false reality —
I want to go back.

Back to the lights —
the artificial sun to warm my soul
sometimes the only reminder that it still remains —
I want to go back.

Back to the curtains —
O, sly creatures of the stage,
the only witnesses to both sides of an illusion too great for man,
hiding each stolen secret until it comes of age —
I want to go back.

Back to the stage —
a battleground that allows only victory, regardless of bloodshed,
a home for the artist and the ill at heart,
a world for the creative to mold to their idea of perfection —
This —
this is where you will find me.

Bradi Heaberlin, Grade 11
Indiana Academy for Science, Math and Humanities, IN

Through My Eyes

I see black bodies in a dark room
I see the whites of their eyes meet as they hover
But the light doesn't ever seem to get through
In time for the eyes to see each other

I see windows and doors in the whites of their eyes
I see the light as it screams to me through their eyes' shine
But the light doesn't ever get through in time
And its reflection in mine does not the darkness divide

I see that they feel not upset as I do
I feel that they see me watching them
But I remember the light does never get through
And away from the scene I walk again

I see no more ceilings I need to reach towards
I feel not the feeling of feet on the floor
I see no more windows, I see no more doors
I see only feeling, serene, unexplored

And I see not the eyes that the darkness absorbed
I feeling like fleeing from freedom no more

Kevin Klein-Cardena, Grade 12
Schaumburg High School, IL

I Remember Meeting the Stranger I Call My Best Friend

An ordinary day,
Evening approaching.
A maroon and gold cloudless sky filled the scenery.
I was sitting,
Watching,
Waiting…
for something, or someone.
Then I remember
she strolled in making somewhat of a clumsy sound.
Almost afraid to look,
And without knowing what would happen next…
Eye contact, laughter —
Instant connection between us.
No memorable words exchanged,
Nothing of importance,
Nothing of true content,
Nothing except our names.
The words we would never forget,
Each others name.
We were complete strangers,
content with the thought.

Megan Harrell, Grade 11
Roncalli High School, IN

The Whine of a Lost Dog

The whine of a lost dog is all I hoped for.
The whine of a lost dog is all I prayed for.
My best friend ran away.
My best friend left me.
My only friend left me.

Every day I'd run up and down the streets, searching.
Every day I'd put up signs reading LOST DOG.
Every day the cut of pain she left me grew deeper and deeper.

I couldn't bear knowing she was gone.
I couldn't bear knowing she was out there alone.
I couldn't bear knowing she could be with another family.

But then I heard it.
I heard the whine of my lost dog.

Lisa Frieders, Grade 12
Oswego East High School, IL

Addiction

A ddiction pulls families
D own and makes you
D eceive yourself and others
I t makes good into bad it
C auses your whole life to fall
T o pieces in a matter of seconds
I t pulls you apart
O ne by one making a positive into a
N egative just by a sniff puff or a little needle

Lydia Dismang, Grade 10
Carmi-White County High School, IL

The Other Side of a Photograph
Forever a moment in black and white,
The smiles, the tears, the love and the joy,
Were ingrained in the film, captured with light.

Though it's faded and torn there still stands the boy,
On an old worn porch that was new then,
No smile in army green off to deploy.

Fifty years have passed and the corner has bent,
since this was taken and they said "I do."
It's all he has until he sees her again.

Now a sepia tone has transformed the blue,
From the day they brought him home, and sixteen
Years later when his truck was brand new.

Shreds of time are saved by this tiny machine
That can replay your life on shiny paper, and
allow you to remember everything.

All those phases you went through, starting a band,
The time you shaved your eyebrow in half,
And then there was you buried in the sand.

The sounds that were captured, a cry, a laugh,
Will not be heard years from now, but imagine
Them like you were the one taking the photograph.
Darby Marinelli, Grade 12
Boylan Catholic High School, IL

Time Flies
I wake up Monday morn,
Eat breakfast at the crack of dawn,
While I wait and watch for the sun to be born,
Dancing like a little fawn.

Then it's off to school to learn,
Just wanting extra time for rest.
The contents of my stomach churn,
While I wait to take my final test.

The whistle blows, practice begins,
My legs already ache.
I really hope that my team wins,
Then the trophy we will take!

Bedtime approaches,
A long day in the past,
No more yelling coaches
The day is done at last.

Waking up the next morning,
Realizing it is Monday again.
Mackenzie Harrington, Grade 11
Roncalli High School, IN

Sonnet #4
When you're around my heart ignites with love.
I wish that I could freeze time when I'm with you
Because it's something I want a lot of.
I've never been so much in love, it's true.

My mind keeps going back to the night we kissed
And my heart starts to fly around each time.
I didn't know this much love could exist.
Your heart is like stairs that I seek to climb.

Every time we talk you make me smile
And I never stop as long as you're there.
I just want you in my arms for awhile.
I never knew love felt this good to share.

How did I end up with someone so great?
You say I'm amazing, but that's your trait.
Lawrence Algee, Grade 11
Neuqua Valley High School Blue Campus, IL

The Winds Whipped Through
The winds whipped through the branches with God's great might,
the brutal intruder disrupted the night,
threatening to knock the power out,
with a loud crack they began to shout,
running for shelter to escape the fight
between God and nature, what an interesting sight
to see a flash, the sky lit up so bright.
The winds whipped through,
the night threatening with every flash of light,
gritting its teeth with every bite,
leaves and limbs whirled about,
threatening to knock the power out.
Everything will be all right,
after the winds whip through.
Madeline Chmell, Grade 12
Boylan Catholic High School, IL

What Are We Really?
Two hearts to hold; A rose to smell.
The wants and needs of a twisted hell.
What are we really?
People of love and of hate; emotions slowly break.
No one knows life isn't a lesson, but just a dream.
We're given ups and downs; we bring life to a scene.
What are we really?
Sweetly untouched or born ready to die,
Blinded from our rights; only we understand in time.
Well you and I, we're only human beings.
We aren't all perfect, but try hard to give meaning.
So you tell me what you truly believe.
Can you answer my question of life:
What are we really?
Ciarra Deadmond, Grade 10
MacArthur High School, IL

The Clock's Not Ticking

There isn't coffee for a caffeine fill
Only to cherish the flavor
And to inhale
The bitterly sweet scent
Once the day's work is done
Nothing but the promise of
A mattress is to be found
In the depths of one's thoughts
There are no more painstakingly long days
And as quickly as the mission is accomplished
The lids will seal shut until
The body and soul
Meet in a sublime place
Where the being is rejuvenated
Relaxed
And ready
There won't be a sunrise and no sunset
Days may have twelve, a baker's,
Two, even four dozen hours
And time is this same thing as downtime.

Mackenzie Borders, Grade 12
Oswego East High School, IL

Crayola Intelligence

A child cradles a crayon in hand.
An idea flaunts within a man's
Mind. Subject to react
Towards their newfound pact:
Creation, goals burn within their minds.
Their image, enough to profess to the blind.
Complementary colors combat concrete
Walls covered by coloring book pages. Obsolete
Mind-blocks barricade the notion from the page.
Armed with sharp weapons: crayon and wit. A gauge
Displays a measurement of higher order. A beat
Flows. Their melody knows not of defeat.
This child's pictures shows keys,
Unlocking evolution in man's mind to cure disease.
No nation can stop man, armed with an imagination.

Jason de Jesus, Grade 12
Boylan Catholic High School, IL

Penny

Isn't a rusty penny
worth the same as a shiny one?
A red cent of hard work
or a new edition Lincoln mold.
Zero point zero one dollars with a name, a history, a story
or a remodeled piece of copper looking for a start.
Heads up, or face down under the couch
or abandoned in the street.
From the purse of a sinner
or from the pockets of a preacher's suit,
a penny is still a penny.

C. Caleb Washington, Grade 10
North Chicago Community High School, IL

The Fear Within

Happiness comes fleeting as a bird,
Sudden and blurred behind whispered words.
Pounding at my head,
Crying instead,
This happiness that disappears,
And is replaced with fear.
Fear of the light,
Fear of the dark,
Fear of anything not perfectly right.
Fear that rules completely,
Tightening its fatal grasp,
Creeping closer discreetly.
Screams from within
While the Devil smiles his evil grin.
Squirming and running,
It's the endless miles,
Over blank white tiles,
Of reaching demons and ghosts
Smiling as I roast
In the fiery pits of hell.

Louisa Fan, Grade 11
Libertyville High School, IL

Can You Sense the Music

Sweet, melodious sounds occupy the room,
the beautiful voices fill the listeners' hearts with cheer.
If the sounds could be described with a smell,
it would smell like sweet perfume.
The songs are something you must hear,
and a story you must tell.

The notes would have a taste that you want to consume,
every word is sung crisp and clear,
the words running off their tongues like sweet caramel.
You watch the performers up on the stage whom,
look like dancing and prancing deer,
see their beautiful costumes in pastel.

Somehow you can feel the magic in the room,
as if the music could reach out and grab you here.
The songs feel like soft silk as well,
as smooth flower petals after they bloom.
Smell, see, taste, touch, and hear.
These are the senses we know so well.

Stephanie Peterson, Grade 10
John Adams High School, IN

Sunshine Is a Blessing

Sunshine is a blessing.
Morning is a blessing.
Agony is less and fear is diminished in the sparkle
And gold of an early morning sun.
Sunshine is a blessing.
Morning is a blessing.

Trevor Cloud, Grade 10
MacArthur High School, IL

Become You

He is a wilting flower hung on the cold wall
He is the man watching the sand
pouring out of the broken hourglass
He is the abandoned building
being pummeled by a rusty bulldozer

Can't bloom and make a life of his own
Can't stop the time as he feels
his life quickly coming to its end
Can't call for help as he is betrayed
by life, God, and those whom he believed
were is loved ones

Speak out for yourself
Speak out for your beliefs
Speak out for those who truly love you

Become the wall, the sand, the bulldozer
Samantha Bonnell, Grade 12
Oswego East High School, IL

Christmas at Home

I'm always the first up
and down the stairs,
eager for Christmas to begin
the day before.

Once all the gifts are open,
we clean up for the evening's party.
My shampoo
holding its smell of fresh mint,
peppermint to be exact.

Family swarms in.
Uncle Brian is always last.
The party is fun
with prayer and a meal
just before we all catch up.

Christmas at home.
Katherine Moss, Grade 11
Oswego East High School, IL

Thinking of You

You
Bright, shining
Loving, laughing, dancing
What I live for
Love
Spontaneous, romantic
Singing, dancing, kissing
With you forever more
Jenny
Zachary Lange, Grade 12
Lisle High School, IL

This Is Home

A canopy of trees creates a curtain above my head as
my toes dig into the soft earth and crunch the dead leaves.
A deep breath in. This is home.
Fresh air against my skin sings softly with the wind.
The smell of autumn lingers in the air as the animals stir from their slumber.
A long look around. This is home.
Alone and towering above the dirt and overgrowth stands
a tree aged with experience.
Broken, decaying steps held up by the strength of matured nails
lead to the unreachable heights of my imagination.
A climb up the tree. This is home.
Hanging from the tree with all the strength of an eternal secret
is a strong rope swing swaying slightly with the breeze.
The weight of my body pressed against the swing takes the
pressure of the world off of me and throws it into the wind.
One swift swing. This is home.
The tree begs me to stay and play. It taunts me
with all of the secrets it longs to tell.
As the years go by, my oldest friend stays by my side.
The one constant in the chaos of change that is my life.
This is home.
Erika Crouch, Grade 12
Boylan Catholic High School, IL

The Owl Prince

i've fallen into a rabbit hole,
buried by blood clots and dirty snow.
with ice in my veins, freezing them close,
(/{h}e/[<art>){er}-i-es] spilt upon the overpass of a city road.
i'm stuck in November with nowhere to go;
trapped by this depression as winter months approach.
upon her sweater she wore an owl broach,
shining with splendor of silver and gold,
all wrapped up in a mouse-furred overcoat.
i said you are the predator and prey as one;
you are the glowing moon and the shining sun.
you are this sickness, you are my disease,
but you are the medicine which also cures me.
she said you are my prince of darkness and love;
you are the chauffeur of my chariot come.
you are my savior from self-proclaimed death,
you are my everything to the nothing i have left.
and so we were there in a nighttime trance,
as i spinned her around and we slowly danced;
so incompletely complete as two lovers could be,
a thousand degrees of heat produced within just two synchronized beats.
Logan Ghast, Grade 10
Newton Community High School, IL

Moving On

Work hard for success
Sleepless nights of studying
Whatever it takes
Robert Kulevich, Grade 12
Lisle High School, IL

Thrill

The future can scare me
but that won't hold me back
no need for spoilers
Cara McLennon, Grade 12
Lisle High School, IL

Letter in the Mail

Senior year has placed quite a toll on my mailman

As squirrels hole up for the winter
With all of their treasures in stock
My mailman does the same
But within our roadside mailbox

With each new letter's arrival
I cannot help but cast a grin
For each message holds a possibility
Of where my future will begin

Beside me, though, my mailman frets
What will happen when I go away
He has remained by my side forever
Preventing me from running astray

I remind him of the challenges we faced
And of all the lessons shared
When I leave for college next year
I will be more than well prepared

One fateful day, the awaited letter arrives
A judgment day of sorts
My dad, the mailman, rushes to my side
We prepare ourselves for what the news reports

Laura May, Grade 12
Benton Central Jr/Sr High School, IN

The Future

Up, up on the moon, so far, far away,
Girls will laugh, and boys will play
To pass the time of a long summer day
Someday in the future, not so far away.

In crowded streets the people will throng
To celebrate with dance and with song
The new cleaning robot that can't go wrong
Someday in the future, it won't be long.

One look at yourself and you say with a smile,
"How handsome am I, and so full of wile!"
But with age you'll land in a state of denial
Someday in the future, in just a short while.

Someday everything which you now hold dear,
A friend, a toy, or that face in the mirror,
Will pass away to eternal pain or cheer
Someday in the future, it's almost here.

So be ready my brothers, and sisters, too,
If you haven't already, start your life anew,
Accept Christ as your Savior, He'll defend you
On that day in the future when God judges you.

Courtney Potter, Grade 12
Home School, IN

Inevitable

Death happens everywhere.
Sometimes people suffer from awful tragedies.
Sometimes people grow extremely old and die peacefully in bed.
However it happens;
Death is a part of life.

Some people live to an old age.
They die peacefully in their sleep.
All of their family surrounds the bed,
Creating a large rainstorm.

Some drive too fast on the highway.
They lose control of the speeding car.
The car breaks into several pieces.
Just like the driver's family.

Everything with life has an end.
What has life knows death awaits them.
Even though we know we eventually die,
The event is still disastrous.

Ian King, Grade 11
Bluffton Harrison High School, IN

Yet Another Teenage Love Story

Yet Another Teenage Love Story
"Forever doesn't seem quite so long now,"
Is what I say as I sit here alone,
No comfort left, a sad fate to bemoan,
Before my melodrama forced to bow.
And yet with these sorrows upon my brow,
I recall the love from you to me shown,
The long hours spent with you on the phone,
And the promises we both did vow.
But what good now comes from those empty words?
After you have left me without a care,
Left me for other pastures deemed more fair.
You had expected me to do likewise,
But my feelings, at least, were not just lies,
Unlike the empty notes of mockingbirds.

Connor Robinson, Grade 10
Libertyville High School, IL

Not Breaking

I remember you saying, "I'll always be here."
And that you would hold me through all of my fears.
You said you loved me.
You said that you cared.
Well if you really meant all that, wouldn't you still be here?
I just don't understand,
You're changing acts at hand.
It's so confusing.
It's driving me mad.
But it will be okay,
I'll bend, but I won't break.

Samantha Murphy, Grade 10
Carmi-White County High School, IL

Fleeting Innocence

It was beautiful.
But then again, so were we.
Before hatred destroyed all hope…
Greenery surrounded us.
The damp of the rice paddies instilled itself deep within us.
Our foxholes swaddled us like newborns
We were the newborns.
Until blood choked the air around us.
White orchids
now stained crimson and decaying
Like the bodies of the men waiting,
waiting to find their way back home.
Sleep is ever fleeting
The unacknowledged fear came with darkness
so black that it swallowed us whole.
Leaving us to pray that we would again see
the dim light of a new day.
And maybe, just maybe
The world's innocence would survive for a few hours more.

Mackenzee Kienitz, Grade 11
Schaumburg High School, IL

A Lament to God

Why is the world the way it is?
Why are you letting the poor get poorer?
Do you expect me to be thankful?
As I see corruption in the world
As I taste the salty tears of a mother mourning her diseased child
As I read about a terrorist killing thousands of people
How do you expect me to be grateful?
As I watch the bodies dissipate like the fallen leaves
You have created me
As a considerate tiny bit of carbon
In this vast universe
To watch the tin man
Conquer the world
Who you are?
Who are you?
I still do not know

Yasemin Oder, Grade 11
Schaumburg High School, IL

Illusions

Illusions!
Illusions are perfect
They disguise the pain
They make everyone believe you are perfectly okay
Illusions
Illusions can be the simplest things
Such as a cute little smile
Or a simple hello
So do your best to be kind to others, as they may be in pain
They may be using an illusion every single day!

Dana Cousin, Grade 10
Harlem High School, IL

Life of an Equestrian

One day, I want to be one of the best,
But to get there, I need to push myself to be
That person, that athlete, that equestrian,
I know I can be.
I have my flaws and have made mistakes.
I learned from them.
It shows me how to handle my obstacles,
How to ride through the issues,
And make them look like my plan.
I have success when I focus upon my task,
Memorize the course, nail my distances,
Use my abilities as well as I know how.
I have bonds with animals ten times my size,
But I control them at all times in the ring.
They must respond to my commands.
They prove to me how strong I really am.
It takes everything you've got to become one of the stars,
One of the people the young kids look up to.
You must put your heart and soul into it, to be able to reach the top.
I am an equestrian,
With the drive to be the best.

Taylor Wienold, Grade 10
William Fremd High School, IL

Family

My face will be forever painted
And my mine will be well educated
I may be an outcast at school
But I have found a family that is so cool
They are there for me through thick and thin
And they love me no matter what trouble I get in
When I need someone to talk to, I just give 'em a call
And if someone wants to fight, they're down to brawl.
Who am I kidding? I have no family
The only person I have is me
All I have wanted is someone to care
I cannot seem to find that person anywhere
I do not ever want to be alone
But towards me, everyone's heart is stone
I do not even see the point in trying
I am the one who always ends up crying

Cailyn Campbell, Grade 12
Benton Central Jr/Sr High School, IN

I Love Harry Potter

I wish I could go to Hogwarts
Ride the Hogwarts Express
Go to Hogsmeade
Hangout with the Twins, Fred and George
Drink Butterbeer
Make potions
All my dreams would come true
But I'm still waiting for my acceptance letter

Maggie Jansen, Grade 12
Lisle High School, IL

Time

Why does it go fast and slow?
It's hard to watch it pass and fly,
To see how time can just go by.
Memories I'll never forget,
And slip-ups that I'd like to regret.
I need not think of what I've done,
But many more good times yet to come.
Why do those fun times have to go?

Today is another instant in time,
As the clocks continue to chime.
I sit here now, deep in thought,
Passing the time, just as I ought.
If any time is hard for you, though,
Sit back, relax, and go with the flow.
Julia Hoyda, Grade 10
Rosary High School, IL

Amity

wrapped in a blanket
eyes shut
never fidget, never fuss
lost in slumber
keep the peace
make no sound
softly breathe
tiny hands
tiny feet
little mouth
oh so sweet
hands grasp
my little finger
lean down and whisper
"I love you, my sister"
Emily Coronado, Grade 10
Bolingbrook High School, IL

Love Is

Love is wrong
Love is right
Love can be the simplest thing
Giving someone a hug or kiss at night.
Love is pain
Love is sweet
Love is pacing
Like a newborn baby's heartbeat.
Love is laugh
Love is cry
Love can really kill you inside.
Love is you
Love is me
And all together
Love makes we.
Asia Spinks, Grade 10
Ben Davis University High School, IN

Being Human

You pull back my flesh,
My skin,
To my muscle,
To my bone,
You'll see that I'm human,
One of my own,
You take that as you please,
But remember,
Through all the differences in the world,
We are all alike,
You and I,
We are human,
Emotions that run wild,
And looks that vary,
From child to child,
So love each other,
And all ways know,
That no matter what race,
nation,
Gay, lesbian, trans, or queer, Straight or bi,
We're all one of a kind.
Krystal Clingler, Grade 12
Knox Community High School, IN

Wind

Trees swaying
Stray leaves dancing
The strings of my heart keeping time
With it all
As it all, unfolds before my being
And soul
Does it love us?
No, it loves no one
It only sympathizes
Warning and cooling
But as it whispers to me
Heeding a warning to me
Of the horrendous monster
That soon follows it
Hovering after its very wake
It fights against itself
With bright, white flashes and loud claps
Making everything bend to its will
Finally with its last sigh of breath
It weakened
Taking the fierce beast with it
Casey Schmidt, Grade 10
Freeport High School, IL

Nature

Vines intertwine.
Your blood and mine.
Leaves dance in the wind.
Trees sway and bend.
Kinn Reagan, Grade 10
West Vigo High School, IN

The Secrets of Leaves

As the seasons pass and the air gets cold,
the trees begin anew.
The secrets of the past that they will hold
are known by a lucky few.

I sit here waiting, watching, bubbling
with curiosity, pacing to and fro.
"Please, O Trees," I say anticipating,
"tell me all that you know!"

One day I shall be one
of those awe-inspiring few,
But for that time to come
I must live my life true.
Miranda Lindvall, Grade 12
Boylan Catholic High School, IL

Bright New World

Black and white,
a deafening silence.
Rushing by,
left behind.
Rewrite the past,
create a new destiny.
Let the color fade in,
light a new path.
No more waiting,
running towards a new tomorrow.
Existing in the strands of time,
the adventure awaits.
Break through the gray,
into a bright new world.
Kylie Cavender, Grade 11
North Judson-San Pierre High School, IN

Passion

Sometimes life can be cruel
Like the harsh wind on a cold night
Everything you do
Or try to accomplish
Erodes like the receding shoreline
You want to be the best
Instead failure knocks at the door
Nothing goes right
I hate living like this
My life tears me apart
There is so much agony in my heart
People do not understand
How I appear to be happy
But I am empty inside
Jesus Nevarez, Grade 12
Schaumburg High School, IL

I Hear His Annoying Voice

When I sit in my math class in the morning,
Everything is quiet.
I am working silently,
Trying to figure out a math problem.
Then I hear his annoying voice and lose all of my concentration.
He begins his usual routine,
Talking and disrupting the other students.
His laugh is like nothing I've ever heard before.
It's annoying and indescribable,
The kind of laugh you hate hearing.
The teacher then begins to pass back our tests.
He receives his and at once decides to share it with the class,
As he is talking to his friend about the test,
I can't help but think of smart remarks that I keep to myself.
Sometimes, I wish he would be quiet for just five minutes.
I overhear him say that he cheated on the test,
Which makes me even more aggravated at him.
Some days, I just wish that he didn't have the same class as me,
But for now, I will just have to deal with him.
I come to class every day in hopes that he is absent
Only to have my hopes crushed.

Mason Tanner, Grade 12
Marion High School, IL

Living Life

To live life is to trust yourself.
Trust your mind and heart.
Let them lead you to where you are going.
Let them guide you away from the past.
Forget about what you wanted.
Dream about all you can.
Choose to act and make mistakes.
Decide to do well no matter what it takes.
Chances occur.
But, it's what you decide that counts.
The good and the bad look equally appealing.
Just remember with what you are dealing.
Choose to engage in a little or in a lot.
Draw your own path.
Create the course that is best for you.
Then, follow it or don't.

Tiffany Brown, Grade 12
Reitz Memorial High School, IN

The Never Ending Wars

Walking through the valley of the shadow of death,
They put on their masks and take their last mortal breath.
The masses of few, the congregation of none,
Charge at the helpless wielding their gun.
They watch as their brother dies, with no resentment in his eyes.
Falling to the ground, a Bible at their breast,
They pray for forgiveness where their brothers will rest.
You cannot leave, for it's the cause He believes,
Only to be killed by this inevitable disease.

Court Thompson, Grade 11
American School of Correspondence, IL

The Four-Year Old's Escape

A clear Sunday afternoon,
Staring at the TV, intently on my knees,
Soon to realize I was left alone, or so I thought,
Panic set in, I ran for the trees.
Running in my socks
OUCH, OUCH, OUCH, pebbles poke my feet,
As I reach the end of our street,
HELP, HELP, it feels like cars are the only things I greet.
I turn to my left, blindly heading for nowhere,
A house, with a couple in the yard.
"Will somebody please help?"
They take me under their guard.
The house friendly and green.
"Are you all right?" they ask.
"My family is gone," I cry.
Finding my parents is the true task.
A call to the police for help.
My name being a clue.
A call to my house.
Leads to the man in blue.

Greg Cormier, Grade 12
Boylan Catholic High School, IL

Moonlight Path

Moon shines, bright and clear
Against the starry night
Petals falling, sweet and calm
Among the moon's steady light.
    The pathway shown, so undisturbed
    So peaceful in one's sight
    The trees, so tall, beside the path
    Lightened by the moon's clear light
        The stones and sticks we used to see
        Amidst the path's soft way
        Will not be and will not show
        While the moon shines over today.
    The breeze that brushes, calmingly
    Among the thinning trees
    Would have shivered frighteningly
    But tonight, it will not freeze
Silence and beauty beyond the calm
With peace, with harmony, no wrath
Will forever spread, unremitting
On this wondrous moonlight path.

Leena Aljobeh, Grade 10
Valparaiso High School, IN

I Never Knew...

I never knew...
    how hard it would be to lose you,
    how close we were before you left,
    how handsome you were as a baby,
    I never knew that I would lose my first nephew
    at five months.

Brittany Hobson, Grade 10
Carmi-White County High School, IL

Swing

Back
The haunting past
Never forgotten
Blood pumping through my veins
Am I alive?
Sometimes it's hard to tell
Forth
How can I go up from here?
Where's there to go?
Uncertainty overtakes me
I am running out of options
Back
The ride is slowing
I am almost finished
Defined by my mistakes
I am so close
Stop
It's over

Mia VanZandt, Grade 12
Elverado High School, IL

Love

Leaves falling from the trees
I say they are very free
They hit the ground
They make no sound

If I were to say I need solitude
You would not understand
Let me have some space
To contemplate your sweet face

Can I have a kiss?
And then another?
Do you think
I am a bother?

You cannot quench my desire
Or put out my amorous fire

Mario Miranda, Grade 11
Schaumburg High School, IL

Alone

When you held me in your arms…
    I felt protected and loved,

When you held me in your arms…
    a smile would appear on my lips,

When you held me in your arms…
    my heart soared.

But when you let go…
    I was utterly alone.

Shania Clapper, Grade 10
Carmi-White County High School, IL

An Open Mind

It hears but does not judge.
When you go out in the world,
All they do is misjudge.
When you stay positive about who you are,
You know you're able to reach the stars.
Look in the mirror, do you see yourself?
Asking what went wrong with myself.
People look at you differently, when you decide to change how you look,
You're thinking, why are they judging a book by its cover?
You have your real friends and your haters,
Real friends will tell you to love who you are,
But the haters are just the dictators.
Yeah, they can say I am a no one;
But look on the bright side, I am loved by the people I call family.
Keep an open mind; you only live once in a lifetime.
You can be who you want to be, no matter how much people dislike what you do.
You're your own person, beautiful, intelligent, and bright.
Don't think anything less, because everything will be all right.
Lessons learned for today. You are who you are, and nothing less.
Always keep an open mind!

Moesha Manning, Grade 10
De La Salle Institute, IL

Night

At night the world seems to stand still
The slightest noise paralyzes you
It seems like night is dark because it makes it easier to focus on your fears
You try telling yourself you're fine, but in your head you know you're not
You hide under the covers for protection
At last, your eyes begin to droop
And finally, you fall asleep

Jacob Casper, Grade 10
John Adams High School, IN

Dear You

What if I took a risk?
Asked you out today,
Would you say no and break my heart?
Or say yes and make it okay?
What if I stopped the games?
No more little flirting,
Would you try again?
Or just give up?
Would it matter either way?
What if I told you the truth?
I love you but I'm scared,
Relationships send me running,
But with you I feel prepared.
Ready to take a risk,
Ready to be with you,
What if I took a risk?
Would you risk it with me too?

Michelle Schultz, Grade 12
Lisle High School, IL

Too Late

So much that I wish I had said
But you have left me behind
Moving forward on your own
Leaving me to cry

What can I say?
What can I do?
You'll never come back
But I continue holding on to that hope
Foolish of me, I know
Yet I can't let go

So much that I regret
Having not the courage to say
Now you've left the world behind
And me too.

Amy Dong, Grade 11
Mishawaka High School, IN

What I Found in the Sea
Even when the sea is far away,
I sense it.
It is not a physical presence,
but a spiritual body.

The sea is alive.
The heartbeat of its waves
spikes the pulses of all
who experience it.

The sea is a thoughtful being.
Its grainy, seashell shores
are the breeding grounds
of men's musings.

One is not so much in the sea
as the sea is in one.
Even when the sea is far away,
its tide rises within me.
Katelyn Klingler, Grade 11
Mater Dei High School, IN

Kalyssa
You were too young to remember
The times we had together.

Slumber parties with
Extra buttered popcorn
Senseless fights
Turn too fast to talking
Once more.

Long weeks turn
To fun summers
Late nights
To great talks.

Now that you are
Older, I cannot imagine
How one day you
Were barely walking
To wearing make-up.
Stevie Cox, Grade 10
Bluffton Harrison High School, IN

Unseen Beauty
What could this be?
Among all thy beauty,
What is this of which I long to see?
Thy beauty is that of forbidden.
Thy voice is that of the heavens.
So tempting is thee,
The beauty of which
The eye cannot see.
Cheyenne Doan, Grade 10
Rockville Jr/Sr High School, IN

Gone
You never really know what you have until it is gone.

That special something that is on the verge of being taken away.
The sweet nothing that keeps you going…gone in an instant. You can

Kick
Shout
and
Cry

But it won't make a difference in their eyes.
You can say it's not fair.   But how many times a day do we say that?
So take your special somethings. And hold your sweet nothings.
Keep them safe until you're blue in the face.
And when the time comes, when they wave goodbye, do not

Kick
Shout
and
Cry

For our special somethings
And our sweet nothings
Will always comfort us.

Because special somethings and sweet nothings live on forever, never really leaving us,
For they stay in our hearts.
Dana Cornish, Grade 10
Providence Catholic High School, IL

Same Eyes
Controversy strikes. His desk squeaks in the dead silence of the classroom.
The boy raises his hand and says:

If everyone had the same perspective…

People would see
What a world it would be
Trees would have all the same branches
Love would take all the same chances
You could match every smile
And the same eyes would scan every mile
Everyone would notice the spots on the moon
Everyone would hear in the same tune
Everyone looks at the clouds in the sky
Every last eye sees the same bow tie
Maybe even racism and sexism would be broke
All misconceptions would go up in smoke
All our pairs look the same
We all see a different game
Every person can see themselves getting older
Every beauty's eyes would be in the beholder's
Katherine Barelli, Grade 12
Boylan Catholic High School, IL

The Ocean of Homework

A wide-open sea.
Opening around me,
sparkling with ink,
dotted with I's sailing around,
but as I watch,
from this beach of life,
the waves come crashing,
up the shore,
threatening to crush my home,
cascading in brilliant reds and blacks,
all around me as I push my boat of life out,
trying to navigate to a better shore,
the testy winds blowing sprays of confetti at my face,
yet I carry on, finding the currents of daily life,
taking these as I can,
towards the sunny weekends,
these peaceful islands where I can take shelter,
ready, for another trip out next week.

Nicholas Bimmerle, Grade 12
Boylan Catholic High School, IL

Julio Is Someone Who…

Julio is someone who…
Is generous at times
You want to hug when he goofs off
Can irritate you when he goofs around too much
Who acts like a teenager when he's only eight years old
Is awesome to hang out with
I remember…
Watching scary movies with him on weekends
Sitting on my skateboard waiting for him at his bus stop
Taking care of him when we were the only ones at home
Ordering a pizza when we were too lazy to make something
Spending hours in the yard practicing for our baseball games
Julio…
Makes me feel proud to be a brother
Make me want another brother
Makes me want to throw him out the window at times
Has kept me out of trouble
Has kept me home

Jorge Ortiz, Grade 12
Lisle High School, IL

Glory of the Night

I see shadows dancing in the pale moonlight.
I see stars flickering in the sky of night.
I feel the chill of the air brush against my skin.
With all the freedom of the dark, I want it to win.
Fireflies are all around; flitter, flutter, play.
The glowing they provide warns of the coming day.
The sun comes up, the moon goes down, the sky begins to burn.
For all we do to damage Earth; we cannot stop her turn,
But down will go the sun again giving us respite.
We welcome back the coolness, and glory of the night.

Donald Cook, Grade 12
Prairie Heights Sr High School, IN

Just Yesterday

If I could go back to this time just yesterday…
How 'bout five years from now, I'd know what to say
If you told me then what was to happen now
I'd ask you why and if possible how
I'll try to take it one step at a time
I know what I do has no reason or rhyme
I'm sorry for the things that I've done,
Which in truth is next to none
Maybe that's the problem, I should stop right here
I keep walking further, but you're nowhere near
Block this out, ignore it somehow
Put a smile on my face I can do it for now
Keep pushing past this place
I won't give up, that won't be the case
Everyone has a battle to fight
You remind me even in the dark you can find a light
So, stay by my side it makes this feel far away
Let's forget about it all just for today
I'm kind of confused, don't know what to do
But at least for now, I'll have you

Nicole Nudelman, Grade 11
Libertyville High School, IL

Son to Mother

Well Mom, let me tell you:
life for me has been a roller coaster ride.
It's had its ups, yeah,
downs too,
but this far it's been a sure success.
I hate to confess,
but the darkest day,
by all means was when I know who was sick,
Cancer it seems,
but nonetheless,
you taught me a life long lesson those terrible days,
though it hasn't the opportune,
for the wisdom there is no repay,
I thank you for the darkest day.

Michael Koscielniak, Grade 11
Marian Central Catholic High School, IL

Unachievable

Nightmares sparkle in dazzling gleams
Compared to betrayals of desirable dreams
Cotton's soft touch collides with the rough
Mangled and lashed by roots in the brush
Glistening promises of something worth wanting
Foul smirks in the fog from a mysterious haunting
Foreign sights seize my will to proceed
Denting the earth by my fast-falling knees
Dragging my heart on the soggy terrain
Slick and hazardous, soaked by the rain
Awakened by growls from reality's shake
Hopelessness grows as dreams slowly fade

Ben Billand, Grade 11
Guerin Catholic High School, IN

A Gilded Meadow

Grasses of the prairie sway in the wind,
The golden stalks watching as time goes by.
Susans with their black eyes let out a sigh
As the shadow of the bison fades away.
They remember the days of the endless plains,
When the lone birch sprouted up from the soil
That now resides by the trickling stream.
The coreopsis is now stained deep red,
From the creatures that came onto their land;
Yet more of their kind continue to grow.
Silently sweeping the stalks back and forth,
A gust moves across the amber ocean,
Whispering to the birch about the last
Cycle and how to survive the next one.
Several have perished throughout the years,
And the aged hawk circles above watching,
Waiting, for his time to regain the land.
The residents know, however, that their
Time is limited, yet accept their fate.
In the grand puzzle they are but pieces,
But life goes on after their lives have ceased.

Emily Dahm, Grade 11
Belleville East High School, IL

Storms on the Horizon

To my Romeo
Each dawn that I wake I recall mem'ries,
Of you running in causing storms to rise,
Crack, boom, fill me up with warmth, light, and love,
It scares and scars me but it feels so right,
I want it but not so much as you want
My heart, my trust, my love, my forever,
I want what no other man but you can
Give me even if it is forbidden,
Romeo do not stop until I'm yours,
To hold, kiss, love, and more, you're everything,
So do not get shipwrecked on your way here,
Avoid the storm, go to the sunlit path,
Grief, hate, revenge, leave it all in the past,
Be mine at the end of the day to love.
Love, Juliet

Missy Anderson, Grade 10
Columbus North High School, IN

I Am Me

I'm loud because I want to be heard
I smile because I'm confident
I'm still standing because I'm strong
I look down because everyone is beneath me
I laugh because I'm happy
I am creative because I express myself
I'm real because I stay true to myself and never
Lose sight of who I am
I am me so who are you

Tia Crawford, Grade 12
Guilford High School, IL

Sea of Sorrows

Lost wallowing in a sea:
A sea of my own sorrow,
Never to escape; never to glimpse the light again

Listlessly sinking downwards,
Wallowing in self-hate.

Drifting on the bottom of an ocean of my tears,
The rasping sound of voices ringing broken on my ears;
Your voice, too, broken and unclear to me.

Silver stars weep for me, weep in an unseen sky;
Tears falling into the ocean depths drown me forever.

Darkness closes across my eyes,
When I shut my ears to your garbled pleas;
Discard the keys to my heart.

Long forgotten by all Gods,
I flounder no longer…
Within my Sea of Sorrows.

Ethan Vollmer, Grade 10
Benton Central Jr/Sr High School, IN

Cold Heart Beating

What has come I shall lose
like a bomb I just can't defuse.
But as I lay here, my last moments of life.
I lie here and think about my children and wife.
Who shall they be? Maybe they don't exist.
Maybe this thing called love is all just a myth.
A thing of beauty for us to strive and slave.
Will I find love by my very last day?
But maybe it isn't something to find.
It's something to give, it isn't mine.
It is a peace, a gift, it is nothing more.
I realize this as I lay on the rough concrete floor.
And then off with a boom, the walls shatter and fall.
There I lay dead in silence and awe.
I died all alone, but happy and clear.
For I died knowing what love was, and I had no fear.

Nick Konieczki, Grade 12
Schlarman High School, IL

I Am the One Who

I am the one who goes to school and doesn't say a word
I am the one who has no friends
I am the one who wears long sleeves when it's hot
I am the one who takes it, so my sisters don't have to
I am the one who no longer dreams
I am the one who screams for help, but no one hears me
I am the one who has lost all hope
I am the one who cries myself to sleep every night
I am the one who gets beaten by my parents

Caitlyn Jones, Grade 12
Elverado High School, IL

Mr. One-Cheek Smiler

Up bluffs the Porcelain man-he lives,
He had those marbled Eyes.
Stiff face and smile he never gives,
The more he tries, he cries?

Old One-cheek smiler always lonely, see him smiling never wide.

Down cliffs the silky woman lives,
She had those cotton eyes.
Benign face — smiling freely gives,
Here see the man tries, cries.

Old One-cheek smiler always lonely, see him smiling never wide.

Along Confetti-town, they're there —
Sweet Boys — girls see the show.
How she could talk to him is rare —
See both, she makes him glow.

Old One-cheek smiler not so lonely, see him smiling wide?

The Woman sees past his inked glass,
Discover — she waits while.
The Man's visage is loose silk grass —
Cheeks move — await the smile.

Old One-cheek smiler not so lonely, see him smiling-two cheeks full.
Tammy Duyen Do, Grade 11
Homestead Sr High School, IN

The Heartbreak of the Fall

Weather starts to become cold
Wind begins to pick up,
Carrying the rainbow of leaves through the air
Fall is approaching
With it brings a new school year

This season is the saddest of them all
For I know what it brings,
Thinking of the upcoming events fills my mind with dread
The time is soon to come,
The time for him to go

Happiness I once felt,
Will soon be replaced with heartbreak
Knowing that one day I will be with him,
As for the next I am left with nothing,
Nothing but the memories

I cannot bear a day without him
Neither can I image never seeing,
Feeling or hearing that sweet calming voice,
Bringing my heartbeat to a slow, strong, steady beat
It is clear in my eyes that a life without him is no life at all
Vanessa Hilson, Grade 10
John Adams High School, IN

The Majestic Island

The breathtaking nature engulfs the land;
an elevated palm tree stands out aloft the surface,
while others are hidden from sight.

The warm blue waters touch the shore,
carrying grains of sand back into the ocean,
leaving the beach drenched with salt water.

The sunny hot air swirls around the island,
while the seagulls soar into the sky,
circling each other over the seas.

The puffy whites float weightlessly in the sky,
casting shadows among the area,
covering the gigantic island.

The peaceful sounds of pale and ashy gray seagulls,
driving into the clear waters searching for their dinner,
of appetizing fish.

A joyous couple spending time with each other,
camping out on the remote island,
their boat left behind.

Footsteps carved into the sands,
trailing off into the unknown world,
the majestic island.
Jessica Martin, Grade 10
Benton Central Jr/Sr High School, IN

Industrious Rains

O n e car drives slowly
 Twothreefour
Zip along — splashing through huge puddles
The young boy in the boots is drenched
  With water
  With laughter.
To that boy — angels are crying
To a weatherman — clouds are saturated
To me? — my soul is refreshed.
Hours progress and the grass is my mood ring.
  The mist through the mesh of the open window.
  The drip
            drip
       drip against the welcoming concrete.
The smell of the worms celebrating the end of a famine.
The taste of the thick air napping.
Taking a day off from its busy, upbeat life.

  As am I.
  I sigh. I settle into the soft folds of my bed.
   My glass window shuts
      And my green ones are to follow.
Emily Way, Grade 12
Boylan Catholic High School, IL

Out of Tune

Sitting in my living room it waits to be played.
The keys are all dusty,
the bench is pushed in, and the top is closed.
Looking at that piano brings back many memories.
Going to lessons for many years,
but never practicing.
Trying to teach my friend to play,
while I needed to be taught myself.
Inside the bench lie music sheets, books, and pencils.
The sheets haven't been looked at,
the books haven't been opened,
and the pencils haven't been used
in many years.
Quitting piano seemed like what I wanted to do.
Now that I look at my old piano,
I feel kind of sorry for it.
It never gets played.
It's a piano without a purpose.
It's out of tune
and out of my heart.

Katie Kelly, Grade 10
William Fremd High School, IL

Different

The worn paths and ruts of conformity become as canyons.
Many are the men, who take the path through the canyon,
They erode the surface even more.
Only to be destroyed by the breaking of the ever so distant dam.
Washing the poor fools who strive to reach the unreachable away.
All who tell the tale are mocked by the new fools,
Who rush to reach the newly built dam.
The rush towards destruction.
The stampede of vanity, envy, and greed.
They erode the surface even more.
And the continuing repetitive cycle of
Trends, fashion, fads, and other desirables.
But I soar above.
Above the canyon of fools.
I climb upon mountains and run high in the sky,
With the ever-present loneliness of being pleasantly different.

Gabe Wohlwend, Grade 11
Elverado High School, IL

The Wind

Swiftly, silently rushing,
It wearies your thoughts away, peacefully hushing.
Tossing the leaves, giving us wings,
Dancing to songs the mind quietly sings.
It intensifies nature without making a sound
And makes us realize the beauty we can see all around.
It swings around us and hangs in the trees,
It cools the hot sand with its cold breathy breeze.
It brings both good and bad, it will rejoice or mourn...
But in the end, the wind always carries away the storm.

Morgan Tighe, Grade 11
Dunlap High School, IL

My Departed Soldier

He tells me the news that he's leaving again.
As soon as he does, I know my time is limited with him.
But time goes on, fast if I might say,
And I have to say goodbye today.
The tears roll down my reddened face,
Because I fear he won't be safe.

The buses come to take him away,
And goodbye becomes so hard to say,
I watch him falter down the short space,
To the bus that will take him to an awful place.

Now he's gone, and my heart feels hollow,
And I'm crying so hard that it's hard to swallow.
I'll miss him so much...it just isn't fair,
That he has to leave me and go over there.

I'll be okay, I say out loud,
Because he makes me so very proud.
He does a lot to keep us free,
I can feel his love blowing in the breeze.

Venesa Colclasure, Grade 12
Marion High School, IL

Unknown Me

Shadow of the other me
Wishful thinking beyond the sea

They say I'm a jerk am I bipolar
Or just giving the ones I love the cold shoulder

A me that I will never know
A dark side that I should never show

Figuring out my self worth
Confused Gemini since birth

Just coming into the new me
Changed for the better how could this be

Wanna be the best I can
But at the end of the day I'm just a man

Every day I get stronger
Unknown to myself no longer

Dorell Wall, Grade 11
Chicago Mathematics & Science Academy, IL

Here I Stand

Here I stand...
    in the rain,
    all alone,
    waiting on someone who may never show.
Here I stand hoping you didn't leave me wishing.

Leah Rawson, Grade 12
Carmi-White County High School, IL

Celebration

A wooden table is placed in the center of a room
I spread a smooth, linen table cloth on top of it
A floral arrangement sits in the center of the table
Bursts of orange, red, and gold glowers sit inside the piece
The smell of peach pie fills the dining room
I walk around the corner of the room and follow the delicious smell
It's coming from the kitchen
I watch my mom scurry about in a panic
Trying to finish all of the last minute dishes
I decide to help her out…
Food is being boiled, stirred, chopped, fried, and baked
Every possible cooking device is in use
Even the toaster
We cook in this chaotic kitchen for hours
One by one the dishes are completed
Once the last plate is filled, we collapse in exhaustion
Our tag team effort actually worked
I grab a plate from our nice china cabinet
I slab a mountain full of food onto my plate
And now it's time for my favorite part…
The taste test.

Alisha Wamack, Grade 12
Oswego East High School, IL

My Mother's Hands

The aroma of smothered chicken breast and steamed broccoli
Covered in gravy
Unfolds within her hands.
Their smooth lavender touch
Rescues the marching tears
That roll down the hills
Of my caramel cheeks.
When I am breaking like a bridge in an earthquake
Her hands cradle me
Like a gorilla cradling her baby.
In the twilight of the night
They run deep into my starry sheets
Tucking me in as I dream
Of her hands forming the moon and the stars.
As she folds her hands
I thank them for their gentle touch.

Charlotte Ivy, Grade 12
Oswego East High School, IL

Friendship

Don't ever be afraid to talk
Don't ever be afraid to cry
Don't ever be afraid to ask for help
Don't be afraid to give me your broken heart

You are my endearing friend
Like the soft gentle rain
That nourishes our earth
Our bond will never end

Mary Palafox, Grade 12
Schaumburg High School, IL

Moon's Point of View

I am bright and beautiful.
I own the night sky and my name is short.
Very few look at me 'cause my surface is vacant.
I can see those who spend romantic times together.
People compare me and criticize me.
During discussions of science, people talk nonstop about me.
My color is white and sometimes it looks like I walk through the sky.
People say I am cold, not cute.
Sometimes a dark shadow expands over me.
Sometimes this shadow is during the night and day.
No noise I make 'cause I do not talk.
My looks some do not seek.
I have many friends but they are small and special.
A man once spoke to me.
He said he did it for those on Earth.
He was the first to talk to me.
And he was the first to step on me and be happy to see me.
It was a big day for the both of us.
My surface has seen few people.
I am not alone for long for my friends come to me.
I am proud of who I am.

Crystal Howard, Grade 12
Northwestern High School, IL

My Savior

The heart behind the shadow
The smile crushed by the stone
The story and life of a girl
Hidden by truth and darkened by reality
Time passes and rain pours
Her memories take her over
She shoves the barrier in her way
But it will not budge
She ends up falling and tumbling
Twirling through a maze of terror
Never ending fright everywhere she turns
Loss of hope and strengthened fear
The lighting dims as she feels her being disappear
Her body becomes weak
Her thoughts become dim
She is losing herself
The world is taking her over
The walls are caving in
She falls to her knees
Mercy leaving her lips as her hands press
"God, save me…"

Allison Crow, Grade 11
Pike High School, IN

Us

It's so easy to be me when I'm with you.
You bring out the best in me and you don't have a clue.
Without you I could never truly be defined.
You were in God's plan when my heart was designed.

Kami Frymire, Grade 10
Carmi-White County High School, IL

A Single Moment

Melting into the lush canvas of the Earth,
I release all my stresses and looming worries.
Nature's ambiance engulfs my presence,
Conquers my senses; overpowers my conscience.

Leaves whisper as the wind kisses them,
And breaks their bond with their mother tree.
The rippling creek babbles as the cloudy water
Slides over each moss-coated pebble.

Towering cattails dance in the breeze,
Their shadows creating a spectacle on the terrain.
Newly sprouted flowers flourish the exposed landscape,
Painting masterpieces with their vivid hues.

Each minor movement inspiring;
Every slight murmur creating harmony.
Spending a single moment in nature…
Priceless.

Shelby Ward, Grade 11
Benton Central Jr/Sr High School, IN

Together

A gleaming fire saturates the room with warm light;
Christmas carols dance throughout the sparkling house.
Aromas of cookies, hot chocolate, and peppermint waft,
And cheer permeates the souls of those inhabiting the abode.

Laughter rings through the dwelling,
As family expresses notable tales,
Of fond memories and unforgettable times past,
Reminding everyone about their lineage.

The evergreen tree towers proudly,
Decorated with elaborate ornaments and garland,
Illuminated with miniature multicolored lights,
Wrapped gifts positioned carefully underneath.

While emotionless snow falls lightly outside,
And the bitter cold shows no mercy,
Inside flourishes the warmth and love of a family,
Together on Christmas Eve.

Maggie Bott, Grade 10
Benton Central Jr/Sr High School, IN

Longing

Observing the beauty of nature fade
Knowing that winter is near
Seeing the bare branches of the trees
Hearing their prayers for the sun to shine
Remembering the wonderful colors of autumn
Listening to the grey sky cry
Hoping spring will arrive
Before winter breaks my heart

Dominyka Salaviejute, Grade 10
Schaumburg High School, IL

What if You Could Touch a Tree and See All That It Has Seen?

To touch a tree and see, all it could see
Not just from now but through all history
Through people's joys and pains and all their tears
Trees have been around for thousands of years
Of questions unanswered from cultures past
With a touch of a limb, no questions last
Who was it that first invented the wheel?
Is the treasure of the Knights Templar real?
How were the pyramids built with such style?
Who was Mona Lisa and why her smile?
What of Stonehenge, how or why was it built?
Did those who killed Jesus feel any guilt?
What happened today when my back was turned?
There is so much knowledge yet to be learned
To touch a tree and see, all it could see
Not just from now but through all history
From the world's trees we could learn all these things
With all the mysteries that life brings

Brooke Harp, Grade 12
Boylan Catholic High School, IL

As I Walk…

I watched her walk away.
I watched the tears fall down from her face.
But for my life, I cannot remember this place.
I hear her voice so beautiful and pure.
It puts me in a trance like a fish and a lure.
Even though I cannot see her or touch her.
I can feel her presence; I know her hurt emotions follow me.
Like a black cloud over my head.
Why did I have to say that I wished her dead?
Now when I think about it I see.
I see what a mistake I have made.
Now all I can do is hope and pray.
Pray that I'll see her again one day…
Until Then My Silence…

Jennifer Carlson, Grade 12
Elverado High School, IL

One Phone Call

It only takes one phone call to
ruin someone's life, metaphorically it
feels like being stabbed with a
knife, that one phone call can be
just a wrong number, that you can get
throughout the year fall, spring, winter, summer,
this shouldn't be the way that it goes, but
no one really knows, tell me can you sense the
empathy of my flow, on this note you think
you're doing a right, but that right turns
into a wrong, and that wrong is something
you can't come back from, and you fall, and are
mad because you answered that
one phone call.

Airiel Johnson, Grade 10
Thea Bowman Leadership Academy, IN

My Love

Shqipe is someone who…
Always makes me smile
Is always there whenever I'm sad
Always cares no matter what
Will spoil me
She is the one whom I will never be able to replace
I remember…
All of the places we ate
Talking on the phone for endless hours
When we went fishing for the first time
When we went on our first date
I will never forget
Shqipe…
Loving
Caring
Happy
Smiling
Love that will never end

Taylor Morten, Grade 12
Lisle High School, IL

Still Bleeding Bondage of Love

Mine eyes are at a mortal war,
All of my being craves your lilac scent at night.
And I know deep within only you can restore,
My harmonious dreams from this torturous fright.
How now does one walk amongst the living,
When no longer can he stand the rhythm of his heart's drum?
How now can one's love endlessly keep giving,
When to loves hears death's sweet lullaby hum?
When your gaze falls upon me and all time is drawn to a still,
The truth crawls, battered and bruised, from behind your eyes.
Then a ripping, tearing, shattering doth start to kill,
My heart limps towards time's healing arms before it dies.
Though when I see you my heart doth bore,
The still bleeding bondage of love's lost war.

Kayla Perry, Grade 11
Todd Academy, IN

Behind the Mask

Hiding from the world she takes off her mask,
Thankful to be alone at last.
When out in the world she pretends to be glad,
Although deep inside she is very sad.
She puts on a mask so her fear won't show,
Wishing time would hurry so she could go.
She looks at everyone and just smiles,
She's been hiding behind the mask for quite a while.
Afraid to tell her true feelings because she is scared,
To do something different that no one else has dared.
She wonders why people are so hateful and mean,
Nobody has seen the things she has seen.
Going back home now, she takes off her mask,
Thankful to be alone at last.

Alyssa Faulkner, Grade 11
Oswego East High School, IL

Cheers to Life

From the air I breathe,
To the ground below my feet.
From the fluid in the sea
To the leaf on a tree.

From every smile on my face,
To every friend I embrace.
From every intimate moment,
To every date postponement.

From my time here on Earth,
To making every second determine full worth.
From the minutes we make count,
To every achievement's priceless amount.

We will never have another chance,
So never neglect to dance the dance.
We grow stronger from our struggles and strife,
To making the moments count: Cheers to life.

Macey Matson, Grade 12
Benton Central Jr/Sr High School, IN

I Don't Understand

I don't understand
Why people lie,
Why people cheat,
Why people steal.

But most of all
Why life has to be so hard at times,
Why your loved ones are taken away,
Why some people live to hurt others.

But what I do understand is
Why people love,
Why people always say live for today not tomorrow,
And why life is the way it is.

Lacey Qualls, Grade 12
Elverado High School, IL

The Brother I Never Knew

Here's to the brother that I never knew
The one who left us all too soon
The memories and laughs we could have made
The fights, the tears, and all the mistakes
I may not know you, you may not know me
But this is to the brother, I never did see
What's it like, dear brother of mine
To watch the world from in the sky?
What's it like, up above?
Do you hear the whispered prayers of love?
One day, big brother, I'll see you in Heaven.
It may be a while but I promise you
One day you'll know me and I'll know you, too.

Paige Duncan, Grade 12
Jay County High School, IN

Into the Dying Light

You are a raven.
Black as coal, beautiful as night.
I am a tree.
Kissed by winter, fragile to the touch.
You soar into the sky while I stay firmly rooted in this Earth.
The wind that floats under your wings also breezes through my limbs at such a chilling degree.
Oh, what I would give to be with you!
If only you would notice my everlasting presence on this barren forest floor!
To give me life, that is all I ask.
I need a purpose for just a moment.
But, all I can do is watch and listen as you fly farther and farther away into the dying light.

Haleigh Carson, Grade 11
Northwestern Sr High School, IN

There's Something

There's something here, but I don't know what it is. This feeling takes my thoughts, makes me feel like nothing. Everything else seems to know where it's headed. And as for everyone else, it doesn't matter. It's the dumb feeling of being alone in a crowd full of people. Faces address me and smiles hide their real sense in reality. The emotion coils itself and puts more sorrow into my heart. Almost like it's something you have to deal with, so I deal with it like it's everyday life. But I know one day I won't have to. As in the way humans don't fly, but they seem to dream or even wish more than any other thing I've seen. We all walk the same earth, were all made the same way…but I still wonder if there's someone there, like me…with a different sense of wonder.

Jasniequia Rendell, Grade 11
Lawrence North High School, IN

Darkness

Every thing you know is gone all is left is pain, well that's how I feel on the inside, my heart hurts. My tears just can't stop; all I want to do is scream. Pass it on to the world I'm leaving them behind in a flood of tears, chocking in a pool if pain. Venting them is of the other question, all I know is gone left in pain. The waters have crashed down on me holding me back but I don't fight for I know there is no hope. Within this place past events seem to fade, Who was I? Where did I come from? Only if it was true I could start it all over too a place filed with peace of mind. I shiver saying I'm cold, but really I'm fighting back tears. Just a hug might make them start. Just a word might bring me to tears. Start to build up, I sighed, but can hide all the time.

Melina Miles, Grade 10
Jennings County High School, IN

Song

Beautiful melodies and perfect harmonies fill your heart. Hear the accompaniment of the piano ring in your ear. Feel the rhythm move through your body from head to toe. Tap the beat on your feet. Let the notes flow from your voice with perfect pitch, the words repeated in your head. Sing your heart out, no matter what the song may be, because you never know who may be listening.

Devon James, Grade 10
Rosary High School, IL

Who Am I?

I am the sum of my experiences.
I am the sum of my ancestor's strength and beauty.
I am the sum of the earth and space.
I am not an imitation or a copy.
I am just me.

Mecca Joseph, Grade 12
Lisle High School, IL

Blue

Blue is the cool water I jump into in the summer.
Blue is the color of the sky on a warm day.
Blue is the peaceful ocean.
Blue is my favorite snow cone.
Blue is how I am feeling today.

Melissa Duvall, Grade 10
Carmi-White County High School, IL

Blacksmith's Masterpiece
Heated to vibrant orange glow,
The blade is lifted from the greedy flames
Of the roaring blaze of the kiln.
Heat radiating off
The blade screams and smokes
As it plunges into a vat of clear water
Only to resurface gleaming
With silver brilliance
Light casting off sequin hues
Across the packed, dirt floor.
Strong coarse hands slide the blade
Into sturdy silk sheath,
Completing the cycle of the masterpiece
Danielle Naughton, Grade 12
Willowbrook High School, IL

You
I remember pushing away…
The closer you got the more the pain
Without a doubt I loved you whole
But you loved my image not my soul
I showed you perfection hid my disdain
You fell for me without cajole
You are pure yet there is a hole
You deserve more than what I have to offer
You deserve the world in all its grace
You owe yourself a better man than thee
That is why I leave today
I remember walking away
Michael Scifres, Grade 11
Roncalli High School, IN

The Color Gray
Wordless
Speaking to the mind
I speak the language of art
Though few speak my tongue
My language is potential

But to those it may concern
I am never alone
Accompanied by two
Absence of color
Two infused; becomes one
My core awakens
Katherine Draper, Grade 10
Rosary High School, IL

You Are
You are loved by everyone
you are a gift from heaven above
you are a bundle of joy
you are our little angel so sweet
I love you Gracie
Nikki Hast, Grade 11
Carmi-White County High School, IL

Renewal Through Flames
There once was a house on a hilltop, with windows far and wide
Good feelings were found when escaping there, bad feelings were buried alive

A view of the crystal clear waters, even prettier in the rain
By day the warmth of the smiling sun, by night the firewood's flame

Plans were made on this mighty peak, for good and not disaster
Till addiction showed its ugly teeth, and set fire to a happily ever after

Too much time was spent there, polluting the air, escaping to an ignorant extent
A man found what he wanted, leaving family behind, though that was not once his intent

He found his place so far away that he didn't realize he burned all his time
He was burning everything around him, not stopping to think he committed a crime

After not long, plans began to bail out, halfway between start and finish
An empty mood set it, wet from soaking in sin, and what used to be good had diminished

The house met its match on the last of June's days, the memories better off burned
Eaten by flames in electric rage, the rule-breaker's fate had been earned

Years had passed
Where there was once ash had grown grass, and after violent flashbacks I was grinning
What stands there now could be seen as proud
For it holds a new beginning.
Janell Corrigan, Grade 11
Home School, IL

When My Coffee Turns Cold
I turn over in my bed to ask the clock the time
8:32 a.m. — tempting me to shut my eyes
Oh no you don't, it's time to awake
So I grumble and stomp downstairs to start a new day

My heavy eyes rest on the coffee maker
A perky aroma teases my nose, luring me to my fresh cup of coffee
Into the porcelain cup the rich café splashes
Faded in the background, the soft ticking of the clock

Steam pouring from the round white rim
I guide the warm mug to my sleepy face
Allowing the smell to fill my senses as I take a sip
Reminding me of its presence, the timer moves its hands

I set the stoneware mug on the marble counter
Suddenly the tick-tock becomes the forefront of my thoughts
One crashing echo after another screams through my ears
Every noise adding age, vanishing through my fingertips

I reach once more for the handle of the cup of heaven
Slowly up to my lips it tilts, ready for the heat to race down my throat
Shocked from the taste of bitter chill from my cup of Joe
Minding myself a double take to the clock reading 9:32 a.m.
Madie Deno, Grade 10
Benton Central Jr/Sr High School, IN

Dreaming of Elsewhere

I sink my toes into the sand,
closing my eyes because I can.
No place to go, nobody to see,
just me and the sun here by the sea.

A playful breeze echoes of
the cry of a gull.
Scintillating waves reflect
the bright azure sky.
A voice in my ear whispers
that summer has arrived.

I dig my hands into my coat,
opening my eyes because I must.
Lists to finish, and places to be,
just me and this cold for eternity.

A roaring gale echoes of
the crackle of ice.
Glistening drifts swallow
the drab fields of grass.
A numbness in my toes confirms
that winter has not left.

Lauren McCleary, Grade 12
Benton Central Jr/Sr High School, IN

You and I

You and I were meant to mesh and melt.
You and I were meant to twist and twine.
And as we danced we began to belt:
Let's runaway to the bright shoreline!
You and I collide like the eclipse.
You and I collide like the planets.
At the pier, we never thought to miss
The countryside, lifting our spirits.
You and I are the grand adventure.
You and I are the rise of the sun.
Our thoughts never could cross our future,
Our lives found an abundant beacon.
This reality is our vision.
Let us live our vision and be one.

Kristyn Childers, Grade 12
Rochester Community High School, IN

In and Out

Birds
Colorful, energetic
Flying, soaring, escaping
Navigators of planet earth
Escape
Free, gone
Running, evading, thwarting
Never seen after that
Invisible

Jake Soukup, Grade 12
Lisle High School, IL

Independence Day

Once a year we gather to celebrate our independence
With family and friends traditions to maintain
Camping with family and friends determines where my weekend activates
Cousins spilling out from the cars, the festivities commence
Helping aunts and uncles unpack
Placing campers and tents in annual spaces
The fire started right before dinner begins
Under the blistering heat, we all gather and mosey to the creek
Down in the woods away from the heat, hours spent swimming with the fish
Returning to camp to acquire the time we are leaving
For everybody's favorite part of the Fourth of July
The oldest packing into the car and heading to the fireworks store
From baby to big, the fireworks purchased
Returning to camp in time with the nap takers awakening
Dinner cooked with eager children waiting
Finally the time arrives and the little cousins commence with their own little show
Followed with the young adults to pre-teens preparing for the main attraction
The rest of the family waiting upon a hill when finally…boom
The first firework explodes with everybody staring in awe
The holiday weekend closing with smiles and laughter until next year.

Holly Atkinson, Grade 12
Benton Central Jr/Sr High School, IN

Peggy Jean

I tried dialing your number,
But the operator told me your line was disconnected.
I knocked on your door this morning,
But there was no answer.
I tried picturing you in my mind,
But your image had already been forgotten.
I was there when you left this world,
And I was there when you were laid to rest,
But in my mind your absence has yet to be whispered.
I am no longer able to hold your hand,
Yet every day I can still feel your guidance.
Never another time will I hear your voice,
Yet your words of wisdom are etched into my every day.
My eyes can no longer see your smile,
But for a lifetime to come, I will feel the warmth.
When you said you were tired,
I told you okay and that you could rest,
But now that you are gone and only in the way you wanted to go,
I will forever regret my decision to tell you goodnight instead of goodbye.

Maressa Ronk, Grade 12
Benton Central Jr/Sr High School, IN

Mesmerize

Someone like me, I couldn't even think it would be.
I always imagine it would be a little form of me.
Almost like a blanket being wrapped around your body for warmth,
like molded-clay shaped as me. When you call me to talk,
I love to listen to the sound of your muscular tone.
Your voice soothes my mind, as I lay underneath my covers peacefully,
mesmerize. As I fall deeply into your words.

Janisha Young, Grade 12
Oswego East High School, IL

My Family…

Some address them as Friends
Selected ones title them Supports
Others regard them as Helpers
I signify them as my Family

There when you need them
To talk and laugh
To experience joyful interactions
Some address them as Friends

There holding me up
When someone knocks me down
When I just cannot get up
Selected ones title them Supports

There assisting
To accomplish a task I cannot perform alone
When I get frustrated
Others regard them as Helpers

There to love me
To care for me
To be proud of me
I signify them as my Family

My Family…

Abi Niccum, Grade 10
Benton Central Jr/Sr High School, IN

Please

Please don't break my heart,
I know it's an impossible request.
But if you must,
then I knew it was inevitable.

I won't ever break your
heart though, promise.
I would rather carry
the pain alone.

If there's someone else,
I don't want to know.
Because I love you enough
to let you go.

Hopefully she will make you
smile. And know when you're
upset. Hopefully she
loves you back.

If what we have dies,
I'll probably disappear.
Go somewhere far away,
and never come back.

Jillian Holtzer, Grade 11
Indiana Academy for Science, Mathematics, and Humanities, IN

The Best Thing Since Sliced Bread

I didn't have to text the girl back,
That I had never even texted before.
I didn't really have to go to the mall that day,
I could have remembered to get the gift weeks earlier.

Yet still, I procrastinated,
Like starting an essay due only hours
Before I have to lay it on my teacher's desk.
And thus began the extraordinary friendship that's ours.

Luck, chance, fate,
Whatever you want to call it.
I think we both had some of each that day,
Or else we wouldn't have ever met, I'm afraid to admit.

But through all the "what ifs,"
It's okay because we're together,
Peas in a pod, two birds of a feather,
Just like I know we'll be forever and ever.

Katie Prochilo, Grade 10
William Fremd High School, IL

The Reality of Fairy Tales

Far away, in a tower up so high,
the beautiful princess let out an exaggerated sigh.
She yearned for freedom from that dark cold place,
not for a boy with a handsome face.
Tradition states that a prince must take her arm,
but none of them proved to have enough charm.
Once a sweet boy seemed to be the one,
but after about 6 months he decided that he was done.
He said he had to leave but soon he'd come back.
The uncertainty about gave her a fatal heart attack.
Time went by and he was nowhere to be found,
After she had promised to him she would be bound.
Fed up, she decided not to wait,
climbed down from the tower, and went on a date.

Kassidy VanGundy, Grade 10
John Adams High School, IN

Stop Is a Super Hero

The stop sign sits and waits, saving people's lives.
Nobody appreciates it for guarding them day and night.
Without the stop sign innocent lives would be in pain.
The stop sign freezes through the rain, snow, and sleet.
Sweats during the summer, but no one really acknowledges it.
It's always standing on its guard, waiting for the next car.
The stop sign is like a super hero without the recognition.
If it had a backbone oh, how sore it would be.
The stop sign is always there to protect us.
This is one super hero that's on duty 24/7.
Cold, tired, and rusty but fights the battle.
The stop always stands tall and proud,
Not even the wind can knock its confidence down.

Haley Valentine, Grade 10
Bluffton Harrison High School, IN

Woods of Despair

Upon this day I am found astray
In the woods, by myself miles away
No reception, no shelter, no blankets to lay
I am truly alone to think, to unwind, to realize, to replay
I fall to my knees, shattered in pain, thought, and tears as it starts to rain
I come to an understanding
I am engulfed in nature and love
I start to make a blanket out of leaves
I have shelter under these trees
I have reception, not the typical kind, by much needed and hard to find
The thought eases, the pain dissipates, and the tears dry
It all becomes clear, even the sky
I am not alone out in these woods
I have an unseen companion
This companion need not to be named, fore there shall be too many to say
I can conceive this companion as never hidden yet never seen, never talking yet never silent, never gone yet never here
This companion has saved many from these woods of despair; shed a light on those who needed it dear
This companion of mine delivers me from these woods of despair to a place of love, acceptance, and those who I hold near
From these woods of despair, I will vanish and never reappear

Priscilla Worstell-Clark, Grade 12
South Knox Middle/High School, IN

Wishful Thinking

Dreams of acceptance into my institution of choice,
Tirelessly toiling for the acceptable credentials.
Me against them, scrapping for the upper hand,
Anxiously anticipating the envisioned response.

Whether a hopeful Hoosier, a beloved Boilermaker, a grateful Greyhound, or a celebrated Cardinal,
The conquered dream is a lifelong memory, never to be forgotten.
Representing my institute of higher learning for the remainder of my existence,
Never misplacing memories I attain along the way.

Apprehensively awaiting word for weeks upon weeks,
Filling time with scholarships applications and essays.
Wondering if the mailbox holds my fate,
Or if another drawn out week must pass.

The day has come; I read the letter,
Congratulations, welcome to…
I recall the hours spent diligently working towards my goal,
Well worth the wishful thinking.

Austin Gretencord, Grade 12
Benton Central Jr/Sr High School, IN

The Ocean Knows

The ocean knows how to cool our warm toes when we dip them into its salty waters.
The ocean knows how to have fun with the tropical fish and jumping dolphins.
The ocean knows how to roll over and over itself, creating undulant waves for us to surf and swim in.
The ocean knows how to gently caress a boat as it drifts across its glassy surface.
The ocean knows how to frolic with its friend, the shore, as they exchange grains of sand as mementos of their time together.
The ocean knows, as it ebbs and flows, how to calm its capricious waters, allowing us to enjoy the beauty of a reflective sunset.
The ocean knows, as it ebbs and flows, that we value its grandeur and honor its majesty.

Jenna Smith, Grade 11
Mater Dei High School, IN

Nest Underneath Tomorrow
Sing them truly, red bird, the panging sins that burst ornately from your heart.
Through the identical religious actors, through speckled themselves, may sneer,
He may allow you to soar still, in the Heavens as you depart.

Obscurant, uniformed preachers clerically congregating in lame coats,
Brood religiously stubborn from their pulpit-like telephone lines.
Their sermon-encrusted scolds and whistles, monotonous by rasped throats,
Peck upon Gaia's children, invasively declaring their sins with holy whines.
Hypocritical, they are but mimickers of the Lord as Starlings are for Henry.
Conformist, the Myna that survives will attempt discipline in man's rebellious nature.
Yet, the scarlet breast of the cardinal will remain a vivid plumage despite wrest,
And, though branded by its defiance, is caught in resistance to a dull arrogance.
The Puritanical murmurations will hum their piercing, yet meaningless, prayers for lest
Of a sinner's salvation, though, our shamed badges spur us to entreat His holy reverence.
Their futile inquiries of Objectionable Vices never shall determine our innocence chastely,
And our complexities of will to fall like Him, not an Armageddon of fragmenting and denature.
Honorably, we still ascend, crimson creatures flawed, to the Pearl Gates like the Son,
While opines of the dismal preachers, conformed, descend like bygone corpses.
Thus, the wanton rose whipped underneath the dreary weed nest, tomorrow, still finds the sun.

Sing them loudly, red bird, the panging sins that burst ornately from your heart,
Though the identical religious actors, though speckled themselves, will sneer,
He will allow you to soar still, in the Heavens as you depart.

Gioia Marzullo, Grade 12
Guerin College Prep High School, IL

Emerging into Radiance
Slowly I am trapped in turmoil against my will.
Only when I vanquish the darkness inside my soul
    Will I become invigorated and immersed in light.
Unquestionably, my duty as a writer remains clear.
Luckily, I receive support from allies, helpers, coaches,
    As well as friends and teachers.
Confronting such a leviathan will require strength, staying on course
    Is my ultimate goal; as well as never surrendering.
Although there may be obstacles such as blocks, as well as inducements,
    I will stay true to my task until finally completed.
Lurking through the shades of my heart, an ever ongoing battle rages inside me.
    My soul quenches for righteousness.
I never grasped why this plague of souls damages my well-being.
    I must find a way to eradicate this evil form my spirit.
But I hear that malevolent voice whisper dark and resplendent riches into my ears.
Undoubting, I conquer those malicious voices of darkness
    That effortlessly want to perceive my quest to fail.
Relief sweeps throughout my body as I travel through a winding road, and with the trial passed,
    I emerge into the light.

Alexander Gick, Grade 11
Benton Central Jr/Sr High School, IN

Mother Nature
I am the wind blowing through the atmosphere making the leaves and trees dance,
I am the sun warming the ground urging the flowers to bloom and make the world beautiful.
I am the bugs busy at work keeping the earth clean.
I am Mother Nature making a perfect world.

Danielle Petersen, Grade 12
Lisle High School, IL

Sometimes Life…

Sometimes life…
Does not go as we want it,
Shows us different paths,
Takes us to new places,
Can teach us new things!
Sometimes life is a continuous road.

Felishia Curry, Grade 12
Carmi-White County High School, IL

Love

More than a feeling
Head-over-heels affection
Selfless agape

Michelle Schmitt, Grade 12
Mater Dei High School, IN

Grades 7-8-9
Top Ten Winners

List of Top Ten Winners for Grades 7-9; listed alphabetically

Leah Berry-Sandelin, Grade 8
Mahoney Middle School, ME

Naomi Davidson, Grade 8
Decorah Middle School, IA

Olivia Estes, Grade 9
University Hill Secondary School, BC

Faith Harron, Grade 7
Horizon Middle School, ND

Lily Lauben, Grade 9
University Preparatory School, CA

Alex LePeter, Grade 7
Oak Knoll Middle School, VA

Sarah Lynch, Grade 7
Holy Innocents School, NJ

Ally Merrill, Grade 9
Hamilton Freshman High School, OH

Shelby Senger, Grade 8
Emmanuel-St Michael Lutheran School, IN

Anna Sixsmith, Grade 7
St Thomas More School, PA

All Top Ten Poems can be read at www.poeticpower.com

Note: The Top Ten poems were finalized through an online voting system. Creative Communication's judges first picked out the top poems. These poems were then posted online. The final step involved thousands of students and teachers who registered as the online judges and voted for the Top Ten poems. We hope you enjoy these selections.

Lonely Tree

Lonely tree sitting on a hill
Clouds forming its shape behind it
Ocean swishing on the tiny lonely island
Long emerald grass flowing in the wind
Leaves lying on the topaz grass
Big bare tree, bright blue sky
Lonely tree, branching out
Big clean ocean
Water bush
Silent
Lonely
Tree
Mike Wenzel, Grade 8
Thomas Middle School, IL

Stillborn

A huge melon
Nine long moths
Born free, stiff, and cold.

No beats of a drum
Nor warmness to the touch.
You were once alive
Yet now you are gone, gone cold and dead.

Never to walk or play, just to lay
Still and cold…
A stillborn.
Emily Smith, Grade 9
Lisle High School, IL

My Best Friend

I have a Twin Tower, yes I do.
My best friend and my sister, too.
Always together,
No matter the weather.
She may not be the smartest,
But she sure is an artist.
Her humor and kindness
Is the true quality of a pal.
When something goes wrong,
Or a disaster strikes my life,
BAM! She's there.
Right by my side, forever.
Kara Puntriano, Grade 8
Red Bud Elementary School, IL

Baseball

Baseball is so very fun
You get to hit the ball and run
It is so fun running and scoring
While listening to the fans roaring
Fielding, catching, throwing too
Baseball is fun for me and you
Patrick Beckemeyer, Grade 7
St Matthew School, IL

A Dark Time in My Life

A best friend by nature, a dog that was a person,
A warrior, a listener, a pal,
Whose time had finally run out, like an hourglass out of sand.
All those nights I despaired,
The tears stumbling down my face,
Like a man without his sight.
I knew you were with me, every night and day.
Dozing dejectedly out that door, drunk with depression.
Remembering all those times you made me giggle and sigh,
Dancing and skipping like a schoolgirl on holiday
Acting only as a warrior would, growling and barking to protect me.
And although I didn't show it much, I sure felt the pain of you gone.
And without you in my life, the grief was a knife right through my heart.
Running readily through this life, not bothering to stop
My heart a pounding drum.
Don't let me let my grief drive me home to crawl up under those covers and die
I'm chasing this life and staying alive today
I was a locked door, never letting anyone down on my little corner of the world anymore.
I'm starting to second-guess myself
But this I know is true
I miss you Bailey, my boy, my best friend.
Deena Baber, Grade 8
Liberty Jr High School, IL

The Flash vs the Roar

I wake up thinking of a sunshine day.
But then I look out and all I see is rain.
My window is foggy because the heater is on inside while the air conditioner is on outside.
Then, flash! All I see is a glow pass by.
I dashed to the window, but then it was gone.
A roar passes by, chasing the flash.
The roar is close by catching it, but the flash is too fast.
All I do is stand there watching the fight go on.
Then the flash passes me and the roar right behind it.
In any second now the roar will get it.
There, the roar is an inch away…
I turn in the other direction, toward the floor.
The flash glows once again and the roar is going in for the kill.
The roar caught the flash, and the storm finished and passed.
Isabel Hernandez, Grade 8
Galileo Scholastic Academy, IL

Playing a Flute

A mazingly hard in the **B** eginning. You **C** an get better in **D** ue time.
E ventually you will **F** orge **G** loriously clear notes.
H owever, **I** t might not be clear every time.
J ust Remember **K** icking a flute won't make it work. **L** ifting your **M** any
fingers isn't all that you do. **N** ever forget to practice. **O** pen your eyes and
P lay the notes.
Q uiet on some parts **R** usty on others.
S ad playing has **T** ransformed into **U** niquely awesome music.
V erge of finding **W** hat you are good at. You have learned **X** actly everything
Y ou wanted to learn. Hoping you have **Z** ero-defect when you play.
Leah Gouwens, Grade 8
DeMotte Christian School, IN

Beautiful Zebras

Zebras,
In my last dream,
Falling from the blue sky,
In groups they make a black and white
Collage

Jaryd Grabowski, Grade 8
Northlawn Jr High School, IL

Speedy Jay

Speedy Jay, while looking through a cave
Had a vary close shave.
He sat on a bear
That had slept there.
I'm glad Jay was fast and brave.

Cobe Miller, Grade 7
Wethersfield Jr/Sr High School, IL

Curious Creatures

In moonlit forests
Live very curious things
They come out at night
And then they explore the Earth
Dawn comes, and they disappear

Jayden Jimenez, Grade 8
Northlawn Jr High School, IL

Music

Music
Expression through words
Speaks to your heart.
Allows you to let out your inner self.
Music is an endless string.

Emily Carmichael, Grade 7
Wethersfield Jr/Sr High School, IL

The Rose

The rose,
Soft and red,
Quiet but shining,
Obediently,
Delicate.

Shiann Ince, Grade 7
Wethersfield Elementary School, IL

Happiness

Happiness
Brings joy and pleasure
Makes people feel good
Is all around us
Happiness is a ray of sunshine

Mariana Ponce, Grade 7
Wethersfield Jr/Sr High School, IL

Gunner Come Home

The monster Great Pyrenees walked beside me,
calm and careless until his amber eyes sought a bunny.
He bulleted toward the rodent like Wile E. Coyote chasing the Road Runner.
Then he disappeared into the massive cornfield, NO GUNNER!
I sprinted into the never-ending army of cornstalks, dodging every one that appeared in front of me.
In the distance, I saw a white dot fade.
Gunner come home, Gunner come home.
My face, red and hot, with a tear rolling down my cheek, sat in the grass wishing I could go back in time.
How could I have made such a terrible crime?
Gunner come home, Gunner come home.
The sun was starting to sleep,
the moon was starting to greet.
My life was now dust in the wind.
Gunner come home, Gunner come home.
I started inside, until I heard rustling from behind.
I couldn't believe my eyes.
My heart came out of hibernation.
I was as happy as a kid opening his Christmas presents.
Gunner came home, Gunner came home.

Sarah Goff, Grade 8
Liberty Jr High School, IL

The World's True Dream

The demon reaches out to me, his face so blurry…what could it be?
Elongated claws swipe at my flesh, blood and tears streak down my face
Staining my new dress of satin lace
He moves closer now, his eyes glowing
They look hungry, but how can that be?
This demon is fed by all those who see the pain and stress
Caused by this one beast who feeds on an abundant feast
Sucking the life of every soul
But he will finally pay the toll
He shoves me to the dirt ground
Our hearts beating in symphony…
Pound…pound…pound
I struggle to my knees and say
"Spare my life awhile longer please"
The demon's course chuckle rumbles through the night air
He say's "Why should I even care?"
I leap up, plunging a dagger through his cold heart
Stumbling back, I weep into my bloody hands
Because finally, I have broken reality
Finally, I have killed the sick demon named
Poverty

Sydney Skillen, Grade 9
Northridge High School, IN

Dancing Rain

As the rain fell they dance to their freedom.
They tap dance on the tin roof, down the drain they twirl – in a ballerina fashion.
Like two lovers they dance down the stream, another pair dance like fighting pirates.
Why do they dance you say? It depends on what the clouds are crying about.

Isabella Castile, Grade 7
Highland Hills Middle School, IN

Pants on the Ground

There once was a boy named Jack.
Who liked wearing his pants with a slack.
One day they fell down.
With everyone around.
And his mom gave his head a whack.

Jack Wert, Grade 7
Concordia Lutheran School, IN

Stars

Stars
Bright mysteries
Illuminating the universe
Bring so many questions
Bodies

Dylan Newell, Grade 8
Bethel Lutheran School, IL

Blue

Blue smells like flowers
Blue sounds fun
Blue looks like the ocean
Blue makes me want to dance
Blue taste like blueberries

Laman Sauer, Grade 7
Wethersfield Jr/Sr High School, IL

Sky

Sky
Blue, beautiful
Cloudy, sunny, rainy
Dark, rough
Sky

Anwyn Payonk, Grade 7
St Matthew School, IL

My Cat

I have a cat,
he is very fat,
he eats and eats and never stops,
he eats until he pops,
my cat is as chubby as a whale.

Daring Didat, Grade 7
Highland Hills Middle School, IN

Autumn

Autumn
Beautiful and colorful displays
Warm, yet a breezy season
Time for playing in the leaves
Autumn is an enchanting fantasy.

Eden Juarez, Grade 7
Wethersfield Jr/Sr High School, IL

What the World Releases as It Breathes

Life can cry, yes, it can sob.
The battle cries of an angry mob.
Tears of a grave situation,
Streams of endless misfortune,
A cinema of stormy rain dripping down human cheeks.
We should close our eyes, shut them tight
Shut out the ugly of our everyday lives.
There are tears and then…There are screams.
Tears can be washed away with a fair amount of ease,
But screams tend to have a sort of residual characteristic about them.
They linger.
Their nauseating pleas reveal travesty and horror.
Once they finish their wrath,
They stay on the scream-polluted ground
…forever.
You were warned, screams, they linger.
Tears, carbon dioxide, and screams,
That is what the world releases as it painfully exhales.
To hide your eyes from humanity
Please I beg you,
Close your eyes.

Gemma Raynes-Rosenthall, Grade 7
Newberry Magnet School, IL

Family the Strong Foundation

When you're upset you cry, and when you're happy you will smile.
When you find something funny you might laugh.
When something is scary you will cover your eyes to hide from it.
Family will be there to pick you up when you're down.
Help you find the right path when you've lost your way.
Family is your foundation.

Family will always be there when you need help and are hurt.
They will be there when you need a person to talk to or when you need to yell at someone.
Family is your foundation.

Family is something you can always count on.
Though you may not see it they are your strong foundation.

Kaylee Harwood, Grade 7
Emmanuel-St Michael Lutheran School, IN

Loved

Formed and molded in God's loving hand.
Loved and cherished to no end.
All of us are different in our own amazing way.
"But does God really love us?" Is all we ever say.
The answer, of course, is yes! He loves you and me.
And He will love us for all eternity.
If He doesn't love us, would we be here now?
He loves us more than anything, just let Him show you how!
We are like a ball of clay.
Formed and molded in God's own special way.
He knows the plans He has for us and His word is true,
So let Him form and mold you so you can be a light shining for Him too!

Taylor Hougham, Grade 8
Light House Academy, IL

Inside This

Inside this photo album
Are memories
It shows a person's life
The pictures tell a story
It shows the highlights of your life
It resembles a chapter book
But doesn't use any words
It's like a timeline
There are so many familiar faces
And people you have forgotten
Maybe you lost contact
Your paths may cross one day
Some of them have passed away
Snap, another picture taken
Ready to be added to your book of history
Millions, billions of memories
Trail across your mind
But still more pages wait
To be filled…
Mackenzie Lynch, Grade 8
Thomas Middle School, IL

Seasons

Spring
New growth fills the land
Flowers bloom beautifully
Trees bud all around

Summer
Steamy temperature
Foliage fills the live trees
Bugs are everywhere

Autumn
Cool temperature
Leaves are shades of red and brown
Squirrels collect nuts

Winter
Trees bare and dormant
Animals hibernating
Snow covers the land
Sarah Virgo, Grade 7
Immaculate Conception School, IL

Grandfather Clock

Tick, Tock
goes the grandfather clock,
reaching the hour,
he begins to sing
ding-dong, ding-dong
the chiming dies
all that follows
tick, tock.
Averie Anderson, Grade 8
Red Bud Elementary School, IL

Lost in Mars

Oh, how I dread Mars,
Red, near and far,
Tis love I seek,
All here but her, seems bleak,
A day on Mars,
So lost and confused,
Seems my thoughts are refused,
Oh Mars,
Oh Mars,
A place where you're looked down on,
All seems to be a con,
Can't see what's right from wrong,
What's my decision?
Very far from Precision,
Oh a life on Mars,
A man cannot stand,
For it is a place, Of lost decisions,
Every being screams for him "AHH,"
No love,
No light,
Sadly, No God.
Jacob Bierman, Grade 7
Highland Hills Middle School, IN

Time Machine

I don't feel any bigger
I don't feel any stronger
I don't feel that my brain has grown
That I'm now a size eight
That I'm getting pimples everywhere!

Where has the time gone?
Last time I looked in
The mirror
I was 3 now I'm 13
I'm in seventh grade

I look at my mom
She has wrinkles
Her eyes still happy

My brother isn't a kid
He's not 14 anymore
My dad has gray hair

Where has the time gone?
Karen Marin, Grade 7
Carson Elementary School, IL

America

The flag
Red, white, and blue
That is my country that I love
My home.
Lizzy Gonzalo, Grade 7
Marquette Academy, IL

Field

Running in a field,
Never stop or yield,
Not crying, sun shining,
Happiness glowing,
Unknowing of tomorrow,
Not caring, no sorrow,
Yesterday is long gone,
Leaves are flowing,
No noise or moaning,
Slowing down,
Walking now,
Going slower,
My knees slowly lower,
Until all fall asleep,
And without a peep,
The sun does too
Gabrielle Greiner, Grade 7
Bethel Lutheran School, IL

The Essence of Fall

Brisk winds,
brush my face,
the green leaves,
are without a trace.
A watercolor painting,
flew off the canvas,
and onto the trees,
as far as Kansas.
Red, orange, and gold,
fill the scene,
a masterpiece
that's fit for a queen.
Glowing sun,
and wind in my ear
I wouldn't rather do anything,
but sit right here.
Amy Janson, Grade 8
St Matthew School, IL

Evening Song

As evening winds sing evening songs
And willow stops its weeping
As wise owl hoots its melody
You know the world is sleeping

As crickets cry to evening skies
And birds stop serenading
For passersby are fireflies
And eventide is fading

When moon has won and day is done
And clouds come overhead
As shadows come and daylight runs
You're glad that you're in bed
Nicole Barnes, Grade 7
St Matthew School, IL

Good Bye
Life goes quick
Someone you love is there
Next moment they're gone
All you can ask is why
All you can think
Are the times you shared
All you can say is bye
Sarrie Graves, Grade 8
Thomas A Edison Jr/Sr High School, IN

The Sky So High
The sky, the sky,
so high and blue.
The clouds fly,
they go ZOOM!
Thunder hits
and goes BOOM!
You fall to bits.
Molly Malone, Grade 8
Red Bud Elementary School, IL

My Life Is Like an Ocean
I get up and go through the motions.
My life is like the sight of an ocean.
It never changes and stays blue.
Nothing ever becomes new.
Then when night comes, I go to bed.
Then I get up and go through the motions.
My life is like the sight of an ocean.
Adam Jolley, Grade 8
Red Bud Elementary School, IL

Scuba Diving
Coral reef
Deep down under, quiet
I surface to the top, amazing
The sun beats down, I go back under
Quiet again
Briley Balding, Grade 7
West Salem Grade School, IL

Music
M asterpiece
U nderstand
S ound
I nspirational
C reative
Emily Smith, Grade 7
Our Lady of Good Counsel School, IL

Trees
Swaying in the wind
Leaves blowing away from me
My branches feel bare
Trevor Knoerle, Grade 8
Bethel Lutheran School, IL

Blade of Grass
The giant oak tree looks down on me like a protective father
The summer sun shines through its leaves and fills me with exhilaration
The warmth surrounds me like a blanket of healing
The silver streaked sky smiles softly,
Soothes my soul, and supplies me with satisfaction

"Woosh,"
The wind blows as I feel the warm summer breeze turn cooler with the coming of fall
I begin to see the colors change and soon after,
A leaf gently lands upon me and my neighbors as a shelter that
blocks me from the sun

Then again I feel the season evolve and I slowly fade away as the snow covers me
I am claustrophobic under the heavy white blanket
I disappear into the earth and wait for the warm spring rain to come
and bring me to life again

As I feel the snow melt away
The warmth of the sun reappears and earth's everlasting energy erupts
The clouds cry spring rain which wakes me from my deep sleep
I am once again a lively, happy, single
Blade of grass.
Ellie Robinson, Grade 8
Thomas Middle School, IL

Heaven Is Real
A bove all the clouds, **B** eyond all the stars
C omes a place where there is always joy **D** ancing angels fill the streets
E veryone is an angel here **F** arther than outer space
G olden streets fill this place **H** eaven is real!
I n the dark **J** esus is there when you are scared
K ing of Kings, **L** ord of Lords
M an does not compare **N** o one on Earth can relate to the glory in heaven
O nce you enter the Golden Gates, **P** raise is all you'll see
Q uite a wonderful sight **R** isen up above
S atan shall never see **T** is' the word of God, most holy
U niting together, everyone praises **V** ery loving, sharing, and caring
W henever you lie, cheat or steal, God sees from here, **X** -mas is Jesus' birthday
Y es, Heaven is more fun than Christmas, **Z** ombies and monsters can't scare you
when you are with God, in heaven.
Faith Fishel, Grade 7
West Salem Grade School, IL

Mother's Love
Your Mother's Love can fill your soul,
She is like an angel watching over your life.
Your Mother can enrich your life to make it full,
She protects you and your well-being from the heavens above.
You may see her and not think anything of her,
You may not know it but the protectiveness is the sign of her feelings.
Your Mother's Love is the everlasting bank of wealth for your heart,
She hopes the Forever Clock will never end,
So she may have you 'till the end of time...
Your Mother's Love.
Willow Johnson, Grade 7
Pierce Middle School, IN

City

I step into
shadows and darkness
as she walks by
she steps in a puddle
the noise of the puddle
rings throughout the still night
lights dim in the darkness
the man in the windows
stares into the darkness
just standing there
nothing to do but stand
his trench coat gives him a bigger being
the street lights reflects the wet street
apartment lights flicker in the dark
rained soaked city car lights
make thick gold lines on the dark street
in the lonely city
Matt Milijkovic, Grade 8
Thomas Middle School, IL

Freedom

Blades of grass, separated
From their sea of stoic companions
Fly in the wind
No longer will they
Be trampled on
No longer will they
Cringe
For now they are free
To move and dance
No longer held down
By the chains
No longer will they look nice for the people,
Working so hard to grow
They have broken their chains,
Ready to board the train
To a land where grass can fly.
Where they will be free
Nikita Prabhakar, Grade 9
West Lafayette Jr/Sr High School, IN

If Heaven Weren't So Far Away

If heaven weren't so far away
I'd hike 10,000 miles your way
Just to see you once again
Is my dream I have every now and then
People say to me "This is the right way"
But I don't listen to what people say
Your voice is music to my ears
That made me forget all about my fears
Only if heaven weren't so far away
I'd swim from sea to sea to be with you
Even if the sky weren't blue
If only heaven weren't so far away
Tanya Watts, Grade 9
Palestine High School, IL

Fall Is Here!

Colorful leaves falling on the ground,
it makes me want to roll around.
The smell of popcorn drifts through the air,
people crowded everywhere.
Pumpkins seemed all a glow,
as the first frost settles in low.
Kids screaming everywhere,
it makes me want to pull my hair!
A child's laughter is contagious,
like a smile that goes from ear to ear.
And that's how I know fall is finally here!
Kristen Woods, Grade 8
Red Bud Elementary School, IL

Pugs

Pugs lay on rugs all day,
They also play, I say,
When they run in the sun,
So tired they are
Pugs rest on rugs all day

Pugs try to sleep at night,
But they roll on beds, bark and bawl,
And still want to play,
But finally they sleep, soft and sound,
Pugs will sleep at night
Benjamin Grim, Grade 7
Concordia Lutheran School, IN

Sunflower

She dances in the wind
with her yellow dress

She likes to fall to the ground
when a wind storm comes

Then the day will come
when she feels ill.

She feels her life being drained from her
then she falls asleep forever
Jordan Beck, Grade 7
Concordia Lutheran School, IN

Doors

Open sesame
Don't miss your chance
Constantly opening
Constantly closing
Choose wisely,
Choose the right door
Every door
Leads to another
Take the right path.
Bobby Liesz, Grade 8
Thomas Middle School, IL

Ode to Spikes

Oh spikes,
Pointy and sharp,
Digging into the cinders.
You made me run faster,
And win the race.
You're lovely,
And comfy.
Light as a feather,
It's because of you,
That I broke my
Personal record.
It was like,
Flying.
With your help,
I won the race.
Paige Plummer, Grade 8
Rochester Jr High School, IL

Lolly and Varnack

Lolly is like a cool Celeste wind
She is oh so peaceful
Giving people a nice breeze
In fall
As she goes whoosh all
Around giving joy to the peaceful city

Varnack is like a ferocious red fire
Killing all joy
Burns down anything he sees
Just a bad part of summer
Can be everywhere
But mostly on his volcanic islands
Just his evil noises crash, and boom
Will disturb you so I advise you stay away
Ayinde' Smith, Grade 7
Concordia Lutheran School, IN

Middle

I am in the middle
It is not a riddle

I am not tall
I am not small

I am too young to stay up late
or go on a date

I am old enough to do chores
Even though it's a real bore

Some say I am wild
I am the middle child
Josh Tipton, Grade 7
R J Baskett Middle School, IN

Nature

Nature is the most wonderful thing you have ever seen
Green grass and plants everywhere
Trees reach the sky
Mushrooms grow below
Wind blows the leaves away
Sun makes everything grow
The rain comes down and waters everything
And when it's dark the stars come out

Rabbits hope about
Wolves are howling
Caribou are running
Badgers are sleeping
There is so much more to nature than anyone supposes

Jasmine Hamelin, Grade 8
Galileo Scholastic Academy, IL

If I Had All the Money in the World

If I had all the money in the world
I would buy a Camaro
Or maybe even a Corvette
I'd be celebrating like I never had!
I'd pay to not be in school and maybe include my friends too
I'd buy a mansion on an island and maybe the island itself!
There would be a variety of stuff in it
It would include items of gold and jewels
And a bunch of other things
Like a basketball court
Or a restaurant or mall or even both of them all
I would also buy the best seats to every game
All that I would do and more
That is *if* I had all the money in the world

Nathaniel Carmody, Grade 7
Emmanuel-St Michael Lutheran School, IN

Gone with the Love

Gone with the cries
knowing he isn't here.
Gone with the lies
we don't need to hear.
Just waiting for him to reappear.
Thinking of him not once,
but million of times a year.
Hearing voices, but not one of them is yours.
The weeping and sorrows are too much please
no more.
But than I realize, loving someone or something isn't
easy to do when the next minute, they leave you.
I guarantee it to you next time we meet again, I will
forgive you.

Karla Ramirez, Grade 7
Galileo Scholastic Academy, IL

Jazz Bar

I sit alone
anxious for the show
the smell of smoke drifts in the air
the solitary taste of blues,
walks down my tongue and dances with my tastebuds
then I am awoken from my daydream
loud music ripples through my ears
and as I see all the couples begin to dance
I sit alone

Catherine Brinkworth, Grade 7
International School of Indiana, IN

Music

Music is bright, music is fire,
igniting a spark in people's hearts,
which listeners can admire.
Music is a doorway, music is life,
breathing an escape from sadness and strife.
Music is dreamy, music is love,
music is peaceful like a beautiful dove.
Music is freedom, music is never wrong,
and at the end, music always comes out strong.

William Pierce, Grade 7
Highland Hills Middle School, IN

Basketball

Watch the players as they go down the court,
Dribbling the ball,
Going down one end to another hoping not to fall,
But in the end they all fall.

With people eyeing the players,
As they said one last prayer,
They keep dribbling some more,
Then out of nowhere, they score.

Madison Nahrwold, Grade 7
Concordia Lutheran School, IN

Christmas Day

C oming together around the tree
H aving Christmas dinner, yummy
R ipping open presents with a surprised look
I nside are presents for which we ask
S urprised when I get up
T hankful for what I get
M aking many holiday wishes come true
A sking to go out and shovel people's driveways
S inging Christmas carols with the family

John Sterling, Grade 7
Wethersfield Jr/Sr High School, IL

Season

The sun peeking out
Warmer weather on the way
Flowers and plants sprout

Sunny 'round the clock
Brings blazing temperatures
Happy times for all

The heat starts to drop
Everything becomes cooler
Crunching of the leaves

Covered by the snow
People share love and good times
Warm tidings to all

Ryan Friend, Grade 7
Immaculate Conception School, IL

Four Seasons

Leaves changing color
This season full of wonder
Soon leaves fall around

Snow is on the ground
Christmas time is coming soon
Fully of jolly tunes

Weather gets warmer
It rains every single day
Flowers start to bloom

Now it's time for warmth
Going to the beach and pool
Getting really tan

Kelly Wright, Grade 8
St Matthew School, IL

Bringing Home Bella

The morning I got my kitty
Cool, crisp
Little brown building angrily creaking
Glass doors are ice
Little kittens' eyes as glassy as a still lake
Spotting her immediately
Fur as soft as a cloud
Meow as loud as a bell yelling
Teeny teeth are razors
Picking up the black box
Big eyes looking up are marbles
Car ride home rambunctious, rowdy
Settling in softly
Loving home
Bella my companion

Caitlyn McGrory, Grade 8
Liberty Jr High School, IL

Something We May Never Know

He sat in the classroom
Looking out the window
Looking as if he
Had never seen the
Outdoors before

He looked at it with
Such care, such feeling,
Like he had never
Seen the outdoors before

We all join him in looking
Why was he so amazed?
We only saw a tree,
A tree and some grass

But we knew that he knew
There was much, much more
More than he knows, loves
And cherishes but something
We may never know…

Leeann Altherr, Grade 7
Our Shepherd Lutheran School, IN

Heart of Reality

When life shows its ugly face
You're supposed to keep your pace
Not to stumble or fall down
But to fight and take the crown
How can this be possible
When all that I have been told
Is that it is not meant to be
The perfect life of you and me
Welcome to the heart of reality

Like a storm that cuts a path
The pain I feel is like that
The time I said that I love you
That's the night that you slipped through
You know forever I will wait
To be brought back by fate
By destiny, so dark and cruel
I'll take the crown, I will rule
These stories that I have let flow
I try to tell so you could know
Welcome to the heart of reality

Spenser Congram, Grade 9
Brownsburg High School, IN

Happiness

Not feeling pain or hurt
No care in the world
Content with everything
Happiness is a warm blanket.

Adam DeWolfe, Grade 7
Wethersfield Jr/Sr High School, IL

Noah's Ark

My name is lightning
I have struck with intense ire
I control the sky

My name is thunder
My voice vibrates everywhere
I echo lightning

I am known as wind
My strong gales ruffle the trees
I whisper, then sigh

I am known as rain
My waters conquer the earth
Great floods mark my steps

I am the bright sun
My rays have brought peace to earth
My smile lights the world

I am Noah's dove
I have found a place to land
And an olive leaf

I am the rainbow
My hues reflect God's promise
Grace has come from Him

Christine Ayabe, Grade 9
Naperville Central High School, IL

Grandpa

Oh Grandpa, Oh Grandpa,
What a life you lived,
You shared anything from
Wisdom to laughter,
It doesn't matter.

Oh Grandpa, Oh Grandpa,
What a life you lived
You were strong and brave,
Which built this country
The U.S. of A.

Oh Grandpa, Oh Grandpa,
What a life you lived,
You made airplanes and birdhouses,
That laid around the house,
That upon seeing were wanted.

Oh Grandpa, Oh Grandpa,
What a life you lived,
Your smile and laughter,
Made everyone's day
I love you Grandpa

Kristina Steward, Grade 9
Covington Community High School, IN

A Butterfly

A butterfly, colors mixing and creating new
while in their cocoons.
A butterfly is beautiful as can be
and delicate as a leaf.
A butterfly, hanging from a branch blissfully,
lightly and carefully.
A butterfly, bright, beautiful,
and, harmless as can be.
A butterfly, light as a feather, flies with grace
and puts a smile on a child's face.

Jessica Nelson, Grade 7
Highland Hills Middle School, IN

Goodbye

I cry, I weep, how did this happen to me,
I tremble, I shiver, what sign didn't I see?
I wish, I dream, that things would turn around,
I heave, I sigh, what's gone cannot again be found.
I shout, I scream, I cry from broken-hearted pain,
I hiss, I growl, I'm so hurt I've gone insane.
I hide, I run, I want to disappear,
I dawn, I realize, my head then becomes clear.
I smile, I shine, I spread my wings and get ready to fly,
I've learned, I know, before I can move on I must say goodbye.

Jenna Smith, Grade 8
Gridley Jr High School, IL

Feelings of Delight

Christmas morning to Christmas night
Oh! Christmas tree full of sweetness and light
Big brown eyes grow bright
They fill with tears of delight

Opening bright color boxes with all might
Finding tops, dolls and a jazzy kite
Let's play with all the toys until tonight
A warm good hug makes it all right
All ending with a blanket of white

Amanda Arroyo, Grade 7
Galileo Scholastic Academy, IL

Autumn Activities!

I love the way the leaves fall form the trees.
The bright colors of the leaves are so pretty.
I love the smell of the autumn breeze.
Even though summer is over and winter is a pity.
We still have autumn, fires and leaves.
And there are hotdogs and s'mores to enjoy.
Also holidays like Halloween and Thanksgiving.
But say goodbye to the birds and bees.
Because winter's on the way along with winter toys.
Say hello to winter and good bye to autumn living.

Falon Wilson, Grade 8
Rochester Jr High School, IL

The Wonder of Winter

The air is getting nippy,
The sun begins to cease,
The roads are getting slippery,
Fluffy snow falls with ease.

The world is transforming,
Into a frosty place with gray skies,
It is pleasing and calming,
To my soft and weary eyes.

I hear the ring of bells,
As delicate as the snow,
I get a gust of Christmas smells,
Whose identity I will never know.

The days are getting bitter,
More frigid by the day,
As the snow shows off its glitter,
And more comes on its way.

I drink hot chocolate with holiday cheer,
It packs a punch of peppermint that's sweet,
I'm glad that winter is finally here,
What a wonderful seasonal treat!

Monica Barany, Grade 8
Corpus Christi Elementary School, IN

What Is Love?

The young girl asks her mother;
What is love?
The mother replies;
Love is happiness.
Love is the rainbows
that come after rainfalls.
Love is the soft wind
that brushes your cheek.
Love is the beautiful sunset,
just out of reach.
Love is the blooming flowers,
that open their petals to a new world,
a new life.

Love is sadness.
Love is remembering those forgotten.
Love is the tears,
rolling down your cheek when you are proud.

Love is friendship.
Love is lending a shoulder to cry on.
Love is helping another get through a tough time.
That is what love is, my dear.

Chloe Woodard, Grade 7
Madison Jr High School, IL

A Puppy to Call My Own
I remember this day like
It was yesterday
I remember the big black basket
It was an angry prison
I still hear
The loud barking, as loud as a train
The fur was a soft blanket
I still imagine the
Ball of energy
Running rapidly and ragingly through my yard
He was a speedy car
The puppy was as soft
As a stuffed animal
His eyes were as bright
As the sun
Now I have a puppy to call my own.

Danielle Bogdanic, Grade 8
Liberty Jr High School, IL

Autumn
The sound of crunching leaves under my feet,
Autumn is here.
The cool breeze taking place of the heat,
Autumn is here.
The season when children dress up for a treat,
Autumn is here.
The changing of seasons is almost complete,
Autumn is here.
The feeling of the ice-cold concrete,
Autumn is here.
The season when everyone gathers to eat,
Autumn is here.
Piles of leaves lining the street,
Autumn is here.
The time of year apple cider tastes sweet,
Autumn is here.

Kristina Urban, Grade 8
Corpus Christi Elementary School, IN

Coffee
O sweet coffee
With your silky pools of brown
One single whiff of you
Can reverse any frown.

You helped me through those sleepless nights
As I typed this poem up.
The only thing that kept me going
Was you in your magic cup.

O sweet coffee
You used to be my pick
But now when I think of you all I think is:
Ick.

Kiran D'Souza, Grade 7
Dunlap Valley Middle School, IL

Life
Life in itself is like a river.
It flows with freedom and wild ambition
and can fracture off into a sliver
with hard and tough times shot out like ammunition
but with the bad comes good
times filled with laughter and smiles
life never turns out like you think it would
the possibilities can go on for miles
but if you just quit life
it can't get any better
because with that knife
you'll close life's letter
and times can't progress any greater
life is a constant quest for answers
but death is the answer key which is even better
but don't look in the back of the book of life
life doesn't share answers to those who quit
because dying intentionally is a bit strife
so don't complain because it's all you get
life is a journey to explore and ponder
so stay on track and please don't wander

Elias Worthy, Grade 8
Todd Academy Inc., IN

The Effect You Have
Every time I look in your eyes I can feel your passion.
I can see how you look forward to life.
With every breath you take, you breathe pure inspiration.
You are power, you are life's best friend.
You are everyone's best dream and goal in life.
You are the things that bring spirits to rise and pain to subside.
The bittersweet memories die in your presence.
Problems collapse at the mention of you.
Everything is right when you blink those amazing eyes.
You said you would never leave me and you haven't.
A fire runs through my heart, adrenaline rushing.
I am fully alive.
What I thought could never happen has.
I can breathe, I know what I'm feeling.
This moment is an awakening moment for everyone.
They realize that they are alive, their bodies rid themselves of pain.
You are the effect the government wishes to be.
You have everything in your hands of good will.
You've discovered the pure happiness of this world.
Somehow you still better everything around you.
It's the effect you have on the rest of us. It's the best thing.

Danielle Morales, Grade 9
Carl Schurz High School, IL

Homework
He thought the war with homework was over
When he opened the next folder, it started again.
It started in first grade. Folder after folder,
Paper after paper, it does not end.

Greg Mertz, Grade 8
Red Bud Elementary School, IL

I Can See Them Watching Me

I can see them watching me
Lying in wait, watching me
Ready to pounce on any mistake I make, ready to attack.
They don't realize it but,
I can see them watching me.
As I watch I realize something
I realize that under all the hate they have towards me…
There's something else.
One little emotion bottled up inside.
Hiding.
This small emotion that is hated,
That is craved.
This little emotion that has driven people to hurt,
To plead.
This one emotion that can choose between life
Or death.
This little emotion.
Fear.
I can see them watching me.

Haleemah Na'Allah, Grade 7
Dunlap Valley Middle School, IL

Oral Factory

Inside this mouth
Wondrous white workers
Smash! Stomp! on food
Silver managers move the workers into place
They must be straight like soldiers
The tongue is a washing machine
Getting rid of any unwanted crumbs
Germs are the villains
Trying to damage and construct cavity homes
The elongated squirts of toothpaste
Distribute minty fresh adrenaline to the workers
The molars use their muscles to grind the last and final
Crumbs left behind
When the factory
Decides to shut down for the night
The components take a break
Awaiting the next task
Given by the President of Operations
Me.

Monica Misch, Grade 8
Thomas Middle School, IL

Apples!

Apples, apples, apples.
They are the best, especially in autumn.
Apples dipped in warm, gooey caramel will melt in your mouth,
But cinnamon makes the apples to die for.
After an hour or two outside, the best thing is coming in,
And chowing down on a couple of crisp slices of apple pie.
Apples are just the thing to eat during the best season of the year,
Autumn

Rene Runions, Grade 8
Rochester Jr High School, IL

When They Fell

What if there was one person left in the world?
The crows screamed atop the black tree,
echoing through the desolate wasteland
that once was all man's.
The crows were gone,
all that was left were the scars
of the bombs and its prey.
But from the ashes and burning fires,
the lone wanderer rises and he limps
through the sea of burnt bodies
and crumbled buildings littered like garbage.
And as he scales the hillside, one step at a time
the image of a mushroom fills the sky.
And so, the final prey
all alone, with nowhere to go,
collapsed onto the cold dirt
with his brothers and sisters
and let out his parting groan.
What if humanity vanquished?

Alex Beric, Grade 8
Thomas Middle School, IL

The Never-Ending Vacation in Mexico

Finally, Mexico, its beauty was a batch of flowers
Furious, the never-ending flight
Tossed us around as if we were in a blanket
Family, friends were as tired as lions after
They caught their prey
Hotel, the chandelier was as big as
15 full-grown elephants
Pool, people screaming with excitement,
A roller coaster of fun
Next day, awake like a snake
Now friends have stomach flu
Staying in hotel, solitary confinement
Family sick, everyone else is sick
Survivors sank silently in the pool
Hotel has flu too
Silent sound waves stirred around the pool
We still enjoyed ourselves
The disease took our bodies
But not our vacation

Timothy Cucci, Grade 8
Liberty Jr High School, IL

Dolphin Contest

I turn around and what do I see?
A slippery dolphin staring back at me!

With a swish of its flipper, and a splash of its tail,
I know that my dolphin surely won't fail.

We turn to the judges and to our surprise,
The judges are holding up gladly the first prize.

Hudson Jones, Grade 7
St Matthew School, IL

Chocolate Bar
As I buy it form the shop,
I unwrap the wrapper,
I look with my hungry eyes,
As I open my mouth,
I hold up the chocolatey goodness,

As I check it over,
I check for any faults,
Then I look if anyone is watching,
The chocolate seems so luscious,
As I drool at the sight of it.

I take a bite,
I start to melt,
My sweet tooth shivers.
As I dive in for more,
The shop keeper yells "Hey, you have to pay for that!"
Niall Sullivan, Grade 8
Rochester Jr High School, IL

Ode to Fall
Pumpkin spice and bales of hay,
Are scents in the air on a crisp, fall day.

Loads of leaves linger in the long-lasting breeze,
As they float to the top of the pile with ease.

visible all season, are colors more vibrant, not mellow,
Like oranges, reds, and even some yellows.

Hearing the cold, bitter winds; through the barren trees they blow,
Autumn is here, and everyone knows.

Baseball's over, football's here instead,
People act as if the Pope has risen from the dead.

I don't know if I've told you this, maybe I've never,
But fall is the absolute best season ever.
Jeanie Freeby, Grade 8
Corpus Christi Elementary School, IN

The Television
I hear you walking toward me.
I can hear you grab the remote.
Then, you turn me on and I can finally see.
I show you many things.
I can show you the shopping channel with a picture of a tote
There is a travel channel to take you to other countries.
It shows you a tower that leans.
There are cartoons and sit-coms.
There are army shows of planes dropping bombs,
And don't forget the weather channel showing weather for counties
There is even one with rhythms and rhyme
But there's a catch, you can only watch one at a time.
Gregory Gould, Grade 7
Bethel Lutheran School, IL

Angela
She said she was fine
As if nothing happened
As if she wasn't hurt
As if she wasn't scared for life
She said it as if it were no big deal
But it is
It's the same every day
When she comes to school
I can see it
Not just the purple bruises
It's on her face
I can see how she feels
No matter how she says it
Just the way her eyes cry for help
Inside of her there's a girl who wants to fight back
But she's smart enough to not let her out
She knows her father would hurt her more
She thinks this is the only way
She's strong, she won't give up
She has hope
All she can do is hope
Shruti Amin, Grade 7
Stratford Middle School, IL

Ode to Chocolate
O, Chocolate,
So rich, creamy, and smooth,
A delectable sensation on my tongue,
A welcome treat anywhere,
Dark, white, milky, any type doesn't matter:
Such a wonderful, tempting, delicious bit of chocolate
Cannot wait to be eaten. It sits in a bowl,
Or on a table, whispering,
"Eat me, eat me…"
Don't try to resist the wonderful morsel of sweetness,
A soothing of the nerves when it hits your mouth,
Ode to chocolate.
Colleen Schena, Grade 7
Stanley Clark School, IN

Tornado
First comes the rain,
Then it is gone.
Suddenly there is an eerie calm.
The sky is black, then it turns green.
You hear a rumbling from somewhere unseen.
The clouds are moving round and round;
A tornado will soon leave its mark on the town.
A funnel descends from the clouds,
Then finally it touches the ground.
It moves in faster and faster as continues on its path,
Leaving nothing but destruction in its aftermath.
Then it is gone—you sigh in relief,
But what it has left behind leaves you in disbelief!
Annemarie Michael, Grade 7
St Matthew School, IL

Manatee

Poor little manatee, drifting in the sea,
  What a lively little thing you used to be.
You used to zoom around, and ate seaweed.
  When all of the sudden, out of a pipe,
 Oil burst out!
      It drifted towards you.
But you didn't know about it at all,
    In fact, you were playing with a seaweed ball.
It came from a gulf caused by a meteor.
     And your death,
 It came from the values of humans,
     Who valued money over your wellness.
Poor, poor manatee, drifting in the sea,
You were killed by oil, the silent killer of the sea,
  which made it so you couldn't breathe
    But humans,
  We suffered too.
     Some were killed in the explosion of oil.
  But our loss is nothing compared to that of the manatees.
And in your time of need,
    No one remembered the manatees.

Tasha Pullam, Grade 7
Todd Academy, IN

Lost

He sits alone, all alone
In an open field
Mourning for the girl he loves
She sits in the dark
Waiting in Talamadden
For him to come for her
He grieves for her smell
Of cinnamon and peaches
And for her long black hair
She grieves for his strong hands
Wrapped tightly around her waist
And for his hot breath against her neck
Without her
He is nothing
His magic is gone
Without him
She is weak, she hasn't the strength to stand
Together, they are stronger, than any other witch in L.O.S.T.
Nothing will stand against them
Their story too lugubrious to end this way
They are to be reunited again

Sabre Campbell, Grade 7
International School of Indiana, IN

Space

When I see space, I see stars.
When I see space, I see planets.
When I see space, I see a mystery.
When I see space, I see things I have never seen before!

Drew Dobbins, Grade 7
St Matthew School, IL

You

My heart pounds at the sound of your name
I test you like it's a never-ending game
I blush, I grin, I hide my frets
I show no affection 'cause you don't know yet
The pictures together are the ones I cherish
But to keep it secret, my affections must perish
You're a little too old; I'm a little too young
So it comes to the fate that we couldn't be one
You have no faults from what I know
It's like I'm Juliet and you're Romeo
Some laugh at the crush that I have on you
But they don't know you just like I do
We tease, we jab, but I wonder the same
Does your heart pound when you hear my name
Fall goes to winter and winter to spring
Summer started this special little thing
My heart goes to you, and never another
Seeing you, my heart goes aflutter
Your smile makes me feel like I'm home
Steady, warm, and never alone
You're an angel from above, holding all of my love

Lauren Johnston, Grade 8
North Putnam Middle School, IN

Blue Sky

A clear blue morning sky
I wondered who these people were as they passed by
I grabbed my luggage, and boarded the plane
Not knowing what kind of people just came
I went to my seat, sitting down as I looked around
Unaware that we were death bound
The plane took off and we were up in the air
There was a man looking at me I couldn't help but stare
Just then a voice came on the intercom
He told us to be quiet and stay calm
Many things were racing through my head
Not knowing that there were people in the towers dead
Worried faces and phone calls
A woman sitting next to me bawled
I got off the phone as I said goodbye
Would today be the day that I was going to die?
I looked out my window to see the New York skyline
Now I know that freedom isn't free
I am sad that I won't see what my daughter will grow up to be
The last thing I saw was the blue sky
I was about to see heaven with my own eyes

Emma Seynemeier, Grade 8
Central Jr High School, IL

Friendship

The dark blue sky of late December
Almost makes me forget but then I remember
All those magical experiences we had
Like golden jewels adorning my head

Cruz Moreno, Grade 9
Schaumburg High School, IL

Can You Judge Me?

Can you judge me?
Can you judge me by the words that come out of my mouth?
By the personality that resonates within me?
By the way I will react?
No. I don't think you can.
You don't know the times I have picked myself up off the ground,
struggled to make it in a situation that would not allow me to,
shake off the caked mud of lies, and criticism,
and harsh slaps that take away my sense of pride.
Do you know the things that have stripped me bare of everything that I had?
My happiness, my laughter, my joy?
You think you know what exhaustion feels like?
Things that I could do, but you, yes you could never do, not in a million years.
I know you see a girl who looks perfect and stumbles through what you call cool and popular awkwardly,
but you know what I see?
I see a girl who knows no fear anymore of what people are going to think or let roll out of their mouth.
Who knows now not to take your attempted falsehoods,
And blows to break my walls of friendship, happiness, and family.
You think you know?
You think you can judge me?
No. I don't think you can.

Olivia Vejcik, Grade 8
Gwendolyn Brooks Middle School, IL

Eyes

There are no two eyes that are the same.
Some eyes may be plain brown while others have vivid colors.
Some even say that eyes describe a person
One with a colorless pair of eyes may be considered as boring, or even dreary
My father's eyes defeat all odds as his are some of the most interesting
His are as green as the Amazon rain forest in the fall but as blue as the roaring waters of a rapid
They change every year like a chameleon changes color
They also have dots
Dots that are always there no matter what time of year
Dots that are there to stay no matter what happens
Those same dots are perfectly adjacent to one another.
Such interesting things like the dots, are just very hard to see
Then there are the things that can be described as never before seen
His eyes have a circle that goes around the iris.
A circle so brightly colored that none can compare
His eyes characterize him as he may be one of the most interesting people
He sees things not many other people see
He sees every single state 4 or 5 times a year.
Those eyes are the ones that see the inside of a semi-truck almost every day
Those same eyes keep me safe during the night
All this is just from eyes, eyes are what makes me dad, dad.

Michael Botchev, Grade 7
Stratford Middle School, IL

I Remember

I remember my old dog Ziggy. He was black as darkest night. He was like a shadow that was always there. His white squeaky ball was his one true love and it flew through the yard like a run away dove. He was only eight when he passed from this place but we will never forget his cute pug face.

Brad Beams, Grade 7
Highland Hills Middle School, IN

The Two Lone Towers

We are the victims of terrorism,
Look at us with the holes in our sides,
Look at the grave site of many in the ash.
What do you see?
Terrorism at its peak.

We are the Twin Towers that burn,
We burn to the ground,
We fill the air with smoke.
What do you see?
Hate and anger beyond belief.

We are the towers that are broken,
Flames raging inside,
People too astonished to move.
What do you see?
Agony that no one should ever have to face.

What do we see?
We see people that bleed red, white and blue for us.

Baylen Paulson, Grade 8
Central Jr High School, IL

The Perfect Place

Tall palm trees like giants in the sky
Swaying in the breeze
Families of five
Crammed on a moped
And people laying in the sun like they're dead
That is Mexico

The sand beneath your feet
In between your toes
The waves, a bucket of popcorn
Crashing on the shore
And people picking seashells
That is Mexico

Chefs cooking like busy ants
Tasty quesadillas
With melted cheese, a burning sensation in your mouth
Homemade guacamole
With crunchy, warm chips, a plateful of tastiness
That is Mexico

Brianna Darlage, Grade 8
Liberty Jr High School, IL

Life

Life itself can be a simple flutter,
It is an epic journey through time and space themselves,
A chapter book about you.
Life is like a flower bud that can last through the toughest winters
Life can be love, hate, lust, or beauty
Till death comes, life is our shower of light.

Maraih Phillips, Grade 8
Bethel Lutheran School, IL

Between You and Me

Between you and me there are words to be spoken.
Between you and me there are secrets that have been broken.
Between you and me there are jokes to spare.
Between you and me there are dares to share.
Between you and me we have fought and loved.
Between you and me we have hugged and shoved.
Between you and me we have remarkable moments.
Between you and me we have never been cruel opponents.
Between you and me have been through thick and thin.
Between you and me we normally win.
Between you and me I'll be your friend till the end.

Jane Dorsey, Grade 7
St Pius X Catholic School, IN

Varnack and Lolly

Varnack is vicious and cold
He lives alone in an abandoned house
Boom! Thunder rumbles while lightning strikes
The sky is always black
While the cool spring weather is never nice

Lolly is positive and happy
Who lives constantly in summer
She loves to twirl around gracefully in her beautiful garden
Ding! The calming wind chimes sing
Sulphureous sunshine falls all around her

Kyla Macaraig, Grade 7
Concordia Lutheran School, IN

An Ode to the Memories

An ode to the memories for all the things you do,
You brighten my day up and make me laugh too.
You tell me the stories that I've seemed to forgotten,
Wishing they'd come back to life and never would have rotten.
You calm me down when I am flabbergasted,
Remind me that anything can happen.
I miss the times you keep for me, but after all the years,
I'm glad they lasted when they did,
Because then I wouldn't have all of the joyful tears.
Oh, all of the wonderful memories!

Loranda Guy, Grade 8
Sandwich Middle School, IL

Fall

The leaves diving into the depths of the Earth.
The flowers no longer give birth.
The sun shines bright, just like the glistening snow.
The birds fly…leave…go.
Listening to the wind whisper,
While sitting under the empty trees with my sister.
I see the mesmerizing pumpkin faces,
As they light the wonderful places.
Fall,
Is the best season of all.

Macy Schreiber, Grade 8
Corpus Christi Elementary School, IN

Smile My Dear*

Troubled thoughts, worried wisdom,
A serene smile. Mona, my love, your grin shows no true bliss.
Would a dozen roses fill that empty space?
What about an entire field of lilies arranged in your name?
What about my heart? I would gladly
Carve it out of my chest, and nail it to the wall.
Smile, my dear.
I am not forcing you to. I'm simply tired of the damned crying
Throughout the night. They deserve to see your smile,
And the angelic brilliance that will shine upon them.
Smile, my dear.
Must you be pleased? What do you need?
Crave? I would do anything,
To just see that exquisite and luminous curl in your lips.
Smile, my dear.
Must I kerf your innocent cheeks?
And stitch them back up? The blood will drip,
Giving you those rosy, perky luscious lips
That I would adore.
Smile, my dear.
Or must I do it for you?

Alex Karwowska, Grade 8
Thomas Middle School, IL
*Based upon "Mona Lisa" by Leonardo da Vinci

The One for Me

The day I bought my first dog,
I was as happy as a clam.
My smile was a permanent crescent all day.
Arriving at the pet store,
I peered into a big, gray cage full of puppies.
A certain one stood out to me,
One that was as cute as a button.
I held him like a mother cradling her baby.
His fur was a yellow piece of silk.
His bark was a small-sounding alarm,
Tiny yelps were jumping out of his mouth in excitement.
I loved this dog.
He was the one for me.

Taylor Jacobs, Grade 8
Liberty Jr High School, IL

Thundersnow

T he booming claps of snowy sound.
H appens up high in the sky.
U nusual in the winter.
N ormally comes in all kinds of colors.
D ark colors are included.
E vents you will never forget.
R eds, yellows, blues, and violets.
S ounds out of the ordinary.
N othing in the world more interesting.
O dd in its own big ways.
W ould anything interest me more?

Benjamin Craddock, Grade 7
Wethersfield Jr/Sr High School, IL

The Beauty of Colors

What if there were no colors?
What would the world be like?
Without shining bright blue skies
Pink flowers with the buzzing bees and nagging flies
Or bright red faces when a person lies?

What if we never knew what colors were?
What would your favorite color be?
If there was nothing to see
Nothing to admire so delicately
Or even describe your unique personality?

What if you woke up and color was gone?
How would it feel?
If you couldn't describe a criminal who can steal
Or the glimmer lights on a Ferris wheel?

What if colors never existed?

Amanda Kowalski, Grade 8
Thomas Middle School, IL

Christmas

Christmas is the time of year
When the snow is crystal clear.
The snow falls from the sky so very bold.
The snow is so delicate and cold.
Now everyone heads inside to warm up
And get some hot chocolate in a cup.
The gifts are wrapped and under the tree.
I wonder what these presents could be.
A truck, a game, a sled, a doll
Some clothes or maybe a football.
The food is so delicious and warm.
Everyone attacks the food in a swarm.
Today is the best day of the year
When everyone has Christmas cheer.
Now the day is almost over and we had lots of fun.
Time for us to go to bed and the party to be done.
My family loves Christmas and you should too.
I love Christmas too just as much as me and you!

David Horn, Grade 8
St Matthew School, IL

Kaitlyn Rosa

Kaitlyn's hair is as red as the bulging hot sun
Burning her pale skin from above,
Her eyes are blue and gray like the sky on a rainy day,
Her smile is as beautiful as a blooming orchid,
Her laugh is soft but wonderful,
Like ice-cream,
Her height surpasses mine,
But only by a little,
She lives in a world of fun,
And she eats the games she plays.

Jonas Rosa, Grade 7
International School of Indiana, IN

Yasmine Davila

Yasmine
Courageous, creative, compassionate, and comical
Daughter of Jeanette and Edgar
Lover of music, cows, and having fun
Who feels helpless without her family and friends, anxiety about starting high school next year,
and excited about Christmas
Who needs love, happiness, and books
Who fears insects, haunted houses and scary movies
Who gives laughter, inspiration, and love
Who would like to see the jungles and culture of Africa, the history of European countries,
and the coral reef
Resident of the Milky Way Galaxy
Davila

Yasmine Davila, Grade 8
St Daniel the Prophet School, IL

Martha Guziak

Martha
Daughter of Stanley and Margaret Guziak, sister of Bart, Mike, Kinga and Veronica Guziak
And twin of Taylor Federici.
Lover of sports, music, family and friends, Anyssa Gonzalez, and parties
Who feels expectations, friendships, and amusement
Who needs comfort, that special someone, and makeup
Who fears rejection, the future, death, losing someone's trust, and grades
Who gives great advice, heartwarming hugs, and smiles on people's faces
Who would like to see the world, the moon, the end of a rainbow, and Northern Lights
Resident of Cook County, Chicago, Illinois, United States, North America, and in Milky Way Galaxy
Guziak

Martha Guziak, Grade 8
St Daniel the Prophet School, IL

Tree in the Sunset

The tree once again stands still on the hill in a warm summer afternoon
The river flowing smoothly sparkling and shining
Showing the vibrant rose, vermillion, gold, tangerine colors from the reflection of the sky
Looking like a fire spreading through the sky almost turning to night
The hills showing the darkness as night is falling
The tree's leaves moving softly from the fresh cool breeze passing by as the branches stay still
Smelling the fresh aroma from the flowers in the background
Then the tree showing the darkness as night comes closer and closer
Making the tree the most serene time in all of day

Maria Cordova, Grade 8
Thomas Middle School, IL

Medals of Honor

This is the moment. This is the moment that I suffer and die. No. My comrade comes to help me up. He informs me that a passing-by ally jeep had flipped on to me and broken my legs. He quickly drags me behind a rock for cover. He runs onto the battlefield and I watch him, with my own eyes, the man that saved my life. I saw him fall to the ground and cry. I watched him bleed from his chest. I crawled across the ground to him. I sat next to him and guarded him with my only gun. A pistol. I don't know how, but I stayed alive long enough for our allies to come pick us up.

I sat with him for 2 weeks, next to him in the hospital. I was healing but unfortunately he wasn't. He was dying slowly and painfully. On the last day and the last hour of his life, I watched him, with my own eyes, the man that saved my life. I saw him die. I saw him close his eyes and leave me.

Stefano Cacucci, Grade 7
International School of Indiana, IN

Every Small Town Holds a Tragedy
As I'm sitting in this chair, waiting for him to speak.
Why is it at this moment, my eyes just feel so weak?

Looking down low, bowing my head.
Starting to whisper, "why are you dead?"

I begin to look up, looking to the sky.
I look back to you, I begin to cry.

I hope you sleep well, I hope you seek rest.
I hope you're doing better, than this tightness in my chest.

We all know you fought, how you gave it your all.
We all understand, we had to let you fall.

I'll look in the mirror, and know what I'll see.
My wretched face, staring back at me.

I'll scream and I'll shout, lo and behold.
You'll speak to me, "Just let go."
Marti Steadman, Grade 9
Palestine High School, IL

Maddy McKinney
Maddy
Athletic, smart, outgoing, and funny
Daughter of Craig, daughter of Lacey
Who loves:
Horses, family, and friends
Who feels:
Injured, happy, and mad
Who needs:
Healing, sleep, and food
Who offers:
Advice, hard work, care
Who fears:
Snakes, crashing, and spiders
Who would like to have:
Horse stable, 100 million dollars, 50 new horses
Who would like to see:
Italy, Hawaii, and Wyoming mountains
Who lives in:
West Salem, Illinois
McKinney
Maddy McKinney, Grade 8
West Salem Grade School, IL

Strawberry Field
I'm laying on warm grass dreaming about tomorrow
And waiting for tomorrow eating each
Strawberry one by one

As I eat each strawberry it counts for happiness
When I pass by the strawberry field it makes my day
Carina Romero, Grade 7
Galileo Scholastic Academy, IL

Unidentified Shaking
His eyes found the back of his head on that Friday night.
Him not waking was my biggest fright.
Bubbling spit rolled down his face.
Yet, he seemed to be breathing at a steady pace.
I started to panic when he kept on shaking.
I screamed his name, but he wasn't waking.

All of a sudden, my head was spinning way too fast.
Was this night really his last?
Downstairs, they heard my panicking cry.
They rushed upstairs, wondering why.
The long, agonizing car ride seemed to take forever.
All I wanted was for him to feel better.

Finally, my little brother was okay.
Our ears were open to what the doctor had to say.
This incident was going to happen again.
Unfortunately, we wouldn't know when.
It's going to be like an endless ride,
But he'll always have me by his side.
Amanda DeJesus, Grade 8
Highland Middle School, IN

Me
Santana
Smart, athletic, funny, and outgoing
Daughter of Revel, Daughter of Randy
Who loves:
Sports, family, and friends
Who feels:
Happy, sad, and angry
Who needs:
Food, water, and sleep
Who offers:
Help, advice, and comfort
Who fears:
Snakes, spiders, and ghosts
Who would like to have:
A dirt bike, a Chevy Camero, and a million dollars
Who would like to see:
Alaska, Australia, and Peru
Who lives in:
West Salem, Illinois
Turner
Santana Turner, Grade 8
West Salem Grade School, IL

Candles
The bright light that guides you through the night
the streams that flow down the side
the streams hot to the touch
but it helps you with delight
it dims through time, trying to serve you
the dim light that guides you through the night
Charlie Raya, Grade 7
Dunlap Valley Middle School, IL

Apology

This is just to say
I have watched
The last *Parenthood* episode
On Netflix.

The one you probably
Wanted to
Watch together.

Forgive me,
It was dramatic.
So nice,
And heart-warming.
Natalie Baker, Grade 7
Rochester Jr High School, IL

What If

Suffering, sunshine
Emptiness, courage
Crying on the inside
Closing the door
And crying out loud
Letting it all out

There are emotions everywhere
Colors in my head
Thinking what could be
What would it be like
Then I realize…
I have a perfect life
Ariel Nix, Grade 7
Galileo Scholastic Academy, IL

Death

Death is cold and lonely,
A watery tear sitting at the corner of my eye,
That trickles down my face,
As I look at the coffin, I see a person,
Lying there as still as night,

I look around,
People sit and cry,
As we sob tears for our loved one who died,
Family, friends, and people alike sob tears

We hope it brings them back.
But it does not.
Xochitl Zavala, Grade 8
Galileo Scholastic Academy, IL

Holidays

Happy holidays
Love, joy and peace in the air
Our hearts filled with glee.
Ethan Sebok, Grade 8
Bethel Lutheran School, IL

Ode to Elevators

I lug myself upward.
I trudge unhappily.
My feet are bricks upon bricks.
When I return to these disgusting stairs,
Something catches my eye.
It is shiny and new.
I step closer to this magnificent invention.
I press the "up" button with eagerness.
The doors slide noiselessly.
I step into the Elevator…
…and enter a whole new world.
In every direction I see myself
In absolute awe.
The Elevator slowly reacts.
And carries me up.
Up, up, up
And up, and up, and up.
When I reach the top,
I see the stairs of the Stone Age.
I laugh and think to myself,
Oh, oh, ode to Elevators!
Muqsit Buchh, Grade 7
Stanley Clark School, IN

Fall

Leaves begin to fall
The ground gets cold
Geese let out their calls
And fly south without being told

Summer is ending
Winter is near
And we are tending
The Christmas cheer spreading

As the geese fly
We watch them leave
And say goodbye
Taking photos for a memory

Orange skies turn gray
Trees are now bare
Summer goes away
It's time for people to care

Fall is beautiful
Sarah Steed, Grade 8
Immaculate Conception School, IL

Hate

A strong dislike towards another
Doing verbal and physical harm
A burdening feeling of danger and anger
Hate is a cycle that never ends
Allysah Morris, Grade 7
Wethersfield Jr/Sr High School, IL

Soccer

I love soccer
When I play soccer I have fun
When you score a goal
You get the best feeling
If you don't score
You are still helping the team
You can be tall or short
Strong or weak
Large or thin
It's teamwork that matters
When you play with your friends
It is so much better
Though you could play in bad weather
I wish I could play all day and night
If I could
I would play with all my might
Branden Billhartz, Grade 7
All Saints Academy, IL

Winter

Winter
Skiers out to ski
Snowboarders rip through the snow
Down a steep mountain

Kids layer on clothes
Pack the snow tight in their hands
Snow forts being built

Snow, snow, snow so cold
Hats, mittens, and winter coats
Winter so frigid

Take off my snow gear
A cozy fire greets me
Mom is making hot chocolate
Aurora Whitmarsh, Grade 7
Immaculate Conception School, IL

Snow Days

As I sit in my snuggie
all cozy and warm
I watch the snow falling
from the big winter storm.

School is canceled
at home I must stay
what should I do
to enjoy this snow day?

I put on my coat
and leaped into the snow
I grabbed my sled
down the hill I did go!
Jenna Elsby, Grade 7
Highland Hills Middle School, IN

Perfection Is Not Here

What if everyone had no type of struggle?
Feeling safe every day
No obstacles in the way
No need for any pay

What if everyone had no type of problem?
Nobody ever sick with the flu
No goals, nothing to do
No second thoughts about what you should pursue

What if everybody was always happy?
Feeling joyous every day …
All children together at play …
Sending smiles along the way …

Not everything is perfect
Nor do I want it to be
Having something to work for
Shapes me into what I want to be

I love what I have
Sure it's never precise
But it's what we have to work with
Sometimes it's better when it's not right.

What if everything was perfect?
Susan Lindstrom, Grade 8
Thomas Middle School, IL

Mowing

The grass was getting tall,
then they heard an above bird call.
Jacob just wanted to lay low,
and he really didn't want to go.

When he got outside he could see the lawn,
but he was so tired he gave out a yawn.
The sun came up to start the day,
and Jacob looked at the lawn with dismay.

He started off with the front,
and he noticed that the mower's blade seemed blunt.
He stopped the mower and went to his dad,
who when saw this, became furiously mad.

When Jacob asked what he could do,
he said, "I will say the choices for you."
The first choice was homework,
And with that, Jacob let out a smirk.

As you can see what I've done,
I did choose number one.
For I wrote this poem,
And I have found my rhythm.
Jacob Logan, Grade 7
St. Thomas Aquinas School, IN

Meet the Rain

I listen to the rain it beats on my soul
I listen to my soul it sings to my heart
I listen to my heart it defies my mind
I listen to my mind it speaks to my life
I listen to my life it thinks of my love
I listen to my love he breaths loving things
Our love that beats like the unending rain
And I realize that love is what we're really searching for
But we don't know it's searching for us
And when we find it we don't appreciate it
Because what we really want is an eternity
Something past forever something more
When we search for love some may be happy
But most want more a pledge that will always bind
A pledge that should never be broken
And when it is love it is shattered until it can be found again
Love wants to be held close to the heart
Where it can thrive and live happily, forever
Ebony Whitted, Grade 8
Young Women's Leadership Charter School, IL

Stars

Stars are extraordinary and unique
They are forms of fire and gas
Stars are tiny light bulbs that stand out against
the dark, endless sky
Stars are completely different worlds, twinkling with light
They tell us myths and stories about history
They represent other opportunities, and all of the
different places that we could go
Stars are drawings, forming bears, dragons and snakes
Stars are white shards of glass lying on a black carpet
Stars are sources of inspiration and imagination
They are little bright arrows, guiding people
through nature and life
They are 'pinholes in the curtains of the heavens'
Stars show us every person that has lived and died
and the souls that watch over us
Stars are keys to the universe and tell us that we may not be alone
Becky Marshall, Grade 7
Stratford Middle School, IL

What Is Love?

Love,
Painful,
Mind-bending,
And complicated.
At some point you may wish love never existed…
But could you picture the world without it?
Could you imagine US without it?
Love,
It's like food,
There are some kinds you just hate
But you need it to LIVE!
Kala Tatum, Grade 8
Red Bud Elementary School, IL

Life of a T-shirt
If I were a T-shirt,
I would chill-out in a closet with other shirts.
The small, crammed, discreet closet would be my home.
I have a unique design of green and blue stripes.
Other shirts tell me it matches my personality.
In the closet it would be as cool as a glass of iced tea.
But sometimes I'm taken out for duty.
It's as annoying as taking care of a 5 year old kid.
They put me on, putting on the buttons improperly.
They sweat a lot and their dampness carries onto me.
They smear their gross chapped lips on my sleeves as if they didn't have enough time to go put a tissue to work.
I know that I have done my duty when I've been thrown into the laundry.
Now I'm trapped with the other disgusting clothes.
After when they finally feel like doing the laundry I get shoved into a jumbo basket.
I get put into the laundry *swish swosh swish swosh* and next thing you know I'm rinsed and cleansed.
After 30 minutes, as I am cold and soggy I get put into another spinny thing that dries me up.
It gets extremely loud in the dryer and it is also very uncomfortable and hot in there.
And the next thing you know I finally get back home into the small, crammed, discreet closet.

Andy Song, Grade 8
Thomas Middle School, IL

Seasons of the Year
One of the seasons is summer
Summer is the warmest season of the year
Most kids look forward to summer because they are off of school
Whenever summer comes to mind I think of ice cream, slushies, pools, and happy kids
The next season is fall
Fall is when all the leaves go from green to burnt orange, like it just came out of the oven,
Apple red, like a freshly picked apple, and sunlight yellow, like it was kissed by the sun
When I think of fall I think of families raking leaves and the kids jumping in the piles
The season after fall is winter
Winter is cold, frosty, and icy
This is the coldest season of the year
During winter there is Christmas and New Year's Eve
When I think of winter I think of kids playing in the snow, sledding, bare trees, and the weather is freezing
The final season is spring
Spring is when flowers spring up out of the ground
The leaves grow back on the trees
Whenever spring comes to my mind I think of the color coming back to the Earth

Mary Landry, Grade 7
Stanley Clark School, IN

Roses in the rain
Roses left in the rain have a great world of pain, sorrow and tainted in black and blue. Washed away petal by petal left on the thorns of the clear red blood dripped rose. That had been tainted by red the color it bled. The green of the stem washed away by the white of the rain. Left on the cracks in the pavement cut by the thorns of the rose. Washed away by the rain makes the rose turn black in torturing pain is it really a rose any more or is it just a waste of time a waste of space left behind. On the concrete waiting, waiting, waiting for the time the time to die the time to sit the time to wait or just more time to disappear from this earth. More and more time passes just sitting and waiting for someone to save it, to rescue it to take it and plant it and bring it back to life. But does it even come, now all there is to do is just to wait and wait to sit and wait for my love to plant me again and bring me back. Day, months, years and years have passed still in the same place waiting for him my Savior in Jerusalem waiting for him to arrive. As I sit and wait I could hear the bells ringing Rome choirs sing, sing please be my savior, my sword, and shield take me off of this dreadful pavement of a battlefield make me up again make me new. Make me like my old self again make me love him I just wish to be planted once again.

Jessicca Rone, Grade 7
Pierce Middle School, IN

Down the Floor

Down the court she ran
Faster then before
Waiting for a pass
Her only chance to score

Yelling here! Here! Here!!
One pass please, here! She did call
Running ready for a shot
Finally shooting the ball
Swish!

Rachel Widenhofer, Grade 7
Concordia Lutheran School, IN

One-r Who-er Is-er Always There-r

Jesus talker
Children lover
House picker-upper
School driver to-er
Personal chauffeur
One who's with me-er
A lot of the time-er
Information giver
Best listener
Mom

Spencer Melgreen, Grade 7
Rochester Jr High School, IL

South Carolina

South Carolina where the sand is gold;
Where the beach is hot, not cold;
Where people wade in the water so warm;
South Carolina, so fun you can't ignore.

South Carolina, with its coconut trees;
That sway in the wind uncontrollably;
South Carolina my favorite place to be;
It's beautiful there, just go and see.

Jordan Smallwood, Grade 7
Concordia Lutheran School, IN

The Graveyard

Thy stillness rises up to meet me.
Thy quietness speaks volumes to my soul.
What is it like without any glee?
O graveyard, what is thy goal?

The bodies that lie within thy ground,
Are cold and lifeless, awaiting the call.
Sleep on O bodies without a sound!
For Christ is coming with judgment for all.

Kanoshia Schmucker, Grade 9
Cuba Mennonite School, IN

Afghanistan

A fghanistan's mountains
B ad people
C ountry full of
D eadly things
E verywhere troops
F ighting for their lives
G renades killing soldiers
H ills making it hard to climb
I llness killing innocent people
J ets dropping bombs
K illing Afghans
L andmines blowing up
M adness controls their people
N ight planning attacks using
O ps flying
P lanes fly above after that
Q uiet roams the area while
R unning for cover
S uppressive fire using
T actics so they can come home to the
U .S. while the Afghans are
V anishing into the mountains
W aiting for our troops to
e **X** amine the area, then they fire at our troops
Y elling then a
Z ap blew over the land then…Nothing.

Austin Feldman, Grade 7
West Salem Grade School, IL

I Am From

I am from a farm were all you see is corn,
I am from a family of love.
I am from a world of happiness and betrayal,
I am from a world where you look around the corner and you'll find a food shop,
I am from a world of nationalities,
I am from the French bread and wonderful sweet chocolate,
I am from the British army that guards their queen for protection,
I am from a world where life isn't perfect,
I am from reality and not a story character,
I am from a world were technology is taking over,
I am from a world that is coming to an end,
I am from a life were every moment is history,
But best of all I am from a family of love.

Madeleine Watson, Grade 7
International School of Indiana, IN

Test Day

My palms are sweaty.
I am not sure if I am ready.
I studied but still just don't understand.
I receive my test and there is a pain in my chest.
I look at the first question but quickly notice it just says name.
I went through the test with a breeze but my mind was still not at ease.
I have to wait for the results the next day.
My mind right now is like a car going one hundred miles an hour.
The teacher walks around handing out tests I hear a yes and then an oh no.
The teacher approaches my desk and hands me my test.
I can't bear to look but I take a peak.
And on this glorious test day I come out with an A.

Chase Stepp, Grade 7
Highland Hills Middle School, IN

Winter Night

The white snow shimmers
In the glossy, thin moonlight
Snowflakes sprinkle down
Peacefully

Zoe Smith, Grade 8
Northlawn Jr High School, IL

I Hate Having a Cold

I hate it when I have a cold
It hurt when I sneezed
Going to school would be mighty bold
And my father would be pleased

Logan Lomas, Grade 7
West Salem Grade School, IL

The Tilt

The tilting table tilted so precariously on the tiny tip of a needle.
It is still there, ready to fall millions of feet off the tiny needle, tied with a thread to not fly away.
Hazardous, needing help to not fall off into the never-ending space, but nay,
It doesn't, it's there, tilting, bigger than the Earth!
On top, it's flatter than a square's side,
It's even flatter on the other side,
It tilts, balancing on Mars and Venus,
It's almost falling off now, don't touch it!
It fell into never-ending space, never to be regained.

Zacharie Zirnheld, Grade 7
International School of Indiana, IN

Being Human

It welcomed me at birth.
It was there when I took my first step, for my first nightmare, first day of school.
It was there when I won. It was there when I lost.
When I picked myself back up again because I refused to lose and I continue to push myself forward.
I know it's there.
I can feel it around me, in the air and it will leave whenever I part from this beautiful planet.
What is this feeling of just being? I can tell you.
It's called living.
It's being Human.

Sara Geiger, Grade 7
Andrew Jackson Language Academy, IL

Where Fall Ends and Winter Begins

Fall, the season where trees are painted with creamy browns, deep reds, bright oranges, and pale yellows. The end of summer and the start of winter, yet the wilderness is still teeming with life. A mature whitetail buck with bulky thick antlers stops rubbing a pine tree and steps out of the rut and brush to chase a herd of does down the trail. A ladybug flees from a starving sparrow to avoid being a meal for the bird and its chicks. A bear sniffs for the crisp smell of fresh salmon in the stream. These all take place between the end of summer and the start of winter. Fall's cold and foggy air has a fresh icy taste to it and feels cool and misty on your skin. A variety of different-colored leaves splotches the grass a fiery tie-dye array of color. The end of summer and the start of winter. Some people do not like fall because it ends their favorite season or begins the one they do not adore, but that is just the way nature is. Fall, where summer ends and where winter begins.

Brandon Allen, Grade 8
Corpus Christi Elementary School, IN

The Melting Pot Girl

I am from three different flavors of countries that mix together into one big soup, honeyed, spicy, and humorous.
I am from a maple tree of glasses, sweet yet strong and stubborn.
I am from a hot pizza, with mozzarella cheese and marinara sauce.
I am from an ancient warrior caste with deadly accuracy.
I am from the bragging, nagging, and teasing of best friends.
I am from the perfect spring days: pleasantly warm and soft.
I am from the sarcastic humor in English class that makes people fall out of their chairs laughing.
But most of all I am from a melting pot of languages, cultures, with a heaping load of spicy-sweet humor.

Carmela Mohan, Grade 7
International School of Indiana, IN

If a Horse Fell Through Your House

If a horse fell through your house he would: Slip on the bathroom floor, fall down the nursery stairs, bump his head on the bed and get tangled up in a thread. He would knock down the door, hit the couch, fall down the stairs and then say "ouch!" He would roll through the kitchen, stroll out the door, run to the fields and yell "NO MORE!"

Cooper Conley, Grade 7
Highland Hills Middle School, IN

Buzz Buzz

Dribbling down the floor
Charging — a closed door.
Swoosh, Swish, Squeak
Time is running out
Tick, Tock, Tick, Tock.
Sweat dripping off players
Drip, drop, drip, drop
Five, four, three, two
Shoot, Shoot
The crowd is going wild!
Dribble, dribble, swoosh
BUZZ BUZZ
He made it!
Aspen Duncan, Grade 8
Red Bud Elementary School, IL

Willow Tree

Willow Tree Willow Tree
where the guardian angels watch over me.
As I lay among the night,
I know that things will be all right.
when I have my ups and downs,
the guardian angels help me turn around.
When I lay beneath that tree,
The guardian angels lay with me.
We talk and talk every night,
talk about heaven's beautiful light.
Guardian angels guardian angels,
when you lay by me under that willow tree.
I know that heaven is right for me.
Gracie Scott, Grade 7
Liberty Elementary/Jr High School, IL

Knock on Wood

knock knock
who's there?
knock on wood
nothing bad ever happens
knock on wood
no one innocent dies
knock on wood
no more war
knock on wood
the hungry are fed
knock on wood world peace
you never know what could happen if you
knock on wood
Alex Roth, Grade 8
Thomas Middle School, IL

Pandas

All pandas so big
Are losing their homes of trees
With no place to go
Ashley Bannan, Grade 7
Bethel Lutheran School, IL

We Are Only Human…

Sometimes we use the phrase, "We are only human,"
But that is only an excuse.

I think we should say, "We are human"
In a way that means we can accomplish anything we set our minds to.

We all have dreams…
So go chase them…then live them.

We all have goals…
So set them higher.

We all are our own person…
So be you.

We all have a presumed thought of the life we desire to live…
But we only live this life once, so make it the way you want it.

We will go through hard times,
But they only make us stronger…

Most importantly, no matter what…
We should always believe in ourselves.
Gabrielle Ludwig, Grade 7
All Saints Academy, IL

Phoenix Feathers

She dances in the foggy dusk as she makes her long
descent, the moist atmosphere is closing in on her.
She heads home on a wistful current, flying…gliding.
The journey is long from end dear phoenix…as thou
passes by, a single feather drops down from the sky…

A boy of nine passes by and sees a sight to behold!
The rare phoenix feather lies abandoned on an old road.
He lifts it in a gentle embrace…walking home on this day.
He now seeks rest and tender care, his quest, far from end.
He steps with grace, a slow pace and turns a lofty bend.

He now has seen an amazing sight, the phoenix!
The fine phoenix who lost a long scarlet tail feather
She gazes upon the boy, who stills and rubs his eyes.
The phoenix takes flight with a beat of her wings,
carrying the small boy, who is carrying his things.

The two reach a fine nest, where they can land,
The boy sits still with most awe and most disdain,
The phoenix roosts and with one stern look, turns…
The years went by, the two grew old and died within the
nest, but now they've found eternal peace…and a quiet place to rest…
Maggie Shepherd, Grade 7
Pleasant Plains Middle School, IL

Something That Was…

She gazed upon the blackened tree
And wondered just who might be
Up, up, up in that big blue sky.
Like a life that always ends,
She lost her tree, her spectacular friend.
They made the decision to brutally strike down
And torch around her the once lush ground.
Her poor tree, now a scorched carcass, still stands.
It remains the most glorious in all the lands.

Morgan Everman, Grade 8
Red Bud Elementary School, IL

Christmas

At Christmastime, we celebrate Christ's birth,
And go to nighttime church.
Stockings are hung, snowmen are made,
We cut down trees to decorate.

Presents are wrapped, large dinners are made,
Gingerbread people are eaten.
Santa Claus slides down the chimney with lots of joy,
Christmas is here, with trees and toys.

Grace Bieberich, Grade 7
Emmanuel-St Michael Lutheran School, IN

Friends

Fight after fight,
You know I'll forgive you.
We are friends,
Considering what we have been through.
People may think it's stupid and pointless,
But it's funny because you bring me happiness.
Flirting, fighting, or enemies,
I still care because I know when it's all over,
You'll still be there.

Sadie Farmer, Grade 8
Red Bud Elementary School, IL

The Catcher

As the ball whistled past the swinging bat
My glove shouted with pain
I saw a runner stealing second
Blinded by the dust the dirt pushed me up to throw

I watched my throw cut through the wind
I waited for it to reach the end of its path
A dust cloud formed as he slid into second
The suspense of the umpire's call killed me

Andrew Padilla, Grade 7
Galileo Scholastic Academy, IL

Grandpa

What is my grandpa?
Loving me more than life itself
Caring for me
Giving me life to my dad who also loves me
He taught me how to act in life
Gave me money for my birthday
Fought in one of the wars and fought for freedom
Died and was buried but went to heaven because he is a believer
That is my grandpa.

Cody Stegenga, Grade 8
DeMotte Christian School, IN

The Finish Line

My heart is beating so loud my opponents can hear it
I listen to the voices that are cheering
At this point I can't and won't quit
At the sound of the gun the finish line is nearing

I feel the wind whipping at my face
I sense the others running behind me
I finish the race with grace
I have won the race and I'm swelled with glee

Kylie Steele, Grade 7
Emmanuel-St Michael Lutheran School, IN

Can't Wait 'Till the Bell Rings

What's the buzz about school?
Is school really that cool?
The bell rings you get your things.
You go to class learn some things then the bell rings.
If you have music the teacher may sing!
Then you munch on lunch 'till the bell…rings.
Between classes there's hooting, howling, and yelling.
'Till the bell rings! Tick-tock it's 3 o'clock.
Boom! School's out right when the bell rings!

Jennifer Villanueva, Grade 7
Pierce Middle School, IN

Inside a Laugh

Inside a laugh to be heard by all, a sound of happiness is awake.
Inside a laugh your heart is open to spread the gift of joy.
Inside a laugh the presence of happiness blooms, like a flower.
Inside a laugh a smile is blossoming waiting to be shared with all.
Inside a laugh there is a sweet, pleasant sound,
contagious when you see the smile on people's faces.
Inside a laugh there is magic, enchanting to everybody around.
Inside a laugh there is more than joy, and happiness.
Inside a laugh there is love that makes the world seem brighter.

Hannah Franz, Grade 7
St Pius X Catholic School, IN

Night

I curl up under my blankets,
as the darkness seeps in.
Through the crack in my door,
Taking over.

I hear,
The pitter-patter of tiny rain drops.
The trees are casting ghostly shadows.
A full moon,
Shines brightly,
Like a light for the entire world.

The night,
Waiting for me to fall asleep.
Like a lullaby,
My lullaby

And I curl up under my blankets,
as the darkness seeps in.
Through the crack in my door,
Taking over.
Roshana Krishnappa, Grade 7
Madison Jr High School, IL

My Pencil

My pencil has had quite a journey,
From German to L.A. to math
It gets sharpened frequently,
And then *skips* across the paper some more
My pencil is like a magic wand,
Spreading words across the page,
Issuing forth my wishes as
It *dashes* across the page
It spies each word carefully,
Counting them one by one
It wants to help my spelling,
But it can't yell "SPELL CHECK!!"
My pencil is like a translator,
It can read my thoughts,
And can translate them,
Into print,
As it *leaps* across the page
My pencil is very special,
Can't you tell?
And there is still halfway
Of the lead left to go.
Sarah Larson, Grade 8
Thomas Middle School, IL

In Trouble

In trouble, grounded
Wanting to be outside playing
My heart seeking fun
Guilty, but still in trouble
Taner Carlson, Grade 7
West Salem Grade School, IL

Seasons

Winter wonderland whirls with white
Whistling wind whips with might
Spring season saturates the earth
Satisfying scents are at birth
Summer sunshine fills the day
Sending slumber on its way
Fall foliage flutters without a sound
Crunching carelessly on the ground
Seasons cycle through the year
Make the most of each while it's here.
Katy Seiwert, Grade 7
International School of Indiana, IN

The Day She Came Home

She came with hundreds of others patiently,
Waiting to see their families very graciously.
They came from very far back from a war,
All of them being in the peace corps.
We cried with joy after seeing each other,
I was so happy to see my loving mother.
After her very long flight,
We took her home that very night.
She was happy to be here,
And I was happy to have her there.
Felice Brokaw, Grade 7
International School of Indiana, IN

Peace and Freedom

What is War?
A time of fighting
A time of sorrow and
A time of happiness
God bless America
When brave people go to serve
Men and women standing proud
Saluting to the flag
Fighting for peace and freedom
That is War
Jake Bowers, Grade 8
DeMotte Christian School, IN

Home

What is my home?
   A place to be comforted
   A safe refuge
   A time to be yourself
   A place for family to hang out
   A private place
   A place of fun
   A place to cry
   A place to relax
That is my home.
Kurt VanderMolen, Grade 8
DeMotte Christian School, IN

Seasons

Cold, blustery wind
Snow falling ever so hard
Fire roasted chestnuts

Great new life cometh
Happiness in abundance
The perfect weather

Sport kids run around
Relax in the chilly pool
Don't die of heat stroke

Trees are changing hue
Gorgeous leaves plummet down
Jump in the leaf pile
Ethan Frobish, Grade 7
Immaculate Conception School, IL

Snow

Beautiful and white
Creates silly memories
Christmas time is here

Each of them unique
Snowmen built; frostbite appears
Family time brings cheers

Melting grayish slush
Beautiful becomes dull
Christmas time has gone

Beautiful at first
As time goes on snow is gone
That's the end of snow
McKenzie Rodgers, Grade 7
Immaculate Conception School, IL

Fun in the Sun

Tanning in the sun
The breeze blowing through my hair
Looking at sea shells

Sun sparkling down
Palm trees swaying in the breeze
Playing in the waves

Dolphins frolicking
Seagulls gliding through the air
Water glistening

Building sand castles
Sand crunching under my toes
Now the day is done
Mattie Meyer, Grade 7
Immaculate Conception School, IL

Sisters

Sisters are like a wall,
The strongest and tallest wall, that you could ever imagine.
The wall that grabs you every time, you fall.
You confide in this wall,
And each second, minute and hour of each day, it supports you.
This wall maintains its support,
Whether you obtain a location of twenty feet, or twenty miles away,
The wall remains persistently.

Sisters are like a blanket, a very warm and gently blanket,
Unless a feather lingers, poking out, offering minimal consent,
With its uncomfortable position.
But the feather persists meaninglessly,
As it gets flicked away, then comfort prevails, once again.

Sisters are like a paperclip, they bind you together,
Unless they snap.
If they snap, you collapse.
Although, the two of you together, reorganize yourselves.
Now the two of you can endure the feeling, of being in sync,
Forevermore.

McKenzie Mauer, Grade 8
Thomas Middle School, IL

My Mission*

Day by day I don't get to see your face.
It might just be a phase,
But I almost want to chase it.
Then I realize it's only a dream,
So every day I've lived without you
Is all a frightening scream.
People say I look like you.
People seem insane.
But everything gets looked at
When I start thinking the same.
I think about you day and night.
It's just an unbearable flight.
I just wish you were here in my arms
And I could see your beautiful face
Like a shining light.
All I have is pictures and very few memories.
It's a mission in my life to live without you,
But now I know you're really here.
Whether I can see you or not,
You're always in my thoughts.

Wesli Welch, Grade 8
Daleville High School, IN
*In loving memory of my mother

Ode to Autumn Leaves

I love the autumn leaves,
Which fall from the nearly bare trees.
The wind blows them around,
You can hear their crunchy sound.
When the air is cool and crisp,
And filled with fall haze,
Their warm and bright colors,
Seem to brighten up the days.
Bright oranges, deep yellows, and beautiful crimsons,
Their beauty is at its greatest during this season.
When the season of fall comes around,
The thing I look forward to is the leaves on the ground.

Maddie Owen, Grade 8
Rochester Jr High School, IL

My Brother

Kicking, screaming, throwing his toys,
My mother screams, "Knock it off, boys!"
But what did I do? Nothing at all!
"He's the one who punched the wall!"
The little jerk is quite a brat,
Running around in his camo hat.
He always says, "You hit me, it's true!"
Then I always say, "I'd like to choke you!"
He always says he's filled with sorrow,
But the exact same thing will happen tomorrow.
My mother sounds like a repeating song,
"WHY CAN'T YOU TWO GET ALONG?!"

Ryan Mann, Grade 7
Marquette Academy, IL

The Apple Barn

I love driving to the Apple Barn,
Pulling in to the lot and smelling the crisp air,
With the leaves swirling like red and yellow maidens dancing.
My family and I tumble out of the car,
Almost running to that warm shelter.
We race through the door,
Smelling all of the warm pies like my Mom's homemade ones.
Dad buys some hot apple cider for us,
While my little sister and I munch on free samples.
Then I grab my bucket and skip outside like a prancing young colt.
We finally finish picking and laughing, we walk inside,
Mom bought everything; including some apples.
Jumping back into the car, I already can't wait to go back next year.

Madeline Campbell, Grade 7
Rochester Jr High School, IL

Thoughts on Thanksgiving

T he families all over the country get together,
H alf the food people have gets put in the freezer,
A lot of people get up early the next day to go Black Friday shopping,
N obody is fighting because it is such a happy time,
K etchup with turkey? People think I'm gross!
S tuffing gets made to put in the turkey,
G ood food is made and families get together,
I ce cream afterwards? Nobody has room!
V alentine's Day love can't beat this!
I am grateful for everything I have,
N othing could make this day bad! (Unless the turkey burns),
G reat thanks to the Pilgrims and the Indians
or none of this would have started.

Maya Patel, Grade 7
Hannah Beardsley Middle School, IL

Will You Hear Me?

will you hear me if I cry,
above the thunder of anger,
over blasts of fear and hate,
when help comes not at all
or when it comes to late?
when streets explode with fire,
and hearts grow dead with grief,
when all the sounds are sad,
and there's no more relief?
will you hear me before I die?

Marlayna Gandy, Grade 7
Galileo Scholastic Academy, IL

An Ode to Holidays

The holidays are everyone's favorite day
Even when the skies are gray.
Creatures emerge that cannot be seen
On the day of Halloween.
A man on a certain sleigh
On a special holiday.
Holidays are so fun
When celebrated with everyone.
So go on out and celebrate
Every one in every state!

Hannah Feder, Grade 7
Stanley Clark School, IN

The Apple Barn

Kids laughing everywhere you go,
As you pass by pumpkins in each row.
The fields will soon be covered in snow,
So go with the autumn flow.
Leaves turning orange, brown, and red,
And soon the trees will all be dead.
Birds flying south for the winter,
Sound of crickets like tiny splinters
Still waiting inline for this apple drink
It's the best taste in the world, I think.

Andria Robinson, Grade 8
Rochester Jr High School, IL

Ode to Autumn Trees

The color of the trees catch my sight,
But the trees are becoming bare,
A gust of wind and the leaves take flight,
It's like it's losing its hair,
They're being blow all over the sky,
Everywhere I go: yellow, orange, red,
The season goes by so fast,
I watch as the leaves go by,
These trees will soon be dead,
Then leaves will be a thing of the past.

Jay Tally, Grade 8
Rochester Jr High School, IL

I Come From

I come from my struggles,
From being beaten until I had no strength left to fight back,
And the darkest caves of silence.
I am from the names of hate and defeat.
I am from the melodies of my mother's sweet, soothing voice,
and the loving arms of my biggest hero,
from rising, and from falling.
I am from the words of faith, love, and hope.
From the great words of Maya Angelou, from the "Still I Rise."
I come from the meekness of a mouse to the courageous roar of a lion.
I am from my struggles, but yet I rise.
I come from the sweet, glorious smile of victory.
From the battle that has already been fought and won,
From the race that is still being run.
I come from my struggles,
From my brokenness and my pain,
From the race
I will not run in vain.

Sarah Scasny, Grade 8
St Marys School, IN

Spring

A zaleas are springing up, **B** lowing from the winds,
C arnations are flourishing.
D arkness disappears, **E** liminating the cold weather,
F ading the memories of winter.
G usts of wind make the entire scene sway.
H ouses again open up, **I** ssuing a comfortable breeze.
J umpy children run outside, **K** ites are taken out and soon fill the sky.
L ight skies promise sunshine.
M eadows' grasses multiply.
N ewly found love for nature, **O** pens my dreams.
P layful birds are chirping.
Q uilts are shoved into the closet.
R equests for warmer weather, **S** now is drying up.
T alk of rain showers.
U nbelievable sights, **V** ibrant colors fill the scene.
W inds play a song to e **X** traordinary beauty coming to life.
Y ields God's expertise.
Z ippers on children's jackets come down.

Alyssa Hoffman, Grade 8
DeMotte Christian School, IN

Sounds of Nature

A bee zips by, murmuring a gentle buzz
I hear cool, stream waters in the distance
While a cardinal sings to her fragile babies, covered in fuzz
A bee zips by, murmuring a gentle buzz
I think about what the butterfly, silently gliding, once was
A soft breeze rushes around, whispers in my ear, then is gone in an instance
A bee zips by, murmuring a gentle buzz
I hear cool, stream waters rushing in the distance

Carrie Jane Reese, Grade 8
Northlawn Jr High School, IL

Time

Time is a reward that is presented upon those of pure souls.
Only those of golden souls may use time wisely.
Others steal time and use it for misdoing.
The only one who can take that time back is the father of time.
He shows them their reward for the theft of time.
Some use time for nothing and murder the time they're given.
Wasting the time that they only get once.
Some use time to help others gain more.
Some use it to steal others' time.
Some complain about it and they get rid of it for eternity.
Time should be given to only those of pureness.
Those who waste time have their time taken away.
Some know that time is a gift and should be used to the fullest
But not many know that time is only given to those of high expectations.
Others believe life is more important.
One way or another we need both.
Time and space must work together to create all.
But even though those who use time badly always are given a second time by the father of time.
No matter what though everything is important
Even things of lesser time.
So remember all deserves time.

Liam Hargreaves, Grade 7
Todd Academy, IN

Autumn

Autumn, Fall, el otoño …no matter what you call it or how you say it, autumn is my favorite season.
I don't know what it is,
There's just something about fall that no other season has.
Autumn is when the heat dies down
And the cooling breeze comes out.
Autumn is when leaves change colors;
First yellow, then gold, then orange, then red…
Before I know it, I'm greeted with all these leaves lying motionless on the ground.
Dead, but so alive.
As the wind blows, I hear the rustling.
Then I see a flash of colors fly past my window.
I sit and stare, taking in this unique beauty
Unlike anything else I've ever known.
I see the mystery, the glory.
The life, the refinement…
I watch the leaves drop,
One by one
Until the trees are all bare.
Autumn, I don't know why you are so special and take a place in my heart…
Is it your beauty, your elegance…or is it only me?

Nicole Sharon, Grade 7
Stratford Middle School, IL

Summer Breeze

The summer breeze feels warm upon my face, gently pulling my hair back and forth.
The summer breeze is as light as a feather upon my hands, lightly touch my arms with care and trust.
The summer breeze slides upon my legs giving me goosebumps, wistfully just touching the tops of my feet, tickling them.
But I know one day I will say goodbye to the summer breeze and hello to the sharp, unforgiving wind, of winter.

McKenzie Todd, Grade 7
Kingsley Jr High School, IL

The Magnificent Sun
I am the supporter of the earth,
I give it heat and light,
My rays come to your planet,
And keep it warm and bright.

I shine during the day,
The moon comes in the night,
And I travel to other side of the planet,
And give it some of my light.

My work is ceaseless,
As I make every plant grow,
And at the start of spring,
I also melt the snow.

While I am still alive,
I am what you should cherish,
Because when I finally collapse,
You will also perish.
Arun Arjunakani, Grade 8
Margaret Mead Jr High School, IL

Climb to Heaven
If I had a choice
On how to get to heaven
A rock wall,
Or an elevator
I would choose the wall
Without any indecision
And climb.

I would climb and climb
Until my arms fall off
Then, I would fall,
Back to the ground,
With a chance to try again.

But this time, I say,
To those living still,
Come with me to heaven.
Come, climb with me,
Come touch the sky.
Sarah Beste, Grade 7
Madison Jr High School, IL

Dark Night
Wind Howling.
Your body shivers.
Streets are blank,
With only leaves walking by.
The trees wave to you,
But don't know what to do.
Hoo, hoo,
The owl quotes.
Claudia Mehring, Grade 8
Red Bud Elementary School, IL

Winter's End
Gone now again to the wind
lost forever until winter's end
hot and cold control her life
caught between fire and ice
wide, youthful eyes
whether yellow or brown
captured in the wolf's face
stealing away the one I love
my best friend, my future wife
my entire life
forever searching, willing to find
your beautiful dark gray hide
and once summer rolls around
your wondrous hair, like golden sound
forevermore lyrics will come
describing you, describing our memories
folded up into paper cranes
waiting for your return
when you once again find your skin
I will be waiting at winter's end
Emme Hays, Grade 8
Southwestern Middle School, IL

Seasons
Summer
Sun is shining down
The day is ready to start
Play outside today

Fall
The leaves are falling
Crackling, crunch on the ground
In a bed of brown

Winter
Dark is early now
The flickering of the lights
It is cold outside

Spring
Tractors in the field
Flowers swaying side by side
New babies are born
Michael Feeney, Grade 7
Immaculate Conception School, IL

Demon
Words of horror filled my head
No one spoke or even cared
Maybe I was better off dead
Everywhere I looked, there was no hope
I trembled, I feared, nothing was pure
In a world so cruel, so dark and evil
It's not fair when everyone's a demon
Sabrina Velazquez, Grade 8
Galileo Scholastic Academy, IL

What My Mother's Like
She's an avid church goer,
A constant bosser,
A don't-bother-me cleaner,
A *Survivor* watcher,
A caring homework helper,
A former farmer,
A plant talker,
A wanna-be Italian speaker,
A not-so-great cooker,
A never stressed-er,
She's an awesome mom.
Lucas Denney, Grade 7
Rochester Jr High School, IL

The Summer Sun
The shining sun in the summer sky
directs his rays at me.

The light is bright, which hurts my eyes
until I cannot see.

In the morning, when he comes up
I know that night is at an end.

But every evening when he disappears
I say goodbye to my friend.
Maddy Ford, Grade 7
Concordia Lutheran School, IN

Balloon
Balloon
I am a gift to a child,
A little boy or girl,
And then when they let me go,
I float around the whole world.
Up, up into space I go,
Seeing people see me from below.
I start to descend,
As my helium disperses,
Pop! I go down, down,
Now I am worthless.
Laila Haydar, Grade 7
International School of Indiana, IN

Candlelight
Flicker, flicker,
Flames, dance quicker.
Please, stay a little longer.
Candlelight, gleam and glow.

Dimmer, dimmer
As the light becomes thinner,
The candlelight starts to go low.
Oh candlelight, please don't go.
Ian Brown, Grade 7
Concordia Lutheran School, IN

Ignorance Is Bliss

On the top of a mountain, the slope gets steeper,
The pain increases, invisible cuts get deeper,
In the dark the light won't show,
And in your mind the thoughts take hold.
Their taunting voices and hands so cold,
Hold you captive and never let go.
The "what ifs" and their chilling kiss,
In the dark, the silence I miss.
I've been hurt too much,
So please don't touch,
Everything I've ever been.
This is my last resort,
It comes down to this.
Now I find,
Ignorance is bliss.

Amber Frost, Grade 9
Schaumburg High School, IL

The Garage

It is not a room but a garage,
As the floor is dark, damp, and cold,
The smell of oil and gas hang in the air.
And the lights are dim; but just bright enough.
This is the place champions are made…

When the players push themselves to exhaustion,
The sweat pours down their faces; going through their routine.
The banging of the weights muffles the grunts from the men,
And the exercises are not for the weak or mild.
This is the place champions are made…

As many dream of being the best
Few are willing to push themselves to the test.
While the training and hard work just be viewed together
Life lessons are learned in this garage.
This is the place that champions call home…

Dalton Handlin, Grade 8
Rochester Jr High School, IL

With All in Life

The sun rises every day,
Though it doesn't always feel that way,
The grass turns brown and the flowers old,
But each day is another story to unfold,
With all in life to love and to hate,
Some things only come down to fate,
Though it might not always seem this way,
there is a little good in every day,
A small gesture from someone who cares,
Someone who lightens the burdens the world bears,
So be there for that friend who is always there for you,
And listen to them, because they have problems too.

Audrey Maicher, Grade 8
St Marys School, IN

Titan

Titan
Little soft puppy
As soft as a blanket
Coming home, he looks around our home
Wondering where he is
We let him outside
It's windy and cold
It's as cold as an ice cube
Tired from playing in the winter snow
Puppy hair so little but soft
As I held him close to keep him warm he yawned
I could smell his puppy breath
As I took a bite out of my mountain-high burger
I look over and there he is
Begging for my mountain-high burger and twig-sized fries
He's bigger now no longer a baby
A full-grown Dane
We named that big beautiful boy Titan
He's as big as a horse, he's mighty Hulk
My perfect playful protector
Titan

Cameron Letsos, Grade 8
Liberty Jr High School, IL

That Odd Orange Cat

That odd orange cat
He thinks he's all that
Munching on mice and moles he maliciously murdered
That odd orange cat
He bites babies and tips over everything
That odd orange cat
Wide as a toothpick and sluggish as a cheetah
That odd orange cat
He is coarse as oil and his nerves are soft as steel
That odd orange cat
I would almost tip my hat to that cat
But he's still just that odd orange cat

Wyatt Lee, Grade 7
Highland Hills Middle School, IN

You

When you look in mirror you refer to yourself as me
You and I make a whole
Together or not we can't be separated
The bond between us cannot be broken
You would think you could just walk away
Before you've found out that we were together all along
You and I are practically the same
But you just don't know it yet
Do you ever look closely in the mirror?
Who does it look like?
Do ever feel lost in the world?
You don't realize that I'm only a fragment of you
I am you

William Lyles, Grade 8
Divine Infant Jesus School, IL

Inferiority

Please don't blame me
For this insecurity
I try to keep a smile
But fail, all the while
Even if it doesn't seem like it
I'm trying my hardest
And just maybe
A flame of self-confidence will be lit

Please don't worry
I know how tough it'll be
But I'll come out of my shell
But until then
I'll just keep smiling
Cassie Romero, Grade 8
Galileo Scholastic Academy, IL

The Light in You

There are days when you struggle,
There are days when you fall.
Sometimes you just want to give up,
And lose it all.
Overcome your weaknesses,
Overcome your fears.
For there are days,
That are not worth the tears.
People may tell you that you are wrong,
Never give up,
And just stay strong.
You are beautiful at what you do,
Just take your time,
And let the light shine through.
Natalie Mueller, Grade 7
Dunlap Valley Middle School, IL

Through Sickness and Health

Six miles to go
It has been a long ride
Nights laying awake
Through the head-aching drives

Falling asleep
And sitting roughly
I already dropped her off
My beloved wife I need

I'm here now
Finally at last
I will sleep forever now
And never forget our past
Jackie Martinez, Grade 7
Galileo Scholastic Academy, IL

A Year Without Rain

I am singing in a concert and the
"Spotlight" is all on me.

My head is spinning "Round and Round"
and I start to freeze.

I feel like it's "A Year Without Rain"
and my mouth is dry.

When I start to sing it's "Off the Chain"
and people are chanting Selena.

The crowd then says that I'm a
"Rock God" and I feel good.

Now I'm singing my number 1 song,
it's "Sick of You,"

And I love, the attention and would
be fine if "There's No Tomorrow"
Katie Vetter, Grade 7
Sacred Heart School, IL

Behind That Smile

Maybe you smile
Just to hide the tears.
Maybe you laugh
Just to forget the fear.
Maybe you seem happy,
or maybe you just seem scared.
We all need to be loved,
to feel cared.
So here I am
Telling you today,
Those people that made you cry?
They will pay.
Don't lose my number,
or forget my name.
What you do to yourself?
I used to play that game.
So be who you want to be,
And sing when you want to sing
Why do I even care?
Because you used to be me.
Devin De Both, Grade 8
St. Mary's School, IN

Cheering

Fans cheering
The smack of the bat
"Hey batter batter, hey batter batter"
The whoosh as her leg sticks out to slide
And me
Cheering along with the crowd
Meghan Lee, Grade 7
St Pius X Catholic School, IN

The Strongest Can't Live Forever

Such a strong woman,
filled with love.
One day filled with so much energy,
the next so ill.

Doctors couldn't explain
why she was in so much pain.

Finally! The mystery was solved!
Cancer was making her fall.

Laying in bed,
the man she wed, sobbing.
With family all around,
she slowly slipped away.

A single tear ran down her cheek,
a symbol she would miss us.
Dawn Bailey, Grade 8
Jennings County Middle School, IN

My Future Dream

Fast city of bright lights
Soaring quickly over the city
Working in the sky
Big buildings soar high
In the bright lights of the city
The noises of the cars
Warmth of the red sun
Sand is blowing with the wind
Earth is shining bright
Reach to grab a star
Warm star melts in my fingers
The future in hand
Rain falls quietly
Rainbow to a tomorrow
Sun around the corner
Life in the fast lane
Hoping for a better tomorrow
While living in the now
Isabella Kaplan, Grade 7
Notre Dame Catholic School, IN

Paradise

Reclining on a warm, sandy beach,
With my SPF 30.
Radiant, dazzling rays,
Shining on me.
Beads of sweat
Pour off my tank top
And face.
Just want to dash into the
crystal, clear water to
Escape.
Alyssa Cowell, Grade 8
Red Bud Elementary School, IL

Brothers of Ruin

Death is merciless and cruel
His grip squeezes the life from men and child
Their hollow screams are gone unheard
As you feel death's hand upon your soul
You begin to realize he is telling you this is the end
Death will claim all in its path of Ruin

War is the brother of Death
He alone sends many to an internal damnation
His sword splits apart family, friend, and nation
The way of man is to fight for survival
Some may think War is glorious
But tell me where the glory in genocide is

These two are brothers of Ruin
You may deny this
You may have a different opinion
But Death and War do not give good graces
People like Adolf Hitler did not get good graces for his War
He thought his War was glorious but as I've said
Those who approve of War and Death
Are those who approve of The Brothers of Ruin.

Brad Nally, Grade 7
Todd Academy Inc., IN

Chocolate Chip Cookie

Smells like Grandma coming for the holidays.
It's as warm as a new summer's day.
It tastes like sugar and everything nice.
Moves as fast as lightning, one glance and it's gone.
When you take your first bite it melts away time,
And when it's all down your throat reality hits you
And you have to come to.
Some are soft like chewy caramel,
But some are crunchy like peppermint candy.
It's the color of base and brown,
But tastes like a rainbow with many flavor pops and booms.
No matter what's your favorite,
You can never go wrong with any kind.

Olivia Portnov, Grade 8
Thomas Middle School, IL

Halloween Time!

The candy collectors on the move,
Batman, Superman, and Cinderella too.
"Trick or treat!" echoing around the neighborhood.
Sweets handed out to the costumed figures.
Shadows waltzing to and fro,
A pumpkin's scary face glowing in the midnight black.
Visions of ghosts jumping out everywhere,
Vampires, spirits and all things scary about.
Boom! Crack! The thunder begins,
The moon hides from fright underneath a billowing cloud.
I wish this night would never end!

Elaine Comerford, Grade 7
Rochester Jr High School, IL

Autumn in Nature

Leaves of all colors swirl around me,
When I take a step you hear them crunch,
Hundreds of them lie around me,
Scattered or in piles,
I can smell the fresh air,
And the breeze in my face
Giving me a kiss upon my chilled cheek,
Face to face with mother Earth,
Nothing can change my feelings of excitement,
Kids carving pumpkins,
Trees changing colors,
Starting to be colder,
Embrace the happiness,
Pass on the spirit,
It used to be spring,
But not it is fall.

Samantha McDonald, Grade 7
Rochester Jr High School, IL

Fire

Flames blazed through the room
We ran to the exit
Too much smoke

But someone fell into an abyss of a hole
That ate through the floor

We jumped with fear at his shrieks
We dashed to him
And bolted our feet to the floor

TOO LATE.
Darkness gobbled my best friend

A few tears came down the nurse's cheek
As I told her what had happened to my beloved friend.

Jose Lozada, Grade 7
Galileo Scholastic Academy, IL

9/11 in 2011

9/11 to you may seem to have no meaning
When actually it means thousands will be grieving
Thousands of lives that day we may have lost
But nobody dies innocently without a cost
In peace those towers stood ten years ago
Why they still can't be standing in peace I'll never know
The people who crashed down those buildings were cowards
Honestly, who crashes down two important towers
While the real murderer went on with his day
Many innocent bodies were left there to decay
One of these days I hope we get world peace
But for that to happen we need all this nonsense to cease
Our heroes kept just a few alive
And those few are the ones who are helping us survive

Ashley K. Egelhoff, Grade 8
Southwestern Middle School, IL

We Stand Together

You're not alone,
Together we stand.
When you're down,
I've got your hand.

As the world gets colder,
You become more and more bolder.
When you believe you can't bare it much longer,
I'm here to help us both get stronger.

Before the door closes and life comes to an end,
You've got me to fight with you and defend.
We won't give in!
We'll make it through,
The cold, toughness and blue.
Don't you know God and I love you?

Dominique Dilworth, Grade 8
West Park Academy, IL

Dreaming of Faith

People say it'll never happen
They say to just give up.
They think that if it happens,
It would be because of luck.
I'd like to ask them to believe in me
And to have a little faith
Because some talents are worth the trouble
And shouldn't go to waste.
This journey has been a struggle,
But its been worth it all the same.
I've wanted this more than anything,
But I haven't wanted it for the fame.
I've had this dream all my life,
And have had enough faith for two.
And if those people had a little more faith in me,
Someday my dream might come true.

Emily Cain, Grade 8
St Matthew School, IL

Stuffing

The table was set
With cranberry red
And potatoes from the garden bed
On silver platters rolls stacked high
And warm spicy pumpkin pie
Green beans and yams, too
So much my brother pretended to have the flu
I placed the turkey at the seat of honor
Much to Grandma's horror
I gave him a plate with food stacked high
When Mom saw she rolled her eyes to the sky
This confused me...
'Cause she's the one who told me to stuff the turkey

Kjrstyn Michalak, Grade 7
Hannah Beardsley Middle School, IL

Forgotten Memories

Pictures bring back memories from the past
Events we wish we could hold onto, but can't
Nobody can grip the time that moves so fast
Pictures bring back memories from the past
Our minds send us into a time warp, but at last
We snap into reality, the adventure making us pant
Pictures bring back memories from the past
Events we wish we could hold onto, but can't

Hannah Warwick, Grade 8
Northlawn Jr High School, IL

Poetry

Poetry is like a sweet harmony without notes
It's like a boat swaying smoothly over an ocean of words
It motions you to read it
You can sit down and let it lead you into words
It'll make you dig a mound of words into a mountain
It can lead you anywhere
All you have to do is dare to go there
And listen to the harmony of words that is poetry but without notes

Regina Maggio, Grade 8
St Matthew School, IL

Friends

Friends come
Friends go
Some leave
Some we hold
Friends stick together until they're old,
It's like PB and J you know it just goes
Friends are like stars, they sparkle and shine
They brighten your life all the time.

Kendall Kaiser, Grade 7
Highland Hills Middle School, IN

Who Can Love?

Some say love is for the wise,
not the meek nor the weak or the ones in disguise,
but for the veterans of the heart,
who've suffered love's painful spark,
yet the young know nothing,
kept in the dark,
'till love's true travesty breaks their heart.

Kyndra Sassman, Grade 9
Dunlap High School, IL

Mighty God

God
Gentle, big
Loving, answering, blessing
Comforter, Lamb, best friend, and Holy Spirit
Saving, listening, coming
Mysterious, strong
Father

Jennifer Ackley, Grade 7
Bethel Lutheran School, IL

Humans

So sorrowful and poor they are, the humans.
Mistreated and threatened by one another.
We have no mercy.
Our thoughts ungrateful.
Our words meaningless.
Our smiles faked.
Our laughs forced.
Our concept of beauty distorted.
Our lies never-ending.
Our pain intense.
"Love" is used loosely.
"Hate" is used mostly.
Ignorance is typical.
We raise our eyebrows in disbelief and protest.
We claim it isn't so.
But once we're alone, we are trapped in a whirlwind.
A hidden storm filled with regret, misery and shame.
Those poor, poor humans.
Their sorrowful little lives revolve around attention from others.
Won't anyone help them?
Can't we help ourselves?

Mia Silva, Grade 7
Stratford Middle School, IL

Thanksgiving

T o have my family with me
H aving a wonderful cooked meal
A sking my family questions
N o problems on this day
K nock on wood, I celebrate Thanksgiving
S haring and caring on Thanksgiving
G reat time with family members
I mpressed by all the joy
V ery special holiday for all of us
I magining the great time people are having
N o school for me
G iving back to the community

Stephen Nalepa, Grade 7
Hannah Beardsley Middle School, IL

All in One Week

A ll summer long **B** illy played sports and baked
C ookies and **D** rew in his notebook and started
E ating grapes **F** or which he had never tried
G ary, his best friend **H** ad a pet
I guana which he and Billy **J** umped around with while they flew
K ites and **L** ooked at books about
M onsters and **N** injas as they tried to
O pen a box with a **P** adlock on it while they looked for
Q uails and they **R** an around the
S treet, one day **T** hey had to use an
U mbrella because it was **V** ery
W et outside and they bought a **X** ylophone and dreamed of
Y aks and **Z** ebras

Jacob Mason, Grade 7
West Salem Grade School, IL

Ode to Dole Whips

Oh, Dole Whip a Hawaiian treat.
Your pineapple flavor so vibrant, so sweet.
The yellow color stands out,
You are the sweetest, the fruitiest without a doubt.
The smooth cold swirls neatly prepared,
Nothing else is my favorite if I even dared.
Vanilla is tasteless if I were the judge.
On Dole Whips there are no need for sprinkles or fudge.
You can be enjoyed slowly or in one bite and you're gone.
It is a bittersweet ending.
I think I will have another one!

Anna Garatoni, Grade 7
Stanley Clark School, IN

To Summer

To waking up to the sun shining through the window
To shopping for brand shades
To sweating like a pig every day
To getting sunburn after sunburn
To sitting in the sun taking in the Vitamin D
To eating every day at all times
To going to Six Flags ride after ride
To traveling high in the air
To party after party
To California girls
To Summer

Nancy Cisneros, Grade 8
Peck Elementary School, IL

Light

As I wake up today, I look at the sky,
to see if there is any light, but all I see is. . .
darkness, insecurity, loss, and emptiness.

It's just plain empty, like my heart.

I ask for forgiveness day by day, but I get no answer.
My life is full of sorrow.

Please forgive me.
Please forget.

Amara Riccio, Grade 8
Galileo Scholastic Academy, IL

Writer's Block

Here I sit thinking, pondering on what to literate,
making a class assignment that cannot be turned in late.
Perhaps, just maybe an essay on migration,
yet sadly I can't come up with a creative alliteration.
So there I silently sat, quiet as a cat when my mom came in.
She handed me a glass wanting me to drink.
So here I sit left alone to think.

The End…until I come up with something to write about.

Charlie Sandifer, Grade 7
Highland Hills Middle School, IN

The Hammerhead

Swooosh! The hammerhead flies past the rock,
Swerving through the cracks,
Crashing across waves.
His head feels like a block.
I'm sure he could smash a rock.
Swim across the rim,
Bash and crash.

Jonathan Marquart, Grade 8
Red Bud Elementary School, IL

Where Family Is and the Fun

Fun is with my family
relaxing and video entertainment
only good could happen,
and there's talking, playing, eating, and even sleeping.
The wind is blowing and it's warm with a very cool breeze,
peace and harmony fill the air with happiness all around me.
I love my favorite place don't you see?

Briyauna McNeal, Grade 7
Pierce Middle School, IN

Get Him, Got Him

Dress in hidden camo, leave home, ready to hunt,
Grab gun, have fun
Bullet soars through the air
Killing deer
Draws a tear
It's all right you got him
Let's head home.

Cody Kennedy, Grade 8
Red Bud Elementary School, IL

Never Give Up

When the crowds get loud
And sing the anthems proud
When the lights go on
And the teams come out
You know it's time to shout

Now you're still young
You're having a lot of fun
But you wish you were out
Playing on the field
The star, the favored one

You decide to try out
You also need to work out
I know it will be tough
But don't ever give up
Because one day you'll be a champ

Be on your best game
People will repeat your name
"Hey, he's in the Hall of Fame!"

Bozhidar Kolev, Grade 9
Schaumburg High School, IL

What You Left Behind

You make me cry
when you lie
you're like E. coli
can make you die

I want a drain
to swallow my pain
but the pain
will remain

You were the cure to my disease
but it all had to cease

But you yet to attain
to give me pain

All I wanted was a hug
to keep me smug

A grin that would win
my heart that you broke apart

If you're in line
to be mine
that's fine

Just remember love is what you make it
take my heart and please don't break it

Gabriela Bravo, Grade 8
Zapata Academy, IL

When I Was a Kid

When I was a kid
I gave myself a trim
I saw some scissors downstairs
So I decided to cut my hair

When my mama saw my head
She started to cry and said
Why did you cut your hair
Now your head looks so bare

She cried and cried
I didn't know why
Because you see
I was only just three

So I really didn't care
That my head looked so bare
I didn't know better
But I will never ever
Cut my hair again
'Cause Mama said
it won't grow back until I'm ten

Jessica Brisbin, Grade 7
Bethel Lutheran School, IL

Soul Searcher

His eyes glistened as he gazed upon the lake,
As a swan awakes with fright in its eyes,
Her eyes like burning coals staring into your soul,
As you feel a hole go through your heart you have felt its toll,
For she has a great power to judge a person's soul,
You are an animal gasping for air at the moment,
For its talent is truthful and potent,
You can never escape its all-seeing eye,
If you try it'll end in your demise,
Its eyes talking to you at this moment,
Have seized your attention and scarred the moment,
Forever you shall remember,
What you have never dared to have forgotten,
The moment the swan was talking to your soul

Samanta Garcia, Grade 7
Highland Hills Middle School, IN

Goodbye Summer

Our stomachs filled with excitement
Our parents kissed us goodbye
We joined our friends and ran away

We ran to our cabins
With our bags in hand
Threw the bags on the bed
And ran off

With our swim suits on we leaped out the door
We cannon balled into the pool one by one
Loving every moment of it

Little did we know our summer was over
We jumped out of the pool, ran back to our cabins
Packed our bags and went home for the summer
Good-bye summer, good-bye

Emma Ortiz, Grade 7
Galileo Scholastic Academy, IL

Thanksgiving

T urkey is one of the most delicious things to eat
H aving your whole family around
A lso giving thanks for all the things you have
N obody gets tired of turkey
K ids eat their vegetables with no excuses
S o many plates on the table to eat
G etting stuffed with turkey all day
I nvite all your family and friends to celebrate
V ery good stuffing the moms do
I enjoy having my family around and eating all together
N o school on Thanksgiving
G et ready for Thanksgiving and all the turkey

Itzel Diaz-Gonzalez, Grade 7
Hannah Beardsley Middle School, IL

Dreadpool

Small abyss filled with my dread and terror.
The pool looked up as if it is frowning.
I sweat from heat and worried of error.
So much fear in me, afraid of drowning.

My first time jumping in the pool of deep.
Reluctant at first, but hungry to learn.
Was I mistaken? This pool is 8 feet!!
My stomach churned, my head turned, my eyes burned.

I came up slowly eager for fresh air.
Finally, I emerge, treading water.
Strokes become easier, I swim with care.
"I'm swimming, I'm swimming," I said happily.

I learned to swim that day, my fear was done.
The battle with the water, I had won.

Caleb Patterson, Grade 8
St Angela School, IL

Time for Tae Kwon Do

In the classes eight kids or twenty,
Kathryn makes it oh so funny.

Self-defense is what we learn,
The colored belts we do earn.

We kick and punch the red and black paddles,
With our sparring gear on we go to battle.

Our grandmaster tells us to go faster,
Especially when we're kicking the heavy Wave Masters.

I am on the Tae Kwon Do team,
This isn't gymnastics, we don't walk the beam.

We bring our enormous sparring bags,
But before we go in, we must bow to the flags.

Julia Frick, Grade 7
Marquette Academy, IL

Thanksgiving

T hanksgiving is a very special holiday
H aving turkey for dinner
A ll relatives should get together
N ot everybody can have a Thanksgiving dinner
K now what you are going to say at grace
S melling the food makes you want to have some
G iving is also good so everyone has something to eat
I nstigating with your brother is not nice
V iolins playing on the radio
I n the night is when you eat
N ow it's time to eat
G etting the food around the table is good so everyone can eat

Brandon Helsom, Grade 7
Hannah Beardsley Middle School, IL

Page 86

Ode to the Pencil

O' pencil, how I love the way you write!
   Your graceful strokes leave me in a daze.
The way there was nothing on the page
   but now there is something.
The beautiful way you curve the S
   or the way you round your O
O' pencil, I have never seen something quite like you,
   so perfect in every way!
You sit like a soldier,
   but write like a graceful swan.
O' pencil, is there anything you do not excel in,
   from letters
     to numbers
       to bright yellow smiley faces?
O' pencil, I envy you, sitting there erect and straight,
   without a care in the world,
     with one purpose: to *write*.

Manny Smith, Grade 7
Stanley Clark School, IN

The Life

I look to the head at rows forgotten,
where the white clouds swim in the morning sky,
and women bend to pick soft, tufted cotton.
Where people are to be sold and to buy.

Where the whip lays heavy on the black's back
and the children were not allowed to play.
When God's guiding hand was taken off track
and demon spirits were allowed to slay.

Where my mother's tears streaked down her meek face
when my father was picked from line to go
and then I was told he would fight for our race.
And that was the fight that soon all would know.

And I was thrilled when we won our freedom,
but I'd rather my dad, a home he'd come.

Sage Iverson, Grade 8
Woodland Middle School, IL

What I Can Do

I can see.
I can hear.
I can hear the cries of all the saddened people.
I can see the need for peace in the world.
I can learn of these tragedies.
I can learn why.
I can smile when I'm happy.
I can weep when I'm sad.
I can be inspired.
I can be accepting.
I can gain maturity.
As all this takes place, I can make a difference.

Jacob Vigran, Grade 7
International School of Indiana, IN

I Hope For...

I hope for a happy ending
Like the ones in fairy tales
I hope for all suffering and pain to cease
I hope that one day no one will worry about finding food
We will all be full and happy
I hope for everyone to have someone to love them
For we need love to survive
I hope that I never have to hear about illness again
I hope for no more war
Why can't we all get along?
I hope for no more racism
I hope for world peace
I hope for brighter futures
Why can't this become true?
I hope for everyone to get everything they ever wanted
It's not fair that certain people get everything
I hope for there to be no more evil
I hope for everyone to have a fairy godmother
I hope for no one to be sad
I know these are all crazy wishes
But wouldn't it be nice if they came true?

Rebecca Munoz, Grade 7
Stratford Middle School, IL

Infinity

Any mind's giant hand can
wrap itself around a stretch of land,
the vastness of space it can encase,
too bad it's assigned and confined to a skulls worth of space.

Einstein could reach the skyline,
but no matter whoever,
no matter how clever,
to put a halt to their great endeavor,
give them an answer that stretches on forever.

Infinity

Ryan Chimienti, Grade 8
Wredling Middle School, IL

I'm Fine

When people ask if you're okay,
They don't hear what you really want to say.
They can't read your mind, so let it all out,
As quiet as a whisper, as loud as a shout.
It's hard to tell the truth.
Whether you're old or still in youth.
It's hard to say how you really feel,
Because sometimes, it doesn't seem real.
No one cares what's really wrong.
They just want you to move along.
You want them to know you're not okay,
But somehow, it's all you can say:
"I'm fine."

Sarah Vendal, Grade 8
St Matthew School, IL

Going Gets Rough (Based on a True Story)
Beautiful girl, inside and out.
She won't hurt a fly. She won't shout or pout.
Straight "A-Plus" student, sweet as can be.
Her hopes and big dreams meet reality.
One day her life gets threatening news.
"You'll get very ill and your hair you will lose."
This comes as a shock. We pray that they're wrong.
We're all devastated. She faces it strong!
"What happens will happen, I'm only 15!
I'll do what I must, to get cool and keen."
No words can describe her and what she'll go through.
But, she'll remain happy, and hopeful and true.
Life will go on, cured or still ill.
But she will get better, I know that she will.
Remember this girl when times are quite tough,
And never give up when the going gets rough.

Adam Raso, Grade 7
Dunlap Valley Middle School, IL

Fire
Fire is *gleaming* and *shiny* with all sorts of colors
From yellow to blue
The *passionate* glow keeps the fire *flaming*
Its light brings hope
It can also *strike* fear
The terror it brings when it gets out of control
But if it is tamed
Fire is *beautiful* and *glamorous*
For every person the thought of fire is different
To some people the thought of fire brings *hardship* and *grief*
But to others it can bring *grace* and *beauty*
The sound of its *sizzle* is unique to every person
It could sound like *burning* forests
Or like the loud *crackle* of fireworks on the fourth of July
So is fire *graceful* or *evil*

Carsen Anderson, Grade 8
Thomas Middle School, IL

The Typewriter's Younger Sibling
Click click the keys go
as our fingers type away on the shiny white keyboard
words flying across the screen
showing us what we just thought in our heads
mouse moves magically
by the touch of your finger
the arrow slides gracefully to where we wanted it to go
It is like a typewriter, more high tech for it now
like a younger sibling, outshining the older one
the computer is like a talkative person,
you can type all you want and it will show up
it beats all the words out, as the keys sweep across the page
The computer and talkative people are much alike,
they both can type or talk,
endlessly

A.J. Scheidt, Grade 8
Thomas Middle School, IL

Friends
Amazing memories and funny moments.
Hilarious inside jokes that last for years.
There's pointless drama that makes you cry over nothing.
They're always there for you no matter what,
and you can trust them with everything.
They keep your secrets, even the big ones.
And they don't tell lies, big or small.
You watch scary movies and you
eat ice cream at sleepovers together.
You have puppet shows and laugh 'til you cry.
They match outfits with you every day.
You can talk to them and they'll give you advice from their hearts.
Friends are like sisters that support you through thick and thin.
They're always there to lean on.
They live, laugh, and love with you.
Friends are like family.

Kaitlyn Jorzak, Grade 8
Thomas Middle School, IL

Friendship Doesn't Always Last
The first day we met, in my mind,
I still see you sitting on the bus looking for some company.
I took myself that day neither of us knowing what to say.
We talked about our lives and quickly
Became the best friends no one else could be.
The closer we grew the more we knew this was a part of our lives.
Each and every day I would pray our friendship would be the same.
As time passed and I guess it didn't last.
Only memories were brought back and a little friendship remained.
I look to my right, look to my left to see there is no you.
Don't you think it hurts me to see you and her together as
Best friends thinking that should be me.
We are both moving on now.
I hope your friendship lasts long enough so you could be happy and
Be the best friends you guys could ever be, but our friendship
Still remains in our memory and good times.

Vivian Melchor, Grade 7
West Park Academy, IL

I Like You!
I tell you I like you.
But would you say you like me too?

If I asked you to hang out,
Would you say no way, I'm out?

I think about you all the time,
But do you think about me or not a dime?

I wish I could tell you that I like you,
But I'm afraid of what you would do!

Oh how I wish I could speak up before you find somebody.
I probably won't find anybody.

Katelin Adams, Grade 8
West Salem Grade School, IL

Song

When all the songs are over
And all the words have been said
The sun grows dim across the sky
And the world prepares for bed

I often can take a moment now
To view the sky above
And whisper God a simple prayer
To thank him for his love

Jensen Hood, Grade 8
Leo Jr/Sr High School, IN

Christmas

Spirits are high, snow's on the ground,
smells of food and pine fill the air.
Family and friends all around,
and Christmas songs and carols blare.

We stand by the Christmas tree,
all full of Christmas cheer.
Every face in the room is full of glee,
and sing praise to Jesus for all to hear.

Emma Sickafoose, Grade 8
Emmanuel-St Michael Lutheran School, IN

Nature

I can hear the rain
Hitting my window I can see
The lightning and hear the thunder
I ask Mother Nature
Why did it have to rain today
Out of all days my beautiful hair
Is now messed up my cute clothes
Are now wet

Tiara Crenshaw, Grade 8
Thomas A Edison Jr/Sr High School, IN

Football

Football is a sport for guys
Football is not for someone who cries
Football is not for weak and weary
Football is not a sport to get teary
Football is a miracle that was given
Football is necessary for livin'
Football is the best sport by far
Who do you think is the best football star?

Tyler Sorg, Grade 7
Highland Hills Middle School, IN

Awake and Sleep

Cock-a-doodle-do
Like a morning mist at dawn
Squint, sigh, sleeping time

Addison Horton, Grade 7
Bethel Lutheran School, IL

A Day in the Sun

A day in the sun,
How simple could it be?
You might think of the gleaming sun,
Or hanging out with friends.
Maybe you think of the beach,
With its rapid waves or rippling water rushing towards the sand.
Or maybe you imagine an empty field with flowers swaying in the breeze,
Or maybe you think of the trees in the distance,
With the leaves ever so slightly changing colors.
Then you notice the bees and the butterflies rapidly fluttering their wings,
And filling the air with a low hum.
Then when the sun starts slowly sinking into the ground,
And the moon appears in the sky,
You think about the day you had and how it could be compared to a dream,
And how you would give anything for it to come back.

Kaitlin Coughlin, Grade 8
Thomas Middle School, IL

FDNY

Rising above the rest, suddenly taking the ultimate test.
I may never see the ground again, as these towers crumble, we roll in.
80 pounds seems like nothing, full of fear, constantly running.
Narrow stairways fighting for air, the thought of this I cannot bear.
Could this have been prevented? The air is now metal scented.
Reaching my objective, I truly realized this event is nothing anyone should ever relive.
My mind says leave, but my heart says stay, as I reach another hopeless hallway.
I told them to fight through this, but the chances of survival were hit and miss.
People on the ground could never imagine; this terrible act never should have happened.
One tower goes down and I cringe in fear and shock.
Ash and dust storms down every block.
I rush to get to whoever I can, trying to save these innocent Americans.
Red, white, and blue will always be our true colors,
From the bunker, to the front-line drummer,
No one can steal our thunder.

Mike Rundle, Grade 8
Central Jr High School, IL

Escalation

It lurks deep inside you
It comes only in a moment of ferocious anger
You don't realize its devastation until the task is done
And if you see its devastation first hand
You'll know what it feels like to die and be resurrected by the aftermath

Rage fills the darkness that was once called your mind
It captures your soul and locks it away for only seconds
But then it is too late
The damage is done

You try to pretend that nothing happened
But it never works
Rage takes your anger to another state of being
Rage soon dies but its mark is everlasting

Aamir Muhammad, Grade 7
Galileo Scholastic Academy, IL

My First Love

Red is the color of your hair.
Oh, your emerald eyes are so rare.
Without you in my life, I would despair.
Daily, you rest on your favorite chair.
You and I are quite a pair.

Rowdy, my fat red cat, you will never know
how much I care.

Ally Wallace, Grade 8
Daleville High School, IN

Santa's Ride

In the silky, white snow
So many things are happening
Santa yells, "Ho! Ho! Ho!"
In the silky, white snow
Santa's reindeer seem to flow
The next house starts to hear a tapping
In the silky, white snow
So many things are happening

Franklin McDonald, Grade 8
Northlawn Jr High School, IL

Light in the Eternal Night

The sun, a ball of fiery power
lighting up the planets.
One of many glowing, majestic stars.
A beautiful solar mass of luminent energy.
So full of power…
And through the eternal darkness,
Its light emerges.
A light in the eternal night.

Kristin Pazera, Grade 8
David L. Rahn Jr High School, IL

Football

F abulous
O utside
O ffense
T ackling
B ig hit
A ll-American
L egendary
L ocker room

Kirkland Jenkin, Grade 7
Wethersfield Jr/Sr High School, IL

Little Dolphins

Dolphins are as blue as the bright blue sky,
Sometimes they might seem to fly,
They swim really fast,
A line is cast,
Eek, Eek,
Is how they speak.

Parish Thompson, Grade 7
Highland Hills Middle School, IN

Victory

The awaited news arrives,
The allied soldiers rejoice,
And their fellow countrymen shout joyfully.
Germany has given up and has laid down her tools of war.
Soon she is followed by her comrade in arms —
The Empire of the Rising Sun.

The axis tyrants have been crushed.
The lamp of peace has been lit.
As the allies rejoice and the enemy mourns,
More horrors of war are discovered —
Soldiers liberate prison and concentration camps
Ending the grizzly nightmare of the Jews and their fellow prisoners of war.

In the victor's homelands, parades and homecomings are abundant.
In Times Square, a celebration takes place.
Thousands of people crowd the streets.
A sailor and his girl celebrate,
And with the photographer watching,
He sweeps her off her feet and becomes a picture to remember.

David Hein, Grade 8
Emmanuel-St Michael Lutheran School, IN

Blackout

Claws reach from darkness
A shadow covers the day
Radiance never comes forth
Not even a blaze stands against its ways
So, the void sucks in all around it
Because not a one would try to stop it
Many sit and wait for the end
Some wish it would come
Few try to carry on with their life
But in the end, there is none
the blackness took it over
And there seems like there is nothing they could do
But no one ever tried, so no one ever knew
So, the years of darkness: "I would rather be burned by a thousand suns than live in
this world!" Thus, the darkness granted his childish wish.
A flame emitted from his body and he lit a fire for all to see
Luckily, he was somehow unharmed, and soon, all of the spirits lifted
Lights shone brightly, fires rose, and all light sources burned fiercely
The whole world awoke and the void of dark and sorrow vanished
They say that the boy rose into to the sky as a sign of hope and peace; the new sun

Paige Hoerner, Grade 7
St Matthew School, IL

Being a Poet

Written with no recognition,
Your face turns white as snow.
Your light gray eyes show more than the poetic disguise,
Time flies by as you stand there like a frozen mime, life can certainly turn on a dime.
The churn of your stomach and shiver of skin makes you see what could have been,
Being a poet is surely an unfair sin.

Johan Rummenigge, Grade 8
Thomas Middle School, IL

The Winter Night

As cool day turns to icy dusk
Powder white snow falls tonight
Forests turn into frigid husks
As cool day turns to icy dusk
Cars bloom with dark rust
Cold frost reflects silver moonlight
As cool day turns to icy dusk
Powder white snow falls tonight
Nathan Kitzman, Grade 8
Northlawn Jr High School, IL

Gobble, Gobble

Gobble, Gobble time to eat
Thanksgiving meal is ready
Turkey, ham, dressing, and beets
I will eat till my stomach is heavy
Gobble, gobble too full for treats
Not even one treat can I eat
I ate like a pig
Can't eat another fig
William Dorsch, Grade 7
Highland Hills Middle School, IN

My Love

My love
Is an everlasting sea
It is like a waterfall
That overpowers you and me
When I say
I love you today
Know I mean it
For eternity
Rachael Bickett, Grade 7
Highland Hills Middle School, IN

Plains

The Plains is like a giant ocean,
vast and rolling always in motion,
with joy in every hill,
it sways in the wind at will,
with waves of green and tidal waves of gold,
finally, an occasional palm tree of old,
on a lonely island,
The Plains is an ocean to me.
Jessica Smith, Grade 7
Pleasant Plains Middle School, IL

Paintball

The rush of adrenaline
The whoosh by my head
I duck frantically trying to find cover
The shooting stops
I pop my head out and fire
I see the paint on his body and cheer!
Blaine Fulton, Grade 7
Stanley Clark School, IN

How We Came to Be

As I left my old home and moved miles away
My mother got ready for her big day
I knew she was happy and he was too
But I couldn't help feeling blue
She said she loved him and did nothing wrong
But I just didn't know if he would belong
I got a new family I didn't know
This place was a fresh start but, I couldn't let go
When the big day came I tried to smile
But, my mother knew I couldn't comply
Why she would do something that made me unhappy
So in her face and many others, I sat still and calm and smiled blankly.

The tears of joy came streaming down her face
And people were smiling all over the place
When the pictures came, I broke down crying not tears of joy, but tears of sorrow
Tears came down a small 5-year-old's face, a sudden blow
That day caused me great pain and fear
For, I did not know what was near,
But, here we are seven years later
Their love so strong, and growing greater
I love my dad and we are happy, one full of love, cheerful, family.
Valery Badio, Grade 7
International School of Indiana, IN

My Indiana Beach

The drive up there, a century long
Seeing all the fields of lazy corn, as blank as a sheet of paper
Looking forward to going up there every blazing summer
Hearing the long-awaited words, "We're here!" from my mom
Sprinting out of the car like a wild boar, stepping on every bag while I was at it
Unpacking the stuffy, compact car, as packed as sardines
Saying hello to the lurking lake I loved, waving back at me
Introducing my best friend to my insane loving family
Looking forward to being able to finally go tubing this year!
Walking up the hill, a mountain high, to the amazing amusement park we all love
Anxious to see the changes that were made to it
Going on the rough, rigid, rides, as fun as can be
My family, monkeys, being their usual selves
Looking forward every calm cool night for the following day
Having the time of my life in the place that I love
Carly Senerchia, Grade 9
Liberty Jr High School, IL

I Am From

I am from 20 acres of old memories; memories of gardening, exploring, and climbing trees
I am from a world of patient learning, where everyone goes at their own pace
I am from the pounding of shoes and the leaping of feet that I know so well
I am from a crazy world of rushing around, one thing after the next after the next
I am from a family that cares and teases and laughs
I am from a mother that taught High School German and a father that can't say "Hola"
I am from a family with a last name that is misspelled on every single letter sent
But most of all, I am from a loving, learning, laughter-filled world,
And I am so lucky to be from where I am.
Margaret Schnabel, Grade 7
International School of Indiana, IN

Puppies

Puppies
Cute as can be
Little, wet tongues lick me
Giving me big, dog-breath kisses
Yucky!
MacKenzie Sharp, Grade 8
Northlawn Jr High School, IL

Prairie Fire

Rushing through the grass
Burning all in its hot path
Heat scorching the ground
Bringing light to the dark night
Leaving nothing but white ash.
Jakob Weiss, Grade 8
Northlawn Jr High School, IL

Fireworks Ignite

They light up the sky
Big and bright, shining at night.
Loud sounds fill the air;
A quiet crackling is heard
As they descend back to Earth.
Cooper Wilkinson, Grade 8
Northlawn Jr High School, IL

The Sun

The yellow sun across the sky,
A light yellow glint on my eye,
Yellow everywhere, it's all I can see,
The yellow sun staring at me,
The yellow, yellow on the sea.
Autumn Leigh Newberry, Grade 7
Wethersfield Jr/Sr High School, IL

Darkness

Darkness
Awareness of your surroundings
Alert to all sounds
Afraid what's going to pop out,
Darkness is a new moon.
Bradley Goff, Grade 7
Wethersfield Jr/Sr High School, IL

Love

Love is an eagle,
It tenderly grips your heart,
And never lets go
Erica Gamboe, Grade 7
Dunlap Valley Middle School, IL

The Never-ending Forest

A ll around me, all I can see, is tree after tree after tree
B ones of the lost wanderers before me lay in **C** rumpled heaps at my feet.
Do the wild **D** ogs not smell the stench of decay, or are they not hungry?
Be as it may that they do not find me on this **E** gregious day.
Do not ever **F** orget me; think of me often, even though I have been led
astray. I will never come out of this **G** argantuan forest, being
H aunted by the ghosts of the confused souls that meandered through the
Ever-changing pathways. **I** nside this magic-filled forest it looks as if the
J oking trees are uprooting themselves and are skulking around like
K naves changing the paths to trick the lost people that are
L eaving behind their previous lives to stay in this forest,
M aking believe that they will get out but in reality they **N** ever will.
O minous beasts lurk behind the brush, on the **P** rowl for another big meal
Q uietly they wait for their prey to fall in their jaws **R** unning away only
when they have been seen. **S** o I stealthily sneak through the forest
T rying not to make a sound, taking the **U** tmost precaution to stay
undetected. If only all the trees could **V** anish, and the danger disappear. I
W ish I could get out of here and live my life without fear. I want to
e **X** tirpate all the trees to set myself free, and **Y** ank out all the weeds that
snag on me, I wish I could **Z** onk all of the beasts that look to me for a feast.
But that is just a wish, in reality I am stuck here full of fear.
Claire Miller, Grade 8
DeMotte Christian School, IN

A Different Place, with Different People

When I moved everything changed
People, places, it was just different
Like apple-and-orange different
I was somewhere new
Somewhere so strangely scary
And I didn't know anything
I was like a fish in a new pond
I missed Chicago and I could feel it missing me
I was afraid as much as I actually wanted to leave
There was just something pulling me back
That night laying in my bed which was a brick hitting my back so hard
Not able to sleep
Just trying to take it all in as if I were a vacuum
Listening to the perfect harmony of the crickets chirping
The white noise, an angry siren buzzing in my ear
Wondering if this was truly my fate
Wondering if my life was a dream and I couldn't wake up
Thinking if it would be different
And it was, and still is
And I see that now
I finally see that change is good
April Lewandowski, Grade 8
Liberty Jr High School, IL

Luminescence

There were beautiful down feathers floating everywhere in the bright light.
The light, ultraviolet it seemed, pierced my eyes; but I couldn't look away from the sight.
He was watching me, smiling as he had before; this couldn't be.
Had I gone to Heaven, or had Heaven come to me?
Taylor Gasper, Grade 7
Rossville Alvin Elementary School, IL

Good Fruit
Apple
Very juicy
Grown in an apple tree
Very delicious and healthy
Soft pear
Chad Hill, Grade 8
DeMotte Christian School, IN

Bible
B rings the word to me
I n my heart
B inds me together
L eads me to the right path
E xactly true
Paige Carpenter, Grade 8
DeMotte Christian School, IN

Mother
Mother
Loving, caring
Helping, teaching, cooking
She deserves my love and respect
Parent
Angela Pugh, Grade 7
St Angela School, IL

Friends
Friends
Caring, Joyful
Helping, sharing, laughing
Friendship is always exciting
People
Artasia Gusman, Grade 7
St Angela School, IL

Happiness
Happiness
Energetic and ready for the day
Joyful for what's soon to come
Smiling for one another
Happiness is the sun in the sky
Riley Tuthill, Grade 7
Wethersfield Jr/Sr High School, IL

Fighting for Freedom
Soldiers
Committed, tough,
Fighting for their country
Staying strong through good and bad times
Freedom
Alexis Black, Grade 8
Northlawn Jr High School, IL

The Track Meet
Today the track meet gave me quite a scare, I think it did to everyone there
There was that one kid that was ten feet tall, one leap in the high jump and he beat them all
And the one kid with his legs so long, walked the track, and still won
Plus the kid with muscles like mountains, threw six discusses at once, I was countin'
When I ran my 100-meter sprint, the guy knocked me down, maybe that was my hint
So I left my track meet defeated and mad, ready to pout and be so sad
I even asked "What's wrong with me doctors"
They replied, "That's what you get for playing with monsters"
"They weren't monsters they were real"
They said, "Don't even try to appeal"
"I know what I saw I know it was true, please let me go and prove it to you"
And that's when I saw:
Nobody was ten feet tall, and nobody won with legs so long
And I knew something had to be wrong
But I just couldn't understand, I couldn't explain
And I didn't know who was to blame, maybe I'll never know the answer
Could it be they used some kind of enhancer?
Could it be a trick of the eyes?
I need more rest, that's what the doctors advise
Then I thought to myself, could it even be true?
I don't know what to believe, do you?

Kate McLaughlin, Grade 7
International School of Indiana, IN

If We Kept a Childish Open Mind
If we kept a childish open mind
We'd still walk on bricks and feel like birds flying in the sky
We'd think we were kings and queens
We'd fight dragons and be warriors
We'd dance with prince charming at the ball

If we kept our childish open minds
The bench would turn into an amazing horse
The pencil would become a magic wand and we'd all have magic powers
The rug would become Aladdin's magic carpet

If we all kept a childish open mind
Everyone would be a friend
It wouldn't matter what you looked like
Or what you wore
It wouldn't matter how much stuff you had
Or if you were slower than others
We'd all be beautiful
Everyone would be a friend
But that's only if we all kept a childish open mind!
Mykala Ulery, Grade 7
Collinsville Middle School, IL

Softball
The amazing sound of the bat hitting the ball
makes you feel like you own the world.
All of the sudden you feel yourself running through the wind, then,
WOOP!
Take out the catcher guarding the plate, slide through their legs, to save the game!
Mackenzie Sharp, Grade 8
Red Bud Elementary School, IL

Flowers

We are like flowers.
Every flower is unique,
And their life
Is the blink of an eye.
One minute they're blooming,
The next they are beginning to wilt.
Every flower has different colors
Like personalities
Bright red
Royal blue
Some are firm under pressure
While some aren't
Flowers have a distinct beauty,
That shines throughout the land.
Flowers are something someone sees,
And instantly feels hope.
Flowers are an example,
Nature's true beauty.

Logan Skildum, Grade 7
Stratford Middle School, IL

A Plane Headed Toward Me

I woke up this morning
Feeling as good as can be.
I took a shower,
And put on my suit.
I went downstairs,
And ate breakfast with my family,
As I walked out the door,
I kissed my family goodbye.
Who would've known,
This would be the last time we spoke.
I went to work,
Sat at my desk,
And a little after nine,
I saw it.
A plane headed toward me,
And in the blink of an eye,
My wife became a widow
And my daughter didn't have a father.

Mariah Elmore, Grade 8
Central Jr High School, IL

Droplet

The rain droplet
Falling down
Watch it, watch it
Hitting the ground.
It's slowly, slowly
Dripping down.
There is thunder
All around as
The rain droplet is
Falling down.

Alex Wierzchucki, Grade 8
Red Bud Elementary School, IL

Love

Love is like a flower.
It can make you feel
joy,
hurt,
confusion,
and anger.
Sometimes love slowly blooms
like the delicate
and colorful petals.
But, eventually
the flower withers away
and falls to the
soft green grass.
The petals shrivel
and become weak.
The relationship comes to an end.
But overall,
love is beautiful.

Carlie Adams, Grade 8
Thomas Middle School, IL

The Deep Sea

Long hair
waving
fluttering in the wind

A girl
falling towards the sea below.
She thought there was no one to save her
so she decided to let herself drown

She hit the deep blue water
Sinking

Sinking at will
she began to let go
but someone took her hand
and he pulled her out of the vast ocean

into the sunlit world.

Samantha Honaker, Grade 8
Our Shepherd Lutheran School, IN

Everything

Friends are like the *air* we breathe.
You *can't live* without them.
They *help* you *survive*.
Friends are like the *ground* we stand on.
You can't *stand up* without them.
They *support* you.
Friends are like *music* to our ears.
You *love* to listen to them.
They make you feel *happy*.
Friends are *everything*.

Caleigh O'Neil, Grade 8
Thomas Middle School, IL

Imaginary Friend

I am a whisper in the wind
I am a jitter in your skin
Feeling safe in my puffy cloud
Waiting for a large laugh out loud

Once I hear that laugh of joy
I can be his playful toy
He's safe in his puffy cloud
He's shocked of what he just found

Knowing that he will be okay
I know that he is here to stay
Making sure he is safe and sound
Playing in our puffyed up cloud

Sometimes I feel so alone
Thinking that he will be shown
He and I are safe and sound
Together in our puffed cloud

Alicia Boers, Grade 8
Immaculate Conception School, IL

Dare to Dream

Dare to dream
I say to you
It's the best
Thing you can do

Once you have
Your dream so dear
Try your best
To make it appear

Live your dream
Make it come true
You'll remember it
Your whole life through

Everybody
Has a dream
So make it shine
Make it gleam

Amber Litteken, Grade 7
All Saints Academy, IL

Sally…

Sally was very smart.
She was also great at art.
She always made her paintings pop.
She even had her own painting shop.
Her paintings were always bright.
They always had a lot of light.
Her paintings were always bold.
She always had her paintings sold.

Brittany Rieke, Grade 8
Red Bud Elementary School, IL

Penguins

P redators chase them
E legant creatures
N ot very big
G oes to escape
U nderwater
I n and out they swim
N ot going to be eaten
Lauren Schmidt, Grade 7
Wethersfield Jr/Sr High School, IL

Smile/Frown

Smile
Grinning, Laughing
Happy, Joyful, Yellow
Positivity, Elation, Despair, Negativity
Gloomy, Miserable, Blue
Pouting, Crying
Frown
Hunter Elias, Grade 8
Northlawn Jr High School, IL

Trees

trees
winter comes
they are cold and bare
like a shaved puppy
summer comes they are a big poofy dress,
big and full
trees dancing in the day's wind.
Mandy Ellis, Grade 7
Highland Hills Middle School, IN

My Dog, Reggie

When he eats he sounds like a pig!
Plus, he is very big.
Reggie is very funny!
And he is soft just like a bunny.
He barks very loud,
"Woof! Woof!"
And I love him very much!
Meredith Collings, Grade 7
Highland Hills Middle School, IN

What You Need in Life

F un people to hang with
R idiculous jokes
I nto the same stuff you are
E xtraordinary adventures
N ever fight for real
D ying in laughter
S tay with you forever
Colin Quigg, Grade 8
DeMotte Christian School, IN

Never Content

She struggles, she feels trapped, weighted
Vying to break free, she feels foreign to the earth.
This thing, this gravity, it holds her down
Earthbound

The sky, how it taunts her, bright, blue, clear.
How she jumps, how she reaches, she can't touch it,
That brilliant, azure pool.

At last with a cry she breaks free, rising up.
The wings she had so long pictured attach
She spins around, alights on a cloud,
But the sky too soon darkens around her.
She flies higher, laughing at the brewing tempest.

The wind picks up, lightning strikes,
Her wings, so carefully crafted, burn to ashes.
Whipping through the air she falls,
But until she collapses upon the ground, bliss of flight.

The shock is great, the pain, mind numbing.
Then…black. Alone. Broken.

She will never fly again. Confined to our cold reality that fits her not.
Jumping, reaching, crying, earthbound
Caroline Gillette, Grade 7
St Matthew School, IL

The Unforgettable Heartbreak

The day was beautiful, sunny and warm.
I'd never had guessed that on this day, my heart would be torn.
As I sat on my balcony, enjoying the breeze,
I heard a loud crash and rushed to the edge to see.

As I stood at the balcony's edge, all I saw was smoke and flame.
I looked for the source, and that's when I saw it,
Sticking out of the north tower,
Was the wing of a plane.

People were gathering in bunches along the sidewalks and streets.
Some were running. Some were hiding. All were dodging debris.
The air was still filled with smoke, and the sounds of sirens blaring,
BOOM! Another loud crash and it was then that my heart started tearing.
For my son, my boy, was at work in the south tower that day.

"Ring! Ring!" I rushed to my phone.
"Mom, I love you, and I promise that through this you won't be alone."
As he said his goodbyes, I started to cry,
Then the connection went dead, as did he.
My son, my boy, my bundle of joy, was gone in the blink of an eye.
Not once did I turn on the news that day, I was in denial I guess you could say.
And now, 10 years have gone by since that life-changing day.
And this mother's heart, and life, will never be the same.
Cheyenne Henson, Grade 8
Central Jr High School, IL

Ode to Autumn's Short-lived Colors

Autumn rains fiery colors, painting the dull ground,
Until the sky grows bare, and has no more colors to render.
I gather the fire in my hands and put it in a big mound.
The chance of autumn surviving is sadly very slender,
But before the fire dies down and before the white blanket can come,
I must savor the season and hope it still lingers,
As I dive deep into the heart of fall.
I soon emerge to find out that my nose is very numb.
With slightly frostbitten fingers,
I watch the season give in to winter's frozen call.

Amelia Lafferty, Grade 8
Rochester Jr High School, IL

My Special Place

The large pumpkin-like sun sets down behind the sea,
Until darkness has overcome me.
The sand starts to cool down from the summer sun,
Hitting it with its warm rays of fun.
People start to sit around the campfire,
Until the guy with the guitar begins to sing what he desires.
The children start to play tag,
But their mothers want to leave and begin to nag.
But when I step back and take a look at this place,
I realize that I love it and a smile spreads across my face.

Quila Dixon, Grade 8
Bethel Lutheran School, IL

Autumn, the Best Time of the Year

Leaves piled on a mound,
Branches moving in the wind.
Squirrels scavenging for acorns on the ground,
As the apple cider season begins —
People are restless with autumn beauties,
Ready for cool weather and bonfires.
Harvest time with big, green monsters zooming through the fields,
Choosing the perfect pumpkin…what a cutie!
My friends and I swinging on tires,
I hope autumn never yields!

Zelinda Taylor, Grade 8
Rochester Jr High School, IL

Autumn Treats

There are so many sweets to eat in the fall.
Orchards are filled with apples waiting to be made into cider.
Pumpkin bread, freshly made from pumpkins in a patch.
Ears of corn look like they're dancing as they're heated and popped.
Using caramel, the popcorn in tuck together for a popcorn ball.
Candy stuffs houses once Halloween comes around.
Sugary cupcakes and cookies made with black and orange icing.
Cranberry ice cream as pink as a rose sold in every store.
A whipped cream topped pumpkin pie that glides down your throat.
These are some of the delicacies I could not live without in the fall.

Julia Mayfield, Grade 7
Rochester Jr High School, IL

Autumn

The sun drifts away,
Disfigured by monochrome clouds of ash and azure.
Burning, musty incense weaves through the air,
Painting with crisp breath, smoke and fog.
The ghosts of vibrant green leaves,
Waltz in their costumes of copper and gold.
Shuttering, rustling, and crumpling,
Like wisps and snips of ancient chants.
I wonder how much,
Autumn knows.

Lily DaFrees, Grade 8
Corpus Christi Elementary School, IN

What Is 9/11?

What is 9/11?
A day that will never be forgotten
A day where thousands of people lost their lives
An anniversary
A day when heroes were made
When the world changed
When people changed
When the world stopped turning.

That's 9/11.

Hannah Miskell, Grade 7
Marquette Academy, IL

Love Me

You loved me today.
But not today, you've stayed away.
But I still love you.
I think about you.
Do you still love me.
Tell me I love you.
You left me to die I died inside you've gone away.
You left me goodbye.
I love you and I will always love.

Sabrina Reynolds, Grade 7
Highland Hills Middle School, IN

Christmas Eve

Cheers of Christmas celebration
While eating Christmas Eve dinner
And when we are done
We will hear the cries of excitement and joy
As the Christmas gifts are opened
We beg to play but it's time to go
Oh, how it has been a good day
We wish we could stay
And we leave with our presents stacked high
As if we just got back from a shopping spree

Kyle Zeinemann, Grade 7
Highland Hills Middle School, IN

My Feelings for My Country
P roudly showing what I believe
A nd thanking some for my liberty
T hinking about Independence Day
R emembering those who fought for me
I magining how things would be different
O nly if there was not that victory
T here is our flag, waving so high
I t is raised for our people to see
S urely God has blessed us here
M aking us a nation that is free.
Kayla Groen, Grade 8
DeMotte Christian School, IN

Dreams
What are dreams?
Hopes for the future
Belief in yourself
Goals to accomplish
Things worth striving for
Fantasies that can come true
Heart-felt wishes
Desired destinies
Confidence in tomorrow
Those are dreams!
Megan Groen, Grade 8
DeMotte Christian School, IN

The Game: Play by Play
Starting with the first serve,
floating towards you like a round butterfly.
Squaring up to pass, a small rainbow,
to the waiting setter.
She is active like a flying squirrel,
placing the ball at the hitter's face.
The hitter approaches the balls,
and hits it until it falls.
As the ball hits the floor it bounces,
winning the point and ending the match.
Kendall Hoback, Grade 7
Highland Hills Middle School, IN

The Bonfire
The warmth of your smoldering fire.
The smell of the sweet marshmallows,
And the savory hot dogs.
The sound of your sparks crackling,
Gives me chills.
You are my lifesaver during the cold.
I love your warmth each fall.
As your flames rise,
I can't imagine a harvest time without you.
Don't forget to return each October.
Kara Burke, Grade 8
Rochester Jr High School, IL

Siblings
My sister likes to chat
In the tub she always sings
Sometimes she a brat
She gets into my things
I love her so very much

My brother is a piano
He plays himself every day
He is like a loose spring
Reacting to whatever I say
I love him so very much

They are caring and sweet
And two people you ought to meet
Though my siblings bring strife
They are treasures in my life
I love them so very much
Kaitlyn Muench, Grade 7
Highland Hills Middle School, IN

Wind
Whispering whistling wind
All night you sing songs of
Loss
Heartbreak
Death
Darkness
Forever cold, forever dark

Sing a sad song on everything you touch
Never a worry, never a care
Just keep singing your songs of
Regret
Sorrow
Tragedy
Lonesomeness
Forever careless, forever shrill
Whispering whistling wind.
Addison Cole, Grade 7
Dunlap Valley Middle School, IL

America's Game
You are Sunday,
You are a fan magnet,
You are a stress causer,
You are a happiness bringer,
You are a party starter,
You are a nail biter,
You are a close game,
You are a day off,
You are family,
You are football,
You are America's game,
You are the Super Bowl.
Josh Segatto, Grade 8
Rochester Jr High School, IL

Luke…
I changed the advent calendar,
To what I like,
Not your way,

I know you will be FURIOUS with me,
And like always,
Scream at me and try to hurt me,

So please just forget about it,
Just saying,
It looks better my way,
But I won't ever do it again…maybe!
Whitney Harry, Grade 7
Rochester Jr High School, IL

The Sea Around the World
From one side to another.
Ever connecting each other.
Filled with more than one memory,
It makes others feel so carefree.
Cold water at night.
Warm water at bright.
One message to a mind
Creates a feel of kind.
At the horizon, equal as the sky.
Different shades at day as time goes by.
Gentle touches in the clear,
You close your eyes, there's no fear.
Kamille Vitor, Grade 8
Chiddix Jr High School, IL

Firework
The sparks in the dark blue sky.
Flashing before your eyes.
So beautiful so colorful.
All the colors flashing up there.
How did they get up there?
You jump when you hear the loud sound.
Sitting outside and you're watching them.
Red, blue, green, and more colors up there.
Watching them from the beginning to end.
The little ones and the big ones.
All of them so beautiful so wonderful.
All the angels get the best spot of all.
Taylor Tuttle, Grade 7
Rossville Alvin Grade School, IL

Ron Weasley
Harry's best friend,
Fought with him until the very end,
Ron, brave little Ginger,
Willing, for Harry, to get injured,
But what can I say?
He gets more brilliant day after day.
Isabella Rossi, Grade 8
St Matthew School, IL

Stormy Night

As I lay me down to sleep,
Every noise turns to a creep.
As the rain pitter-patters,
The thunder makes a big shatter.
Lightning flickers off and on,
Like a light switch that's gone wrong.
Tornado sirens whistle loudly,
Everything turns dark and cloudy.
As the winds howl,
The dog stands up and growls.
As the hail falls tonight,
I am hoping everything will be all right.

Rheanna Kennybrook, Grade 7
Highland Hills Middle School, IN

Backyard Bonfire

The moon shining full in the sky,
Below the lacy clouds
Under the flaming trees.
Embers burst pop pop pop,
Pounding a steady beat.
Flames dance and leap,
Smooth as Indian dancers.
Logs burn and fall,
Thundering like drums.
Smoke drifts above,
Wispy as a ghost.
Backyard bonfire!

Megan Murphy, Grade 8
Rochester Jr High School, IL

Thanksgiving

T urkey is what we eat on the day
H umor is all around the family
A rkansas is where we go
N ever stop loving your family
K ickoff! It's time for the Bear's game
S it at the table until everyone is done
G ames to play outside
I n my cabin with my family
V ery happy time with my family
I love cranberry sauce, it is so good
N ice! Right before Christmas
G iving thanks for everything we have

Noah Swatscheno, Grade 7
Hannah Beardsley Middle School, IL

4th of July

The Fourth of July is fun.
It's like stars are bursting in the sun.
We have a lot of fireworks, a TON!
Our fireworks are dragons.
My family tells me "Be careful hun."
I love the Fourth of July.

Morgan Mobley, Grade 7
Highland Hills Middle School, IN

Against That Wall

Feelings are like splatter paint —
Every color a different emotion, wild and free and unexpected.
Each stroke releases passion,
Anger, love, but most of all,
The ability to not be contained in
Something. The one time where there
Are no rules. Whether you're smearing
And splattering paint, or blood, or heat, or ice,
Or wind, or sorrow — you're free. You can breathe —
Not what we usually call breathing — not to
Survive. More to let go of all things bad, and clean
Out your soul, mind, heart. You can breathe
Without a breath, smell without an aroma, and most of all see
Without sight. You can paint without an image in your head,
But more with a message in your heart. A message that's a closed bottle;
Put away for someone else to rediscover.
To interpret. To make new. For you
To look upon in later days, and reminisce
In wonder. For you will never quite remember
Exactly how you felt as you threw that paint
Against that wall.

Samantha Sury, Grade 8
Yorkville Middle School, IL

The Forest

It was a late night
The smell of rotting leaves filled the forest
As I walked
I felt the trees watching me
The light from the moon was dim
Only a silver crescent shown high in the unforgiving black sky
The wind seemed to whisper to me as it whipped my hair around my face
It was a cold, treacherous night
My hands trembled as they passed over the stumps that were once beautiful trees
I pressed on, knowing I had to escape this nightmare
As I approached an open plain, I realized that I was not alone
Right there, in front of me, were black, hooded figures
They stood in silence, as did I
I was mesmerized
I awoke to my bedroom, crying, glad it was all just a dream

April Powell, Grade 7
Highland Hills Middle School, IN

A Day Away

It is a Saturday. I can take my time, spend my time my way.
I arrive at the beach, and I feel the warm, gritty sand massaging my feet.
I look out to the ocean; I can see the horizon where it seems to last on forever and ever.
I inhale; I smell the salt in the water, and the food of the people nearby.
I eliminate the people around me as I find a seat near the water.
Whoosh! Is all I can hear as the water slams into the nearby rocks
I walk closer to the waves as the coolness of the water tickles my feet;
I walk right in, because I know there is never an end when there is nothing but peace within.

Lauren Stanley, Grade 7
Pierce Middle School, IN

The Tornado
It was like a dark dark top.
Swiveling from house to home,
rumbling and tumbling
over and over
up the hills
through the lakes

NOT STOPPING!

Towering over tall mountains.
Slithering through long valleys.

SHOWING NO MERCY!
Lydia Bird, Grade 8
Our Shepherd Lutheran School, IN

Falling
I feel as if I'm falling
falling through the dark
but I'm not hitting the ground
there is no end, there is no bottom
an endless fall
wishing it would just stop
my minds a rush, it's all a mess
tearing at the walls
trying to slow down
this speeding roller coaster
this earth-shattering fall
that stops my heart in my chest
and rips away my last breath
Charity Bishop, Grade 9
Mount Zion High School, IL

Life
life takes care
life takes time
life is time
not knowing when time's up
or what jobs you're going to work
life is a...
m
y
s
t
e
r
y
Aaron Raymond, Grade 7
Our Shepherd Lutheran School, IN

Winter Trees
Deserted of life
Yet beautiful as diamonds
Twinkle in the light
Neeti Warhekar, Grade 7
Dunlap Valley Middle School, IL

Football
Audacious attempts to keep the Ball from falling onto the Cold ground
Daring to Escape to the end zone
Faster and faster they run on top of the Grass
Hitting others In order to pass through the thick wall of players
Just soon enough he has to Kick the ball because he was Lifted and tackled.
They kick the ball to Minimize the other team's chances
Of getting Near their goal
Opposing Players run swiftly and Quietly
Retrying to Score a Touchdown.
The Underdogs Vie with their Winning rivals
eXerting more energy and Yearning to win.
They are extremely Zealous for this sport.
Nick Arnold, Grade 8
DeMotte Christian School, IN

Ode to Summer
To summer
To air conditioning that keeps us cool during summer
To ice cream that is so creamy and delicious
To parks which you could run in all day
To a sandy day at the beach
To sunburn which you try to avoid all summer long
To juicy and delicious mango's that grow all summer
To water parks that allow you to have fun and scream
To the fun exciting rides that cause you horror and terror at Six Flags
To my wonderful pool that kept me fresh all summer
To camping which allows you to explore nature
To summer, ahh why does it have to end
Cristina Hernandez, Grade 8
Peck Elementary School, IL

Be You and Be True
Be you and be true...
Don't let others tell you wrong
Be as pure as water and as bright as the sun
You can be like a butterfly...beautiful and free
No one will bring you down as long as you believe
You'll be to fast to catch...whoooossshhh...you will blow them all away
As I say once more, then I'll be through be you and be true...
And your true colors will shine through
Sophia Palmer, Grade 7
Highland Hills Middle School, IN

a midnight trip
the end of the day a peaceful sound of burning fire
pop! the fire reached the sap
it is midnight the stars gleam on the water.
a shooting star speeds through the night sky it was as if someone had thrown it
a cool chill passes by my head and back it makes me shiver
time to get some fire wood I said in the back of my mind.
the fire cracks in delight of fresh cut wood.
Reagan Richey, Grade 7
Highland Hills Middle School, IN

It's Christmas!

It's Christmas, it's Christmas!
What else can I say?
I've been waiting all year for this particular day.

It's Christmas, it's Christmas!
What do I see?
I see so many wrapped presents under the Christmas tree.

It's Christmas, it's Christmas!
What do I do?
I open the presents wrapped in blue.

It's Christmas, it's Christmas!
What have I revealed?
An orange fat cat name Garfield.

It's Christmas, it's Christmas!
Have I heard the doorbell ring?
I open the door and see my cousins smiling.

It's Christmas, it's Christmas!
What do we do?
We go eat our delicious chicken and stew.

It's Christmas, it's Christmas!
Have I had fun?
I've had fun with everyone!

Nanette Chapa, Grade 7
Dunlap Valley Middle School, IL

Wind of the Seasons

The wind
Lightly, it brushes my skin.
Whispering, it cools the sweat of my brow.
Mischievously, it turns the pages of my book,
happy for me as I read on this perfect summer day.

The wind
Sadly, it cries in my ears.
Mournfully, it blows halfheartedly against my back.
Grieving, it sobs over summer's loss and autumn's beginning,
pushing me along as I trudge onward to school.

The wind
Angry, it tears at my clothes.
Furious, it claws at my face and hair.
Raging, it screams as my feet slap the ground,
determined to blow me away as I sprint through this winter storm.

The wind
Laughing, it sings in my ears.
Joyously, it blows back my hair.
Deliriously, it rushes through the budding branches,
rejoicing with me in the freedom of spring's return.

Shelby Senger, Grade 8
Emmanuel-St Michael Lutheran School, IN

The Birds of Winter

Fall has finally gone by,
Winter is on its way.
all the winter birds have finally come to stay.
Once again the feeder
welcomes feathered friends to come
eat and play!
Oh listen to them chirp every day!
You can see many colors of them all,
the blue, the black,
and let's not forget,
even the gray!
oh how I love the
birds that eat for all,
just look at them,
having a ball!
Like these days that have come and gone,
oh the beautiful birds of winter!

Ryan Noles, Grade 7
Highland Hills Middle School, IN

Fall

As the leaves start to fall
I hear the season's call

Crosswinds blowing leaves to and fro
The burnish colors I see seem to glow

The playful feeling of jumping in a pile
It always seems to make me smile

Pumpkins all different shades and hues
Lights flickering inside as if on cue

All sorts of smells and sweets
Doorbells ringing, kids saying "trick-or-treat"

It is getting cool, and seasons start to shift
The snow will come down and the leaves will slowly lift

Mackenna Vander Tuin, Grade 8
DeMotte Christian School, IN

Fall

The greatest season of all,
Surely must be fall.
Seeing all the colors of the leaves,
Spread out through all the various trees.
It may be really cold,
Even though the sun shines bold.
Many don't like this time of year,
Only because the bitter cold nibbles at their ear.
This is the time of year when daylight is short,
And it's too cold to play any sport.
This season is very great,
So come one, everybody, let's celebrate.

Alexander James Faherty, Grade 7
Emmanuel-St Michael Lutheran School, IN

The Ghost

There stood the ghost
The ghost of
    Present
      Past
        Future
The ghost, like an annoying mosquito
Buzz, buzz, buzzing in your ear
Reminding you of past
And frightening you of the future
Watchful like a mother
Pursuing you like a stalker
The ghost saunters toward you
You come face to face
Looking your life straight in the eyes
The ghost stands there
Waiting for you to make the first move
What do you do when your life is right before you
Do you regret, or do you brag? Do you walk away?
Or take a deep look at who you are?
Take a deep look at the ghost
Of past, present, future

Michelle Pindrik, Grade 8
Thomas Middle School, IL

Where Would I Be

Where would I be without them?
As comedians do, they always make me laugh.
Like a raging storm
They are completely insane,
Yet keep me from going crazy.
Most people wouldn't consider
A six hour bus ride fun.
Yet when I'm with my friends
I find myself wishing it were longer.
Two coach busses filled with tons of kids,
And nearly infinite sounds
Of laughter, happiness, and enjoyment.
A huge explosion
Everyone laughs at once.
Where would I be without it?
Music is something I need.
I am so different from others in what I find fun.
Like spending all day sitting
Learning music with people I don't know.
I find it fun while others find it boring.
But all the same, music will always be my game.

Mark Macha, Grade 8
Liberty Jr High School, IL

A New Year

Smoke and rainbows flash in the air
In Red Bud, New Years is here.
Bright spirits and crackling fireworks touching my soul,
Illuminating freedom as festive bells toll.

Nathan Salovich, Grade 8
Red Bud Elementary School, IL

Perky Pekingese

Begging, begging, finally a yes!
New Year's Eve, off we go to get a puppy,
A perky Pekingese of course!
From a breeder, not the best,
But we are taking her to a better place, a palace,
Driving up, sad snow smoothing under the tires,
I jump out of the car,
Running to the door, like a marathon runner,
Ringing the doorbell, the key to the treasure inside,
Upon the door opening, I heard…quiet?
A library, we walked into a dark, quiet room,
With a small cage along one wall,
Like a small dark cave, 6-8 puppies piled inside,
Click, as the light goes on and they all wake up,
The little bears obviously excited,
Jumping all over like rabbits,
She opened the cage door, after a delay,
A flood of little, bright-colored foxes,
I look around then down,
They all look beautiful,
But she had chosen me!

Bre Van Eck, Grade 8
Liberty Jr High School, IL

Mirror Twins

Two girls of a kin,
The Mirror Twins.
One in red, green, and black leather,
the other in bright white and gold.
They're opposites but are exactly what they look like.
The bruised kid who gets in fights, right.
He takes the blow for other kids.
The sweet little girl dressed up in pink,
she smiles to adults faces but hurts others behind their back.
The kids wearing black and ink,
help unknowing kids on the street.
The golden boy on the football team,
is really the bully in the schemes.
If you ask the mirror twins to,
part their hair and show their wings.
The sister in red, green, and black would have wings of white,
and above her head a ring of light.
The sister in white has thorn-covered wings of red,
and dark horns on her head.
The angel looked bad and the demon seemed innocent.
The lesson look beneath the skin and see the true person.

Jacquelene Lehrman, Grade 7
St Charles Borromeo School, IN

Life

Doesn't know what's going to happen next
Afraid you'll go to sleep forever
Knowing every day's a bonus
Life is as good as a cold drink in the summer.

Alex Bryan, Grade 7
Wethersfield Jr/Sr High School, IL

Day Is Night

The sun started to rise
Minute by minute
The stars started to shine
Second by second
The moon started to glitter
In all that is silver and gold

In time and in space
Where all is new and old
Memories and feelings hold
Together the pieces of life
The center of the universe
Where everything's untold

Kamille Vitor, Grade 8
Chiddix Jr High School, IL

Spring Showers

On sun shining days,
my tree is still growing,
soaking in warmth
and snoring with glory.

Though, when raining and storming,
branches fall straight down,
leaving leaves littering
my tree is now frowned.
The next morning, however,
she will be sleeping.
Smiling and happy,
a beauty re-blooming.

Mileena Cannella, Grade 7
Galileo Scholastic Academy, IL

A Hero

People say I'm a hero.
Saving many lives,
For those who could have died.
Putting out the fire,
That blazes higher.
Carrying innocent people,
Out to the street,
To where their family's they seek.
Going back in,
Till the very end.
The towers may fall,
But we still stand up tall.
I am a hero.

Zack Hogan, Grade 8
Central Jr High School, IL

November

The leaves are changing
The hours are shortening
Thanksgiving is here

Randy Janson, Grade 7
St Matthew School, IL

Popcorn

Pop! Pop! Pop!
Can't you hear that yummy, buttery, slippery popcorn popping away?
Good for watching movies and tastes like heaven.
Great to eat and you'll eat more than seven.
Because once you start you just can't stop,
Those slippery kernels will make you drop.
Opening the bag to see what's inside,
You won't even think to share or divide.
Popcorn's great for listening to drama,
Or even riding on top of a llama.
So before I go, I have to say,
Popcorn's good for every day!

Ashleigh Trujillo, Grade 8
Red Bud Elementary School, IL

Gone Forever

What if we had to leave earth?
The ground will crunch with a step.
Small cries.
But high hopes.
As we enter a world unknown.
Many thoughts fluttering like butterflies.
But no echoing answer.
Tiny kids board.
The silent wind, disappeared from the world.
The rushing river, almost deserted of the plowing water that once was.
Gone.
What if everything was gone?

Sarah Gardner, Grade 8
Thomas Middle School, IL

I Never Thought…

I never thought this would happen…
Us being together…
My chances of being with you, could blow away like a feather…
You really did surprise me, you shocked me more than anything…
You are my everything…I don't know what I would do with out you…
You know I'd never doubt you, as long as we are together…
Here… now… always… and forever…

Tayah Luckadoo, Grade 8
Lane Middle School, IN

My Favorite Day

Wow! I'm here at the beach
when I look up I see the hot sun big waves and people in swimming clothes
Boom! I hear waves splashing people laughing and babies crying
Fantastic! I feel hot dry sand sweat running down my back
and I feel cold ice cream dripping down my stomach
Amazing!! I smell hot wings pizza cheese fries and pretzels all cooking
Fun! I'm glad to be here!

Keayzia Holliday, Grade 7
Pierce Middle School, IN

Fire

You look at the fire and wonder
You look at the fire and ponder
Stare into its blazing logs
And through its smoke and fog
You see the wonder inside
And none of its secrets to hide
The destruction it has wrought
The help that it has brought
The lives that it has taken
The age it has awakened
The cities it has brought down
Beneath its golden crown
The people it has enslaved
The lives that it has saved
You look at the fire and wonder
You look at the fire and ponder
Raymond Moylan, Grade 8
All Saints Academy, IL

Haunted Trail of Horrors

"Ahhhhh!"
Follow the trail
and hang on to the rail.
Night is coming
and the stench of death
chases weary souls.
Ghouls, goblins, and ghosts
give goose bumps to brave heroes

going down the haunted Trail of Horrors.
Scream, scream
as loud as you can!
No one can hear you.
No one can hear you
anymore.
Muhahaha!
Justin Juelfs, Grade 8
Red Bud Elementary School, IL

Fall

I love fall
Leaves, colors, and all
For me,
It never grows old
Well at least until it gets cold
It's the best time of the year
To me, it's a time to cheer
When I think of fall
I think of the trees that are tall,
Of the leaves that are pretty
Oh, I'm so glad I don't live in a city
But most of all
I think of the time I spent
And everywhere I went.
Kathleen Tracy, Grade 8
St Matthew School, IL

A Fun, Yet Not Fun, Pool Party

Every year there was a pool party,
At my Aunt Lynn's house.
But ever since my aunt died,
It has never been the same.

The pool party was heaven.
Everyone was laughing,
As hard as a child after a funny joke.
The huge house,
Like a mansion on stilts.
The water felt great,
Like swimming in the clouds.
Big plates filled the deck,
It was a feast for a monster.
The pool had room for everyone.
Playing volleyball,
Big splashes of water coming to life.
The bad barking of Maddie, the dog.
And the taste of the food was a home run.
But it will never be the same,
Without my Aunt Lynn.
Jason Roesing, Grade 8
Liberty Jr High School, IL

Late Night

Steady night
Darkness engulfing the horizon,
Couple sitting at the bar,
Discussing whether or not,
To get back together,
Or stay apart.
While chewing on,
5 cent bread, at Phillies.
Bartender serving them,
After a tough night,
And his pay getting cut,
In the depression.
Lawyer, getting a drink
After a difficult day on the job,
Trying to figure out the case.
Time ticking away as he gets,
Closer and closer,
To getting an answer.
Dogs howling in the moonlight.
Serious, interesting, awkward, Reuniting,
Night at Phillies.
Mark Milligan, Grade 8
Thomas Middle School, IL

Waterfall

Water runs quickly
Flowing down a large mountain
Crashing into rocks
How gorgeous!
John Krasnican, Grade 8
Northlawn Jr High School, IL

Running All My Life

Wind in my hair
Crowds all stare
I only care
Running all my life

Running in the trees
Through the nice cool breeze
Past the willow trees
Running all my life

Smell the sweet nature
Feel the hard ground
Hear the joyous birds
Running all my life

Running in the morning
Running at night
Anytime every time
Running all my life

Injury may stop me
It will cost a little fee
But I will always be
Running all my life
Thomas Lechtenberg, Grade 7
Marquette Academy, IL

Ode to the Spy

Oh, how I love my family,
But how I miss the deceased,
So why won't you tell me
When you'll be released?

We were always together
And it felt like forever,
But now that time passes
I realize that it was never.

I would always talk to you
And you would just say "k,"
But I wouldn't mind it
Because you were that way.

You always found a way to make me smile
You always told me that life was a gift,
That most people didn't respect,
And we just need a little lift.

You always said that when you grow up
You would be spy,
And I've been thinking you are a spy
Who lives in the sky.
Carlos Bedolla, Grade 7
Divine Infant Jesus School, IL

My Last Day

Fear, fear rung out everywhere,
As a plane struck the tower next door
Boom!
The tower came crashing down
I on the 64th floor began to panic
Running, running down the stairs
Crash!
Shaking then silence
Faster I ran
Smoke, smoke everywhere filling the air
Screams rang out
Chaos everywhere
Pushing, shoving down the stairs
Coughing, coughing
I'm on the ground hurting
Ash falling, tower crumbling
Glass shattering, metal melting
Then all was silent
I was no longer coughing, no longer trapped
I was free from my horrible last day
But my wonderful new beginning awaiting

Emma Helms, Grade 8
Central Jr High School, IL

Thanksgiving

T hank you for the things I have
H aving Thanksgiving dinner with my friends and family
A lways knowing I have food to eat
N ew things I get for no reason
K nowing I'm loved
S howing my family I love them
G iving to people who don't have a family
I nviting people to celebrate
V enturing out to help people in need
I nventing ways to spend time with each other
N ot being selfish
G iving thanks for what you have

Olivia Linder, Grade 7
Hannah Beardsley Middle School, IL

Golf

A warm, balmy weather today,
perfect for playing a few holes, let's say.
We drive to the first hole with our bags in the back.
I go first to hit the ball.
I tee it up, and concentrate.
Focusing on the ball, I have a knack.
I swing and make contact with the ball,
reverberating a metallic "ting!" as it sails and falls.
I stand back to let you hit,
but you made a greater shot than I did.
You made a birdie, while I made a par,
and goes on in this manner.

Christopher Yun, Grade 8
Stanley Clark School, IN

Putting on a Show

When reading all my lines
The thrill I have
I feel like I'm Amanda Bynes!
I can be any person
The opposite of myself
This one is barely getting along
She's not in good health.
This man is funny
This one is sad.
The girl is crying
That woman is so mad.
Why do I feel like this?
I don't really know
Maybe I was born
To put on a show.

Kaitlyn Ammerman and Jahnari Pruitt, Grade 7
Pierce Middle School, IN

Pet Peeves

I hate it,
I can't take it anymore.
The sound of annoyance and screams
In my head.
I run to the place I like the most,
my bedroom.
I make it
but I still hear it.
I go on my drum kit.
Still hear it.
I screamed and screamed until I couldn't take it anymore.
Then, I stomped across the hallway
into my brother's room
and told him,
"Will you stop with the guitar?"

Mikey Williams, Grade 7
Madison Jr High School, IL

Learning in School

Learning in school is really great,
I do not hate, hate, hate.
I love learning math and science,
From the Metric System to heredity,
To 2 times 10 equals 20.
Learning this stuff makes me grow in knowledge,
I cannot wait 'til I go to college.
If you don't like school that's a bummer,
If you don't pay attention you will get dumber.
Sometimes you fall and get hurt,
Then you can go see the nurse.
Someday when you have kids,
They will give you a great big kiss.
You will say what was that for?
For sending me to school, to learn more and more

Erin Firestone, Grade 7
Our Lady of the Wayside School, IL

Anyssa Gonzalez

Anyssa
Eyes of the color green, brown haired, athletic,
and gracious.
Relative of Nadia and Aziel
Lover of comedy, bacon, soccer
Who feels terrified, puzzled, content
Who needs affection, compassionate friends, anticipation
Who fears bees, rejection, a short life time
Who gives joy, trust, and care for the needy
Who would like to see Rome, Italy, Eric and Lina
Resident of the Windy City
Gonzalez

Anyssa Gonzalez, Grade 8
St Daniel the Prophet School, IL

A Rose Flower

A rose, sweet as honey
It is like a colorful rainbow
Precious as gold at the end of the rainbow
Grows like a 100 year old tree
Communicates with the people with its beautiful, gentle little petals
It cries when there is no one around
It dances with wind as it blows
It creates gorgeous necklaces out of its petals
It shares its precious beauty with everyone
Whoosh, whoosh, slowly its petals start to fall
It lets go of its ten million petals to fill the sky
A rose, reminds me of the great times I had with my family!

Shruthi Ponnada, Grade 8
Thomas Middle School, IL

Mysterious Me

My heart holds all the secrets of my past
It keeps them under lock and key
They are not meant for anyone but me
I live in my imagination and eat all the stories that I hear
My eyes are under the influence of my mind
My eyes can be sad and yet they always smile
My eyes see things others don't
My hair is the color of an autumn night
The curls hold the stars and the moon
My smile can be sweet like hot chocolate
But it holds a mystery in its calmness
I live to love and learn, and imagine even more

Isabella Roberts, Grade 7
International School of Indiana, IN

The Game

Through the brightness of day.
Through the darkness of night.
I will eat, sleep, and breathe baseball.
All I hear in my head is the crack of the bat.
Followed by an explosive cheer from the crowd.

Kevin Banks, Grade 7
Highland Hills Middle School, IN

Always Watching

I am the girl who never spoke up
never seeing it as my problem
never even thinking of what was happening
watching I was always watching
I am the girl who could have never done anything
Or that's at least what I told myself
I am the girl who witnessed self esteem drop to its lowest
watching never letting my eyes stray
What could I have done?
Or maybe I should change that to, what should I have done
there was so many things that people changed
their personality, their friends, everything
I truly am sorry for not saying anything
for simply standing there and watching
watching yet never doing anything to stop it

Jahnari Pruitt, Grade 7
Clifford Pierce Middle School, IN

Grandma Puncyski: An Angel Above

I admired my grandma like another mother
Her mind was like a craft book
Spending time together, knots tied next to each other
Talking on the telephone, typing e-mails, or even fun text messages
Enjoying what a wonderful life we had
Hearing the horrible, heartbreaking news
Changed everything, turned my world upside down
Unable to do everything as we used to do
On a dark, gloomy morning when the clouds began to cry
He knew it was time for her to go
From the day she left
Everyday has been too slow, a clock ticking backwards
People refusing to leave her grave and stone
My heart fell as if a ship had sunk to the deep, blue ocean floor
But noticed she's still with me wherever I go

Kayli Wolf, Grade 8
Liberty Jr High School, IL

It's Like…

Sadness is in all of us
It's a fear
That flows through the veins
It's a depression
That lingers in the air
It's like a sickness
That you can feel running through your body
It's like an anger that tears out your heart
It yells in your face to give up…
But you don't
You keep on kicking
Come out swinging
And you know that the crying won't help
But the pain is so overcoming
That you want to deal with it another day

Seth Johnson, Grade 8
Liberty Jr High School, IL

Indy 500

In the humid heat people sit,
with headsets, hot dogs and drinks.
They watch the cars lining up on the grid,
but the men mostly look at the Safety Car,
a prospective buy, in which they would look "cool" at the bar.

As the race starts
everyone leans forward,
eyeing their favorite racer with an eagle eye,
shouting loudly when they get overtaken and
cheering even louder when they overtake

Tires at the side of the track,
And spare helmets and gloves all on a rack
Drivers are pulling in to the pit
And when something goes wrong
the team manager throws a fit.

As the end of the race draws near,
some people shed a tear,
and some are drinking beer,

But the racers keep racing, competing,
until the final flag waves,
for the glory of winning cannot be replaced.

Jakub Vohlidka, Grade 7
International School of Indiana, IN

My School Day

At the beginning of the day
We all begin to say
A nice little prayer
Then Intentions we share

Off to Math we go
To show the world what we know
Social Studies is such a blast
I love learning about the past
Then to the Special of the day
It's my favorite class, if I may

Next we go to Religion class
And learn more about the Mass
Once the bell rings for lunch
We all begin to munch

Then it is vocab time
Wow, I need to learn how to rhyme
Soon we visit the Land of Nouns, Verbs and Prepositions
Then we write our compositions
In Science and Lit
We learn about the elements and works that were writ'

And that's an average day in the 8th grade

Monica Clapp, Grade 8
St Matthew School, IL

Ewwwwww! Peas!

I was facing a terrible fate
My peas sat on a plate!
I was ready with a water glass, prepared to drink, fast!
I opened my mouth and readied my tongue
I took a deep breath with my beautiful lungs
The peas so ugly, so bare, how was this fair?
The peas so squishy, so soft, so green
How could my parents look so keen?
I chewed and swallowed, then coughed and hacked
I could've sworn I had a heart attack!
I choked and spat, as my family stared and sat
I made a funny face, from that killer taste,
I gulped and gasped for air, I wish I had a lung to spare.
Where was my water?
I had placed it right there!
As fast as I could think, I ran to the sink
I gulped the liquids, thank the gods!
I could cry, I could die, I want pie
I breathed in relief and sighed, I was alive!
I counted to ten,
I was ready to go through with death again.

Sabrina Cupryk, Grade 7
International School Of Indiana, IN

Can Anybody Hear Me?

Can anybody hear me?
I'm drifting away.
I'm swimming in sorrow.
My heart in decay.
Can anybody hear me?
I'm in my bed.
No one will ever know the thoughts in my head.
Should I say something?
I think not…that gives me a headache, like a blow from a pot.
Can anybody hear me?
Please take my hand.
I will show you my thoughts, a wonderful land.
Can anybody hear me?
I'm trapped in this darkness.
I feel so helpless, forced in a harness.
Can anybody hear me?
I'm right in your face.
But whenever you see me, you pick up your pace.
Can anybody hear me?
I know you do.
You only care about things that benefit you.

Jayana Dailey, Grade 9
George Westinghouse College Prep, IL

A Christmas Tree

A Christmas tree is like a starry night glowing over you.
Until one day it gives its gifts with open arms.
Children's joy shining brighter the stars.

Kyle Woods, Grade 7
Highland Hills Middle School, IN

Coldness

Cold
A uninviting feeling
Appears strongly at night
Strong
Cold is the door closing in upon your life
Evan Witte, Grade 7
Wethersfield Jr/Sr High School, IL

Jill and Phil

There once was a girl named Jill
She got married to Phil
They bought a cat
They named him Pat,
and everything they got was God's will.
Meredith McDonough, Grade 7
Bethel Lutheran School, IL

Families

Families bring friendship and memories
They are inviting and secure
Always there to encourage and support you
They bring importance and care
They will always love you
Shelby Berg, Grade 7
Emmanuel-St Michael Lutheran School, IN

Leaves

Leaves are everywhere,
up in trees or on the ground
they're all different
either in color or shape,
brown, yellow, green paints the scene.
Jacob Boswell, Grade 7
Wethersfield Jr/Sr High School, IL

Fireworks

Fireworks
Loud, booming
Booming, exploding, crackling
Colored streaks of elements
Bombs
Zebulyn Phillips, Grade 7
Wethersfield Jr/Sr High School, IL

Feelings

Feelings are colors
Splashing like paint on a page.
Blue for when you're sad,
Red for when you're mad.
Dancing through your head all day.
Ann Marie Swiskoski, Grade 8
Northlawn Jr High School, IL

Technology

What if technology took over the world?
Would we all stop talking to one another?
Would we have technology do everything for us?
No one would care about the world,
Things wouldn't be the same anymore,
Robots would do all the work for us
As we sit and do nothing in our own lazy way.
The silence is as cold as a winter day.
We would spend all our days wasting away on computers
Instead of enjoying the warm weather on a nice summer day.
People would rely on technology to have all the answers for them.
The human society would be different forever
All we would care about is our technology
Click Click Click
Hear as people type on keyboards.
If technology took over look at how our society would end up turning into.
What if technology became our new world?
Alysa Zurlo, Grade 8
Thomas Middle School, IL

Street Dreamer

As I stand, I dream and pray for me that this dream will one day become my reality.
Standing on a field in the middle of my squad, listening to my fans as they chant Hurrah!
Singing a song that will be heard by all rising to the occasion
I dunk the ball winning a gold medal that's shining because of very stainless playing.
In a movie where I am the most famous
Painting a portrait even greater than the Mona Lisa
Starting my own credit card company like Platinum Visa
Sail the oceans, seas, and all the Great Lakes
Travel the world from country to country and state to state
Stop all the violence with an outstanding speech
Travel into space and go where no other man could ever reach
All of these dreams are far from within my grasp
I enjoy this moment because I know that it will surely pass.
It's the dream of our lives, that's why we struggle.
I am a *Street Dreamer.*.
That's why I keep on Hustlin'
But I still find myself asking God, *"What must I do to make my many dreams come true?"*
London Taylor, Grade 7
West Park Academy, IL

Miracles

Ella was my miracle
A miracle, that she was
She didn't bark a lot
She would tell me when she needed to go out
She was a good listener yes she was
A doll from beginning to end
I wish I could have appreciated her more while I still had her
Because we imprinted her paw in some clay then I never saw her again
And scattered her ashes in another miracle from God
A rose garden with pretty roses just for Ella
Hopefully a red fern will grow right between Ella and my Lacy
Rest in peace Ella and Lacy
Alana Pries, Grade 7
Concordia Lutheran School, IN

Farm Life

Farm Life
Feeding the livestock
Packing fifty-pound bags of feed
Picking corn, bucking bales
Dusty, sweaty summer days
Grinding cattle and hog feed
Freezing winter mornings — thawing icy water tanks
Breaking calves to lead
Hard, backbreaking work

Showing pigs and calves at the fair
Responsibility
Operating machinery
Nuzzling a soft horse's muzzle
Calves' tickling, sandpaper tongues
Man's best friend — my beagle
Hog's flopping ears as it runs to greet you
Fresh, spring rains
A fun way of life

Alan Warden, Grade 9
Beardstown Jr/Sr High School, IL

Glistening Mystery

As I looked across the sparkling sea,
something caught my eye.
I looked really hard, but what I saw,
was more than words could describe.
As it floated closer, and came into view,
there was only one thing my instincts told me to do.
I swam out to meet it, and see it face to face,
but surely when I got there,
it decided to race.
Out to sea we went, swimming toward the sun.
I didn't see it anywhere; I hoped the race was done.
Out of breath I stopped.
It had come back.
It hurt my eyes to stare at,
I had realized what it was.
Not a mermaid or diamond,
Alien or fish,
but my own reflection.
Who would've guessed?

Olivia Prudhomme, Grade 8
St Matthew School, IL

My Favorite Foods

Pie, cookies, macaroni and cheese!
Fried chicken, baked chicken, pizza with pepperoni!
Cornbread, broccoli and also rice!
Baked potato, sweet potato with a little spice!
Ice cream, waffles with a little cinnamon!
Don't forget to add my blueberry muffin!
Those are the foods I like to eat!
Come back next time and make sure you're hungry!!!

Maxwell Moore, Grade 7
Clifford Pierce Middle School, IN

The Battle

An army of six versus an army of six,
The separation line so thin.
So many different attacks, land and air.
The weapon of choice: a striped grenade with no explosives.
It is thrown to the front lines,
smacked over the separation line,
instead of everyone diving away,
they dive toward it.
It hits the floor with the force of Superman.
Whistle blown.

She is shaking, weapon in hand.
Her army in front of her, she quivers.
She knows there is still work to be done.
A line of land mines sits in front of her.
The trophy sits, mocking her.
She pulls the pin on the grenade.
5
She tosses it up.
4
Stress is crushing her.
3
The army relies on her.
2
She swings her arm.
1
It soars over the separation line.
0
Instead of it erupting…the crowd does.

Kaila Kasper, Grade 7
Galileo Scholastic Academy, IL

I Love You Daddy

Youthful innocence gone
Destroyed
She now has to grow up
For who else would sew her family back together
Stitch by stitch, all the seams were unraveled
By just that one car
That one night
That one crash
That one life lost, the one that meant the most
Now who would she go to in times of need
In times of needing someone there
That someone is now gone
He can only watch over her now
She wishes she could just see his face one more time
Give him a proper good-bye hug
A proper good-bye
That's all she needs
To know he is okay
To know he is always there
To know she heard her final words to him
"I love you daddy"

Emily Poynter, Grade 9
Greenville High School, IL

Black, Black Rose*

O, my love is like a black, black heart,
That's newly broken in stride,
O, my love is like the vampire,
That's wasting away inside.
As dark art thou, my heart hurts,
So deep in love am I,
And I will love thee still, my friend,
Till a' the pigs gang fly.
Till a' the pigs gang fly, my friend,
And the rocks float wi' the birds!
And I will love thee still, my friend,
While the milk o' life shall curd.
And fare thee sad, my passed love.
And fare thee sad a while!
And I will love again, my friend,
Tho' it were fifteen hundred mile!

Madison Brock, Grade 9
Palestine High School, IL
*Inspired by "O My Love's a Red, Red Rose"

Bring Me Home My Love

My eyes wander up to the moonlit sky,
looking at you I get butterflies.
You've been just my friend for so many years,
you've comforted me,
through the heartache and tears.
Yet I can't shake the feeling I've felt this before.
This feeling that I've long since opened the door,
to a world so beautiful, silent, and wise,
all hidden beneath your silvery, sky eyes.
Looking at me with much more to see,
it's funny how you bring out the best in me.
We gaze at each other with stars in our eyes,
but you live in Heaven,
so I am your prize.
For tonight we can glance down at the world from above,
so bring me home my love.
Bring me home my love…

Cierra Patrick, Grade 8
Red Bud Elementary School, IL

Inside This Clock

Inside this clock all of the gears are as confusing as a maze.
Inside this clock there are more gears than people on earth.
Inside this clock I hear "tick tock tick tock."
Inside this clock all of the movements are as precise as a robot.
Inside this clock the arms move like marching soldiers.
Inside this clock cobwebs flutter in the corners.
Inside this clock I stand alone in the dark.
Inside this clock I never miss a beat.
Inside this clock there is always enough time.
Inside this clock it is now two o'clock.
BONG
BONG

Alex Norris, Grade 8
Thomas Middle School, IL

Answers

What if there were no answers?
The world would seem dead,
Not knowing the truth.
Once an answer, now a black, fuzzy picture.
Once a thought, now a question floating in the air
Never to go anywhere.
Once a school, now an empty building
Filled with ghostly memories.
What is the purpose to be on earth?
The person who would ask this question will never know.
No one would know.
Why do I see people suffer,
Starve,
Die?
I don't know.
Why am I living?
What if the world never knew?
What if no one will ever know?

Claire Niemczyk, Grade 8
Thomas Middle School, IL

Death

I am death
I am everywhere
I am fear inside you
I take away your loved ones
Reach out with a bony hand
And when I touch them they are forever gone
I am your worst nightmare
I strike without warning
I am an assassin
I am invisible
I cannot be stopped
Nor killed
I have no emotion
I kill millions every day
I am your deadliest enemy
I am death
I strike without warning
Forever I'll exist

Nicolas Rossi, Grade 7
McClure Jr High School, IL

Turtles

Turtles hatching on the beach, easy prey for some to reach.
Watching, wading, winning the race to the water.
Powerful legs propelling them towards their first swim.
Seagulls soaring through the sky, dolphins diving close by.
Swimming slowly down a trail following others behind their tail.
Hugely hungry hoping to eat, seaweed I see at my feet.
Growing gradually, getting bigger.
Searching currents far and wide taking a break on the tide.
Finally full circle I have come
Back to the beach I am from.

Bryce Blakemore, Grade 7
International School of Indiana, IN

Swimming

Swimming is difficult,
But it is still fun.
It's better than baseball,
And easier to run.
Butterfly, backstroke,
Breaststroke, freestyle,
They're all too difficult
To crack a smile.
Butterfly's the hardest
Freestyle's the least
But only I can swim
Like an aquatic beast.
I start out in the air,
Then dive into the water.
I love swimming.

Otto Stark, Grade 7
All Saints Academy, IL

Seasons

When winter is near,
Coldness is here,
The seasons will never end

Spring has a lot of showers
But they bring tons of flowers
The seasons will never end

The summer sun is helping
To make things melting
The seasons will never end

Fall is a time for leaves
To fall off their trees
The seasons will never end

Sarah Neuhalfen, Grade 7
Immaculate Conception School, IL

My Day at the Beach

I like to go swimming,
It often leaves me grinning.
I went to the beach,
And ate a nice peach.
I got in the water,
And saw an otter.
I got salt in my eyes,
Which I truly despise.
Then I saw a shark,
And my world went dark.
I passed out just like that!
When I finally came to,
I was on top like a canoe.
I made friends with that shark,
And we played until dark.

Natalie Schisler, Grade 8
Bethel Lutheran School, IL

Winter

Chilly and freezing
My preferable weather
Good times for myself

Children always laugh
Sleds and toboggans about
Good times for myself

Icy and snowy
People should not be driving
Good times for myself

Radio roaring
Schools are canceled for today
Good times for myself

Icicles hanging
Licking the cold wet water
Good times for myself

Danny Black, Grade 7
Immaculate Conception School, IL

Mirrors

Is this me?
Then again…
who is me?
It's unclear in this world of mirrors.
The closest shows empty space…
I'm see through,
or am I?
What exactly am I?
Am I a person?
Like, say,
a flower?
Or would I be a doll,
unresponsive and unmoving,
merely posing?
My eyes have no depth,
only fog.
Why is that?
Who am I?
Who are you?

Sydney Matthys, Grade 8
Stanley Clark School, IN

Trust Me

Trust me.
No one is perfect.
If you were perfect,
Life would be boring.
If your life was boring,
Can you be happy?
If you're not happy,
Then you're nowhere near perfect.

Mackenzie Icenogle, Grade 9
Beardstown Jr/Sr High School, IL

The Birds

The birds fly
Enjoying their freedom

They make a soft cry
To the ones who can't see them

Gliding in the air
Floating in the wind

They look so fair
Happy they're not pinned

They swoop to the trees
And soon become hidden

Shooting out from the leaves
As if the trees are forbidden

They make their last call
When the sun starts to dim

Saying goodbye to all
Then they're gone on a whim

Laila Mitchel, Grade 9
Elk Grove High School, IL

Christmas Tree

Christmas tree, oh Christmas tree,
Covered in a snow white,

Christmas tree, oh Christmas tree,
Oh so shimmering bright.

Christmas tree, oh Christmas tree,
The things on you pulled tight,

Christmas tree, oh Christmas tree,
Oh your great massive height!

Christmas tree, oh Christmas tree,
So tall you might take flight.

Christmas tree, oh Christmas tree,
You don't give me a fright.

Christmas tree, oh Christmas tree,
I wish with all my might,

Christmas tree, oh Christmas tree,
Oh the glorious sight!

Kaitlin Verchimak, Grade 8
Immaculate Conception School, IL

Cars

Slim, sleek and beautiful.
They roll down the road.
In a rainbow of colors.

Their engines purr with power coursing through it.
Their outer shell shines with a metallic gleam.
Inside they smell like sweat and air fresheners.

They spin and swerve on the asphalt.
Leaving streaks of burning rubber.
They are seen with amazement or welcomed with scowls.

They prey on the earth and harm it.
On dark days the prey on our end by harming themselves.
They are awake sometimes during the day or sometimes at night.

They die when a key is pulled out.
When reborn they awaken with a roar and restart their life.

Sarthak Singh, Grade 7
Madison Jr High School, IL

What If

what if
the Earth stood still?
what would happen to humans?
would everyone just *freeze* in their place?
would the very spot you're standing in right now
be your *final* resting place *forever and ever*?
would it forever be night somewhere and elsewhere day?
would their be nations concealed in shadows or exposed by light?
would any tears being shed be shed forever, and then…
the shed-er would forever feel the sorrow and pain that
they felt at that moment? would there forever be…
questions left unanswered? there would be lots
of boys and girls left playing in the park, mid-
swing, with still so much to learn about…
we all know that the Earth is always
rapidly moving, but you can still
wonder…what if the Earth
stood still?

George Ayoub, Grade 8
Thomas Middle School, IL

Love Peace and Happiness

I am from a world of sweetness, love, and HAPPINESS
I am from a country where the delicious food is tasty
I am from a city where la Tour Eiffel, comme toujours est belle.
I am from a family of happiness, love, art, and music
I am from a little town, where friendship is strong
I am from a school very close to my house
I am from a beautiful family with two fun older sisters
I am from a friendly, peacefully world that I love very much
I am from a world of sweetness, love, and HAPPINESS
But most of all I am from a family of love, peace, and happiness!

Alice Delahaye, Grade 7
International School of Indiana, IN

The Meadow*

Swirling
The whisking winds
Aqua and azure
Brushing my face
Whispering
Alone
Standing alone
In the empty meadow
Standing
In mustard amber wheat
The pistachio trees and bushes
Drift in the wind
Coldness
Creeping down
From the curved mountains
Behind me

Elizabeth Moran, Grade 8
Thomas Middle School, IL
*Based on "Cypres dans un champ de ble" by Vincent Van Gogh

My Best Friend

My best friend's name is Taylor.
We always eat lunch together.
We have been best friends forever.
I always go over to her house
And we always hang out.
My friend Taylor and I have only had each other for friends.
We think each other is pretty and we never say anything rude.
We always have sleepovers at her house.
And we are the best friends you could ever see.
We always hang out
And we always shout and we make her dad mad.
He is big and bad (just kidding he is always grumpy)
We love to watch movies
We are just alike.
We like to eat spaghetti and cheese,
Omelets, candy, and ice cream.
We are best friends Taylor and I.

Kathleen Lister, Grade 7
Rossville Alvin Elementary School, IL

The Men Who Do It All

These people do this on a regular basis.
Running jumping to hit blocks.
Getting power up from a smiling mushroom.
Squashing angry brown mushrooms.
Jumping onto flags.
Avoiding ping pong-ball-shaped ghosts.
Chucking heaps of fire.
And battling an evil reptile.
Saving a princess who leads talking fungi.
Doing 25 years of this and not quitting.
It could only be…
SUPER MARIO BROTHERS!!!

Jack Anderson, Grade 7
Madison Jr High School, IL

I Come From

I come from smiles and laughter,
With tears and fears.
I can be found in the dark depths of song,
From iTunes to the radio. I grew up with the sound of Toby Keith,
But came to love Three Days Grace.
I come from poked and blood-stained fingers.
The beeps of highs and lows are all I've ever known.
I come from the smell of spaghetti in November.
The hustle of crowds and smiles on kids' faces.
I come from pizza and a movie on Saturdays,
From comedies, romances, and histories.
Each movie with a moral.
I am from a piano
That started with "Mary Had a Little Lamb," and became
A 5 flat solo piece.
I come from Crown Point.
A quaint town with little shops and sidewalks.
I know I will leave to go to Washington D.C. someday,
But I come from this place.
The people I've met and the things I've done will never leave me.

Megan Jones, Grade 8
St Marys School, IN

The Things I Don't Understand

The things I don't understand
Are as difficult as a person running barefoot through the sand,
Like love, hate
Is there such a thing as fate?
Life, death
Why waste your breath on meth.
I have had people tell me their reasons,
And they are as difficult to put together as the seasons.
Love is the greatest passion you can feel for someone.
Also love can be the greatest pain for just about anyone.
Hate is just another version of love.
Hate is when you dislike everything, even the beautiful turtle dove.
I have heard many things about life and death.
Can you die of death?
Life is what some people waste away.
Life is the thing people enjoy at the end of the day.
Death is a state of painlessness.
Death is a period of sadness.
These things I don't understand
Are as difficult as a person running barefoot through the sand.

Cienna Knights, Grade 8
Daleville High School, IN

Winter Bliss

Winter is the time of care
When Christmas joy is in the air
The perfect time to pray to God
To thank him for his wondrous love

When Christmas comes, it is a time of cheer
To be proud of Jesus, the Lord of all here

When all the presents are under the tree
That is the time of glee indeed
When kids wake up the next morning
To see what they have got
They find things to keep and love
And be thankful to God

But that is not all what winter is about
The snowmen, the cold brisk, the fresh mistletoe
The homemade things that taste so delectable
Winter is the best season of them all
I can't wait till the end of fall.

Akshat Tyagi, Grade 7
St Matthew School, IL

My Big Brother

I'm sorry big stupid lovable brother
for believing that you'd choose me over her,
think of me as worthy of your time
remember how we used to be partners in crime?
Unaware that your friendships are now taboo
and that you hurt all your friends that were around you.
Who does she think she is, taking you from me?
Everything is broken and everyone agrees,
that choice wasn't very smart
am I the only one with a broken bleeding heart?
Oh big brother, big brother you know I love you yes,
I want you to see that everything turned into a big mess.
I want to help you very badly
however you've hurt me and sadly
I think I don't adore you as profoundly
but keep me where I belong somewhere soundly
around the place she will never go.
I just wanted to let you know,
before my eyes become a wet blur
I'm sorry big remorseful forsaken brother

Tammy Bell-Bey, Grade 9
Carl Schurz High School, IL

What You Have Done to Me!

I was marked by your selfishness.
Betrayed by your hidden lies.
You say you have chosen me by your untamed temper.
Your words haunted me, so I was tempted to leave.
Now I'm burned here, into ashes I sleep.

Abigail Favela, Grade 7
St Frances of Rome School, IL

Racing

Race cars go blazing by.
People screaming loudly.
Cars flying against the wall and into the infield.
Fireworks blast across the sky.
And me…enjoying it all.

John Hurley, Grade 7
St Pius X Catholic School, IN

Prejudice

Prejudice is a word that I learned one day.
And one good example is calling someone gay.
If only they knew what that word really meant.
So let's start off by saying this one good hint.
It does not mean bisexual, it means lively in fact.
Also known as merry or bright.
So why do you call someone this, at the point of their sight.
A word that you have mixed up, or so called tweaked.
Prejudice is what this is, very prejudiced indeed.
To have mistaken someone because you can so call read.
If you can read, pick up a dictionary one day.
Look up this word and see what it says.
Prejudice is mean, it's not at all great.
To prejudge someone, and put a label on them that's fake.
So be careful what you say, and be careful what you do.
You might even be prejudged too.

Jeremiah Shepard, Grade 9
Academy for Learning, IL

The Game of Baseball

Heart beating,
Beating,
Faster than ever,
The next play happening right in front of you,
Being freaky fast,
Reaching,
Seeming like it's miles away,
Though you seem to stretch just far enough,
Collecting the ball,
Releasing the ball,
It seems to be mocking me,
Floating in slow motion,
You give up and hang your head,
He's out!
Regaining hope,
Realizing that you've made the winning play!

Joshua Lolan, Grade 8
Red Bud Elementary School, IL

Thanksgiving

The day to be with your family and relatives,
to have a big feast while giving thanks
to all people who fought for our country,
not having regrets or bad feelings,
a time to be kind and generous to others, and
give special thanks to people who have kept us safe.

Giving others food and cheer,
instead of being selfish or cruel to people who
very much need food or money,
don't be mean,
instead give thanks to people like family or relatives.
Nobody should be left out of Thanksgiving.
Go and tell them what they mean to you!

Jaime Javier, Grade 7
Hannah Beardsley Middle School, IL

Gold

Yesterday I told my friend, "I Have a Dream"
that one day I would become a famous dancer.

"Well Does Your Mother Know?" she asked.
"No, I haven't told her." Then at school
I won tickets to an "ABBA" concert.

So I took my best friend; the first song
was "Super Trooper" and I started to dance.

No one really noticed how good I was
until they played "Mamma Mia,"
my favorite song.

Everyone circled around me and
started chanting "Dancing Queen."

Then I thought to myself, oh dear God,
"Thank You for the Music."

Catherine Thornton, Grade 7
Sacred Heart School, IL

The Good Days

What ever happened to the good days,
when everyone used to laugh and play.
It seems like it all started to go away,
when everyone grew up to today.

When I was little it was all fun and games,
Jumping on trampolines,
and having sleepovers with my friends.
But as I got older it all started to fade away.

I'm older now,
more friends,
more freedom,
more responsibilities.
I gain hearts,
I break hearts,
and when I'm down, my friends always have my back.
But the good days I have now,
don't compare to the good days I used to have.

Melanie Robinson, Grade 9
Homestead Sr High School, IN

Graveyard Shift

Staring, stationary statues startle silly standers,
Ghouls, grim and gray, startle pint-sized kindergartners,
Bam, Ka-zam, automated statues and ghouls,
Acting like a sanitarium full of fools,
Working the graveyard shift in the dead of night,
But when the sun comes out,
The ghouls and fools have to return into the cold, stone body,
That they have to use 'til sun down.

Brandon Imming, Grade 8
Red Bud Elementary School, IL

Kicks in Motion

Such grace, such beauty
So many turns and twists
The elegance, the perfection,
So much power it consists.

We use kicks for fighting
We use them for show.
It takes precise practice,
Those kicks high and low.

There are many different kinds
Like hook, round, and side,
Together spectacular
When all are combined.

Perfection takes time
You stop and you start,
Practice makes perfect,
To master the art.
Bethany Knox, Grade 8
St Matthew School, IL

White Snow Day

The snow glistens in the light
As I gaze outside the window
The sun shines extremely bright
Around the land of the meadow

The large trees blow toward the right
And carries the light snow around
Even with all their might
As the eerie night carries on

Footprints trail off in the night
Into the frightful dark cold night
I hear the wailing of wolves
Seek into the forest of fright

Snow piles on the windowsills
Finding it hard to see outside
The plow comes around to pile
Everyone wants to shout winter
Anne Enright, Grade 8
Immaculate Conception School, IL

Love Freely

The love is thick
I am freely alone
Frightened of the love worshiped
Smiling at the small things in life
Joyful for my freely thinking
Scared of my own thoughts
Sick of the hurt I endure
I sit and wallow in my self pity and pain.
Brittany Snapp, Grade 8
David L Rahn Elementary School, IL

Stuck

Ugh…I can't think,
writer's block is back,
my brain won't budge,
not even a step,
just like floating in space.

Ideas won't flow,
not even a trickle,
it's like a traffic jam,
that never ends.

Wait! My brain's getting an idea,
it's coming slowly,
but as soon it gets there,
it shies away.

I've tried my hardest,
to get some ideas,
they may look like a dish rag,
pathetic, torn, dirty,
but still alive.

It may taste like a cup of dark coffee,
bitter, and oh so boring brown,
but it is an idea.
Eric Lo, Grade 7
Madison Jr High School, IL

What Happens?

What happens
when a raindrop
falls?

What happens
when rain
pours out?

What happens
when lightning
slices the sky?
When thunder
shakes the earth?

What happens
when wind
whips through
the trees?

What happens
when all is calm?
When the heavens
open up
and pour out
light onto the soaked ground?
Bethany Krupicka, Grade 7
Madison Jr High School, IL

Spring

Watch the flowers,
Blooming
Listen to the birds,
Chirping
See the nature,
Coming back to life
Watch animal eggs,
Hatching
Listen to a lamb go,
Baa, baa when it's born
See the snow,
Melting
Watch those gorgeous
Spring days, get longer and longer
Listen to the children shout,
Spring Break as school lets out
See the lovely sites,
There are to see
In that lovely spring time!
Abbey Zielinski, Grade 8
St Jude Elementary School, IN

Songs

Notes rise and fall
All across the page
Like a rolling ball
My notes never fade

Try to get an idea
A spark of greatness
Nothin' ever comes
All just blackness

I fumble with words
I tumble with verbs
I think of a noun
Then I write it down

Now it's all complete
I'm tapping my feet
To that awesome sound
That never fades
Raine Odom, Grade 8
Immaculate Conception School, IL

The Girl…

The girl who seemed tough, cried.
The girl that bullied, was bullied.
The girl that was smart, failed.
The girl that was nice, exploded.
The girl who was everything to one person,
was nothing to another.
So why is it that people get titled,
when no one knows the real them.
Emily Lahey, Grade 7
Emmanuel-St Michael Lutheran School, IN

Be Inspired

Be inspired.
Dream.
on…and on…and on
FOREVER.
Follow your dreams, no matter how hard it seems
Chase them.
Dream.

Be inspired.
Be your own person
and stay true to yourself.
Be who you are.
Don't change
  for ANYONE or ANYTHING.
You are who you are. You make you…YOU!

Be inspired.
  Be inspired.
    Be inspired.
you can do anything
just BELIEVE.

Taylor Vergara-Wright, Grade 7
Galileo Scholastic Academy, IL

Giving Tree*

Giving tree
standing all alone
holding itself in perfect posture
its almond body stretches to the sky
then explodes out into brilliant branches
which pop with ochre and tangerine leaves
the lemon sun slides
behind the long heart of the tree
the topaz sky slow fades to a harsh steel
the giving tree holds the secrets of hundreds of years
every vein on every leaf
can tell its own story
it can tell you about the summer lemon sun
the drop to the ground in fall
the giving tree lets the tawny squirrels
climb its branches
slowly doze off on its branches
the giving tree puts the world
before its own self.

Karla Diviesti, Grade 8
Thomas Middle School, IL
Based on "Sky Tree" by Thomas Locke

Bird in the Sky

I wish I could soar
Like a bird in the sky.
What would it take to fly this high?
To be courageous or give up all the way?
You will never know 'til you try to fly like a bird high in the sky.

Lexsis Carner, Grade 8
Red Bud Elementary School, IL

Hurricane

As the wind speeds up,
so do the people.
They take cover,
like a turtle sneaking into its shell.
Animals leave,
because they sense it.
Rain plummets to the ground,
waves crash to the shore like two buses without brakes.
And in the middle of it all,
silence.
Blank as a fresh sheet of paper,
nothing is heard.
And once again,
explosions of waves like fireworks,
and cracks of lightning as loud as bombs.
Water fills the ground,
creating a bigger ocean.
Only the tops of the trees can be seen as the rain moves on.
And after it all,
complete destruction and devastation.

Ryan Bayerle, Grade 8
Thomas Middle School, IL

Night

It was dark,
You could hear the dogs bark,
And when you step out,
Everyone takes you out,
You could hear the babies cry
People moaning in despair
Knowing that not a single soul will be spared,
Complete extermination
Yet no sign of determination to survive,
What is living like this?
Trapped in work,
Family members dead,
And all the souls waiting to desist,
No hope for life
But just when things were getting bad…
This nightmare became a dream…
One dark, Horrible,
Memory…
Elie woke up from that night that started it all,
The years of the Holocaust.

Jennifer Jimenez, Grade 9
Carl Schurz High School, IL

I Don't Know How to Write a Poem

I don't know how to write a poem.
There are lots of them written I just don't know 'em.
So I sit here thinking about how to write a poem.
Writing a poem for me is as slow as a snail.
But definitely not as quick as lightning.
Hey! I did it, I just wrote a poem.

Peyton Pierce, Grade 7
Highland Hills Middle School, IN

Jesus

J oy He gives us
E verlasting life with the
S avior of all of
U s forever we
S erve Him

Brandi Bisping, Grade 7
Bethel Lutheran School, IL

The Streetlight

Streetlights
Turn on at night
Waiting for the daytime
Lighten the surrounding darkness
For now

Elizabeth Jones, Grade 7
Marquette Academy, IL

Twirl Girl

There once was a girl who loved to twirl.
Her favorite shape was, of course, a swirl.
She twisted and turned,
And soon she learned,
Her head was in a whirl.

Maggie Brennan, Grade 7
Bethel Lutheran School, IL

Butterfingers

Tasty chocolate
In the form of candy bars
Peanut butter with
A sweet taste that lingers long
After the last, crunchy bite

Kyle Schoenekase, Grade 8
Northlawn Jr High School, IL

Dad

I love you Dad
Always making me smile
Would walk a mile
I love you Dad
Someone I can always count on

Emma Cable, Grade 7
Wethersfield Jr/Sr High School, IL

Scarf

Scarf
colorful, long
blowing, warming, covering,
soft, silky, fuzzy, furry,
warm

Mollie Krueger, Grade 7
Bethel Lutheran School, IL

People*

Fast people
Slow people
Smart, funny, cool people
Short, tall, big people
Those are just a few!
Flying people
Walking people
Driving, running, riding people
Biking, skating, rolling people
Scootering people too!
Strong people
Weak people
And don't forget fast people!
Last of all
Best of all
I like friendly people!

Mitchell Odom, Grade 8
West Salem Grade School, IL
*Patterned after Beans, Beans, Beans by Lucia and James L. Hymes Jr.

Boring as a White Wall

What if humans stop interacting with each other?
They would sit, and text.
People would watch TV some of the time,
Maybe play a video game or two,
Surf the internet, or listen to music. But only on headphones.
Occasionally someone dared to ask a question.
And. They. Would. Talk. Like. This.
When people got tired, they would sit and stare
At a wall in front of them not saying a word. Maybe lay down.
You would not hear a sigh, or a yawn.
The earth would be as silent as an empty room.
You would not hear a bam, or a boom
Because humans would stop interacting with each other.
They would eventually lose any facial expressions, and their ability to talk.
People would end up being breathing, unlively blocks
Sitting in a room full of people doing the same thing, like robots.
What if the word fell in silence.

Emily Wolniewicz, Grade 8
Thomas Middle School, IL

Picking a Pumpkin

We are on our way to Chatham,
We can guess where we are going.
We pull into the rocky road,
I hop out and look all around,
And say, "Look what I've found!"
The biggest pumpkin in the patch was like a whale in a school of fish.
My mom admits it's huge,
But then I look to the left and to my surprise,
I see the best pumpkin; all fat and wide.
I pick it up and we buy it.
Now I am as happy as a little boy on a roller coaster,
I wish they had pumpkins all year long.

Remington Roy, Grade 7
Rochester Jr High School, IL

Perfect So You Think

What if everything was perfect?
No separation between good and bad;
Everything would be equal.
Trying to find traits
To define right from wrong.
Nothing would be interesting
Like a dark and lonely world
Surrounds you.
No decision making;
Everything
Would be planned out
In your whole life.
Nothing to look forward to.
Just disappointment and soon…
Imperfection
What if everything wasn't perfect

Paul Tokar, Grade 8
Thomas Middle School, IL

The Big Test

I must do well on this test
The score on the last was not the best
If my grade is not better
My report card will show a bad letter
I am known to nap through class
But not today because I have to pass
I listened to my teacher
My pages of notes could not be sweeter
My dance shoes are at rest
I'm too busy studying for the test
My nose is stuck in my book
I have memorized all the notes I took
The day of the test is here
My mind going blank is what I fear
The test is in front of me
I know I will ace it. Just wait and see.

Amanda Pelnarsh, Grade 7
Immaculate Conception School, IL

Time Heals All Wounds

As tragedy strikes
Sorrow
Covers everything like a blanket
Forever smothering the fire that is
Happiness
Tick
Tock
Time stops for nothing
Neither *happiness* nor sorrow
Neither life nor death
Time
Slowly
Continues
Healing even the deepest wounds

Sean Frenzel, Grade 8
Thomas Middle School, IL

Ludicrous Libby

Click, clack, click, clack,
The sound of her little nails,
Ticking tiles triumphantly,
Slipping and sliding left to right,
Bounding in leaps with all her might,
Speaking all day and into the night,
She bounds like a bunny,
Flopping down like a frog,
She is a bird outside when it's sunny,
And eating as if she were a hog,
She is a little noise machine, and is funny,
She is such a little clown,
Oh boy, how I love that hound!

Kayla Madey, Grade 8
Liberty Jr High School, IL

Thanksgiving

We thanked the giving.
Turkeyed our plates,
cranberried the dressing,
hammed our faces,
fooded our gut, filling it to the max,
finally couching our bodies for a relax.
TV'ed our eyes,
while pumpkining the pies,
stomached the dessert.
Goodbyed the guest,
hello-ed sleep,
goodnighted that night.

Trenati Baker, Grade 8
Galileo Scholastic Academy, IL

Thankful

T hankful for a house and food
H aving my RC stuff
A lot of food on Thanksgiving
N ever stop caring
K ing of eating
S pending it with my family
G iving food to the people who need it
I nviting my friends over
V isiting my cousin's house
I will be good on Thanksgiving
N ever stop sharing
G obbling my food down

Alec Waugh, Grade 7
Hannah Beardsley Middle School, IL

Cold and Warm

Winter
Cold, white
Snowing, sledding, throwing
Grow, play, mow, riding
Summer

Dylan Jones, Grade 7
West Salem Grade School, IL

To Judge Another

Dearest child,
Do you not see what is above?
Do you not see, what others love?

Is it right
to judge another?
Just upon, their own skin color?

Do you realize
how you live?
That you take, instead of give?

So dearest child,
listen here.
Lean in close, lend me your ear.

I have a secret
to be told.
Share it with others, when you are old.

Many people
here today,
Judge, just like you may.

However dear, I must confess
I do not love you,
any less.

Alyssa Hamrick, Grade 7
Woodland Middle School, IL

Babysitting

Whenever I babysit,
As soon as I wake up,
Before I eat,
After I do my chores,
I am ready to go.

While my mom drives me,
As I listen to music,
Rather than homework,
Now the car stops,
I come out and go to the door.

As long as they are good,
Once they sleep,
Supposing they will,
Now that they are old enough,
I have no worries at all.

After I babysit,
Even though they are cute,
Wherever I am
While siblings fight,
I wish I said no when she asked me.

Sheradan Foster, Grade 8
Rochester Jr High School, IL

Mourning of the Timberland

I have fallen today.
I used to stand strong in the woods so tall,
My soul though fell to decay.

My leaves are to fray,
My bark is to thrall,
I have fallen today.

The sun's mighty ray
Glances down to recall
My soul though fell to decay.

The pow'r of the day
Has said to appall
I have fallen today.

My trunk goes to lay
Though once and for all
My soul though fell to decay.

A tree stands to stay
Its roots to go sprawl
I have fallen today.
My soul though fell to decay.

Katharine G. Ruegger, Grade 8
The Orchard School, IN

It Is…

Deadliest of the deadly,
appreciated and unfair,
feared yet protected,
sworn to be there.

Mindless and closed in,
something let off the chain,
curious you are and saunter
to the window of pain.

Nothing can hold it,
mighty the beastie is,
brilliant at the time,
not a void – an abyss.

But brilliance is horror,
and horror is true,
nothing is mentioned
but what you once thought you knew.

The time has come,
and you can't turn it back,
some might even say,
"It is…you've met your final match."

Nellie Haug, Grade 7
St Matthew School, IL

The Friend

I had a friend
Trustworthy comrade
Great soldier in battle
My 2nd in command

The day we were promoted
He showed his true colors
He was late for his meetings
He wasn't optimistic like he used to be

During our meetings he wrote lots of notes
There were notebooks full
He didn't drill his men like he should
His morale rotted his crew

One day he was on the phone
It wasn't the commander or home
As I listened in,
I heard all our secrets
He was a traitor

Jason Tilman, Grade 7
Rossville Alvin Elementary School, IL

Too Far Away

this isn't for publicity,
this isn't for the fame
something bad is happening
it's not longer just a game

we watch these things happening,
we wish we could help
but there's a little piece inside
saying we wouldn't make it out

the TV does no justice,
but it's happening just the same
civilians are going fast
terrorists are to blame

we are marines,
we are marines,
yet we're sitting in our platoon
wishing that these people,
wouldn't die so soon.

Ellea Schmidgall, Grade 8
Central Jr High School, IL

Trees

Wind howls through the night
the trees fight back with all their might.
Snow falls gently and trees are now bare,
their freezing branches cry in despair.
Sunlight shines through the black
the leaves of trees have now grown back.

Jenny Li, Grade 7
Dunlap Valley Middle School, IL

Which Way?

What way should I go?
Left or right
North or south
Where is the trail?
How do I know?
There is no map
or signs.
Nor a wind.
How do I know?

How do I know what way to go?

Caitlynn Long, Grade 8
Our Shepherd Lutheran School, IN

Running

Feel the wind
Going through your hair
See your teammates
Cheer and stare
The ground below
The sky so high
As you pass
The others by
Finally you're done
Accomplishment…
Along with fun

Taylor Jockisch, Grade 7
Dunlap Valley Middle School, IL

Baseball

"Tink, Tink!" The second and first,
Outfielders dying of thirst,
A bat sings hitting the ball,
Then soars like an eagle,
"Slam, tink,"
The runner sinks,
As he darts to first,
Ball like a missile,
"Bam, slam, crash, crinkle!"
Runners' safe,
Window broken.

Jaromy Birkner, Grade 8
Red Bud Elementary School, IL

Broken Pieces

Tears gathered like a rain storm,
Words hit me like a train,
They stabbed me like a knife.
Searching for a pulse line,
Praying it was fake.
The problem reached its peak,
I turned weak.
I couldn't speak,
I crumbled to pieces.

Cecelia Cowell, Grade 8
Red Bud Elementary School, IL

The Forgotten Heroes

A normal day,
Until I hear the news.
"A plane has crashed into the World Trade Center."
I rush to my locker.
And grab all my gear
And load up on the truck.
We arrive on the scene
The building is engulfed in flames.
We run inside.
And run up the stairwell.
To check every floor for survivors
I climb up the stairs,
As people run past me.
Then we get the news.
The other tower has also been hit.
We know it's only a matter of time.
Before the buildings collapse.

Matt Runyon, Grade 8
Central Jr High School, IL

A Brave Soldier

One aching day,
In a massive, majestic gymnasium,
In the town of New Lenox,
The girl's varsity basketball team
Was going for the gold.
One of the girls, Kay,
Was a brave soldier.
She went to do a lay-up,
and BAM!
Collapsed to the hard, wooden gym floor,
Both hands on her left knee,
Screaming as if she were in a horror movie.
The game paused,
People were frozen.
The girl's mom
Watched the college scholarship run away like a little puppy.

Antoinina Witkowski Albright, Grade 8
Liberty Jr High School, IL

Life

I'm misunderstood.
I stay in my hood.
You get me in trouble.
You are so crude.
Bright is your day,
and dark is my mood.
My day is so bad I hate this day,
while you in your yard just run and play,
but wait awhile and you will see,
all the good stuff will happen to me.
So good luck with your life mine isn't great,
but wait until your older and live in a crate.

Daniel Padgett, Grade 7
Rossville Alvin Elementary School, IL

The Battle of Us

The battle of us was the Civil War
About our nation that once broke apart
A war that strongly showed blood and gore
The battle of us was the Civil War
Brother versus brother was nothing to adore
This war, number one in deaths on the chart
The battle of us was the Civil War
About our nation that once broke apart

Logan Bundy, Grade 8
Northlawn Jr High School, IL

Where Do I Come From?

I am from a warmhearted household, with helping hands.
I am from a huge tree of close family.
I am from the exuberant cornfields that represent our state.
I am from the country, with liberty and justice for all.
I am from a world of peace and war.
I am from a galaxy that was unknown before.
I am from a universe still to be searched.
But most of all I am with the people I love.

Sasha Wilson, Grade 7
International School of Indiana, IN

Fall

The colorful leaves get blown in the air,
The autumn air is crisp and fair.
Raking and jumping in the leaves,
During fall we put on our pants and sleeves.
With fall brings Halloween,
You can be anything you want: A bee or even a queen.
Fall is the most beautiful season!

Katherine Perille, Grade 7
Our Lady of the Wayside School, IL

Friends

Friends are like fuel you need them to keep you going.
They stay with you until you're finished growing.
They are with you,
Through thick and thin.
And in the sun and in the rain.
No matter how big the fight,
You guys will always be all right.

Michaela Seders, Grade 8
Red Bud Elementary School, IL

My Mother

My mother's smile is soft and pleasant.
Her eyes are dark like black cherries hanging from a tree.
Her hair is like dark waves crashing against the shore.
Her skin is soft like clay and molded by a hug from me each day.
Her nails are long like the a conversation between me and her.
She lives in the covers of peace and eats prayer.
Her heart beats to the sound of a turning page.

Kelsey Randle, Grade 7
International School of Indiana, IN

Plant

The baby is growing into a child.
Her feet are growing into the soil.
She is drinking up water from her feet.
Her limbs reaching for the sun.
Here her house is giving her shade.
She is blooming into an adult.
She is shivering from the wind.
She dies after a harsh frost.
Then she came next spring.
Then it happened again.

Rachel Saunders, Grade 7
Concordia Lutheran School, IN

Basketball

B ouncing a basketball on the court
A nnouncing the starting line up
S hooting before the game
K ernels popping in the popcorn machine
E nding the season of 2011
T eam getting pumped before the game
B asketballs flying through the air
A ll the fans cheering
L oud chants and screams
L oud cheering from the cheerleaders

Bryce Anderson, Grade 7
Wethersfield Jr/Sr High School, IL

Christmas

It comes and goes every year.
I cannot wait, Christmas is near.
Because it's Jesus' birthday
We get together and celebrate.
Opening presents and showing care,
I know Jesus is everywhere.
Christmas is a holiday
So we should cherish it.
In the name of the Father,
Son, and the Holy Spirit.

Caleb Manzella, Grade 8
St Matthew School, IL

Fall

In the fall,
It can be a ball.
Outside the wind blows by
Making the leaves fly,
Chasing those leaves,
That blow in the breeze.
Jumping on the pile,
With a great big smile.
The wind whispers that winter is near,
This will be the last fall, until next year.

Haley Graham, Grade 7
Emmanuel-St Michael Lutheran School, IN

Different Planet

What if we were able to go to a different planet?
A planet where its entire surface was a barren wasteland,
Of only red and brown sand and dust that covered everything
And sharp mountains cut into the sky that was always dark,
Dust storms were as common as a shower of rain and water was barely existent.
The only thing living there was the howls of the wind
And the avalanches of the uncontrollable snow
That never seemed to stop falling from the tops of mountains.
As if all existence had vanished and time had stood still.
A place that is lonely and quiet, and the only voices that were left
Were the ones that had echoed from the people who had last lived there
What if this was our planet?

Drew D'Astice, Grade 8
Thomas Middle School, IL

The Escape

She looks into it,
She doesn't know why,
But she hates it.
Why must it mock her?
Why can't it just leave her alone?
She must get away,
So she starts to run.
She runs as far as she can go
into the darkness.
Finally she has escaped it.
But has she really escaped?
No, she has forgotten something
That the wise woman said.
She sighs,
Safe for now.
She rests awhile,
For she knows that soon,
She must run again.
Away from herself.

Kendra Escudero, Grade 8
A-C Central Middle School, IL

Freedom

I walk out of the door
Begging for more
Of what I lack
High on the rack

No one wants me to have it,
My parents, my friends,
And while they guard it,
Captivity never ends

As a teen girl with wants and needs
I'm not a child, just mud and seeds
I'm no weed, when I see them, I leave them
What I search for is Freedom
Sweet Freedom

Kayla Hawthorne, Grade 7
Merle Sidener Gifted Academy 359, IN

My Wintering

My boots are out
My scarf is purple
Blue gloves warm me
A green fuzzy hat

My runny nose
My eyes water too
Throbbing ear pain
My cold feet on floors

A big red sled
A tall white snowman
Green trees frozen
The rock solid pond

The lights are bright
The Christmas shopping
Silver bells ring
Angel ice sculptures

Lindsey Schmidt, Grade 8
Immaculate Conception School, IL

Fishing

The day looks fine
It's all mine
Why am I wasting my time?

Now I'm done wishin'
It's finally time
It's finally time for me to go fishin'.

Softly cast the bait
Sit and wait
Why do the fish seem to always be late?

I got the perfect fish
That was my wish
This will make a rather tasty dish.

Eli Gile, Grade 7
Immaculate Conception School, IL

Life Is a String
The long piece of course string
Smooth once started
With ends frayed and short
The knots twisted and disoriented

Going up,
Curling down,
Tangled in the wad
Going on for miles

Sudden moves swirl about.
Time stops and turns to watch
The knot, this horribly wretched blob,
Interrupted in mid-churn,

With the flash of a knife,
Severed the sorry sight
With a scream echoing into the night
Thrown into the brawl of blight
Jennifer Yeh, Grade 7
Galileo Scholastic Academy, IL

All I Am Asking For
All I am asking for is
peace to the Earth
food for the hungry
water for the thirsty

A guardian for a kid
warmth for the cold
shelter for the homeless

Clean for the human nature
health for the sick
money for the poor

Kindness for the mean
happy for the sad
love for the hate

All I am asking for is
for dreams to come true
Camille Adao, Grade 7
Galileo Scholastic Academy, IL

All Alone
Now it's just me all alone.
I don't need his help.
I'm good on my own.
It's far too over now.
There is no looking back.
I won't regret.
You crossed the line way too soon.
So now I say goodbye to you.
Tia Gramelspacher-Zehr, Grade 8
Jasper Middle School, IN

Big Hit
I yank up my socks,
step into the batter's box.
Wipe the sweat from my forehead,
see the players in red.
Take my stance,
give Coach a glance.
There's the pitch,
see the stitch.
"CRACK!"
It's heading way back.
Passed one, going two.
Run! Run! That ball flew!
Touched three, one more.
Now I have to try to score.
Hear the cheers,
home plate is near.
There's the throw,
like a rocket.
Dust and dirt puff up in the air,
Blue takes a look…
Safe!
Olivia Bievenue, Grade 8
Red Bud Elementary School, IL

Standing Still
9/11
Another day
in New York,
on the way to work.
The crowded sidewalk,
bright blue sky.
Suddenly hearing
a thundering sound.
Looking up to see
a plane.
Flying
very low.
Hearing a crash.
Broken glass,
Unbelievable screams; crying.
Staring at once was
two beautiful towers.
Now one falling.
One standing still.
Once perfect
Until.
Morgan Hobbs, Grade 8
Central Jr High School, IL

Sail
I wish I could sail away
To a far away land
Just be gone for a day
Only with you hand in hand
Olivia Loudermilk, Grade 7
West Salem Grade School, IL

Bull Riding
I hear the door shut close,
the angry, anxious bull waiting
to buck me off before the 8
seconds. I feel my legs shaking
furiously, just thinking what
dangers are willing to hit me.
My hands being squeezed by
the rope, hoping not to be
injured by the 2,000 pound
monster, with the deadly sharp
weapons called the horns.

When the door opens, I fly up in the air,
diving into the horns going through
my body feeling the pain and hearing
the crowd shouting to help me.
Oscar Munoz, Grade 7
Galileo Scholastic Academy, IL

Fam'ly
My helping hands
Hugging and supporting
They will adore me forever.
Loved ones

Parents
They understand
Generous and thoughtful
They are my dearest role models.
Wisdom

Siblings
Sister, brother
Texting and playing sports
They bring joy and happiness.
Smiling
Megan Davy, Grade 7
Immaculate Conception School, IL

Christmas
Christmas is the best time of year
You just better wish the roads are clear
Spending time with family
Is obviously better than candy
Waking up on Christmas morning
Even though the clothes are boring
I always love seeing the cookies eaten
And the hot coffee we have to sweeten
I remember when I got socks
Then I opened the X-box
Christmas is amazing
But then again I'm still craving
Those Christmas cookies
Christmas sure is the best time of the year.
Zach Stratton, Grade 7
Highland Hills Middle School, IN

The Best of Brothers

Brothers are here to support
And to always keep you on track
They will never let you go
And they will always have your back

When a boyfriend is lurking
They will likely turn them away
Thinking they are protecting
Not letting them lead you astray

When you feel down in the dumps
They will always be there for you
Giving you their attention
Like friends such as Piglet and Pooh

Brothers can be annoying
And really be a pain at times
But most of all I'm happy
To have such good friend to call mine
Maren Bashor, Grade 8
Immaculate Conception School, IL

Warriors of November

As Men disperse running to their team
The kickoff begins and there is no mercy
Going for it all everyone wants it
Every play going until the whistle is blown

Every play teammates got your back
If you mess with one you get the pack
Tenacious, Ferocious and Fearful
No one mess with them at all

Teams give them a run for their money
But nobody comes even close
There is no fun and games in November
Every complete game is always a nail-biter

When reaching for that brass ring
Finally until the last whistle is blown
Everybody will always remember
The Warriors of November
Ryan Niewinski, Grade 8
Immaculate Conception School, IL

Inside This Pizza

Inside this pizza
The pepperoni dance
Red sauce sings a melody
Strings of cheese all prance
A lonely mushroom plays guitar
Little sausages jump and run
The perky crust chats cheerfully
Who knew food could be this fun?
Margaret Nickerson, Grade 7
St. Pius X Catholic School, IN

The Woman I Call Sister

The woman I call sister
Is someone who is there
The person I call sister
Is someone who always cares.

The woman I call sister
Can make me smile when I'm blue
The woman I call sister
Is someone very true.

The woman I call sister
By choice, is my best friend
The woman I call sister
Will be there till the end.

The woman I call sister
Is the blessing from God above
The woman I call sister
Is the sister that I'll always love.
Kaylin Korte, Grade 8
Immaculate Conception School, IL

Night of the Nativity

The sleeping babe lays
In a manger full of hay
An angel choir sings
A few shepherd now waking

The shepherd arrive
Barring nothing but their lives
They bend on one knee
Praying to the savior baby

A star lights the sky
And it catches three kings' eyes
They come on camels
To worship Emmanuel

Kings bear three presents
For the child and his parents
The angels still sing
Of Christ our new born king
Kendra Thuente, Grade 8
Immaculate Conception School, IL

Mind

Inside this mind, little red people working.
Muscles creating.
Emotions jumping.
An empire of imagination and wisdom.
Cells dividing.
Thoughts are fighting.
I.Q. points growing like weeds.
A mystic vault cradling our lives.
Nicholas Huntine, Grade 7
St Pius X Catholic School, IN

Batter

I'm standing at the plate
Ready to bat
You might think I suck
Because I'm actually kind of fat
But don't mind that
I'm really good at this
Here is a little secret
I barely ever miss
When you stand at the plate
Your adrenaline's flowing
The pitcher winds up
My smirk is showing
When I hit the ball
It is out of my sight
Now you see the force of my might
The inning's now over
The sides were now switching
The coach now tells me
I am the one pitching
Zachary Belles, Grade 9
Yorkville High School, IL

Life

Life can easily lift you up,
And then after, knock you down.
I'm tired of it pulling me over,
Then pushing me around.

For when the storm has lifted,
It lifts my spirit as well,
And when it tumbles straight downhill,
It takes me right down with it.

But I've learned throughout my life
To enjoy myself a bit;
To have fun in the joy of the journey
Before I pout or cry;

To be brave; to stop and fight
Before I run and hide;
To just sit back and take in the view
And just enjoy the ride.
Megan Alms, Grade 8
Zionsville Middle School, IN

My Dog

I have a dog,
Her name is Daisy.
And, oh man, she is lazy!
But darling Daisy did do something.
She yawned and she stretched,
But alas,
She's back on the ground.
Daisy is such a lazy hound.
Journey Burdell, Grade 8
Red Bud Elementary School, IL

Parties

Music almost making you deaf.
Your favorite songs blasting throughout the air.
The house shaking.
Speakers echoing.
Walls vibrating.
Dancing.
Jumping up and down.
Throwing your hands all around.
Pitch black.
Except for the glowing black lights, and the blinding strobe lights.
Your friends laughing and having a ball.
Food spilled out all over the table.
Everybody drinking from the same liter of Pepsi.
More people pile in.
Everyone crowded, having a blast.
Now that's a party!

Dana Smosna, Grade 8
Thomas Middle School, IL

Self Portrait*

stern face
no one knows
what's going on
in his mind
he creates a masterpiece
in his head
before he creates it
on paper
the curvy lines of
the self portrait
and the starry night
unique style
only seen once
on his
expressionless face

Vanya Navratil, Grade 8
Thomas Middle School, IL
*Based on "Self Portrait" by Vincent Van Gogh

Dribble, Dribble

Pass to me, pass to me.
Dribble, dribble

Down the sideline I go.
Dribble, dribble

The ground is wet and soggy with mud splattering up.
Dribble, dribble

Towards the goal I go.
Dribble, dribble

Whack! I kick the ball with a mighty force
Swish into the net the ball goes.

Sami Sears, Grade 7
Highland Hills Middle School, IN

On My Mind

On my mind, every day.
On my mind, every day.
All the time, you're on my mind.

You're the clouds in the sky,
Watching over everyone you love;
Up above in your new home.

You're like a flower filled with love.
Look up above you see a dove.
That reminds me of how caring you were.

You got taken away into the sky, I believed it was a lie,
But then you were gone.

You're a diamond in the sky, you're like a million stars,
A special bright star running away.

Many more messages were meant for you.
You were as bright as the sun.
You're the flower that never gets down.
You were the buzzing bee that believed in hope.

On my mind, every day.
On my mind, every day.
All the time, you're on my mind.

Ree Brown, Grade 8
Liberty Jr High School, IL

Family Means Together

Families are for caring
Families are for loving
Families are for playing, laughing, and hugging
Family means together.

You play with your sister
You laugh with your brother
You always do the best for your father and mother
Family means together.

You try to make memories that will last forever
So when everyone moves out it will make your life better
Family means together.

Then when you get old and you find in a sack
A picture book that brings memories back
It's a picture of when you're all young
It's when all of the fun in your life begun
Family means together.

No matter what you do your family will always be there
Even if you're in trouble somewhere
Your family will make your life better because
Family means together.

Cate Thompson, Grade 7
Marquette Academy, IL

Mirror
A mirror is like a parallel dimension,
you see yourself but in a different way.
What if your reflection was a whole different person?
A person who lives in a different world,
along with everything else you see inside a mirror.
Would it be possible to trade places with the person in the mirror?
Could you take their place and they would take yours?
There are many mysteries that lie within a mirror.
Ethan Croke, Grade 8
Thomas Middle School, IL

Light
Light is what we all await
During the eternal hours of the night
For light to shine, we cannot wait
Light is what we all await
As light fades, comes the time we all hate
Darkness appears and light is nowhere in sight
Light is what we all await
During the eternal hours of the night
Rodrigo Lopez, Grade 8
Northlawn Jr High School, IL

Moonlight Worries
As she look up at the sky
She begin to wonder why
The moon seems to be too bright
But yet it brings a feeling of light
The moon brings her into a daze
Only if she could remember those days
But those days are gone
Nevertheless she questions how it went so wrong
Autumn Mockensturm, Grade 9
Prairie Heights Sr High School, IN

Cameron
His eyes are as brown as milk chocolate melting in the sun
His fur is as light brown grayish as well a Weimaraner
His loyalty is as loyal as a dog to his trainer
His smile is as happy as a giggling baby
His personality is as joyful as 2 kids in a candy store
His heart misses those in his life before
He lives with his kind and eats the sadness that haunts him
Jana Haschel, Grade 7
International School of Indiana, IN

Crystal Ball
Inside this crystal ball,
It's glittery and glorious,
The glitter floats up in one shake,
The clear shell stops you from escaping, trapping you inside,
The future surrounds you it's spontaneous and fun,
But remember this, you cannot tell anyone,
This is what's inside a crystal ball.
Mazzy Huser, Grade 7
St Pius X Catholic School, IN

What I Will Do
I'll take life as it is to come
which is too hard for some.
I won't dwell on the past,
and I won't go too fast.
I'll go with the flow;
just take it slow.
I'll live life for each day
because that's the only way.
I'll always have a blast
because each moment's one more than the last.
For right now
I'll tell you how
to succeed in life
through every strife.
Just do your best
and then the rest
will fall into place
in each and every case.
Brittany Pace, Grade 8
Holy Family Catholic School, IL

Prayers
What if there were no more diseases?
We wouldn't need antibiotics,
No picky children to hide from
Taking their medicine,
People living longer,
No more shots,
Everyone would walk around
With a smile on their faces,
Their lives as carefree
As a bird,
The prayers of suffering families
Would be answered,
The tissues would breathe
A sigh of relief,
The people suffering would finally be at peace,
No more suffering or pain,
What if we could find the answers
To our prayers?
Alyssa D'Onofrio, Grade 8
Thomas Middle School, IL

To Fall
To raking and jumping into leaves.
To eating broccoli soup when I am sick.
To borrowing your boyfriend's sweater.
To pulling back out the skinny jeans that fit so tight.
To pigging out on Thanksgiving.
To my dad stealing my Reese's Pieces from my candy bag.
To watching scary movies with Josie.
To camping in the dark.
To roasting marshmallows.
To me crying on Halloween when I see a clown.
Jessica Gutierrez, Grade 8
Peck Elementary School, IL

Snow
Snow
Slippery, shiny
Snow
Like a white blanket over the town.
Snow
Chilly and freezing,
Snow
Sledding down ginormous slopes,
Snow
Happiness lying on the ground,
Snow
Happiness laying on the ground.
Brenden Stellhorn, Grade 8
Red Bud Elementary School, IL

Conditional Thinking
Condition
Condition yourself for the journey
Condition yourself for the run
Condition yourself for life
Condition yourself for the little things
Like grades, beauty, and high school
Be yourself
Wear what you want
Live how you want to live
Let your true colors fly
Condition yourself
Chrissy Loera, Grade 8
St Marys School, IN

What Winter Left Behind
It's spring now
The chill
That nipped at noses and fingers
Has begun to vanish
The color
That was hidden by blankets of snow
Has begun to return
But spring
Forgot me
I'm still
Cold and gray
Claire Rorick, Grade 8
St Charles Borromeo School, IN

Spring
Tiny green stems
Peek out from their white blanket.
Small buds on the branches
Burst into new life.
Chill gives way to warm breezes.
Birds chirp in the trees.
The silvery world turns green again.
At last, Spring is here.
Matt Ernat, Grade 8
Sacred Heart School, IL

One Day
One day in class our teacher said
that we would be putting on the play "Sound of Music."

I decided to try out for the lead role
"Maria" and I got it.

We started with the song, "Climb Ev'ry Mountain"
and found out I can't sing.

After I got some tips we moved on to the song,
"The Lonely Goat Herd." I sounded much better.

After practice I went home and started to sing but I lost my voice —
maybe "Something Good" can come out of this.

On the day of the play I got really nervous and I told myself,
"I Have Confidence in Me."
I went out there and did the best I could.
McKenzie Meadows, Grade 7
Sacred Heart School, IL

Storm
Malevolent forces join together, to create this hazardous type of weather.
The wind starts to howl,
As autumn leaves brush against my ankles.
The faint sound of children, laughing, hollering,
As they retire to their safe homes.
Suddenly, a funnel appears.
Take cover! Take cover!
Boom! Crash! Whoop!
Lightning blisters through the sky.
The funnel grows,
Forming the ravenous tornado!
It eats up quaint, small towns.
Ripping, tearing,
Shredding, murdering.
Aftermath follows,
All is calm again,
Until, the rain visits us once again.
Aishwarya Palekar, Grade 8
Chiddix Junior High School, IL

Bullying
Bystanders need to stand up for the person being bullied
Understand that person personally
Love and care for them even if they're different
Let them know you're there to help them out
You know if just a few more people tried to stop bullying, you could help that person
In your own school bullying happens every day
Nobody knows what their life is outside of school
Go! Go help out whoever needs you, cause I'll be there when you need me.
Taylor Gleave, Grade 7
Concordia Lutheran School, IN

Camping

The fun summer nights
They flew out the window
The minutes, birds soaring free
Sitting still, surrounding smoke
While the flames warm the air
Roasting fluffy marshmallows
Like white daytime clouds
The dew-covered grass
Slipping between my toes
The moon shimmering on the black lake
Wood crackling like little fireworks
Raccoons moving smoothly under the moon
Soundly sleeping, softly snuggle
Our tents acting like shields against the wind
As the creepy creatures of the evening emerge
The night, a sleepy fellow
Awaits the dawn of day
A flower waiting for spring
Oh those fun summer nights

Ellie Paul, Grade 8
Liberty Jr High School, IL

Who Am I

Who am I
I am softhearted
This does not mean I'm a softy
But I am thoughtful and kind

Who am I
I am an athlete
This doesn't mean I am a jock
But I am respectful and a good sport

Who am I
I am a strong leader
This does not mean I'm bossy
But I am a good listener and I help guide others through challenges

Who am I
I am a son
This doesn't mean I am an only child
But I am a brother of a softhearted, athletic, and strong family

Keagan Sobol, Grade 7
Immaculate Conception School, IL

All About Me

All about me that's all I ever hear.
Through my eyes and through my ears.
People always think everything is about them
When most of the time it's not.
Stop thinking the world revolves around you.
You are on the earth so you are revolving with the earth
with everyone on it too.
So just stop thinking everything is about you and you only.

Zarria Moss, Grade 7
Pierce Middle School, IN

The Girl in Red Jeans

She walks down the street with a sway in her hips.
Swinging her arms and nodding her head.
Music in her ears, dog by her side.
Feeling the kiss of the wind.
Cars zoom by, people pass.
Keeping her head up high,
She walks on.
Down the hill, past the pond,
She walks on.
Pulling on the leash, plugging in her head phones,
She walks on.
She's the girl in red jeans.
Swinging her arms and nodding her head,
She walks down the street with a sway in her hips.
Music in her ears, dog by her side.
She walks on,
The girl in red jeans.

Madison Collins, Grade 9
Clay High School, IN

New Land

"Yesterday" I had a great idea
To set sail.

I told my friends to "Come Together"
To build a boat.

"Here Comes the Sun," I said
As we finished the boat.

I thought being at sea would be boring,
But "Something" is always happening.

We could only "Imagine"
What the new country would be like.

It was a long and painful week,
But I got through it with "A Little Help from My Friends."

Matt Leonard, Grade 7
Sacred Heart School, IL

Friends

They are honest, care and love you
they are there when you need them
they care for you like you care for them
you see them every day
Talk, text and laugh
I mean who doesn't share a laugh

It's nice to see their smile once or more a day

You don't even bother listening to them
because you know they will always be
your friends

Adareli Ojeda, Grade 8
Galileo Scholastic Academy, IL

My Little Secret

I have secrets, like everybody does.
Used to keep it hidden, with all that it was.
To make sure no one knows, that no one will,
Wonder about my past, my fears, and my thrills.
"What is this secret?" you probably ask.
Friendship will not reveal what I mask.
Could I hold it forever? Most likely not;
Be like me, if you did, you probably forgot.
Until that day comes, this secret is mine.
You will discover no clue, no hint, no sign.
All secrets, however, will come to an end,
Shared among others, or by texts that we send.
This secret is spilled, but not by thee.
Magic or persuasion hasn't coaxed it out of me.
With all things special, this secret is done.
Me, Myself, and I have hid clues since line one!

Michael Lin, Grade 9
Schaumburg High School, IL

Christmas Time

Christmas time is almost here
Time for snow and gifts is here
My mom will tell me I can sled to my hearts desire
As long as I don't set the house on fire
School is out you will hear shouts and glee
No more worries about getting a D
Time for friends and family has come
By the time you get home your hands will be numb
We get a big tree you get a small tree
We can get them both there isn't a fee
There will be snowballs flying in the air
Sooner or later you'll get one in your hair
I can see snowmen all across town
And if you listen closely a caroling sound
Christmas time is finally here
Hanukah too for all to hear

Patrick Connelly, Grade 7
St Matthew School, IL

Movie Theatre

The aroma of warm butter and popcorn
Preserved my thoughts
Room full of laughter and tears
Comedy and romance
Perceiving the emotions trapped in the dense air
The warmth of the seats comforted you
The darkness
Trapped you
The immense screens' lights
Beamed on the audiences' faces
The loud speakers enclose you
The movie
Is
A beauty

Lorena Murati, Grade 8
Thomas Middle School, IL

Ode

Ode to slalom skiing
as I put my wet foot into your slippery wet boot,
my foot wiggles and squirms as it slowly drops in the boot,
as I jump off the ski platform into the warm water,
I try to keep the skinny single ski under my body,
I put the nose of the ski directly in front of me,
I tightly grip the rope and hold on tight,
as I open my eyes and I'm on top of the water
crossing the wake one to another,
when I'm done I simply let go of the rope
and slowly sink back into the water.

Nathan Cripe, Grade 7
Stanley Clark School, IN

Christmastime

Christmas trees, sugar cookies, candy canes,
Santa Claus, hot chocolate, presents,
Sledding, snowmen, sparkling lights
Reindeer, mistletoe, gingerbread.
These things are fun at Christmastime.

But these things are important at Christmastime:
Wisemen on camels, a guiding star, joy to all,
Shepherds in the fields, peace on Earth,
Angel choirs, singing praise.
The baby in the manger — the birthday of Jesus.

Kami Rieck, Grade 7
Emmanuel-St Michael Lutheran School, IN

The Dark Night

Pitch black evening
Unknown noises in my head
Crows flying around in a perfect circle
Empty streets, no cars, no motor sounds…nothing
No one around to hold my hand and keep me safe
Broken street lights flickering on and off
I am all alone
The voices of the wind blowing through me
Cricket sound, sounds like a scary coo-coo clock, someone or
something going to pop out and scare me
I am all alone in the dark night.

Destiny Juarez, Grade 7
Galileo Scholastic Academy, IL

Purity

Light is not always pure,
As darkness is not always evil,
Both a blend,
A life,
A death,
A timeless agony where hate is chosen over love,
The realization of hate as its true form,
Love is the only purity,
And hate, the only evil.

Rebecca Velez, Grade 8
St Boniface Catholic School, IL

We Belong

We are two leaves
that float in the breeze.
We dance together,
we glide with ease.

We are two flowers
that reach for the sun.
We'll grow together
and die as one.

We are two waves
that ebb and flow.
We're one and another
moving to and fro.

We are two hearts
and one soul.
We are two halves
that make on whole.

We are two voices
that sing one song.
We are two lives
that together belong.

Kaela Joslin, Grade 9
Clay City High School, IL

The Hindrance of Dusk

The bairn of suns past,
Lies in wait of the dawning
Of yesterday's tears,
Enlightened of such dangers.

His ray, a hand to hold,
When the damnable oppress
My happiness,
My courage, my capability.

His smile, happens onto me as
The only sight I wish to see,
When the answer to my ailing wish
Lies within his comfort.

His warmth, as a touch,
Bestowed upon me
When the depth of this world,
Insinuates the contrary.

But, of most importance,
It is his very soul
That lies within you,
My light, my salvation.

Hannah Schroer, Grade 8
Central Jr High School, IL

Winter

I can't believe it's here
All the children cheer
Christmas feelings everywhere
I can't believe it's here

Christmas bells ring and ding
Cold snow starts to fall
Santa Clause will be here soon
I can't believe it's here

Snowmen are being built
Snow looks like diamonds
Silently, sparkling, falling
I can't believe it's here

I hope it never ends
I love this feeling
Of the cold breeze all around
I can't believe it's here!

Julia Cutler, Grade 8
Immaculate Conception School, IL

Christmas Day Surprises

I awake with a jolt
Out of my bed I do bolt
As I started to pace
A smile appears on my face

I run to my brother
After I wake my mother
We quickly run downstairs
Almost tripping on the stairs

We see the wrapped presents
Bought by our lovely parents
Christmas day means great fun
Out into the snow I run

To go make an angel
Cold hearts I do untangle
Christmas joy I do bring
To my family I do cling

Emma Dingbaum, Grade 8
Immaculate Conception School, IL

The Pitcher

A fall day with a chilly wind
Wind whipping at your face
You grip the ball and get your sign
Bring the glove up and start your motion
Let it fly.
The batter takes a mighty swing
But a change up always gets to the glove
with a POP!

Jonah Rumbold, Grade 8
Bethel Lutheran School, IL

Boy Scout Popcorn Delivery

Putting on my uniform
Neckerchief around my neck
Red Radio Flyer wagon full of popcorn
Unbelievable butter, butter light
Cheese lovers, chocolate lovers
Popping corn, kettle corn
Looking over the order form
Door to door to door
Down the street
Around the neighborhood
Ringing doorbells
Excited dogs
Hoping they are home
Red wagon getting lighter
Happy customers
Money for my troop
Thank you.

Tom Brya, Grade 7
St Matthew School, IL

Fate, What It Means to Me!

Fate is waiting at your door,
To show you, your dreams and more.

Come willingly to meet your fate,
Don't close your eyes, it might be too late.

Fate is the twinkle that's in your eyes,
Fate is the color of your cries.

Fate is the wonder in your voice,
Fate is the perfection of your choice.

Fate is important to one and all,
Just stay strong so you won't fall.

Sing a song, and dance along,
Fate means everything.

Taylor Davis, Grade 7
Dunlap Valley Middle School, IL

Thankful

I'm thankful for my loving family
I'm thankful for my life
I'm thankful for being in school
I'm thankful for being in soccer
I'm thankful for the food I eat
I'm thankful for the friends I have
I'm thankful for the electronics I have
I'm thankful to be able to go to Spain
I'm thankful for having freedom
I'm thankful to have rights
I'm thankful to have a nice home
I'm thankful to be alive

Dominik Chece, Grade 7
Hannah Beardsley Middle School, IL

Count the Stars

I walk down the old dirt road, that leads me to my past.
I was never alone, but those days didn't last.
Paint a picture with my tears,
Then dry it with the rain.
Count the stars 1000 times,
Before they fade away.
Lead me to the ocean,
Where the waves sing a lullaby.
Count the stars forever,
Before they say goodbye.
I whisper in the darkness, crying to the night.
Home lays far behind me, in a different life.
Take me to the edge of earth,
Toward nothing and beyond.
Count the stars an eternity,
Before the break of dawn.
Dance with me till twilight,
In a forest far away.
Count the stars with me,
For forever and a day.

Olivia Buck, Grade 7
Center Grove Middle School, IN

Practice

Tuning my guitar,
like winding up a clock,
I wait and start to practice.
The drum sticks count off,
tic, tic, tic, tic.

Chord after chord,
sliding my fingers up and down the rough-edged strings.
I mess up and I need to start over,
I stop for a moment then start again.

I get past where I messed up,
but I fear it could happen again.
I wonder how to change the song,
and make it the best I can.

I practice, practice, practice,
until my hands are red,
and if I keep on going,
I feel like I'll be dead.

Eric Adamany, Grade 7
Madison Jr High School, IL

Ocean Paradise

Reflection of the moon almost blinding at the sight.
You can hear the crash of the waves.
Swoosh!
Glimmering like stars in the night sky.
Not a single soul in sight.
The ocean is quite beautiful at night.

Mady Brown, Grade 7
Highland Hills Middle School, IN

My World*

This is my hideaway this tree this sky
The world all around it I love this place
Where I can feel free to be myself
Away from the world
And the rest of its people
I can run away from my problems here
And create my own world
In these branches
I don't have to worry about rules
Or what other people think
Or any of my issues
When I am here I can step away from all of that
Some don't understand
Why be up there with the bark and the leaves
But I feel free here
Among the strong sturdy branches
I feel comfortable and safe and protected
I like to get away
And be with the things that I love most
Where I don't have to be or do anything I
Don't want to because I belong here

Fiona Collins, Grade 8
Thomas Middle School, IL
Based upon "Sky Tree" by Thomas Locke

Floor 29

I was in the tower.
The tower that fell down.
I will never forget that day.
All the screams and all the cries.
The plane crashed right above me.
Blazing flames came roaring.
I ran to the exit.
Everyone crowds around.
Thank you to the firefighters that saved all our lives.
Once I got out I started heading home.
To tell my family that I loved them.
I took one last look at the tower where I worked.
And saw the tower fall down.

Elizabeth Peterson, Grade 8
Central Jr High School, IL

Basketball

Boom! Goes the dribbling of the ball.
A lot of players are tall
But some are small.
I feel the ball in my hands;
I see it with my eyes.
It's round and small
Orange and black
Lay-up,
Free throw,
Whatever you know
That is a round, orange, and black basketball.

Kaleigh Johnston, Grade 8
Red Bud Elementary School, IL

Nature's Diamond

Snowflakes so small and perfect
Glistening like the lights of a Christmas tree
Each one different and unique
Delicate patterns and designs magical in their mysterious ways
So perfect they hide from the judgment of human eyes
Melting so fast even a microscope can't catch
The full extent of their mystical essence
A snowy jewel come to say:
"There is hope, there is beauty
And when it comes your way
See it not as something cold and unimportant
But as a sign, life will go on."

Mersadies Pierce, Grade 9
Lincoln Sr High School, IN

Tiger's Quest

There was a quest.
That quest involved a tiger,
That tiger involved a girl,
And that girl involved powers.
Those powers were Lightning and Love.
That quest tested courage, bravery, and love.
The quest was treacherous, violent, and deceiving.
The quest decided what was right and also what was wrong.
That quest was love.
That quest was humanity.
That quest is life.
That quest is a Tiger's Quest.

Kaylee Davis, Grade 7
Henryville Jr/Sr High School, IN

Zip Lining

I just kept going, and going, and going,
It was like it was never going to end,
I was soaring across the galaxy,
The sky was the most pure blue I had ever seen,
And the clouds,
Oh the clouds were made of cotton balls,
Big, fluffy and white
When I looked down,
my heart skipped a beat,
I was up so high!
Blowing in the wind
The most peaceful thing on earth, zip lining

Helen Moran, Grade 7
International School of Indiana, IN

Paper

White: crisp, like a juicy apple I want to bite into
Untouched, like uncharted land waiting for me to explore
A chance to do something magnificent; a canvas for my mind
Swiftly moving my pencil; composing my work
An opportunity to do something amazing

Abigail Martin, Grade 8
David L Rahn Elementary School, IL

Winter

Air so cold
Outside white as a blanket
The great warmth inside like a bear hugging you
Snowflakes coming down one by one
Sunlight melting my joy

White angels all over my yard
Pressing my face against the window
Feeling the coldness on my cheek
Tongues sticking to the poles
Realizing it isn't summer anymore it's
Winter instead

Hot chocolate running down my throat
Chapped lips from the cold air
Sledding down the hills with so much excitement
Slipped on ice
Wow that cracked my back
Winter Wonderland is all around me
We end the night by having a Winter Wonderland dream

Anneliese Daley, Grade 7
Galileo Scholastic Academy, IL

Angel Cat

Sitting in grass, fur blowing in breeze,
Dust tickles my nose, I sneeze.
A hawk cries above me,
What would it be like to fly free?
Suddenly, a strange feeling on my back,
A sudden pain, like I was given a whack,
When it was almost gone,
I thought, "My peace has come."
Then a strange sensation, kind of tough,
A light something I couldn't shake off,
I looked behind me, and almost cried,
There, on my back were great white wings, stretched wide!
Then I gave a great heave,
I was up in the air, free, free!
Gliding and flying in the air,
I am carefree and slicing the air,
Who am I, you might ask?
I am the Angel Cat,
That is me,
That is me.

Kathleen Boelens, Grade 7
Bethel Lutheran School, IL

Best Place

I see palm trees and flowers and stores
I hear people talking, laughing, and screaming
I feel the sun, the cool breeze, on my face, I feel relaxed and calm
I taste everything while I'm there, sweet, salty, grilled you name it
I smell all of the restaurant's food, aromas in the air

Karrington Davis, Grade 7
Pierce Middle School, IN

Invisible Boy

He sits and he waits
even though he doesn't know
what he's waiting for.

DaiQuan Ford, Grade 7
Pierce Middle School, IN

Sun

The sun kisses me
The rain pelts madness at me
The wind dries me off

Delshaun Garner, Grade 7
Pierce Middle School, IN

Tweeting Turtle Doves

The pancakes were seized
By two tweeting turtle doves
Cawing victory

Heather Junge, Grade 8
Red Bud Elementary School, IL

A Fall Day

The long breezes blow
The leaves are changing color
Then the leaves they fall.

Brianna Henry, Grade 7
Concordia Lutheran School, IN

Wind

Wind, softly blowing
Lightly tickling my ear
Whispering softly.

Alizjah Crockett, Grade 7
Wethersfield Jr/Sr High School, IL

Stork

The majestic stork
Standing on the fragile branch
With clean white feathers

Jonathan Crummy, Grade 8
Thomas Middle School, IL

Mountain

Snow-covered rigid peaks
the kings of the land looking
on the green prairie.

Connor Burhop, Grade 8
Thomas Middle School, IL

A Summer Day

As the wind blew by
The clouds danced across the sky
While the sun rose high.

Jada Kirby, Grade 7
Dunlap Valley Middle School, IL

Dolphins

Leaping in the distance,
gone with a splash,
tails whipping through the air like a fan on a sweltering, summer day.
They whistle, warble, and wheeze,
backs gleaming with minuscule droplets of water,
glossier than any fragment of glass can be.
Their mouths have a crooked grin,
like gossipers with valuable secrets they can't wait to tell.

Together they dive,
plunging into the world below,
swimming swifter than a plane taking off for flight
in the deep and distant depths.
Schools of fish, anemone, and crabs,
show that life is a bustling phenomenon.

Coming back up,
they break through the lucid, blue surface,
rippling the water like creases on crinkled paper,
and shattering the reflection of the sunset.
But they don't care,
for together they are invincible and bound with love.
That is all that matters.

Julie Park, Grade 7
Madison Jr. High School, IL

A Better Life

A hungry cat with purring kittens lives under a house alone.
There are unwanted dogs running in the streets or mistreated at home.
This doesn't seem fair and this just isn't right.
They want a better life.

They may not be perfect or of pure breed.
One thing in common is that they all have needs.
A warm place to stay and enough food to eat.
They need a better life.

They are like babies and need to be cared for and loved.
We all were created by God above.
They want someone to be their hero and to give them a chance.
Homeless animals deserve a better life.

Savannah Conrad, Grade 7
Highland Hills Middle School, IN

Homework

You could board the QE 2,
And sail across the ocean blue,
I'd still be stuck on problem number 2.
You could trek over the whole Swiss Alps,
I'd be sitting at my desk, trying to find a rhyme for scalps.
You'd find a way to make the Titanic function,
I wouldn't yet know the difference between convection and a conduction.
Homework takes up all of my time,
Right down to this very line.

Mary LeClerc, Grade 7
International School of Indiana, IN

What Would It Be Like?

Don't you wonder?
What would it be like to fly?
To soar carefree through the wind
What would it be like to be rich?
To have your wish list completely fulfilled every year
What would it be like to rule the world?
Everything you say, is law
What would it be like to be beautiful?
All eyes following you with your every step
What would it be like to have a true friend?
No matter how far you are you will always be close
What would it be like to find true love?
To have someone to live for and someone to die for
What would it be like to run away?
To turn your back on everything and everyone
What would it be like to be free?
All burdens and worries…gone
What would it be like to give happiness?
What would it be like to finally be happy?
To truly smile
I wonder…what it would be like…to die

Muqaddas Farooqi, Grade 7
Stratford Middle School, IL

Lying

To lie or not to lie,
That is the question.
To lie and escape punishment,
Or speak truly and gain trust.
When you lie there is no twinkle in the eye, yet
When you speak truly you speak fully.
So when the time comes decide very carefully.
For the consequence may be larger if you lie,
But if you do, you should be sly.
If you speak truly you may have a lesser consequence,
Because you have more sense
To tell the truth rather than lying.

Keagan Finkenbine, Grade 7
Dunlap Valley Middle School, IL

Winter

Winter is my favorite of all the seasons
There are lots of things I like about winter
Christmas is just one of the reasons
Making snowmen in the cold
Rolling up snow balls to be thrown
And hearing the Christmas stories of long ago
Drinking hot chocolate by the fire
Hanging up the stockings on the wall
While watching the Christmas tree being built higher and higher
Decorating the beautiful tree
Hanging ornaments here and there
You see Christmas isn't just about you and me
It's about how the Lord and savior came to be

Autumn Reed, Grade 8
Emmanuel-St Michael Lutheran School, IN

What Can I Say I'm Just Being Me!

People say I play too much
What can I say I'm just being me
People say I talk too much
Well I'm just me
Some say I'm not who they want me to be
Well what can I say I am me
You don't like it and you leave
I'm not changing me for anybody
Accept me don't knock my style
Don't hate on my flow
You don't like it oh well
I am told I'm not good enough but look I am doing just fine
I am not accepted well guess what
What can I say I'm just me.
Nobody else not that I would want to be
People tell me I'm their everything
I'm adorable
Hey I like it
What can I say just being me!

Robyn Gary, Grade 8
Young Women's Leadership Charter School, IL

The 25th of December

Of all
the many days of the year,
Christmas is full of cheer.
All of the sights are so very bright,
Strung all with lights.
The loud music rings
That will soon bring happiness and joy to all.
Rather it is the snow so cold
That feels so very bold and will give you that Christmastime feel.
Or it is that special gift
That will make you shift that glum frown upside down.
The festive taste of the food, including the pie,
Will make you want to sigh.
The special holiday that only comes once per year,
Let it be filled with great amounts of cheer to end the year
On a great note
Because of this
holiday poem
I just wrote.

Haley Sutton, Grade 8
Daleville High School, IN

Inside a Dream

Inside a dream,
It's full of knowledge with stories untold
Feeling ready to tell its tales to the young and old
With evil villains that haunt your sleep
And heroes that render their defeat
Fairy tales, romance, action and memories
Wishes, magic and all that is shimmery
Inside a dream.

Maura Clark, Grade 7
St Pius X Catholic School, IN

Sizzle

Fire
Starting, Sparking
Hot, Colorful, Blazing
Smoke, Wood, Hose, Bubbles
Cool, Clear, Damp
Absorbing, Soothing
Water

Travis James Phelps, Grade 8
Northlawn Jr High School, IL

Issue

S uicide is an
U gly act
I ncident that is major due to many things
C oncern for many people
I nappropriate way to end life
D eath takes place
E vil way to die

Josephana Ma, Grade 7
Concordia Lutheran School, IN

Sad Stick Man

Up and down the road alone,
He sees no one's face but his own.
He hopes for something new to come along,
But when nothing amazing pops up in life,
He sings a sad and mournful song.
This man has no fun or risk,
And wishes for the end of this.

Luke Smith, Grade 7
Dunlap Valley Middle School, IL

Brownie Apology

I am sorry,
I ate the last brownie,
You were probably saving for dessert,
It was so good,
And so chocolatey
I hope you can forgive me...
And maybe bake some more

Katie Archey, Grade 7
Rochester Jr High School, IL

Nature's Love

Snow so white.
Trees so green.
I love the way he looks at me.
I close my eyes,
I feel it's a dream.
But I awake to see
It's reality.

Daniela Ortiz, Grade 7
Galileo Scholastic Academy, IL

Like a Puzzle

Before we were born, we were two pieces to a puzzle
God squished us together, and it was a perfect fit
We never had to go a second without someone to call a best friend
We fill in each other's gaps, and make each other's rough edges seem smoother
She makes me happy, and could make me sad, but that only means that I love her
She supports and understands me better than anyone
Whenever we talk about our futures, we are always a part of each other's
We are like an Oreo, as close as a sandwich, but with the sweetness of a cookie
She makes me feel at ease, and always has some way to help when I have a problem
I never have any doubts when I am with her
She is a wave of relief, and a crackling fire of warmth
She always has a hand to lend, and will always be my best friend
She always has a way to make everything fun
She is one of the best things God gave me
She will always be the key piece of my life's puzzle
She is my twin sister, and best friend

Anna Lowney, Grade 7
Highland Hills Middle School, IN

A Night at the Opera*

A large elegant chandelier dangles above hundreds of heads focused on the stage.
The soprano's aria echoes into the crowded theatre.
Chills run through my body as I sit at the edge of my velvet seat in awe.
The spotlight shines on the soprano as she proudly showcases her outstanding talent.
I look up at the ceiling painted so detailed and beautifully.
Everything is so peaceful, so lively.
The orchestra plays a breathtaking melody as the soprano walks off the stage.
Gold lines the stage.
Along with the rest of the auditorium.
The crimson curtains close and I realize the show has come to an end.
I stand up and clap as the curtains reopen for a curtain call.
The performers receive a standing ovation.
Bravo!
Everyone calls out as the curtains slowly close again.
As I walk out of the house, I know this is how I'll live my life.

Jayne Diliberto, Grade 8
Thomas Middle School, IL
*Based upon "Wheeler Opera House" by Red Grooms

Friendship Is Like an Apple

Just like an apple you need to peel away a friendship.
You will learn their inside jokes, favorite things to do
And how to turn "each other's frowns upside down."
You can sometimes have a green Granny Smith moment,
Where friends are sour and get in fights.
Other times you might have a Golden Delicious moment,
They have a thin skin and a juicy texture,
Friends can be shy at first but deep down inside they have a heart of gold.
Most times you have the greatest of all a Red Delicious
Which is the most famous apple.
It is known for being
Sweet tart and crisp.
Just like a friendship, that will last a lifetime!

Madelyn Baboian, Grade 8
Thomas Middle School, IL

Thanksgiving Break

On Thanksgiving, we sat around,
Eating like a pig
All talking to our family
My cousins,
Driving me insane
Surrounded by dozens,
We started playing games
On this beautiful Thanksgiving Day
Mackenzie Kaiser, Grade 7
Highland Hills Middle School, IN

Doors

There are many doors awaiting me
They are portals
To either dread or success
They lead me
To a path
A path in which
My future
Anticipates…
Arlind Murati, Grade 8
Thomas Middle School, IL

I Dreamed a Dream

I dreamed a dream
Of what love should be
Just like a flowing stream
I dreamed a dream
Of what love should be
And someday would find me
I dreamed a dream
Of what love should be
Elish McCann, Grade 8
Northlawn Jr High School, IL

Nightfall

As light fades to night
Others become a misty shadow
I start to fill with fright
As light fades to night
I begin to lose sight
I can see only what my eyes allow
As light fades to night
Others become a misty shadow
Brandon Delaney, Grade 8
Northlawn Jr High School, IL

Water

Drip-drop, drip-drop rain is falling
Bam! Bam! Bam! Rain is pouring
Drip-drop, drip-drop
Rain is slowing down.
Slowly flowing down the hill,
Quietly down the hill.
Jason Chausse, Grade 8
Red Bud Elementary School, IL

Seashell Shore

When I was younger, I gathered seashells
Enormous ones, tiny ones, all sorts
The crystal white *sparkled* from the rays of the sun
White reflections *shot up* from the water
My favorite sound is hearing the waves *crash* into the sand

When I was younger, I would build
The most incredible sand castles
I would spend hours on end
Sculpting, digging, and shaping it
And once I'm done I lay down inside
And fall asleep to the peaceful calming noises like heaven

When I was younger, I tasted salt water in my mouth like a peanut
I inspected each shell carefully with my naked eye
The ridges remind me of potato chips
The salty and sweet taste in every bite
Just like the *bubbly* salt water
The white seagulls land next to my kingdom
I *burst* out sprinting, knocking down my beautiful creation for cover
Disappearing into the sunset is like running into a movie scenery
Delaney Parker, Grade 8
Thomas Middle School, IL

A Lost Idea

Crumple, throw. Crumple, throw,
Another idea tossed out a window,
And hitting the trash can, flies on the floor,
A lost idea has just been lost behind a door.
Maybe a better thought was found there,
Or maybe a blank wall has gone up in despair.
Defeated, balled up pieces of paper hit the wall
And crinkle to the floor, just an idea; that is all.
Maybe that paper deserved some sort of second try,
For more in that paper, more paths do lie.
That half-erased, torn drawing could be something new,
That half-written poem could be something you rue.
Not all is not gone, so just take a look,
Hey, this poem was a lost idea, and now I'm submitting it in a poetry book.
Emma Goddard, Grade 8
Bethel Lutheran School, IL

Friends

If there is one thing I can't live without, it would be my friends.
They're with me when I laugh and pout; in trouble they're here to defend.
When the tough gets going, they're right by my side; they make me feel at home.
From coast to coast, hallway to hallway, I know I'm never alone.
Though busy schedules and tempting distractions try to keep us apart,
We've stayed strong together and even when we fight, we make up with a fresh start.
I can't even name all the movies we've seen, or fun weekend times we've spent.
Realizing that someday they won't be here turns me into a wreck.
So I savor every moment we cherish together and always keep them in check.
I just want to say thanks for being in my life, all you dear friends of mine,
I love you more than you'll ever know and you'll always be worth my time.
Ashley Wax, Grade 8
St Matthew School, IL

Running

Bang!
The shotgun's loud voice,
Piercing my ear,
Commanding my feet to run.
I fall into the rhythm as easily as
Slipping under the veil of water in a pool.
Left, right, one, two,
Listen to the beat of the track.

The rubber is hardening before my very eyes
Pounding on my soles, filling my legs with fatigue.
Jumping each hurdle is climbing a mountain;
The effort drains me.
But I keep on running
For what else is there for me to hold onto?

My feet are no longer feet.
They are wings — flying, gliding,
Clearing each hurdle as if
They were only stair steps
Carrying me higher and higher,
Into the pale, bittersweet sky
And over the finish line.

Elisa Jensen, Grade 7
Dunlap Valley Middle School, IL

I'm Thinking…

I'm thinking of two words.
One might have minutes or seconds, too,
but that's not what I'm after.
Take another clue.
They have you and me together,
always side by side.
I'll be there forever;
in me you can confide.

Can you tell what I'm thinking?

Next, comes a small word.
It is used often, and I just used it again.
Finally, this word tells about a long, long time.
Forever and ever,
oh, I did it again.

Can you tell what I'm thinking?

You've had your clues so now it's time,
to unravel this confusing rhyme.

I'm thinking: our friendship is forever!

Andria Pace, Grade 8
Holy Family Catholic School, IL

Victory Is Sweet

I'm oh so very sorry I won,
Victory was sweet.
Too bad you were embarrassed,
When you thought I'd taste your dust.

Luckily for me, you won't run the race next time.
I guess you'll be done for the season.
At least you can watch me win again,
When I run 1600 race.

Unfortunately, you finished five seconds after me,
You should've pushed yourself to do your best.
I'm sorry you lost your race,
Hopefully you'll try again another time.

Abby Reichen, Grade 8
Rochester Jr High School, IL

Summer

There is a time once per year
Where the children run free
And the sun is near
Where we are away from the horrors of school
Where you have no fear
You can run and scream
As the school year nears
You can streamline through the pool
As you watch the day disappear
You can bask in the sun
Or laugh and sing, for that's all you hear
These are the sounds of summer
The next thing we know, it will be a brand new year
With pencils and papers and frowns on the faces.

Sam Spina, Grade 8
Galileo Scholastic Academy, IL

A War

War is an awful and
Disruptive disaster,
Many people lose their families
And their lives,
You are called and soon are holding a gun
And fighting because two countries just can't get along
Every night you lay in the wet hole you dig
Hoping this nightmare would come to an end.
Thinking every day how stupid you had to be
Just to join the army
To look cool in front of your friend,
That is if you ever see them again.
Every night you write letters
Hoping a few words will make it better

Antoni Lipski, Grade 7
Galileo Scholastic Academy, IL

Intruder in the Night

It was a dark, stormy, and frightful night.
All of sudden, there was a noise that gave me a fright!
BOOM! SNAP! CRASH! BANG!
I got out of bed, my heart at a pang.
I grabbed a flashlight and looked around.
I found nothing, but heard a loud POUND!.
From my closet, I brought out a baseball bat,
only to find that the noises were from my cat.

Jacob Taylor, Grade 7
Highland Hills Middle School, IN

Fire Storm

The trees of which there are many
Cedars, Oak, Redwood, Maple, Evergreens
All with ember flames leaping overhead
The glow of which can be seen for miles
Sparks like millions of fireflies float
Consuming everything in its wake
There is still hope for the forest
Millions of dots in a black and barren landscape.

Donovan Cantrell, Grade 8
St Thomas the Apostle Elementary School, IL

Socks

When I don't find mine I steal from my sister.
The warmth of the sun tucked neatly in my drawer.
Keeping my feet from getting blisters.
When I come from school they end up on the floor.
They smell like Swiss cheese warm in the sun.
With holes to match as if mice have been here.
The colors are bright, cheery, and fun.
And soon will be hung hoping Santa is near.

Claire Copenhaver, Grade 7
Highland Hills Middle School, IN

Life's Intention

If you fall down,
bring yourself up.
Never say never, even when you're not so clever.
We all make mistakes,
but we can't act like fakes.
Don't give up,
and don't give in.
And always be a great friend.

Miranda Sellers, Grade 8
Gifford Grade School, IL

My Favorite Monument

S uper huge monument
P haraoh built this
H uge enough to make the Eiffel Tower cry
I nvincible to all nature's attacks
N ever goes away
X -rays show it made of rock

Nikolas Gonzalez, Grade 8
DeMotte Christian School, IN

Thunder Ball

The ball is thunder,
As it claps every time it rebounds off the floor.
If it is swiped from under,
The crowd will make a triumphant roar!
She drives to the hoop,
Eyes stuck to the rim.
The ball goes through the net,
As they make the win!

Madelyn Weber, Grade 7
Highland Hills Middle School, IN

Chocolate

Unwrap me
Taste me, Feel me
I will dance on your tongue, Taste me, Feel me
I wait for you
You wait for me
GO ON, You know you want to.
Oh hello, I see you looking at me, GO ON
Unwrap me

Eloise Richardson, Grade 7
International School of Indiana, IN

Weather

Summer, winter, fall, and spring
This is what the weather will bring.
Rain, hail, snow, and sleet
All of these fall to our feet.
Windy, cloudy, foggy, and sunny
The weather changes so fast that it's not funny.
What will the weather be today?
I don't think anyone can say.

Carson Banghart, Grade 8
St Matthew School, IL

White Snow

The snow is very white!
How white is the snow tonight?
As ivory as a heaping bowl of vanilla ice cream,
With huge caramel swirls that I eat in my dream.
Oh! How the snow falls so fast,
Like NASCAR #8 zipping past.
The frosted mounds pile up by the hour,
That one there is the Eiffel Tower!

Lucas Hertle, Grade 7
Highland Hills Middle School, IN

A Goal

I see a ball
It's black and white
It flies through the air
Like a bird in flight
It only lies still
Past the goalie's will

Luccas Greco, Grade 9
Schaumburg High School, IL

Music World

It's a new world right before my eyes
Something magical and unexplainable, I can't believe it.
It's so real and it never lies,
Always there, explaining every different feeling I have bit by bit

Roses are red
Violets are blue
Oh how I love it
How about you?

Headphones on and I'm set to go again
To the world of music, the real world ends
Imagining how it would be like if it were real,
It would be awesome, is how I feel.
You might just call it sounds
Or sentences with verbs and nouns,
But its more than that.
It's my Music World.

James Gaytan, Grade 7
Galileo Scholastic Academy, IL

Christmas

Only nine days left, it's almost here.
I can hardly help but cheer,
but before then I have to shop for presents to give my mom and pop.
"Can I decorate the tree?"
I ask my mom with glee.
I can just hardly wait.
I really want to decorate!
The week went by in a haze, now there are only two more days.
Yesterday some carolers came knocking,
and today I have to hang my stocking.
It's Christmas Eve,
so now we leave
to go to church.
We learn how they did search.
It's Jesus' birthday!
Let's shout hurray!
So Merry Christmas one and all,
I hope you all have a ball.

Breanne Mason, Grade 8
Bethel Lutheran School, IL

Summer Days

When summer comes around
It's time to play around with friends
Waking up to the sound of birds chirping
Parents head off to work
Going outside to laugh and play
That's a way to spend a wonderful day

Feeling sweaty and very hot
Jumping in the pool would surely hit the spot
Wearing flip flops, bathing suits, and eating ice cream
Feels better than a dream

When the stars and the moon begin to show
My energy level starts to go down
Time to go to bed and get some sleep
As I lay in bed I start to count sheep
Excited for tomorrow waiting for the day to come
It's another summer day filled with fun and joy

Carmen Mora, Grade 7
Galileo Scholastic Academy, IL

Ode to Halloween

The cool breeze chills my hands,
Oh the dark night!
Different doorbells ring in my ears,
The cheerful chirps delight.
The smell of candy wafts into my nose,
Sweet victory at last!
Rhythmic stomps of feet,
Sound off like horses.
The shadows from moonlight are cast.
I run home dying to open my treats,
The sweets crackle in their wrappers,
Let me out! They say
Chocolate slowly melts inside my mouth
Like a warm, sweet, puddle of goo
Wafers crunch like dead leaves on the ground.
Hello cavities and sugar rush
Halloween only comes once a year,
So I have to make it last!

Lizzy Olmsted, Grade 8
Rochester Jr High School, IL

Rainbow Drops

Drip! Drop!
Plip! Plop!
Rain rushing down roads and rivers.
A runt ray of radiant sunshine
Slips through the sheet of white rain.
Striking every drop.
Creating color.
Bridging out across the sky in an arch.
An act of God, for hopeful humor.
During the first rain of the season in March.

Alicia Nunn, Grade 8
Red Bud Elementary School, IL

Football, All Nighters, and the Joy of Books!!

I am from the great outdoors of my backyard
I am from the wonders of a wonderful book
I am from evenings of reading under the covers
I am from a bright orange world inside my room
I am from driving to football games in the middle of fall
I am from all nighters with my best friends
I am from the joy of swimming in backyard lake's
I am from ISI the school I grew up to learn languages at
I am from my crazy family
But most of all I am from an awesome English class!!!

Kensi Knowling, Grade 7
International School of Indiana, IN

The Bright Blue Sky
I look up into the air,
And flick back my spiked hair.
And through my dark brown eyes,
I see the bright blue sky.

I see a plane fly by,
While looking at the sky.
My mind says it is mine,
That plane in the blue sky.

There's thunder in the sky,
Now lightning in the sky.
The blue sky is now gray,
No bright blue sky today.

Today the sky is white,
Winter season affright.
Now a snowstorm will brew,
Hear the ambulance woo!

The long sky is so great,
But sometimes full of hate.
And as the birds fly by,
I see the bright blue sky.
Matt Borgstrom, Grade 8
Immaculate Conception School, IL

The Darkness
Out of the darkness, I come for few.
Among the few, I know there's you.
A sealed, locked box for many years,
I stored away all my anger and fears.

My life is slowly drained away.
I feel all reality begin to sway.
Happiness and memories start to regress;
As my depression tends to progress.

Into the light, I finally come;
Only to see that there are some.
In the some there are a lot;
Friends I wanted and foes I fought.

Pry open the box, now, I must;
Hopefully there's something there to trust.
I unlock and open it ever so slightly.
The top bursts off and doesn't land lightly.

First comes out my anger and hate;
Then there's sadness, a little late.
Below the destruction and dark recess,
Hidden there is faith, hope, and happiness.
Destinee Pence, Grade 9
Streator Township High School, IL

It Is
Like a full moon at midnight,
or a beautiful china plate.
With its nonexistent corners,
and never-ending edge,
It is round.

Like churning thunderstorm
clouds, or the endless sky
on a winter day.
Like the speculative stare
of a detective on an old mystery show,
It is gray.

Like skeletons from an ancient time,
resting in the ground.
Similar to friendly wrinkles
on your grandma's face,
It is old.

Like the angelic face of a newborn child,
It is small, it is smooth, it is perfect.

Sitting on my desk,
for my eyes to love,
It is my special stone.
Emily Zhang, Grade 7
Madison Jr High School, IL

he waits
winter   the quiet man sits
his home   family   world
            lost
   he waits
and bill-and-jill make every snowball
and play in the snow 'til they fall

when the world is snow-covered
the man sits on the chair

he waits
     waits
          waits
for something   anything

to happen
   he waits

and vicky-and-ricky come through singing
and making snow angels and sledding and
the weary
   homeless
   freezing
   man
wishes hopes dreams
Michael Deek, Grade 8
Immanuel Lutheran School, IN

I Still Love You
I don't see why you have to be this way.
Do I not have a say
in anything you do?
You're real nice to make me blue,
but I still love you.

Your eyes are like the sea,
it's just you and me.
So why don't you get a clue?
No matter what you say or do,
but I still love you.

Crack, there goes my heart.
Even though we are miles apart,
you're the one who said, "We're through."
Maybe you should get a clue,
but I still love you.
Tiffany Hull, Grade 8
Triopia Jr/Sr High School, IL

My Grandma, a Survivor
I came home from school,
My mom with a frown on her face.
The bad news to finally arise.

My grandma had cancer,
The most common of all.
She had breast cancer twice,
The chemo to come.

Her hair all fell out,
But she was okay,
And she survives every day.

Her hair has grown back,
All out and strong.
If you didn't ask her,
You wouldn't know what was wrong.
Morgan DeNeve, Grade 7
Madison Jr High School, IL

Skittles
Some are sour,
Some are sweet,
Everybody loves this tasty treat,
Skittles
From the crunchy outside layer,
To the chewy middle,
They make your taste buds wiggle,
Skittles
Flavorful and small,
A sugary treat,
Buy some today they can't be beat,
Skittles!
Jaxon Ince, Grade 7
Wethersfield Jr/Sr High School, IL

The Outside Me

I grow one day only to die the next
You take me from my home with a snap
Put me in a cup to admire my beauty
My life is short, that's plain to see
How could I stay undamaged, fragile me?
Dainty as a princess,
Sweet like perfume,
But that is all you will ever see,
The outside me

Madelyn Neal, Grade 7
International School of Indiana, IN

Don't Stop Now!!!

College, school, what's next
Elementary, can't quit now
Lawyer, doctor, WOW
Household, drama, huh
Mother gone, father gone
Can't quit now, just can't
AIDS, diabetes, no
Father died at show
Life what's next, life what's next, OH

Alexandra Dee Chambliss, Grade 7
Pierce Middle School, IN

Free Throw

The silent sweat slipping,
As she takes her free throw shot
Screaming fans, there are a lot.
Whistling, yelling, cheering, too,
But the shooter has no clue.
Slowly dribbling and glancing about,
The net on the hoop better look out.
The swoosh goes in just like that.
Almost as if the rim was fat.

Breanna Hoffman, Grade 8
Red Bud Elementary School, IL

Problems

You are
Far from alone;
There are many others,
People just like you, who have some
Problems

Brandon Jacobs, Grade 8
Northlawn Jr High School, IL

My Laughter

I am laughing.
My face turns red.
I am laughing.
My eyes start to water.
I am laughing.
My laugh is infectious.

Samantha Culver, Grade 7
Wethersfield Jr/Sr High School, IL

Community

Community means people together, talking, sharing, caring
It means friends forever, no stalking and staring.

Friendship is Dr. King's vision, no racial remarks
He has completed his mission, black, white, Latino, Asian, African never apart

This is what Dr. King wanted, this is what he got
Never having to be taunted, people no longer fought.

People called him Dr. Martin Luther King, he fought for civil rights
We will remember his last day. He stopped a lot of violence and fights.

Dr. King says freedom at last, this is true to say
We had freedom ever since the past, no more foulness anyway.

This is Dr. King's dream, we have freedom
It is like a stream, this is why we move on

He saved us in the past, we are together
Thank God Almighty we're free at last, we'll live here peacefully forever

Thaddeus Odom, Grade 7
Whistler Elementary School, IL

It Makes Me Wonder

Inside this there are millions of conversations waiting to happen.
There are many contacts contained inside this.
How does it store these?
Are there little copies of my friends talking to me inside this?
Inside this there are many games to play.
How does it remember the games I downloaded?
It is big and bulky.
The pink cheetah case makes it more like me.
When I text, the keys talk to me.
The words I type come naturally.
When someone calls me, my phone dances as it vibrates.
Inside this, there is a little camera.
When I'm with my friends, I take photos to capture my memories.
Inside this is homework help all around the world.
You can use a calculator, and the internet too.
Your answers can be found in less than a minute,
So you will still have time to watch Bring It On: In It To Win It.
All of this information galore, makes you want one that much more.
Inside this there are many apps, to gain information and have a blast.
My cell phone is a part of me, once you have one you will see.

Courtney Cayton, Grade 8
Thomas Middle School, IL

Living the Dream

Whack and the ball goes soaring
The ball starts to scream and the crowd roars
The pitcher stares in amazement as that was his best pitch
The batter trots around the bases tipping his helmet to his dugout
The batter jumps on home plate and does the sign of the cross to the heavens
Then the next batter has his chance to live the dream

Adam Rutledge, Grade 7
Highland Hills Middle School, IN

I Love Henry

He was the slowest out of them all,
And couldn't even catch a tennis ball.
But, I love Henry.

He always sleeps in my doorway.
Just to make sure that I'm okay.
I always feel safe with him around,
He never lets his guard down.
I love Henry.

As Henry got older so did I.
Time seemed to fly right on by.
The memories we shared were in pictures,
words, and everywhere.
I love Henry.

Pretty soon he got really old,
Even started to get a cold.
Something always seemed to be wrong,
My parents told me it wouldn't be long.
I love Henry.

Henry is one of my favorite dogs for sure.
I'll never forget the memories that have occurred.
I will always love Henry.

Maddie Dougherty, Grade 7
Marquette Academy, IL

Fishing

Casting. Every thing's ready for a day of fun.
Cock the reel, flick the wrist.
The shimmering gossamer line flicks off the reel…plunk!
The bobber has landed!

Waiting. Set the drag, adjust the line and begin to settle in.
Watch the bobber, watch some more.
Ever so slowly the bobber begins its descent…wham!
The bobber has vanished!

Catching. Feel the tug, the line goes tight, flick your rod!
Reel it in, rod tip up.
Anxiety builds, the line draws near, a flash of silver…splash!
He breaks the surface.

Unhooking. Draw back the whiskers and avoid the barbs.
Open the mouth, find the hook.
Carefully decide the best way out…slish!
Catch and release.

Casting. Every thing's ready for a little more fun.
Cock the reel, flick the wrist.
The shimmering gossamer line flicks off the reel…plunk!
The bobber has landed. Again

Kevin Hinders, Grade 7
St Matthew School, IL

Inside This Instrument

Inside this instrument
You hear laughter and melancholy, all in one.
You hear pounding sounds
That drum against your head.
You sense love as soft and soothing,
Like a mother's comforting care.
When it strums its strings,
There is sunshine.
When it plays its piece,
There is a beautiful sunset.
There is passion but emptiness
When you hear its melodic tune.
Inside this instrument,
Inside the violin,
It's music will touch your heart and soul.

Afroz Razi, Grade 9
Schaumburg High School, IL

Baseball

Baseball is an intense game
You work hard and get hurt
But it is worth it
Because baseball is full of rewards
You can win awards like the Triple Crown
Every position has many responsibilities
Like the shortstops who control the infield
Every position has an important role
Like the catcher who helps the pitcher decide pitches
You can be short or tall
Large or thin
Strong or weak
Talented or untalented
And you can still be trained to be good at baseball
I love baseball

Cole Sellers, Grade 7
All Saints Academy, IL

Ode to Friends

When you're with your best friend
You feel loved and cared for

When you're with your best friend
You can spill all your secrets

When you're with your best friend
You know you have a shoulder to cry on
And someone to rely on

When you're with your best friend
You have someone to lend you a helping hand

When you're with your best friend
You know you will be friends forever and always

Reagan Taylor, Grade 7
Stanley Clark School, IN

Linger

"Our love anew but soon be doomed."

Innocent smiles, a cheery mask, seeming flawless but only an act.
This weakness I have I try to hide, but sadness it lingers, it never subsides. An aching wound that lies concealed, I fear this heart may never heal. My faith in you has never wavered, now you've left me lifeless and tattered. I linger alone in the essences of your touch. Rekindling memories that seem endless of us. I cannot rate this love, I cannot hate this love. But I will wait for this love. I will wait for the words I fear. I will wait for the words I long to hear. "I'm Here"

Mariah Edwards, Grade 9
Pekin Community High School, IL

Ode to a Wii Remote

Oh Wii remote, you connect me to the Wii in an invisible wave.
You and the nun chuck unite in a blend of musical harmony.
You make the gamer and game one.
One of the first in a new generation; a generation of electricity and science.
Oh Wii Remote, with all your buttons that satisfies the user when pressed, you are convenient;
you do not mind when you are left alone, but when you are used you buzz and hum with life.

Mason Lee, Grade 7
Stanley Clark School, IN

Art and Bullies

What inspires me,
Might not inspire you.

It is skillful, elegant, and imaginative,
To be it, is called creativity.

When it comes to imagination,
Originality does inspire someone.

What inspires you,
Might not inspire me.

It is mean, rude, and goofy,
To be it, is called stupidity.

When it comes to annoying,
Irritation doesn't inspire anyone.

The idea of my hobby,
Is my feeling of creativity.

The idea of boredom,
Is my feeling of being hurt.

When you call my creativity: dumb, retarded, or stupid,
I still call my hobby, creativity.

When I call your creativity: mean, unkind, and cruel,
You still call your hobby, creativity.

Art and Bullies.

Maria Do, Grade 8
Jordan Catholic School, IL

Cloud

I am a beautiful creation.
I soar through the air like a bird overlooking everything.

I am as white as the first snowfall in December,
and as puffy as a marshmallow.

I soar up way above blocking rays of sunshine,
that look down on the face of the earth.

I look soft like a feather gently floating down,
although it's hard to feel me.

I float there waiting for the perfect moment
that can amaze you.

On some occasions I'm a
soft purple, rocking the world into a peaceful night.

Other times I'm a blazing spectrum ranging from
a cheerful yellow to a deep violet.

And frequently I'm gray,
that makes the sky depressing.

I let loose walls of water,
that nature soaks up like a sponge.

Even though I have my down points,
all that is made up by the moments I take your breath away.

Emily Donohue, Grade 8
Thomas Middle School, IL

Waterfall
bright blue
water streams down
mossy mountainside cliffs
like lightning across deep green sky
alive
Jane Quinn, Grade 8
Thomas Middle School, IL

My Life
Softball
You field and throw
all it takes is three strikes
In the huddle you cheer and shout
Bat ball
Breanna Toppen, Grade 8
DeMotte Christian School, IN

My Horse
Riding my horse
I feel free as the wind
Mind set, focused, relaxed, free
Time comes, we both are tired
We lay down and together sleep
Paris Comegys, Grade 7
West Salem Grade School, IL

Checkas' Please
Red stationed.
Black aligned.
Red kinged.
Black panicked.
Red annihilates.
Trevor Barbeau, Grade 8
Red Bud Elementary School, IL

Slot Canyon
orange
rocks turning dark
sun shining through the cracks
walls are very pointed and flat
and tall
Matt Peterson, Grade 8
Thomas Middle School, IL

Water
Mirror
Ripples tear through
Ruining the picture
Different from at home, I live this
Picture
Maura Twohig, Grade 8
Thomas Middle School, IL

People, People, People*
Big people,
Little people,
Sad, happy, silly people,
Mean, grouchy, upset people,
Those are just a few!

Boy people,
Girl people,
Awesome, smart, funny people,
Weird, peppy, neat people,
Enthusiastic people too!

Thoughtful people,
Rash people,
And don't forget squirrelly people!

Last of all
Best of all
I like cool people!
Caitlynn Summerfield, Grade 8
West Salem Grade School, IL
*Patterned after Beans, Beans, Beans by Lucia and James L. Hymes Jr.

Animals, Animals, Animals*
Animals, animals, animals
Big animals
Small animals
Messy, cute, white animals
Those are just a few!

White animals
Brown animals
Sad, abused, mean animals
Lonely, brave, nice animals
Adorable animals too!

Canine animals
Sea animals
And don't forget your smart animals!

Last of all
Best of all
I like colorful animals!
Sarah Carter, Grade 8
West Salem Grade School, IL
*Patterned after Beans, Beans, Beans by Lucia and James L. Hymes Jr.

First Communion
First Communion is a great new beginning.
It brings us one step closer to God.
First Communion is when you receive the body of Christ for the very first time.
Receiving Christ is a very important thing in life.
First Communion is something that happens only once.
It is a great new beginning.
Jake Komel, Grade 8
Sacred Heart School, IL

Flowers

They smell like a fresh spring day.
Some feel soft as a blanket,
And some feel as prickly as a porcupine.
Their beautiful colors,
Are like a brilliant sunshine.
You always have to stop,
And take a look while they last.
Before you know it,
Autumn has come,
And they are washed away
Like little drops of rain
Just slammed upon the windshield wipers.
They are a masterpiece that must be enjoyed
For their true beauty.

Melissa Mauer, Grade 8
Thomas Middle School, IL

Family

Your family is always there for you,
When you're feeling sad and blue,
They will always love you,
No matter what you do.
They comfort you when you're defeated,
And they rejoice when you succeed.
They will always help you,
And they will satisfy your every need.
Even though they may fight,
You never have to fear,
Don't kick, scratch, punch, or bite,
And you won't shed a tear.
Just love your family with all your heart,
And you and your family will never grow apart.

Joey Krampen, Grade 8
St Mary's School, IN

The Meadow

I strolled into the meadow,
And the flowers beckoned me with a "hello."
I examined the sky,
Wishing I knew some things I didn't know.

When I told the world goodbye,
It replied with a sigh.
I reached the clouds,
Wishing I'd done some things I didn't try.

I looked down on the crazy crowds.
At my funeral, my body was covered with a shroud.
I stared at my loved ones below.
Still, of the short life I lived, I am proud.

Melissa Stellhorn, Grade 8
Red Bud Elementary School, IL

A Dream Is Like a Butterfly

A dream is like a butterfly,
at first it was only a caterpillar.
It's a small burst of desire, before it transforms.

A dream is like a butterfly,
a bright and colorful hope.
Further and further it flies, tormenting you with longing.

A dream is like a butterfly,
as you follow it you age.
Along the journey you prosper, and gain the knowledge of the roads.

A dream is like a butterfly,
once you capture it the fun is gone.
The joy of accomplishment remains, until the creature perishes.

A dream is like a butterfly,
it has a short life span.
Bittersweet in taste, to keep away any predators.

A dream is like a butterfly,
because after every death, comes a birth.
A dream is like a butterfly.

Mehek Sethi, Grade 8
Madison Jr High School, IL

A Part of Me Is Missing

My missing piece is not just a rhyme
It's my heart all broken up inside
Like an ocean I'm spread out wide
I'm missing, I need someone to guide

My missing piece is gone for good
Never to come back
Never to again arrive
Missing to never be found
Missing, like me, I'm bound

It's me
Just wanting to be set free
Under the oak tree
I wish to be
Just and only me

I don't know me
And that's not how its suppose to be
I used to be on top of the world
But now I'm falling and cracking, slowly breaking…

Down.

Emily Charny, Grade 8
Washington Jr High School, IL

Love

So special and unexplainable
Brings smiles and happiness
While you spend time together
With the one you love
Your feelings take over
The feelings of importance, nervousness, and friendship
Laughing and talking until 3 a.m.
And never forgetting one another

Daniela Kloes, Grade 8
Thomas Middle School, IL

Midnight Waves

Crisp, ocean waves flow slowly at midnight
Light reflects the surface from the rising moon
Birds with bright, colorful wings take flight
Crisp, ocean waves flow slowly at midnight
Fish swim close enough to be in my sight
While I'm looking at the big dipper, which is like a spoon
Crisp, ocean waves flow slowly at midnight
Light reflects the surface from the rising moon

Sam Lesak, Grade 8
Northlawn Jr High School, IL

The Morning After Christmas Eve

Christmas Day is a box of surprises
Children love to open each gift
With each growing moment, the tension rises
Christmas Day is a box of surprises
While kids open presents, they observe their prizes
The joy Santa brings is an emotional lift
Christmas Day is a box of surprises
Children love to open each gift

Walker Reinmann, Grade 8
Northlawn Jr High School, IL

Basketball

From the Fab Five to the Big Three.
Ray Allen will hit the game winning three.
John Wall will ball till he falls,
While Chris Paul will make his defender fall.
The Heat can't be beat.
The lockout is like a bad dream.
Basketball is my favorite and the best sport in the world.

Zach Cavins, Grade 7
Highland Hills Middle School, IN

Not Quite Fate

I have much to digest, but my stomach is already filled.
Filled with anger, love, envy, and hope,
Hope that I find him.
The one that understands me half as
Good as the man I love now.
But he doesn't have the feelings for me that I have for him.
Love is a tragic, fragile thing.

Danielle Pace, Grade 8
St Marys School, IN

A Poem and the Meaning Within

Inside a poem is a message.
Like an envelope, its true contents are sealed within
With no tools to open it but the mind.
But the mind itself needs to open wide
Or it is a dull blade against the thick paper
Useless.

Inside the poem is a bomb.
When it is set ablaze, there's no telling when.
When what? When the knowledge will blast out
With a quiet bang
And the mind is filled with riddles and clues
Answered, revealed.

Inside a poem is a mirror.
Reflected light shines through the letters
Dancing out different meanings.
Lingering light lets us look
Into the deep reservoir of answers
Waiting to be found.

Inside a poem is opportunity.
A writer's say about the world.
Bow down, it will be found
Hidden underneath the marks on the page
And only a reader can see its light.

Erin O'Donovan, Grade 8
Thomas Middle School, IL

Forest

The forest cool and damp,
Teeming with life,
Rivers rushing through,
Trees towering overhead like monsters,

Eagles flying sky high,
Bees buzzing around logs,
The wolves prowling like a fox,
Were scavengers,
Hornets chasing out hikers,
Defending the forest from invaders,

The smell of marching water,
The fish sunning themselves,
Were golden brown,
The sound of a tree tumbling,
Like a gymnast,
And come crashing down,

The river
Like an open wound heals itself,
It washes away the log,
The forest all-natural, self-healer and defender,
Preserver of life.

Kevin Turay, Grade 8
Liberty Jr High School, IL

Thanksgiving

T hanksgiving is a
H oliday filled with joy
A nd it's a time to give thanks
N o one should be bored on this special day
K orina enjoys this holiday very much
S o she can be with her family
G iving thanks together
I t's never too late to give thanks
V ery special time to spend with family
I t's a holiday in November
N o school on this day
G ive thanks for all you have

Korina Avila, Grade 7
Hannah Beardsley Middle School, IL

Thanksgiving

Thanksgiving is great
Always so much food on my plate
Spending time with my family is fun
All of us eating a ton
Stuffing and turkey are yummy
Grandma's jello fills my tummy
Look outside my Grandma's window
I watch the colorful leaves blow
We give thanks on this day
Which we should do anyway
Every year I get that warm touch
Oh, I love Thanksgiving so much!

Alexis Petersen, Grade 7
Hannah Beardsley Middle School, IL

Thanksgiving

T hanksgiving is awesome,
H aving fun while it's cold outside,
A time to give thanks,
N ow it's time to feast,
K icking and screaming
S ometimes laughter,
G etting hyper on dessert,
I nvited guests begin to leave,
V ery quiet but more noises soon emerge,
I continue watching football,
N ow I'm leaving, goodbye to all,
G et together next month for Christmas!

Kevin Noonan, Grade 7
Hannah Beardsley Middle School, IL

Fall

Fall
Biking, running, raking
Beautiful, cold, happy
Amazing, wonderful, Thanksgiving
Family, friends
Fall

Grace Hansen, Grade 7
St Matthew School, IL

Forgotten

I walk through memories in a quiet way.
Seeing you in them,
Washing away my sorrow,
through your lips.

Yet one memory holds me back.
You forget that I'm here in these shadows.
I am forgotten to you,
forget my past.

To save me from darkness is a light I could choose.
Forgotten here in the rain, pouring like blood from a wound.
Tears fall from my eyes
because of my fears,
You don't care as long as my blood spills into your darkness.

Bring me to those memories of happiness and light before I am forgotten.
But you already have forgotten…
You broke my heart and let me be forgotten.

Hannah Hillier, Grade 9
Prairie Central High School, IL

Flying

A nxiously waiting to **B** oard the plane.
C urious to know what's inside?
D eciding to take the leap.
E nergetic yet scared!
F rightened of what's to come.
G o, go, says my family!
H opping up the stairs I go, **I** magining the beauty I'm about to see.
J umping into the Co-pilot's seat, **K** nowing this will be fun.
L aughing is excitement.
M achining to the pilot.
N ot to do loops!
O pening a pop, **P** ilot Pete starts the engine.
Q uivering with excitement, **R** eady to go, **S** tart going, I said, before I change my mind!
T enderly the plane moved forward.
U nscared now, I said let's go!
V ibrating in my seat from the engines, **W** aiting for lift off.
X -ing the four way.
Y ielding at the runway!
Z ing, off we go!

Derek Schurman, Grade 8
DeMotte Christian School, IN

Football

Starts with a kick
Go back to defense and get a pick
Watching the ball fly through the air is like a bird soaring through the sky
Run for the touchdown and try not to get hit
Being hit is a dream and you're wondering when you'll see light again
You go to the sideline and everyone cheers
Soon the game is over and your team has won
You go out to celebrate for what you have done

Luke Pruitt, Grade 7
Highland Hills Middle School, IN

Fall

Fall is the drop of leaves
And summer grieves
Fall is orange, yellow, and red
And summer goes to bed

It is when we give thanks
For the event that took place at the river bank
Fall is when we play
And it never stops that day

Meredith Jackson, Grade 7
St Matthew School, IL

The Hayrack Driver

Apples falling everywhere,
Brown pieces of hay in my hair.
Corn is thrown at our hayrack driver,
Dave is his name.

Entertained, all of the little kids laugh,
"Funny," they think as Dave got out of his tractor.
"Great," says Dave as all the kids snicker,
"Horses are eating my toupee."

Hannah Zachman, Grade 7
Dunlap Valley Middle School, IL

Nature

Trees up high sunlight
Shining over a rainbow
Of colorful flowers.
A field of flowers sparkles
And shimmer like the sun in the soft wavy grass
Violet roses pretty and bright,
Shine oh so brighter than the light,
Perky, preppy, pretty violet rose

Ivory Jones, Grade 7
Pierce Middle School, IN

Dove Hunting

Pick up my shotgun and some shells,
I need some doves for me to sell,
BOOM! BOOM! Down they fall,
Then you call and call and call,
Some come in and I blast some more,
You don't even need a decoy or a lure,
I grab my doves and start heading back,
Then turn around and shoot one more to add to the stack.

Matthew Gregson, Grade 8
Red Bud Elementary School, IL

Sundown

As the sun goes down
All life seems to fall asleep
When the light turns off
The moon shines.

Tony Gonzalez, Grade 8
Northlawn Jr High School, IL

This Cold World

when she cries they laugh.
no one helps not even the school staff.
her mother died and her father's gone.
no one's around she's just alone.
no one knows what she goes through
they don't help like real citizens are suppose to.
I pray for the girl and hope that she's okay.
no little girl should feel that way.

Destiny Hill, Grade 7
Pierce Middle School, IN

Fall

I watch as the leaves blow by.
The wind carrying them to far off places.
I watch as the grass changes color.
Winter approaching fast.
I watch the sky as the sun drops.
Filling up with so many colors.
I watch as fall goes by.
The season changing to winter.

Christian Rice, Grade 8
St Thomas the Apostle Elementary School, IL

Those Ballet Slippers

Those ballet slippers, quite a few pairs,
Through the years, have seen their fair share,
The first class, the first recital,
After dancing for eight years, pirouetting is vital,
But those shoes, although all worn out,
Have helped me all these years, without a doubt,
Spinning and leaping, all throughout the day,
I will keep dancing until the final Plié

Paulina Piwowarczyk, Grade 7
Our Lady of the Wayside School, IL

To Summer

To be playing soccer out in the fields
To be going to the beach and having fun
To go swimming at the pools
To going to the parks and sliding from the slide
   and falling and getting boo boos
To going to Six Flags and almost falling off the roller coasters
   and screaming at the top of my lungs
   To Summer

Marlen Mendez, Grade 8
Peck Elementary School, IL

Light Bulb

Inside this light bulb.
It is so bright.
It hurts when you touch the filament.
There are little atoms flying everywhere.
They get excited and give off light and heat.
If the filament breaks it lives no more.

Jarrod Stiver, Grade 7
St Pius X Catholic School, IN

Sometimes I Feel Like an Ant
Sometimes I feel like an ant.
Underestimated,
overlooked,
easy to overcome,
no one ever hears,
no voice at all.
But then I remember that each and every
underestimated and overlooked,
no one ever hears,
easy to overcome,
Ant, has a very important job to do.
Sara White, Grade 7
Christ the King School, IN

Hiding and Seeking
Flat on your belly,
silent as the night around,
you must not be caught.

He's looking near you,
but you are invisible,
and cannot be seen.

He nearly passes,
but sees the slightest movement,
and now you are It.
Howard Fisher, Grade 8
Rochester Jr High School, IL

Art Is...
Bright colors of acrylic paint
Pencils sharpened to a fine point
Paint that blackens the sea
Brushes perfect for detail
Chalk like the sea after a storm
Oil pastels that blend with every color
Drawings with perfect shading
Pictures made of the finest detail
Lines as curved as fish scales
Wood as smooth as butter
Perspective as far as the eye can see
Lucas Willman, Grade 7
Highland Hills Middle School, IN

Death by Night
The wind rustles in the treetops
Like a forgotten whisper
The stars burn brightly
Against the darkened night sky
Like sharp daggers unsheathed
The smell of death hangs still in the air,
A heavy cloud of choking perfume
Enveloping my senses…and
Coating my tongue with its bitter taste
Rida Ali, Grade 9
Bartlett High School, IL

Paint Me Like I Am
Paint me like I am.
And not how people say I am.
Paint me white.
Around lots of lights.
That are too bright.
Which hurt your eye sight.
Paint me like I am.
With a frown on my face.
Which has been replaced with a smile.
Paint me like I am.
Under a big Amber tree.
That's over the sea.
Braiding with beads.
That are all types of greed.
Paint me like I am.
Paint me…
Dystany Scott, Grade 9
Jeffersonville High School, IN

Christmas
Christmas time is here
The trees are decorated
Candy-canes hung high

It is Santa Clause
Sleigh bells ringing in the air
Bringing presents there

Snowflakes falling near
Snowball fights and snowmen made
Sledding down the hill

Presents are given
The children smile with joy
Christmas time is here
Veronica Johnson, Grade 7
Immaculate Conception School, IL

Winter
White snow falling here,
Snow angels blossoming over there,
Cold snow everywhere.

Bare trees staring at me,
Christmas trees with lights all around,
Light up the winter sky.

Sledding down a hill,
Wiping out at the bottom,
With snow flying in our faces.

Fires burning brightly,
Hot against our cold faces,
Burning until there is ashes.
Nina Funk, Grade 7
Immaculate Conception School, IL

Gold
I am as precious as a diamond
But greater than silver
I get by rather quickly
Through fighting and warfare
I am as rare as an armadillo,
But as common as a hare
People have died for me
Driven crazy in greed
But no matter
I am still found with creed
I am a needle in a haystack
Duplicated by my enemy
But that is just for fools
Like my friend Midas
I have come a long way
Bartered with money and stones
Those who have lost me moan and groan
I am a king above all others
An element superior to Mother Nature
A god before a god
I am gold
Neel Matiwala, Grade 7
Stratford Middle School, IL

The Biggest Sacrifice by Mankind
He gave his life for others
And found the Lord in his brothers.
He heard the shots
Fired from empty lots.
He cares.
He dares.
His family asks
When he'll be back
For their love for him
Is full to the brim.
Who is he?
He is a veteran
Who carries the lantern
To guide our path
Away from this broken world.
We need to respect him
And all he has done
For he has trudged through the grim
To help others survive
And help us thrive
God Bless America and America's Warriors
Jess Beyer, Grade 7
Dunlap Valley Middle School, IL

Red
Red is the roses in a patch of flowers
Red is the blood after you scrape your knee
Red is the sparks rising from a camp fire
Red is the sun as it sets over the horizon
Nicole Schalk, Grade 7
Marquette Academy, IL

Snowglobe

Who am I?
Not a question easily answered, even put to the sands of time.
Perhaps I am someone else's dream.
A hazy patch of existence rooted firmly in a wish,
a wish swirling in the stellar cosmos of a mind.
Is everything I do a reflection of another?

A wishing well, that's what I am.
Absorbing other's visions, I am a never-ending pattern of distorted lives,
images I have twisted and taken as my own.
In my glinting waters lie a parallel universe, a face, tempting chances, what might have been.
Past, present, and future, a potent brew.
But yet I am fragile, only an echo rebounding off my circular walls.
Down, down, down.

What if this world is my own creation?
In a fit of drowsiness, madness crept into the burning edges of my soul,
and lives, ideas, universes were born.
Am I alone?

I hope that you are as real as anyone, that I am not carving this path through the stars on my own.
I hope that our world isn't just a snowglobe on the shelf of a greater something.
But mostly, I hope that I am allowed, by whatever force governs me, to continue being…
for I have become too enchanted to leave it all now.

Katy Dyer, Grade 8
The Stanley Clark School, IN

The Sun

I taste the pollution that the humans give off in their motor vehicles.
I rise and then I fall.
Then I rise again on the other side.
My brother the moon is small and cold, while I'm am huge and hot.
I see everything that they puny human race does.
I sometimes make people sweat then they complain that I am "way" too hot.
Then when I am farther away little white ice, falls out of the sky, then they complain it is too cold.
Then it happens again.
I feel very lonely, sometimes but the stars and moon sometimes keep me company.
While my friends die out I live on and wonder when my time is up, I wonder, I wonder…

Will Rigby, Grade 7
International School of Indiana, IN

The Beautiful Beach

When I was young at the beach, I sprawled onto my towel and let the sun bake my skin. Later my friend and I tossed around a beach ball on the hot boiling sand like food being cooked on a frying pan. After that, we slowly strolled into the cool water that gingerly caressed the sand and flew back into the rest of the lake. Then, we formed a gigantic sand castle as big as a mountain.

When I was young at the beach, I read magazines under a blue and white striped umbrella bigger than a cloud. Under the umbrella we nibbled on lunch and licked our ice-creams.

When I was young at the beach, I scavenged for seashells in the confusing many layers of sand. "Snap!" We took pictures of the beautiful shells and perfectly laid out beach that spread out in front of us.

When I was young at the beach, I turned up the booming loud music and played with a Frisbee in the hot summer sun, as the day grew old. The beach was my favorite thing to do over the summer and I go every summer to discover more of nature's wonders.

Margaret Chwalinski, Grade 8
Thomas Middle School, IL

Fall

As I leisurely strolled through the bright amber, burgundy colored forest
which was highlighted by the intense rays of the incandescent sun
I sniffed the marvelous aroma of nature and the beautiful vicinity which it complemented
The fragrances had the scent of newly fallen leaves from a maple tree
with a slime layer of sap painted on them
As I admired the gift of fall I peered at a pile of little green, gold yellow, scarlet red,
and umber brown colored leaves which must have recently descended from the tree
Suddenly the peace and quiet, silence stop
An adorable infant squirrel with a bright brown tip nose, little brown pointed eyes,
and a fluffy pale tail had poked his tiny head out of the old evergreen tree
The cute, petite squirrel slowly, but gradually climbed down from the sticky bark of the tree
During the squirrel journey down the tree I noticed a ripe acorn situated near the perimeter of the path
When I walked over to grab the acorn it had a durable outer shell
which appeared too rough for the baby squirrel to eat
So I graciously cracked the nearly unbreakable acorn for the squirrel to munch on
When I grabbed the acorn the squirrel had given me the most adorable face ever
his eyes were shimmering, reflecting the sun, and his mouth was twitching as if he would cry
Being kind I carefully, gingerly tossed the acorn to infant squirrel
It appeared that the squirrel was extremely grateful for my gift
The squirrel hastily climbed back up the evergreen tree and I never saw the squirrel again

Will Varrin, Grade 8
St Matthew School, IL

Winter

W ind whips through me and steals my earmuffs from my halfway frozen head.
I stick out my tongue to taste the clean, white snowflakes.
N eglected lawns are hidden from my sight; covered by powdery whiteness.
T rees stand out boldly against the skyline in all of their stark white glory.
E nticing snow banks beckon me to burrow inside of them and to create an underground kingdom.
R ed-nosed carolers go from door to door harmoniously singing tales of flying reindeer and epics of three generous kings.

Mallorie Kendzicky, Grade 8
Corpus Christi Elementary School, IN

Reflection

I look in the mirror every night
wishing we didn't have to fight
why do you hate me?
is what I ask
my reflection replies
you have unanswered thoughts
you have discoveries to make
while I am trapped you are free
I hate being your soul
can't you see?
you have so much to live for
while I am dead
why am I trapped in your head?
This isn't fair
why won't you trade me?
And I reply every night
because there is much I still must learn
one is finding myself
and you aren't her

Karoline Coryea, Grade 9
Northeastern Jr-Sr High School, IN

Winter

The winter breeze swirls
Throwing snowflakes everywhere
Snow hits me, I'm cold.

Bryce Bumphrey, Grade 7
Wethersfield Jr/Sr High School, IL

The Beach

The beach's waves hit
Sounds of the flooding water
Soothes aches all over.

Jordan Lerschen, Grade 7
Wethersfield Jr/Sr High School, IL

Snow

Falling to the ground
Slow and gently in white flakes
Soft puffs of wonder

Jackie Masiunas, Grade 8
St Matthew School, IL

Christmas

Christmas time is here
'Tis a joyous holiday
Candy canes and mints

Jan Ramirez, Grade 8
Divine Infant Jesus School, IL

Love

Sometimes it will hurt
You may not understand this feeling
Sometimes it will last

Brandy Reyna, Grade 7
St Matthew School, IL

Rescue Swimmer

Guardian Angel,
Gambling every last chance,
So others may live.

Courtney Levitt, Grade 7
Dunlap Valley Middle School, IL

Snow
The white snowflakes fall
And flew with the dancing wind.
Snow seasons indeed.
Johnny Min, Grade 7
Concordia Lutheran School, IN

Grades 4-5-6
Top Ten Winners

List of Top Ten Winners for Grades 4-6; listed alphabetically

AbdurRahman Bhatti, Grade 5
Cambridge Friends School, MA

Katie Dominguez, Grade 4
St Joseph School, PA

Avery Fletcher, Grade 5
Balmoral Hall School, MB

Foxx Hart, Grade 4
F L Olmsted School, MA

Maximiliana Heller, Grade 5
Stanley Clark School, IN

Sarah Kim, Grade 5
Avery Coonley School, IL

Grace Lemersal, Grade 6
Meadowbrook Middle School, CA

Julia Peters, Grade 4
Toll Gate Grammar School, NJ

Lucas Tong, Grade 6
Chinese American International School, CA

Mallory S. Wolfe, Grade 5
North Knox West Intermediate/Elementary School, IN

All Top Ten Poems can be read at www.poeticpower.com

Note: The Top Ten poems were finalized through an online voting system. Creative Communication's judges first picked out the top poems. These poems were then posted online. The final step involved thousands of students and teachers who registered as the online judges and voted for the Top Ten poems. We hope you enjoy these selections.

Life
Silent is the waves of the ocean
Silent is the swing waving back and forth
Silent is the rain rolling down my window

Loud is the crowd at the football game
Loud is the people at my birthday
Loud is the potato chips in my mouth

Eternal is the Lord with my heart
Eternal is waiting for eternal life
Eternal is the life in Heaven
Sophia Blevins, Grade 4
Churubusco Elementary School, IN

Frank
Frank
Cheerful, helpful, energetic, peaceful
Sibling of Brian and Josephine
Lover of animals
Who feels happy
Who needs nothing
Who gives love and care
Who fears nothing
Who would love to see my uncle
Resident of Westchester
Gambino
Frank Gambino, Grade 6
Divine Infant Jesus School, IL

Snow
The snow falls from the sky
slowly at first, then faster it blows
I walk outside to watch it fall
off trees and roofs of houses
I feel the cold bite my skin
and I zip my jacket higher
The snow keeps going
faster and faster
The wind starts to feel
colder and colder
and I walk inside.
Megan Hosinski, Grade 6
Stanley Clark School, IN

Valentine's Day
If I were Valentine's Day,
I would have love.
I would love kisses.
My pet would be a dove.

If I were Valentine's Day,
I would make cards.
They would be pretty.
That wouldn't be hard.
Andrea Gonzalez, Grade 5
Edison Elementary School, IL

Georgia
Georgia
the one place
the one place I can get away
my relaxing place

waking up in Georgia
is like a new life
it's so peaceful
I feel at home

Georgia
the one place I love
Jackson Mathias, Grade 5
Manchester Intermediate School, IN

A Snowy Christmas
The frosty snow you see,
the hot chocolate to smell,
pine trees with pine to smell
and touch,
stars flashing on Christmas
trees with lights on them.
At night, warm in bed, thinking
about when Santa will come.
On Christmas morning, opening
presents, whatever you want,
filling you with happiness,
to have another good day.
Jonathan Simon, Grade 4
Copeland Manor Elementary School, IL

Colors, Paintings, Drawings
I can be black or white,
you can use me to draw or write.
If you like to use me,
an artist you will be.
After you use me,
you will see a bright
amazing painting.
I can be pink, green or blue,
I could be yellow too!
You can make me whatever you
want me to be.
Only if you use your creativity!
Cameron Hamilton, Grade 4
Copeland Manor Elementary School, IL

Soccer
S o fun to play
O ver fall or spring
C oming together as a team
C oaches are helping you become your best
E veryone wants to watch you play
R unning fast to get the ball
Hannah Surber, Grade 5
St Michael School, IN

Are We Friends?
Are we friends?
I'm not sure.
You would think I would know,
but I don't.

You say that all I care about
is boys, boys, boys,
but I don't.
I care about you, you, you.

Can I just ask you,
are we friends?
Brooke Enyeart, Grade 5
Manchester Intermediate School, IN

The Adventure of the Bald Eagle
He flew through the woods.
He saw a cat.
He came in close.
He put the cat on the mat.
The cat fought back.
The cat lost.
The eagle had a feast.
The cat's bones got tossed.
The eagle was full.
So he flew away.
He went home.
He will hunt another day.
Jeremy M. Spina, Grade 4
St Matthias School, IL

Reflections
The sun shines
in the darkest of moments.
The moon glows
in the darkest nights.
We wouldn't feel happy
if we haven't felt sad.
Everybody needs hope
once in a while.
It's your choice to go
up or down.
Every once in a while,
people need a friend.
Elisa Wynn, Grade 6
Three Rivers School, IL

Books
Books are like hooks
they wind you in
they let you out
at the end
wondering
should I read it again?
Logan Isbell, Grade 5
Manchester Intermediate School, IN

Tomorrow Is Not a Given!
Tomorrow is not a promise. Neither are we.
You never know when He is going to take us.
So it's time to wake up and see. See what out world has become.

See what Hurricane Katrina did and what happened in Haiti.
Think of the people we lost and remember.
Remember that today is a gift and not a promise.
Tomorrow is not a given.

This poem is dedicated all the people who ever lost a loved one
from natural causes or natural disasters.
It's time to wake up and start living,
and always remember that tomorrow is not a given!
Chardae Compton, Grade 6
U S Grant Middle School, IL

God
He will always be there for you.
And everything you do He is watching over you.
As He said He will always love you
For what you are on the inside.
No matter what.
Be truthful to yourself
And everyone around you.
Believe in one God
Maker of Heaven and Earth.
Father of all things.
He has always loved you
And will always love you.
AMEN.
Victoria Stout, Grade 5
North Knox West Intermediate/Elementary School, IN

Fall
The town is turning red, gold, and yellow
Rainy season of color
Is upon
The delicate flags
Of the balding poles of motionless life
Flutter to the ground as the gentle breeze blows
There are little monsters to the flags
Stomp, jump, and crush them
Rushing inside afterward
To drink the drink of the season
Giant orange balls everywhere
Hunger for the yellow vegetable has ended
The season of color is here
Eric Chen, Grade 4
Highlands Elementary School, IL

Clouds
Glancing over worlds
Fluffy, white, sometimes dark gray
Pillows in the sky.
Alayna Eismin, Grade 4
Frank H Hammond Elementary School, IN

Computer
My family is a computer;

My mother is the system unit;
She's the one that makes the rules.
In other words she's the boss
She makes me think better things.
But sometimes she makes my dad mad.

My dad is the mouse;
He's always fast and in a hurry.
The only thing he says is hi, bye and I love you.
Isn't it time to tell him to spend time with us?

My grandmother is the speakers;
She just sits there talking and talking.
She can't stay quiet for a minute;
Till somebody tells her to be quiet.
It gets annoying.

My older brother is the keyboard;
He likes to copy what somebody says.
It's time to tell him to stop copying other people's words.
Eduardo Botello, Grade 6
Florence Nightingale Elementary School, IL

Jellyfish
The sea is blue and salty
Jellyfishes and stingrays sting persons
Purple and slimy at the same time
And the jellyfish stings
Little fishes are swimming around
All of the jellyfishes have jelly legs
Sharks swim in the sea also
And the jellyfish stings
Swimming away into the deep sea
Into the pitch black darkness
I will go to sleep
and the jellyfish stings
Briana Hernandez, Grade 5
North Knox West Intermediate/Elementary School, IN

The Cycle of Life
At break of dawn
New life shall leap,
Out of the darkness deep.

New love shall come and despair shall fall,
At the Almighty God's feet.
O thank thee, Lord, for thy great blessing,
Of new love in our world full of grief.

But day shall end and darkness come again,
Despair shall return and people shall mourn,
But the cycle of life shall start again.
Alexander Quiroga, Grade 6
Our Lady of Peace School, IL

Car

My family is like a car.

My mother is the steering
wheel, who steers us to
places, and steers us to
do chores.

My sister is the radio,
once you turn her on
you would want to turn
her off.

My dog is the horn, she
is as small and as loud
as the horn.

My dad is the engine,
like the engine he
works the hardest
and runs the family.

Marlen Gongora, Grade 6
Florence Nightingale Elementary School, IL

The Miracle of Lightning

Lightning is a miracle,
how it bends and lashes in a split/second,
 it strikes down to earth
like a hand of God,
like a portal was quickly opened to a distant land,
with hills of thunder and people made of pure energy,
diving to earth and hitting the ground
sending an explosion of light and sound
to the center of the earth.
Great beasts cower when the lightning hits the ground,
and great fires rise when the great power absorbs into the ground.
Men take cover in their homes
to shield them from the great power.
The royal warning of thunder
summons ghastly figures to float through the trees,
and the spirits of the deceased come out
and banshees' screams echo through the night.
But, lightning lights up the land
and man's greatest fear is destroyed,
as the sun comes out.

Baerett Stone, Grade 6
Stanley Clark School, IN

A Sparkly Sensation

On the peak of my Christmas tree
Hangs an elegant ballerina.
You truly can see
That she's special to me, Carmina.
Her appearance is thrilling,
Dressed in a thrilling, turquoise tutu.
Her beauty is blinding,
She might inspire you.
She's been with me since age three.
For her my heart is like a sports arena.
You truly can see
That she's special to me, Carmina.
My tree's light illuminates her face,
A crystal flower is placed in her palms.
Her body is filled with such grace,
The stress of mine she calms.
She is the key
To beauty because she's a stupendous Bonita.
You truly can see
That she's special to me, Carmina

Carmina Ballesteros, Grade 6
Our Lady of Peace School, IL

One of Those Days

It was one of those days
where you don't want to do
ANYTHING
NOTHING.
It's one of those days where you want
SOMETHING
ANYTHING
to do.
It's one of those days
THAT YOU HATE.
It's one of the
LONGEST
MOST BORING
DAYS OF THE YEAR.
It's one of the days
of the year where
YOU DO NOT LIKE DOING
ANYTHING.
This is perfectly normal
So if you're having one of those days, GOOD LUCK!

Grant King, Grade 4
Lincoln Elementary School, IL

Winter

W hite snowflakes fall!
I ntense snowball fights!
N ever do I get hit!
T oo bad I don't get cold!
E veryone hiding in their forts!
R un run run snowball fights here we come!

Katie Schmidgall, Grade 5
Dee Mack Intermediate School, IL

The Inventions of the World

Gatorade, pretzels, doughnuts, and cheese
Sunglasses and Kleenex for every time you sneeze
Popsicles, peanut butter, candy and more
So many inventions from the ceiling to the floor
There are so many inventions beyond our wildest dreams
So many that can bring wonderful things!

Abby Damge, Grade 5
Ranch View Elementary School, IL

Sports

Baseball softball sports galore,
I still wish there were more,
I play until I get a good score,
Sometimes you get really sore.

Baseball and Softball let's start with that,
Half the time you get to bat,
Once you hit the ball you have to scat,
If my friends do good I give them a pat.

Next is tennis that sounds fun,
You barely even have to run,
You like it so does everyone,
The fun has just begun.

There are so many more,
Go out your back door,
Try to get a good score,
I hope you do not get sore.

Mikayla Cassidy and Kaylee Kosulic, Grade 4
Grande Reserve Elementary School, IL

Game Day

We suit up
I'm excited, happy to play.
Wide receiver is my position,
What I do is catch the ball
In any weather condition!
In the huddle
The quarterback barks out plays
Go long, cut right!
The ball is snapped, HIKE!
I run fast, I feel my heart beating in my chest,
I want to catch the ball because I am the best!
My hand's out front,
I snatch the ball from the air
Tuck in my arm,
Run like the wind flying into the end zone!
TOUCHDOWN!
The crowd goes crazy
Game day over!
Yes, we win

Brandon Perrin, Grade 5
Walker Elementary School, IL

Shadows

Only one color,
but not one size.
Stuck to the ground,
but easily flies,
present in sun,
but not in rain,
doing no harm,
and feeling no pain.

Noah Leever, Grade 6
Alexandria Monroe Intermediate School, IN

Walking Dead

Blood and guts the door shuts
The zombies are here I scream "Oh Dear"
When I see a zombie appear
At the door of my second story room

The creepy monster gave me such a fright
So I grabbed the hammer I kept under my bed
I smacked him right in the head
I ran down the stairs and out the door

I ran across the street into the graveyard
A zombie burst from its grave
He charged at me he was very brave
I picked up the hammer and swung at him

I hit him right smack dab in the head
He fell over like a dead yak
I turned and started heading back
Soon I was in my house safe and sound

Nicholas Bivens, Grade 4
Grande Reserve Elementary School, IL

Couch

My family is a couch.

My mother is the makeup;
she loves putting it on,
she looks pretty with it on.

My father is the money;
he supports us as much as he can,
he's always there with money on him.

My older brother is the crumbs;
he's always coming and going.

My little brother is the juice stain;
I can never get rid of him,
he just gets more permanent.

My sister is the lip gloss;
she's always wearing some on her lips.

Leea Rodriguez, Grade 6
Florence Nightingale Elementary School, IL

Snow in Christmas

It is a Christmas day,
I am on my way,
I am going to play in the snow,
I want to feel the wind blow,
It is fun to play outside,
I don't want to go inside,
We are going to make a snowman with a frown,
Let's make his mouth go upside down.

Noami Lopaz, Grade 4
Summit Elementary School, IL

Family

My family's like a jewel
One that shines so bright
They comfort me when I cry
And when my ups turn down.

We do fun things together
Like jump-rope, tag, and Uno, too,
Our favorite thing to do
Is have a blast together.

My family is so awesome
We always have fun with each other
I will love them forever and ever.

Bari Lutz, Grade 5
Stanley Clark School, IN

Aunt Paula

I miss Aunt Paula
Her laugh, her smile, her self.
The way she hugged me.

I was very young
And very devastated
When we got the news.
Aunt Paula had neck cancer.
Cancer took a lot from her.

Her hair and her life.
But she is in heaven now
Watching over me.

Tori Snyder, Grade 5
Northern Heights Elementary School, IN

Sidra and Kaitlyn

Sidra and Kaitlyn
Always are my friends
We never fight
We are chained together
Too much stuff
Not enough space
We always unite

When the sun goes down
We go down

We are one for all
And all for one

Natalie Merza, Grade 5
Walker Elementary School, IL

Hunting

Quiet, we're hunting
Here it comes, the deer, my first
The hunt is over

Gracie Mills, Grade 5
Northern Heights Elementary School, IN

Football

Step on the field
I'm ready for some fun
Strap on my cleats
I'm ready to run

Mouth guard in
And my eyes ablaze
Hitting you so hard
Waking up in a haze

With the game in hand
Ready for the taking
Because I'm running the ball
Like Walter Payton

The score 20 to 20
In overtime
After the win
They all busted out a rhyme

Kamdyn Lester, Grade 5
Manchester Intermediate School, IN

Me as a Singer

I am a girl who loves to listen
To a different kind of music
And dance to the music.
I don't care how others feel about music.
I love to listen to pop music.
Two great singers are
Beyonce and Selena Gomez.
Sometimes I listen to music in my room
Or when I am walking
To some other places.
I sing from my heart out loud
Like nobody is around.
When I sing
It makes me feel happy and excited.
I sing out loud with a
BIG smile on my face.
When I watch people sing on YouTube
They inspire me to sing and dance.

Beza Pernecke, Grade 5
Walker Elementary School, IL

Loved Colorado

The mountains in the sky
The birds fly so high,
The soft white snow falling
Oh loved Colorado!

Skiing down the steep hill,
You shiver in the cold
And great huskies in the snow
Oh loved Colorado!

Daphne Hurthle, Grade 4
Copeland Manor Elementary School, IL

The Polar Bear Show

I went into the
arena where the
polar bears roamed.
I sat in my seat
and squirmed.

Then the trainer came
out and threw meat
in the corners.
The bears came out.

Soon the trainer
was making people
laugh like crazy.
I loved the show.

Ainsley Johnson, Grade 4
Copeland Manor Elementary School, IL

I'm Thankful For…

My family
Food
Shelter
School
Life
Peace
Birthdays
Freedom
Thanksgiving
Happiness
This pencil I am writing with
My sister
Books
Knowledge
I am thankful

Eva Huang, Grade 4
Lincoln Elementary School, IL

Joy of a Child

With my baby in my hands;
Who I won't abandon.
Try to give her all I can;
And soon she will understand.

I teach her to always care
To be very nice and to always share.
Though you are not aware;
Special love throughout the air.

Though she'll drive me up the wall;
We'll stand big and tall.
Many try to make us fall;
And find that we love each other after all.

Brianna Embrey, Grade 6
St Angela School, IL

A Car
My family is like a car...

My dad is like the steering wheel
he wants us to go forward and
he guides us threw everything.

My mom is like the engine
with out her we can't move
or go anywhere.

My brother is like the car
windows he doesn't want attention
but likes to be out doors.

My sister is like the air freshener
she smells good and she always
wants to be in front to get some
attention.

My twin sister is like the bumper
she doesn't mind where she's
heading towards as long as she
doesn't fall apart.

Estephanie Garcia, Grade 6
Florence Nightingale Elementary School, IL

Refrigerator
My family is a refrigerator

My mother is the yogurt;
she is healthy and good
she's the favorite of us.

My dad is the salad dressing;
I don't really like it much
he's good to some people not all.

My sister is the rice pudding;
she is sweet and flavorful
she never goes bad
she'll always be good.

My brother is the onions
he's bitter and makes you cry
he really just stays there
alone.

My cousin is the meat;
he's strong and cannot break hard
he's very good and artistic.

Julio Mendoza, Grade 6
Florence Nightingale Elementary School, IL

Hunger for Thanksgiving
My stomach hungers for Thanksgiving
I'll love Thanksgiving as long as I'm living!
My family is here,
They're all very dear
People far and near
Eating turkey and proving
They can eat no more and still keep moving!

Grant Jackson, Grade 6
Holy Family Catholic School, IL

Doors and Windows
Door
woody, solid
opening, moving, closing
push, twist, break, move
opening, closing, locking
clear, glass
Window

Kyle Krawczyk, Grade 5
Washington Township Elementary School, IN

Fall Is Coming Soon
The cold wind in my ear
The leaves make a CRUNCH sound
Flowers are dying and don't grow back
Summer is going away and fall is coming
Trees become abandoned and get sad without leaves
The wind makes the leaves go everywhere
When is fall going to end.

Maricela Dominguez, Grade 6
Zapata Academy, IL

My Life
My family calls me Sparky.
I'm real playful I love my family they smell great
They give me treats and little bones
I am a Chihuahua I like when they take me for walks.
Humans are very nice to me because I'm cute and tiny
When they take me outside I run and bark and play in the next door
neighbor's yard with their dog.

Payton Brough, Grade 5
North Knox West Intermediate/Elementary School, IN

Night Party
In the night when you go to bed
the stars are having a party.
The moon like a disco ball to light up the
party and the stars like people in sparkly
dress ready to dance the night away till morning
comes to say hello.

Cheyenne Mathews, Grade 6
Our Shepherd Lutheran School, IN

Cow-Tipping

Cows are grazing peacefully,
There's not a noise that's near
The cows are chewing on their cud,
Staring into the gully with absolutely no fear
The gully's home to lots of fish
Especially the gold,
And it is also my great place
To hide and call my Great Stronghold
I sneak up to a great big cow,
So innocent it's funny,
I wield my blow horn from my pants,
I can't wait for the prize money!
I lay my finger on the part,
Where you would honk
I prepare for the moment
And listen as the thing goes BONK!
Two seconds later I realized,
That this was a mistake,
I honked so loud that the cow,
Fell over like an earthquake…

ON ME!

Chris R. Kaetzel, Grade 5
North Knox West Intermediate/Elementary School, IN

A Fate Worse Than Death

There is something that most fear
But never come most near — Cancer
"It's a fate worse than Death,"
They all say with their own breath — Cancer
They put you in these dark, dark rooms
They are so cold,
They feel like doom — Cancer
The beds feel sad and lonely
Just waiting for you to depart — Cancer
And while you wait
It feels like they're tearing your soul apart — Cancer
But, please!
Do not fear!
Not all cease from here!
Sure there are a few
That are not as lucky as you
But think on the bright side!
Think you are a kite
With many ups and downs
But do not take it for granted,
Because Cancer still looms near.

Maya Toffler, Grade 5
Hawthorne Elementary School, IL

Signs of Autumn

Summer to autumn
Clouds moving, leaves changing again,
Picturesque fall scene.

Gracie Helmer, Grade 4
Frank H Hammond Elementary School, IN

A Time of Hope

You turn off your light to your bedroom.
However, you cannot sleep,
For your brain's too full of zombies, bullies,
Banshees, ghouls, trolls, and mummies.

But far, far away, you can smell the smell of lavender.
It makes all those scary creatures jump out of your brain.
You turn on your night light,
And go into the night.

You get knocked over by a tree of thorns.
You pass through rivers, plateaus, and valleys.
You spot the lavender flower.
You run up to it and breathe into your nose.

The lavender has the best smell you would ever smell.
You go back to bed and snuggle down into your covers.
All the scary creatures are forever out of your brain.
So you drift off to sleep and dream of lavender.

Lauren Roth, Grade 6
Creekside Middle School, IN

Fall

Unusual colors, just like
Small treasures float gently toward
The ground. Orange Balloons with green knots
Spring out from the healthy
And Moist
Earth. Orange
Paper forged
Completely
From Flames…
Small children High-dive
Into the burning piles of flame
a strange, but pleasant feeling
fills my heart. It's an Inferno everywhere…
The flames, however,
are cool. Unusually
cool, as if magic…
everything is
calm. The
treasure reaches the ground.

Matthew Naughton, Grade 5
Highlands Elementary School, IL

Overcoming Bullies

I am a lunch helper, or should I say was,
People were making fun of me and it is tough.
Younger kids laugh "Ha ha ha!" they say.
But sometimes they hit, punch, kick, and just get rough.
Now that I quit, I can go to recess.
It is a lot better than being with rotten kids.
I like it out there, as I see happy children
It is an offer that no one else should win the bid.

Austin Brown, Grade 5
Hawthorne Elementary School, IL

Draw of the Bow

Early in the morning
Out in the cool breezy woods
High in the tree
See everything up high in the sky
Hear something coming
The path in the woods
A big albino buck up the
Hill, draw my bow and pull the
Trigger, arrow flies and
Hits the deer, in the shoulder
Deer drops, four-wheeler
Barely pulled deer out of
Woods, deer hangs in
Garage, getting all meat
Off possible, taking the head
And antlers to taxidermist
Got buck now 3 does to
Go, now have big albino deer
Head on wall
Jason Schaeffer, Grade 6
Nancy Hanks Elementary School, IN

The Baby Is Born

It's 2:00 p.m. and we're
In the car on the way to
The hospital. Mom is whimpering
And trying to hold back
Yells of pain.
Mom is carried in; I have
To stay outside the room.
She isn't screaming until
30 minutes after she got
Into the room.
Then it stops.
The baby is born.
2 hours later
We're in the car
On the way home. Mom is
Happy. Her baby's name
Is Cynthia. She's just
Invented her own
Baby.
Erin Fang, Grade 5
Ranch View Elementary School, IL

Life

Trees are green
Night is black

Wind blows
Water flows
And the
Sun shines as
Yellow as life
Wilson Nettleton, Grade 5
Manchester Intermediate School, IN

Dinnertime

I arrived at Country Buffet
I can feel my taste buds grabbing
The delicious food
I can hear forks tapping
On plates
Most of all, I hear mmms of perfect
Perfection
On the outside I'm smiling
But on the inside I'm having a food party
I go get some
Sizzling fried chicken,
Crunchy fries,
And juicy steak
My tummy can't wait
Dinnertime
Selalah Scott-Pettway, Grade 5
Walker Elementary School, IL

Lazy

I'm tired
Need sleep
Please don't wake me
Sweet dreams
Bad dreams
Don't care
Just leave me asleep
Go to work
Not fair
Need a break
Maybe go to Hawaii
Sweet dreams
Bad dreams
Don't care
Let me be
Kayla Henning, Grade 4
Lincoln Elementary School, IL

My Sister

I love my sister so very much
We love to play
And have some fun
Each day I get home from school
I tell her stories and read her books
But each time she doesn't listen
I ask her "Who are we reading about?"
She answers with an "I don't know" shrug
I'll never be able to tell you
How much I love my sister
I love her so much it is amazing
Whenever I go to spend the night at a
Friend's, she comes along with me
I'll never be able to tell you
How much I love my sister
Madyson Ulrey, Grade 5
Manchester Intermediate School, IN

S'mores

marshmallows cling
to my teeth,
heat enters my
mouth,
chocolate melts
inside me,
graham crackers
are like ice
demolishing
when I bite,
can't resist the temptation
to eat more
another, after another
bite, after bite
just want more of this
crunchy, gooey
treat

S'mores
Megan Furness, Grade 6
Our Shepherd Lutheran School, IN

Pets Oh Pets

Pets, oh pets,
Where have you gone?
Are you underground,
Looking for me?

Pets, oh pets,
Where have you gone?
Are you in the sky,
Looking for me?

Pets, oh pets,
Where have you gone?
Are you in outer space,
Looking for me?

Pets, oh pets,
You are mistaken.
I'm here at home,
Safe but lonely.
Bryce Powell, Grade 5
Van Rensselaer Elementary School, IN

Hunter J.

H unting
U nder a
N ew moon
T ingling
E ating
R ed hot buffalo wings and

J umping
Hunter Jones, Grade 4
Shoals Elementary School, IN

The Ten Little Birds

Ten little birds sitting next to a porcupine,
One slipped, then there were nine.

Nine little birds went on a date,
One didn't go, then there were eight.

Eight little birds on a house,
One fell and went to heaven, now there are seven.

Seven little birds sitting on some sticks,
One lost his balance, now there are six.

Six little birds were next to a hive,
One got stung, now there are five.

Five little birds sitting on a door,
One fell off, now there are four.

Four little birds sitting in a tree,
One flew off, then there were three.

Three little birds went to the zoo,
One liked the lions, then there were two.

Two little birds played in the sun,
One got too close, and then there was one.

One little bird went searching for fun,
He never came back, well, that's the end of that!

Maya Ware, Grade 6
Holy Family Catholic School, IL

Friends

Friends are the rare people who ask
"How are you?"
And wait for the answer
Not having your friend is like no turkey on Thanksgiving
No presents on Christmas
And no candy on Halloween
Like branches on a tree you may live in different ways
But your roots remain as one
They are sweeter than candy
Brighter than the sun
Larger than the galaxy
Friendlier than the world
A companion is the one who knows the words of your heart
And can recite it back without thought
Friends are everything
Enemies in war
But will come back as allies
Friends walk in when the world walks out
Gold, silver, and bronze are a speck of dust
Compared to the Jewel of your life
A Friend!

Jonathan Chan, Grade 6
Bednarcik Jr High School, IL

Summer

I like summertime because it is fun
I like summer because we do not have school
The days are long because of the hot sun
Playing in the water keeps me very cool.;

In the summer, we get to play all day
I get to do what I want in summer
No worries, no homework, relax! Oh yay!
Going back to school is such a bummer.

In the summertime, I get to go fishing
If only it was summertime all year long
Is it summer yet? I am sure wishing
I cannot wait to hear the summer song
To me it is the best time of the year
Summertime blues, there is no known cure.

Alex Rouse, Grade 5
Northern Heights Elementary School, IN

Inventing

These are the things you need to be an inventor,
creativity and the ability to be a mentor
You need to take risks using all senses,
with your hands, eyes, ears, nose, and lips
You need to find humor
don't think too hard or you'll get a brain tumor
You need to question your thoughts to make them right
and be open to other people's hearts
You need to keep trying,
with ideas to be on fire because you know,
you will go higher and higher.
But most of all you need imagination
because you know,
"Our heads are round so our thinking can change direction"
And THAT"S! what you need to
Make an invention

Olivia Howard, Grade 5
Ranch View Elementary School, IL

Goal

I like to play a sport that's called soccer
My favorite part is scoring a goal
The hard part is getting past the blocker
You might be scared that it will hit the pole
The grass feels like wind under my fast feet
The sprinting makes my legs feel like jelly
Now that I scored my mission is complete
After my run I am really smelly
Tweet-tweet! Goes the whistle after it's in
My team groups around me in a flurry
Way to go Rene I think we can win!
We only need one more so let's hurry!
Scoring a goal may seem like it's no feat
But you must think you can and move your feet.

Rene Sieracki, Grade 5
Hawthorne Elementary School, IL

Music
Who invented music?
I'd really like to know,
That thing that makes our daily lives sparkle
And glow.
Was it Bach, Beethoven, or Mozart too?
I wonder what makes them
think like they do.
We sing, we dance
We laugh, we cry
Music will never
Leave our lives.

Lisa Johnson, Grade 5
Ranch View Elementary School, IL

My Aunt Stacey
The doctor said the cancer was eating her alive.
She is only twenty-five.

I pray that Stacey will be okay.
I pray every day, I pray, I pray.

And to this very day.
My Aunt Stacey is doing okay.

And that is the way she will stay.
I hope and I pray.

Olivia Rice, Grade 5
St Thomas the Apostle Elementary School, IL

Candy
My family is candy.

My mom is a chocolate bar
because of how sweet she is and my dad
is a huge fan of her because he LOVES chocolate!

My dad is a sweet and sour path kid
because he is always sweet, sour, then gone.

My brothers and sisters are skittles because they are
all their own different colors and flavors.

Andrea Valadez, Grade 6
Florence Nightingale Elementary School, IL

A Baby's Cry
A baby's cry is as beautiful as a baby's eye
Once she is brought into the world you thank the good Lord

It's as good as a baby's eye so please Lord let her be born,
Once she is here thank the good Lord

You are thankful for her
You cry about it, so you are blessed that the good Lord
Brought her into this beautiful world

Quardarious Freemon, Grade 6
U S Grant Middle School, IL

I Am a Pet Rescuer
I am brave and I care about animals.
I wonder what just happened.
I hear loud noises of screaming people.
I see running people with their faces covered in ash.
I want to wake up and say that was a nightmare.
I am brave and I care about animals.
I pretend this never happened.
I feel so panicked.
I touch the poor animals that don't have homes anymore.
I worry about people and their pets.
I cry for the dead and unfound.
I am brave and I care about animals.
I understand that I have to do my duty.
I say these poor pets will find new, good homes.
I dream for world peace.
I try to save as many living things as possible.
I hope this will never happen again.
I am brave and I care about animals.

Chikako Barnes, Grade 5
Stratton Elementary School, IL

Where I'm From
I'm from my old dog Casey
From milk and cookies
I'm from my old crib
And bawling and snoring
I'm from my favorite dog that's buried in the yard
Whose trees grow so tall
I'm from video games and books
From the Kellems and the Meunier family
I'm from hot rod cars and being a fast runner
I'm from loving video games
From eating a gigantic Thanksgiving dinner
I'm from my old house in Evanston
I'm from my Mom and Dad
I'm from my Mom's cheesy potatoes and Thanksgiving turkey
From my Dad's attitude
And my Mom's stubbornness
My baby rattle
I'm from those moments of being a child

Cole Kellems, Grade 5
Perry Central Elementary School, IN

Coyote
I smell a prey close by
I hear birds chirping
I see my prey and I'm about to attack
I feel leaves and branches touching me
I taste the prey I attacked
I sleep in a den
I hunt at day and night
I run very fast
I am big and strong
I love to eat deer, rabbits, and other animals.

Sam Berry, Grade 5
North Knox West Intermediate/Elementary School, IN

David Lamb

D og lover
A lways busy
V ery athletic
I ce cream lover
D oes his homework

L oves God
A lmond Joy lover
M &M lover
B asketball lover

David Lamb, Grade 5
North Knox West Intermediate/Elementary School, IN

Photographs

Photographs
Bring back memories
That slowly fade away
They're always there
But the ink will fade away
That's what they say
Photographs remind
Not remember
It is your mistake if you expect the photograph to remember
Because the ink will always fade away

Alex Potts, Grade 5
The Orchard School, IN

My Pets

My pets make me happy and filled with glee,
I love on them and they always love on me.
My pets are the cutest things you'll see,
Whenever I leave them they always forgive me.
My precious little puppy-dog has a beautiful coat,
My cute little cat can take out a goat.
My pets are wondrous little creatures,
And they have many unique features.
I hope they stay here for a long, long time,
With me knowing they are part mine.

Maddy Detzer, Grade 4
Chrisney Elementary School, IN

My Grandpa

My grandpa was a tall robust man.
He worked with oil bits. He covered the land.
He made lots of money fixing a bit.
If people really knew how much, they would throw a fit.
My grandpa would travel from east to west,
Hauling to rigs to give it a test.
"Big Bill" they called him everywhere he went.
He worked so hard he'd even stay in a tent.
My grandpa will be remember by loving us all.
I take a glance at his room as I walk down the hall.

Noah Singer, Grade 5
North Intermediate Center of Education, IL

Wolf

I am a wolf
I touch the winter ground
I see a darting rabbit
I hear my pack running
I run after the rabbit
I taste my fresh prey
I am dangerous
I am related to dogs
I run in a pack
I take care of my pups

Hannah Dillon, Grade 5
North Knox West Intermediate/Elementary School, IN

Winter

It is my favorite time of year,
The bitter coldness fills the air.
Houses decorated with lights that glow,
As we wait for that first snow.
Wearing hats and gloves trying to stay warm,
Getting ready for another storm.
Boots are on and shovels are ready to go,
I am ready to face that snow.
When paths are made and all is done,
It's time to sled down the hills for fun.

Ryan Esquivel, Grade 6
St John the Baptist Catholic School, IN

Mother Earth

Mother
Earth is very
kind. If you met her
you would know. She makes
the sun shine in July. And in December
makes it snow. And she makes the peaceful
brook flow. Mother Earth is very kind, if you met
her you would know. She makes the seasons
beautiful and if you look around
you'll see it … WHOA!

Duvessa Faulkenberg, Grade 6
Alexandria Monroe Intermediate School, IN

A Gloomy, Gloomy Day

Gloomy, gloomy weather right before the snow,
The snow will come and the sun will go.
Waiting, hoping the snow will fall,
So I can go and throw a snowball.
It rains and rains way too much.
Snow will come so close I can touch.
Gloomy, gloomy weather right before the snow,
The cold, cold breeze will always blow.
Gloomy, gloomy weather please just go,
Please, please just snow.

Annie Weithman, Grade 6
Stanley Clark School, IN

Cryptids
Cryptids
Unknown, creepy
Yelling, creeping, and sneaking.
Watch your back!!!
(Bigfoot, Loch Ness monster)
Sage Veisberg, Grade 5
Van Rensselaer Elementary School, IN

Dog
Dog
Fluffy, cute
Exciting, protecting, scratching
Jumping on new furniture.
Pal
Ethan Gastineau, Grade 4
Van Rensselaer Elementary School, IN

Havanese
12 pounds of love,
Running towards my school bus,
Tail wagging with anticipation,
Joy flooding through my heart,
As we run inside together
Isabel Rosen, Grade 4
Highlands Elementary School, IL

Football
We stand tall and brave
We win we lose we fight
We play right with might
Kick, tackle, fight for winning
We play to win, we're Hornets
Aden Dennison, Grade 5
Henryville Elementary School, IN

Spiders
I saw a spider web.
With a spider in it.
I screamed and ran.
To my mom and dad.
I was bawling my eyes out.
Bethany Lents, Grade 4
Shoals Elementary School, IN

Me
Dreams are where I start
as inspiration passes me by
some daring ideas come along
good ideas lead me to a pool of imagination
then I realize it was me all along
Amanda Feder, Grade 5
Stanley Clark School, IN

Sea of Life
The waves of Change, roll in with the tide, out again, all is calm,
The calm before the storm.
Each wave, for better, for worse, for loss, for gain, it happens to us all.
The calm before the storm.
Every so often, a jewel of Change, so tremendous,
Leaving everything fresh and new, leaving your life, to start a new one.
Some of us, have jewels more than once, yet given the chance,
The sadness and joy, hope and despair, flow out unto paper.
The calm before the storm.
Any day, in any way, Change is in the air,
After so much, Change is our friend, yet still our foe,
The calm before the storm.
Small things, simple things, mean not, a bit of sea foam.
Each renewed, we lay a brick wall, a strong foundation,
To have it crumble before our eyes, and slowly be rebuilt.
The calm before the storm.
So long so calm, Change is making a hurricane,
A hurricane to make tears, scars, love, memories,
And that life just a ghost now, filled with sweet memories,
Bursting with sadness and longing, hope and joy.
The calm after the storm.
Lydia Jaskowiak, Grade 5
Highlands Elementary School, IL

Mommy's Way to Heaven
I see beautiful butterflies as beautiful as a red rose.
All around me in the air, they land on the trees, flowers and ground when they are tired.
The leaves fall from the sky like beautiful tiny raindrops some may think.
But no, they fall from the trees that our Lord made.
My mommy, she loves the grass because it's so green, like the stem that holds the flower.
Mommy and Daddy lay in a field of yellow tulips on a hot summer day.
But then all of sudden, the wind blew hard,
As hard as a rock, and the clouds grew dark.
My mommy looks up at the sky and says, "I can see God asking for me!"
She said she saw a stairway as bright as a room of light bulbs.
I wish she didn't. God says to me, "She will be watching over you."
That's how my mommy found her way to Heaven.
Shelby Christie, Grade 6
Cloverdale Middle School, IN

Ode to My Mother
Ode to my mother taking care of me.
Love her Chinese noodles with spicy chicken, she cares
When I get a cut she applies a
bandage on my knee.
Ode to my mother
when she says "It's okay I love you anyway."
When I'm sad she makes me happy and gives me a soft teddy bear hug.
When I'm scared or frightened at night she comforts me.
ode to my mother to help me with my homework
I give a big ode to
My mother
My care bear.
Nasim Ellahi, Grade 5
Walker Elementary School, IL

My Family Is a Car

My dad is the engine, he can go fast.
He can go slow he can go where ever he
wants us to go.

My brother Juan is the back passenger's
seat. He's always laid back not looking
so neat.

My brother Henry is the front license
plate wondering if someone will ask
him on a date.

My brother Richard is the window wipers.
He's always moving from let moving to right.
wondering if he's ever going to get it right.

My mom is the oil inside the car, so slick
and so fine like the family of mine.

Jennifer Guzman, Grade 6
Florence Nightingale Elementary School, IL

Closet

My family is a closet.

My mother is the coat hangers,
she supports the family and
can carry us when we fall off

My oldest brother is the door
to the closet, always swinging
in and out.

My younger older brother is a
pair of shoes, always with
his pair, meant for leaving but
he still comes back.

My little sister is the shirt,
always trying to be by the
coat hanger.

Jaqueline Ortiz, Grade 6
Florence Nightingale Elementary School, IL

Fall

Fall is coming, fall is near
let's all let out one big cheer.
Fall is here, so let's go play
because I know for a fact
that today will be an exciting day.

Leaves are changing colors
in October and November,
but I always keep in mind that fall is a season
we will always remember.

Darie'l Holmes, Grade 6
U S Grant Middle School, IL

What Was the Noise on Christmas Eve?

I awoke when I heard a sound
I didn't know where it came from, so I looked around
I saw presents under the tree
I found three with my name on it
I heard the noise again
It sounded like a plane
It came from the roof
I could be a tough burglar
I went to investigate
It was too late
He was gone
His voice had a good tone
It was SANTA CLAUS!

Cody Prifogle, Grade 6
St Michael School, IN

And the Chasing of the Cat Went On

And the chasing of the cat went on
Whoosh the cat ran past the dog
Whoosh they ran past the mini mart
And the chasing of the cat went on
Whoosh they ran past the highway
Whoosh they ran past the White House
And the chasing of the cat went on
Whoosh they ran past the pyramids
Whoosh they ran past the Eiffel Tower
And the chasing of the cat went on
Whoosh they ran past the arch
Whoosh they ran past the four corners
And the chasing of the cat went on

Briar Leigh, Grade 5
North Knox West Intermediate/Elementary School, IN

Fall

The breeze steps in,
sending scarlet raindrops to the ground.
Trees prepare for hibernation,
peepers and darters gather provisions.

Scarlet raindrops push into puddles,
shadows come quicker,
the corona fades faster.

Scarlet raindrops scatter with the four winds.

A breeze steps in,
the whiteness is coming.

Nicholas Liu, Grade 5
Highlands Elementary School, IL

Grass

The grass rustles now,
A small breeze whispers softly,
A pretty green sea.

Jamie DeJoan, Grade 4
Frank H Hammond Elementary School, IN

Halloween

H alloween is the opportunity to get as much candy as the candy store.

A ll the kids in their colorful costumes: some pretty princesses and even some dressed like a goblin.

L ick lick lick! Yummy lollipops are the best treats to eat on Halloween.

L eaving for the whole night just to get candy — exciting.

O w! is what you will say if you eat too much candy.

W ebs — lots of webs from spiders! Be careful or you might run into a spider web.

E mbracing your Halloween spirit with all kinds of decorations and crafts.

E ntertain yourself by watching silly spooky shows with special effects on Halloween.

N egative thoughts about Halloween are bad; always think about how good it is that kids get candy for free.

Taylor Moore, Grade 6
Three Rivers School, IL

Leaf

I am a leaf as green as the freshly sprouted grass. As the wind blows me, I fall from my tree like a bird soaring through the air, making every swift sway back and forth count. I can travel around the world in the air, river, and streams visiting countries I've not been and making people happy like a dog seeing his owner again. I am food for animals and bugs. Caterpillars think I taste like candy for a newborn child. Some people never cease to watch me, for I am very pretty in the fall. I change colors so warm it touches the hearts of many. I die in the winter, and grow back again. I see so much it's like a movie that never stops. I travel fast like a cheetah in the Sahara, back around past my tree that now looks like a TV turned off. I touch down so soft it's like jumping on a mattress. My life went by quickly like a drink in the hot summer. I turn brown as a newborn bear, and slowly die. But don't worry; I'll grow back in the springtime.

Jordan Berardi, Grade 6
Cloverdale Middle School, IN

Squirrel

As I scurry up a stone as smooth as ice, I look out on to the forest. I see leaves, as cryptic as space, and the dirt, soft like rubber. As I admire the pristine view, I notice something rummaging around in the grass. I swiftly head into the weeds, after whatever it happened to have been. It ran this way and that, and then I caught up with it. A bug as corpulent as a bear, stands before me. I start to languish it, and eat it. As I head back on a path as twisted as a corkscrew, I start to get thirsty. I head to a nearby river and drink from the water flowing like air. I head on my way. I go over a log that is long like a pole, and go back to my tree. This tree was porcine like a swine, with twisted and messy bark. I climb up to the only straight branch and found a nut, sweet like corn. So I cracked it, and ate it. After a long day, I rest in bed. I am a squirrel, amuck like a headless chicken in the daytime, but quiet like a mouse at night.

Evan Williamson, Grade 6
Cloverdale Middle School, IN

Water

My water flows through the long stream like leaves sway in the wind.

A large toad takes a humongous leap but misses by a few inches, and splashes water everywhere like a small child.

As I flow along, I see a spider spinning its web, a beautiful sight like a baby taking its first steps.

I have more grace than a butterfly. I am sweeter than an honest little girl.

I am older than the dinosaurs, longer than a mile, but shorter than two, bluer than the bluest ocean.

Smarter than Einstein, and prettier than a rose bush.

I am water.

Hannah Williams, Grade 6
Cloverdale Middle School, IN

Around the Bridge

There's a gravel path as bumpy as an alligator's skin. The path leads to hundreds of trees as tall as mountains. A simple feather falls as graceful as a ballerina. I walk upon a bridge as rough as sandpaper. I start to hear the sound of water as quiet as a mouse. A dragonfly comes by me as delicate as a baby. A rose stands alone between weeds. I go to take the weeds out, but I see the rose is as prickly as a porcupine, so I leave it alone. A bridge as smooth as a new road is ahead. I run as fast as a cheetah to the bridge. Just below the bridge is water that glistens as if it were glitter. Moss sits upon the water as green as an ogre. I look at the sky and see it is as black as coffee. On my way home, I think about all the things I saw around the bridge.

Kyla Baker, Grade 6
Cloverdale Middle School, IN

Waterfall

The
   Water
      Falls

        Down to the
          rocks below.

The mist feels
   cool on my
     face.

The ROARING
water pierces my
    ears.

I just want to
   swim in the

Cool
  Relaxing
    Calm

Water.

Lauren Elizabeth Courtney, Grade 6
Our Shepherd Lutheran School, IN

Trick-or-Treat

H alloween is scary,
A lways in a cemetery.
L ollypops and skeletons,
L ots of smiles on everyone.
O wls and ghosts,
W ells and posts,
E els and goblins,
E ating candy and cobblers.
N ice and chewy.

Elijah Fisher, Grade 4
Chrisney Elementary School, IN

My Basketball

This is my basketball
It's as bumpy as a wall
It is very fat
And I got it at the mall.

This is my basketball
Not bright as a light
Although it is orange
You can't see it at night.

This is my basketball
It is very round
And I like to bounce it
All over the ground.

Rachel Metzger, Grade 5
Forreston Grade School, IL

Fun at Halloween

Halloween is the best time of the year.
Little kids are running around with fear.
The door bells will ring,
The kids will scream.
The candy is sweet,
The bats will tweet.
I just love Halloween!
It's our time to scream!

Kyler Williams, Grade 4
Summit Elementary School, IL

Christmas

Christmas is fun,
Christmas is joy!
Christmas is great
For the girls and boys.
Christmas wasn't made
For sadness to be sent,
Christmas is love,
That's what Christmas meant!

Leah Tyler, Grade 4
Summit Elementary School, IL

Valentine's Day

It's Valentine's Day let's scream and shout
Because everyone knows what it's about
Chocolate, flowers, pink and white
It's really sweet on Valentine's night
You see all the love that's in the air
And all the couples here and there
It's Valentine's Day it's time to say
Everyone Happy Valentine's Day

Jordan McDonald, Grade 4
Summit Elementary School, IL

Valentine's Day

You see love all around,
Some are out of this town
You see some people are sad,
But some people are glad
You see stars in the sky,
You sit down with your guy
Talk about who you love,
You see a white bird that's a dove.

Darianna Crowder, Grade 4
Summit Elementary School, IL

Robots

I wish someone invents
robots that did my chores
robots that made video games
for me to play
and best of all
they would do my homework

Abhinav Bawankule, Grade 4
Ranch View Elementary School, IL

Adorable as a Puppy

Adorable as a puppy
Afraid as a newborn baby
Astonishing like a movie star
Cheerful as a cheerleader
Lucky as a four leaf clover
Mature like my sister
Magical like a magician
Likeable as a teddy bear
Fabulous as an actress
Heavenly as an angel
Lovely as a daisy
Protective as a body guard
Helpful as a teacher
Honorable as a president
Talented as a singer
Pretty as a flower
Joyous as Mrs. Claus
Quiet as a tree
Successful as a millionaire
Secretive as a spy

Miriam Gonzalez, Grade 5
Edison Elementary School, IL

Saying Goodbye

Crash boom
down she went
with her face as white as snow
tears streamed down
her beautiful face
some cried
some gasped
some just stood
stuck in a stance
thinking of what they had just witnessed
she was a loving daughter
caring friend
some tried to help
and did all they could
until it was too late
for she was already gone.
some were shocked
some were confused
and some didn't understand why
she had been taken from them.

Kira Pratico, Grade 6
Stanley Clark School, IN

Understandings

The sun smells the scent of the universe.
The tree eats apples off his branch.
No one knows why they do what they do.
They might want to be like us.
Or even yet they want to be better than us.
After all we are all one.

Kaelan Wright, Grade 6
St Angela School, IL

The Sycamore

The Sycamore is like a dad to all the trees.
Its branches are like strings in the wind.
The bugs make a home in the tree like a hotel.
The water falls like dancing swans on its branches.
Its leaves are like a Sunday vest.
Its bark is as sleek as velvet.
The grass grows around it like a skirt.
The bird is like a fish out of water on its branches.
The bird's nest shakes and shakes like an earthquake in its trunk.
All the trees in the forest are knights, and the Sycamore is a king.

Tyler Harrison, Grade 6
Cloverdale Middle School, IN

Me

Yes, my name is Lizzie,
Not Sarah, Tiffany, or Izzy.
I like to sing, dance, perform,
And I might get scared during a storm.
Me, I love sparkles and glitter,
And I'm not the best at softball, not as a hitter.
Pandas are my favorite creature,
When I grow up I might be a teacher.
Or maybe a dancer, singer, actress, find King Tut,
But I am Lizzie, no matter what.

Lizzie Flaspohler, Grade 6
St Michael School, IN

My Bicycle Ride

I like to play outside,
I like to take a long bicycle ride.
I like to glide, hide, and watch the tide.
I let my friends be the guide.
It is fun to skid and slide and hopefully not collide.
I always keep safety at my side.
When it gets cold, my bike is put up until the winter has died.
I cannot wait until my next bicycle ride.

Daniel Morris, Grade 6
Holy Family Catholic School, IL

Cookies

I think cookies are great,
My brother took eight!
There aren't many there,
My brother doesn't care!
Look at the mess he did create!

Cassidy Garner, Grade 6
Alexandria Monroe Intermediate School, IN

Frogs

Frogs
Slimy green
Frightening flipping jumping
Slimy gooey but unique
Amphibian

Roury Farnum, Grade 5
Washington Township Elementary School, IN

Winter Winds

You storm through the air
Winter wind
Your mission is to capture me
With icy hands
Making me frigid and lonely

Jack Frost's army comes skimming
Like the faintest hand writing along the road
Trying to get me
Reaching out with icy hands
Coming closer
But
My crusade of mittens and wool hats fight
Blocking Frost's catching hands and blows

I walk back to my house
Knowing that I have fought the wind

I have defeated Jack Frost's army!

Jake Rees, Grade 5
Walker Elementary School, IL

Computer

My family is a computer.

My mother is one of the most important things,
the monitor.
She can't be left out.

My father is the keyboard,
all he does is work and rest,
work and rest.

My brother is the speaker because,
he shouts and he screams,
he is very noisy.
He could pop an eardrum,
but he can also be quiet.

My smallest brother is the mouse,
he is everywhere,
he also touches everything.

Aimee Lopez, Grade 6
Florence Nightingale Elementary School, IL

Dream Until Your Dreams Come True

Dream until your dreams come true,
Ocean blue to ocean blue.
Yes it's true, you like to dream, from ocean to stream.
From afar you don't look real,
But from close you steal.
You steal the thoughts of everyone.
Because you are a dream come true,
So come on, I'll visit you.

Jordan Smith, Grade 4
St Matthew School, IL

Blue Eyes

You look me in the eyes with your blue eyes.
You sing a sad song into mine.
I'm sorry I have to leave you.
So why don't I just tell you the truth.
I still like you.
I do.
So how am I going to be without you.
I want to be more than friends.
But I can't let this friendship end.

Emmi Gramelspacher-Zehr, Grade 6
Jasper Middle School, IN

Vending Machines

The first one ever seen
was in England in 1615. With a
pipeful of tobacco which would have
been delightful for people who liked
that stuff. It even could be filled with
dozens of eggs. Who would beg for an egg?
But the silliest one was installed in Macy's
in 1960, that no one bought anything
from because they thought it was silly.

Victoria Chamoli, Grade 4
Ranch View Elementary School, IL

Sleep

I lay in my bed
my eyes starting to enclose
my pillow cushions my head
as my tiredness grows.

I start to count sheep
all in my mind
as I fall asleep.
How many will I find?

Savanna Farren, Grade 5
Grande Reserve Elementary School, IL

My Dad

My dad is in Joliet today.
I miss him when he is away.
It makes me feel sad.
It makes me mad.
But I'm still glad he's my dad.

Sophie Tomaso, Grade 4
St Matthew School, IL

Impossible

I'm as quick as a cheetah.
I'm as slow as a turtle.
I'm as short as an ant.
I'm as tall as an elephant.
I'm as skinny as a stick bug.
I'm as fat as a hippo.

Malachy Martin, Grade 5
Henryville Elementary School, IN

Similes

Cool as polar ice
Healthy as brown rice
Green as grass on the countryside
Fast as a horseback ride
Blind as a bat
Scared as a cat
Slimy as a snail
Hard as a nail
Tall as redwood trees
Fun as writing similes

Ariana Paunovic, Grade 4
Lincoln Elementary School, IL

Babies

Babies are quiet
Babies are small
Babies cry all day long
When they don't cry, they smile
When they smile, they laugh
When they laugh, it makes
their mothers smile
It makes their whole day
They are tiny
They are newborns

D'Yonna Dawning, Grade 5
Stanley Clark School, IN

Sledding

The snow is nice
Except the ice
The moon is bright
In the sky at night
Sledding is fun
Just not under the sun
Just try and miss the trees
As you feel the night breeze
Hope you don't fall
Or hit the brick wall

Evan Brown, Grade 5
Stanley Clark School, IN

Dog

He's off
chasing the cat down the street.
He's off
chasing a leaf down the driveway.
He's off
chasing his toy through the house.
He's off
sleeping 'til tomorrow.
He's off
doing it all again.

Alex Good, Grade 5
Manchester Intermediate School, IN

The Day We Get Out of School

I can't wait to get out of school in May
On that day I will say yay

We will have 100 days
To have fun and run and play

Maybe we will go away
To have fun every day

That will be my favorite day
The day I get out of school in May

Carter Payne, Grade 5
Dee Mack Intermediate School, IL

Forever Mine

You look into my eyes
I throw mine into yours
The glare from the sun hits my face
A tear comes out of my blood-red eyes
Plenty of thoughts dash through my head
You squirm your head into my arms
Touching your fur is like feeling snow
I touch your tiny paw
Nails scratch my hands
But I don't care you are mine
Forever mine

Naomi Sanchez, Grade 6
Zapata Academy, IL

Outside

The wind is blowing.
You can smell the
Flowers in the
wind. The sun
Is out.
The kids are playing.
And they play all day.
Until they have to go
Home and sleep the
Night away.

Sarah Anderson, Grade 4
Van Rensselaer Elementary School, IN

You Americans

Time to go
Time to fight
Time to win our nation's rights
Left, Left, Left, Right, Left
As we fight
All through the night
It's time to fight for our nation's rights
It's time to fight
It's time to win
It's time to be free again

Grace Garner, Grade 6
Staunton Jr High School, IL

Mom and Dad

Mom
Nice, lovable
Cares for, loving, helping
Genius, honesty, friend, loyalty
Understanding, caring, listener
Handsome, bright
Dad
Alyssa Marquez, Grade 5
Edison Elementary School, IL

Opposite Animals

Dog
Fluffy, furry
Barking, running, playing
Fast, exhilarated, slow, tired
Meowing, walking, sleeping
Silky, soft
Cat
Julia Gregor, Grade 5
Edison Elementary School, IL

Rigid

As stiff as a board.
Very, very strict.
Unbendable
unchanging
unarguable
unbreakable.
Rigid.
Henry Visconsi, Grade 5
Stanley Clark School, IN

The Fall

It is fall!
In the fall,
I like to play ball.
I call my friends to play in the leaves.
I like to feel the nice cool breeze.
I love the fall.
I love the trees.
Haley Hartleb, Grade 4
St Matthew School, IL

Chickens and Ducks

Chicken
White, brown
Clucky, produce eggs, crispy
Corn, beaks, swim, bill
Quacky, feathery, eat fish
Good swimmers, migrators
Ducks
Ashlyn K. Smallan, Grade 5
Edison Elementary School, IL

Homework

Homework, homework
You're a child's worst nightmare
Homework you're a child's job

Homework, homework
You stink
More than a skunk
Homework
You ruin a kid's freedom

Homework, homework
The worst part of school
I could write a bunch of bad things
About YOU!!
Homework, homework
You're the weights
In my backpack

Now I better hurry
Or I will have more homework to do!!!
Alvin Huynh, Grade 5
Walker Elementary School, IL

Christmas

It was a gloomy night.
The sky was gray and dull.
The family in their house.
Spreading Christmas cheer about.
Hanging decorations by the mantelpiece.
The family hanging by a thread. They saw
the swirl of snow going
windward. They hardly
had enough money
to pay the bills. Their
grandparents paid
the bills yearly.
Their faces were
crooked. Though
they had little,
they simply didn't
care. They just
cared that they
were together for
the last time.
Giavanna Wilson, Grade 6
Christian Academy of Indiana, IN

Halloween, Christmas

Halloween
Dark, scary
Trick or treating, dressing up, eating candy
Masks, bloody, fun, awesome
Cold, colorful
Christmas
Adrian Casimiro, Grade 5
Edison Elementary School, IL

Tooth

Wiggly, jiggly tooth
Oh so very loose
You wiggle it and jiggle it
but it won't come out

Just be patient
and it will come out
You have to be patient
and don't pout

Eat your dinner
You won't regret it
You take a bite and…Pop!
Out comes your tooth!
Brylee Kerr, Grade 5
Manchester Intermediate School, IN

Angels

Angels are white
Angels are bright
They help me fall
Asleep at night

Angels guide me
Day by day
They make my bad dreams
Go away

They are my shepherd
I never flee
Because these angels
Are watching me
Paige Patterson, Grade 6
Emmanuel-St Michael Lutheran School, IN

Thankful for God

God is the right way,
God is my guide so that I don't stray,
He lives inside of me,
He is in my dreams,
He makes me do good things,
Following God's rules is a must,
And in God, I will always trust!
Enijay Averyhart, Grade 5
Walker Elementary School, IL

Opening Morning

A long walk in the pitch dark
Brown and yellow leaves
crunching under my feet.
I climb the frozen metal bars of the ladder.
At daylight squirrels come out to play.
I'm sitting, waiting, watching
for a big, monster buck.
Brayden Casper, Grade 5
Manchester Intermediate School, IN

My Sister

She shines like the sun, when she walks into the room.
When she enters, you hear a pitter patter on the floor.
She has a little voice when she sings her
favorite song, "Twinkle, Twinkle, Little Star."
When she eats something she despises,
she'll make a sour face.
Hearing her name, she looks and says, "Hi, hi, hi"
In her imagination, she feels that tree are
waving at her when she goes outside; she
has to wave back.
When she looks at you, it seems her eyes are stars.
If she is crying, it makes you want to cry, too.
Her smell is like a little baby.
Her skin is so soft.
My baby sister is like an angel to me.
Loving her is all I can do.
Her name is Nataly Rose Flemings.

Kimberly Lopez, Grade 6
Florence Nightingale Elementary School, IL

Where I Am From

I am from the fluffy waffles,
Dark brownies, and chewy Skittles
I am from watching The Walking Dead

and Grimm a drama show were they retell Grimm's fairy tales, and
watching Cinderella as a little girl

I am from the trophies won, jewelry boxes
I am from a delicate tea pot collection
I am from "Did you do your chores?" and "Don't slam the door!"
I am from the disgusting cheeseless broccoli that haunts my plate,
and the rude bullies that scare me to even be around them.

I am from helping cook a delightful dinner for my family
and playing trivia as we eat,
I am also from reading my favorite series
By Beverly Cleary, the Ramona books.

Hailie Collins, Grade 6
Knox Community Middle School, IN

Summer

From the time the sun reaches middle sky
All of us children wake up in a flash
We feel so great we could just jump and fly
We quick run outside in a silly dash
Summer!
There! All of our friends, let's go get some ice cream!
What flavor what flavor, we're free to choose.
It's a perfect Summer day in kids' dreams
A day when nobody could ever lose
Summer!
Oh! It's back! It's back! Can you believe it?
Three cheers because the loved Summer is here!

Holly Fjeldstad, Grade 5
Hawthorne Elementary School, IL

Car

My family is a car.

My dad is the battery;
he keeps us together
he gives us energy for the day.

My mother is the gasoline;
she makes us go and believe in our dreams.
My mother is the seat belt;
she always keeps us in safe.

My sister, Kassy, is the radio;
she's always listening to the radio
she's always singing
she is always talking
she is also entertainment and she makes
us have a lot of fun.

My sister, Erika, is the seats;
she is the seats because when
you sit by her you feel comfortable
she makes you feel like a comfy pillow

Carolina Favela, Grade 6
Florence Nightingale Elementary School, IL

I Wish I Had a Horse

I wish I had a horse
So beautiful
Their shiny coats and flowing manes
Are all I could ever wish for
I wish I had a horse
Don't you understand?
A sleek bay horse with a star on his forehead
His name would be Beauty
I would ride him across the fields
And feed and groom him every day
I wish I had a horse
His name would be Beauty

Emma Burlingame, Grade 5
Manchester Intermediate School, IN

The Best Hot Chocolate You Ever Had

A wave of milk chocolate hits my tongue
Making my heart feel like
A silky river of moonlight floating in the sky
Suddenly, a fluffy white cloud
Takes over the bursting hurricane
Marshmallows make my tastebuds stand up tall
Then a thunderstorm of cinnamon
Rains down, adding a bit of edge to my white fluffy cloud
All together, the wave, the cloud, the thunderstorm
Mixed together
Make
The best hot chocolate you ever had.

Liana Wallace, Grade 5
Walker Elementary School, IL

Kenny the Parakeet

Squawk! Squawk!
He soars like a hawk.
He's a parakeet named Kenny,
But he still doesn't talk!

He crushes up a snack
With his beak that is black.
He loves eating peanuts;
He could eat a whole stack!

He chews all our mail.
He has a red tail.
He's as cute as a puppy
But as loud as a whale!

Squawk! Squawk!
He soars like a hawk.
He's a parakeet named Kenny,
But he still doesn't talk!
Brian Williams, Grade 6
Our Lady of Peace School, IL

I Am

I am smart and great at basketball
I wonder if I could be a NAAS car racer
I hear lots of great news
I see me in a mansion
I want a DSI with *Zelda*
I am smart and great at basketball

I pretend I am the son of Dionysus
I feel happy
I touch my Christmas present
I worry about not getting all As
I cry when I am majorly hurt
I pretend I am the son of Dionysus

I understand how to read
I say, "I'm cool!"
I dream I am a NASCAR racer
I try to work hard
I hope I will be the richest man!
Enijah Averyhart, Grade 5
Walker Elementary School, IL

Pizza

Pizza night is tonight
I can't wait
I got home
And I screamed,
"What kind of pizza are we having?"
"Are we getting
Cheese pizza
Tonight?"
Madeline Brown, Grade 4
Lincoln Elementary School, IL

New York City

New York City shines
When I step out of
My cab I see the street
Lights and people.
I hear beeping and honking
And screaming and yelling.
I see homeless and garbage
And filth galore.
But just beyond the seashore…
I see the Statue of
Liberty all gleaming and blue,
Even brighter than the water.
Man that looks cool!
And that my friends was New York City.
So visit me sometime
And we'll all see the
Statue of Liberty!
Mary Wetterling, Grade 4
Copeland Manor Elementary School, IL

Fall

Arise
The blossom of happiness
As music of color dances in the air

A gentle kitten
Pawing at the world
Changing green to gold

The Pied Piper blows his pipe
All living things fall into his spell
Diversity and Beauty
Reign once more

As the frigid claws attack
And the land turns bleak
I look back on the golden days
And smile
Karen Ge, Grade 5
Highlands Elementary School, IL

School

I love school!
There's so much to do
Jump up and down
and get your wiggles out
Play at recess
Come inside
Get your homework out
Then go to gym
Eat lunch
Do math and science
End the day with a hug
Out the door.
Elizabeth Manley, Grade 4
Copeland Manor Elementary School, IL

My Sister and I…

My sister and I are different
Different it is
Different it is

My sister and I are not alike
Not at all
Not at all

My sister and I do not resemble
Yes, that's it
Yes, that's it

We are different
We are not alike
We are not similar

I have problems with her
Sometimes
Sometimes

I have fights with her
All the time
All the time

I have her
and
She has me
Aashiyana Patel, Grade 5
Stanley Clark School, IN

Ice Cream

Yummy!
Melts in your mouth like snowflakes.
Dreamy.

Makes your taste buds dance,
You want to drool,
Yummy!

I get in the freezer, yes! Confetti cake!
I dip in the spoon and like it clean.
Dreamy.

I dip it in again, and I'm in heaven!
Then I go in the freezer again, chocolate!
Yummy!

I dip in the chocolate
And I melt away in the creamy river.

I dip in, and another, and another!
Until the carton is all gone.
Yummy!
Dreamy
Aleece Geiger, Grade 5
Northern Heights Elementary School, IN

Where I'm From

I am from a household full of children
From cat hisses and puppy kisses
I am from fighting brothers and sassy sisters
And praying every night before dinner
I am from Sycamore trees swaying above
Whose leaves danced their way to the ground
I am from football games and hidden treats
From the middle name Renee and the nickname Misty
I am from Chili on New Years and staying up way late
And from showing no pain during ball games
From watching super bowls together
I am from catching fireflies in the midnight
I am from Patrick Keown and Misty Bussell
From homemade meatloaf and cheesy Mac and cheese
From hard work to keep the family happy
And from surviving illness
From cuddling with my Winnie the Pooh blankets
I am from those moments when the Sycamore tree drops her leaf
Right on my nose

Skyler Keown, Grade 5
Perry Central Elementary School, IN

It's Best to Live in the Midwest

My favorite place to live is in the Midwest, it beats the rest
North, South East and West.

Summertime is so much fun, hanging out with my brother
in the hot sun. I love where I live, because of the lakes.
They give us so much fun, during our summer break.

Fall is full of beautiful leaves. Best of all is the Halloween breeze.
I look forward to my last trick or treat day, as I get older, but it's OK.

I love winter with its clean white snow. It tells me Christmas is near,
which is the most magical time of year.

When spring arrives, I realize the end of my school year is near.
As I walk to school, I get to see all the pretty flowers
and leaves on the trees.

The Midwest is the best place to live in this great country
that I so love.

Lenny Lubas, Grade 6
St John the Baptist Catholic School, IN

Presents

P eople love to get
R eally nice presents.
E veryone thinks good gifts are
S uper expensive.
E ntertaining presents are fun, but it's
N ot the expensive gifts
T hat are the best; ones from the heart are
S o much more special.

Mira Fefferman, Grade 4
Frank H Hammond Elementary School, IN

Plant

My family is a plant.

My father is the dirt;
He helps the plant grow.
He holds the family together.
But he also sometimes dries out.

My mother is the stem;
Who holds the leaves from falling;
She loves her family,
But sometimes she's feeling down.

My brother is the leaf;
He makes the plant beautiful.
He always has a smile on his face,
No matter what he always sticks together
And never falls.

Analisa Castaneda, Grade 6
Florence Nightingale Elementary School, IL

I Am From

I am from the Chicago Bears
and Atlanta Falcons
I am all about NFL
And going to my uncle's every Sunday for football.

I am from SpongeBob on Nick
and Walking Tall on Starz.
From long movies to short episodes.
I am from get up and stop being lazy!
From sitting to riding a bike.

I am from jamming music from Hollywood Undead
to Eminem.

I am from my cousin dying in a car crash at age 17
and scarring my knuckles and cut bone from rust.
I am from those memories.

Ethan Cooper, Grade 6
Knox Community Middle School, IN

Nature

Trees etching the blue sky,
Flowers blooming at lightning speed,
Colors coating everything in sight,
Grass as soft and light as a blanket,
Whoosh! The wind blows by leaving a trace of coldness,
Leaves as crinkly as paper,

The animals whispering to you saying, "Come join us,"
Dirt looking as if it were brown sugar getting mixed into a bowl
To make a batch of cupcakes,
The sheer crystal sky gleaming and spreading joy around the world,
So go outside and take a trip of a lifetime!!!

Taylor Cyr, Grade 6
Frederick Nerge Elementary School, IL

Camouflage

Waking up early,
So excited.
Waiting for a deer up in the stand.
Hear the crunch of leaves.
Camouflage.

The gun is armed.
I see a deer and think to myself.
So excited.
I wait before I make a move.
I hold my breath.
Camouflage.

I shoot the gun.
Did I hit the deer?
So excited.
I'm afraid to look.
My heart is thumping.
Camouflage.
So excited.

Tyler Henry, Grade 5
Northern Heights Elementary School, IN

The Story of the Twins

High up in the sky
the huge towers rose up high
twins in the large sky.

The sun shone brightly
the twins glistened in the sky
the world was peaceful.

The evil spread fast
soon the twins were crippled bad
and down they traveled.

Soon evil vanished
from it came new creation
and new twins were made.

The new buildings rose
high up in the bright blue sky
the seven returned.

Fezaan Kazi, Grade 6
Stanley Clark School, IN

Kaley

K ind
A wesome
L oving
E xcellent
Y ou are the
    most kindest
    person.

Abalena Hampton, Grade 4
Shoals Elementary School, IN

Germs

I'm with you every day
I'm with you when you play

I'm in your drinks
I'm even in your sinks

I'm living in your hair
I'm even in the air

I'm in your car
I'm everywhere you are

I'm a germ!

Hailey Johnson, Grade 5
Dee Mack Intermediate School, IL

Fall

A beginning of an end,
but the end of a beginning.
A crisp force to wash away the torrid heat.
Almost a pleasant warning
to inform of a frigid weather to be.

A time of change,
joy, and peace to bring
the body to rest.
No matter what sense is at work,
the feel is miraculous.
Mistrals come and go,
but they always soothe my stresses.

Adam Jerzy Spitzner, Grade 5
Highlands Elementary School, IL

Waiting

Days and days of waiting
    waiting for the snow.
Days and days of waiting
    waiting for nothing.
Sitting and sitting staring
out the window hoping for white.
Sitting and sitting bored out
    of my mind
    feeling trapped inside
    behind bars or
behind a never ending wall
    waiting and waiting for
    the snow.

Meggie Weithman, Grade 6
Stanley Clark School, IN

Fang

Sharp, white, and shiny
Pierces like a gold dagger
Red with blood from prey

Olivia Campbell, Grade 5
Northern Heights Elementary School, IN

The Flee

Today I think I will just flee,
Jump outside and feel so free.

Make a friend at the rough made sea,
Walk around and meet what I see.

People will listen to what I say,
I might even see a horse and hay.

I will stay there to jump and play,
I will also swim, if said I may.

Paul Ragon, Grade 5
Dee Mack Intermediate School, IL

Chocolate

Who invented chocolate?
An intelligent person you must
    Agree. It must have taken
    Them years and years
    To invent something so
    Yummy. Chocolate has its
    Ups and downs, I like
    Chocolate year round.
It shouldn't take much time
To see how much chocolate
    Means to me.

Saachi Kumar, Grade 4
Ranch View Elementary School, IL

The Amazing Zoo

At the zoo I hear lions
    roar. I see cheetahs run.
Also tigers eat and monkeys
touch their bananas. I smell
the elephants they stink. Kangaroos
are hopping. There are giraffes
eating. Also pandas climbing. I see
    seals swimming and penguins
    diving. I hear parrots squawking.
I see polar bears swim. I hear
    peacocks pecking.

Cate Dudley, Grade 4
Copeland Manor Elementary School, IL

What Is a Soldier?

A soldier is...

S trong
O ver there
L oyal
D angerous work
I ndependent
E xtraordinary
R isk takers

Zach Dilley, Grade 6
Herrick Grade School, IL

Apples vs Humans

I am sitting in my favorite tree
I am in the country.
Then a big gust of wind whoosh
Knocks apples down from my tree
They hit the ground blam! Thwap!
I feel bad for those apples because
Their only fate is to be savagely ripped apart
But what is a better fate —
Being eaten or staying on the ground,
Rotting?
Then I had a thought
Why couldn't those apples be born as oh, let's say a human?
Answer, because if there were no apples, the food chain would break.
So we humans are lucky nothing eats us.
We are the top of the food chain.

Lilly Karwowski, Grade 5
Hawthorne Elementary School, IL

The Avett Brothers

The Avett Brothers are a very nice band.
Everybody knows them throughout the land.
I went to my first concert with a friend,
I was wishing it would never end.
Scott is the banjo picking king,
Nobody could top him not even Lightning McQueen.
Seth is really tall and skinny,
A lot of his songs are dedicated to Jenny.
Bob plays the bass.
He plays it at a very nice pace.
Joe Kwon plays the cello,
He is a very nice fellow.
Jake has a very nice beat,
He makes you want to move your feet.
The Avett Brothers are the coolest!!

Carli Morris, Grade 5
North Intermediate Center of Education, IL

Friends

Friends are always there for you.
They may get in fights but they are still always there for you.
Friends are people who you share memories, laughs,
secrets, and jokes with.
Friends are always there for you.
They spend the night and go on vacations with you.
You sometimes have crazy, funny, or shy friends.
They hangout with you at recess and sit with you at lunch.
Friends are always there for you.
If you can't forgive them then you'll end up with no friends at all.
You can have best friends, not so close friends, or
friends that you sometimes hangout with.
Best friends are people that are there for you
no matter what happens.
Friends are always there for you.

Makinzi Meurer, Grade 5
North Knox West Intermediate/Elementary School, IN

We Remember

Fire, Burning, Horror, Screams,
We remember.
We saw many lives taken away,
And the people who saw terror that day,
We remember.
We heard the blasting alarms and torturous cries,
And we saw the firefighters sacrifice for other's lives,
We remember.
But, we saw our country come together like a knot,
And regained hope, which we all forgot,
We remember.
Today— we remember — but we still stand tall,
And some believe we will never fall.
We will not forget September 11th.
We remember.

Jack Rosenberg, Grade 5
Hawthorne Elementary School, IL

Everything for a Poem

Paper,
Pencil and eraser,
Ideas,
The starts of a poem.
Similes,
Metaphors,
Being like this, or being that, or being a poem.
Happiness,
Sadness,
Feelings for a poem.
Onomatopoeias, personification, and imagery
Figurative language to add to a poem.
Compact language,
Great for a poem.
Everything for a poem.

Alexandra Barishman, Grade 5
Hawthorne Elementary School, IL

My Grandpa*

When I was very young, grandpa and me
Played a basketball game called h-o-r-s-e.

Although I was just learning and I didn't play that well,
Grandpa said I'd get better or at least I'd learn to spell.

My grandpa is getting old now, but he stills plays with me.
He does it even though he can no longer run, jump, nor see.

I am the better player now, but I sometimes let him win,
Just as he used to do for me time and time again.

When I asked if it would be okay to dedicate this poem to him,
He smiled and said it surely was and he'd get even at the gym.

Bret Doan, Grade 5
North Intermediate Center of Education, IL
*Dedicated to my Grandpa

I Am From

I'm from where the deer steak
fills the house with spicy, juicy smell
I'm from the house where they say "Get a job."
I am from where I'm the boss of the candy
When I'm not busy I'm on the love seat
Watching "Ghost Whisperer"
Or reading

I'm from the family that loves Uno Flash
to watching the movie S.W.A.T.
all night long.

These things make me who I am.

Alyssa Smith, Grade 6
Knox Community Middle School, IN

Basketball Fun

The game has just begun.
It's time to have some fun.
We start out with our five starters.
The game is going to be close,
but we might be toast.
Without a doubt we will still have some fun.
Now it's the second half,
The other team is starting to laugh.
We are down one point.
The game is almost over,
but we comeback and win the game.
We all shake the other team's hands and say good job.
So we won the first game!!!

Hunter Jackson, Grade 6
Alexandria Monroe Intermediate School, IN

Tyrannosaurus Rex

Lasers that scan every single tree.
Supersonic eardrums
looking for the slightest sound
that will give up the position of dinner.
Wheels that carry the body to its goal.
Glistening, razor-sharp, elephant-tusk knives,
waiting to rip flesh to shreds
Then...
a sound! The dinosaur's engines charge toward the noise.
A car is no match for a monster truck.
Soon the half-eaten carcass attracts bigger trucks,
And the killer must run or be killed.

Prateek Dullur, Grade 5
Highlands Elementary School, IL

The Big Croc

He lives in a swamp
Stalks his prey in the water
His big jaws will snap
You in half if you are close

Colton Boger, Grade 5
North Knox West Intermediate/Elementary School, IN

Benjamin

Benjamin
"The First American"
Author, politician, scientist, and inventor.
Whose face is on the 100 dollar bill.
Who invented the robot arm, bifocals
And the lightning rod.
Who helped us write
The Declaration of Independence.
Who said, "A penny saved is a penny earned."
Franklin

Braeden Smith, Grade 4
Ranch View Elementary School, IL

I Don't Run Away

Bullies, mean dogs, and tigers
Who want to hurt me.
I don't run away.
Zach and Wesley try
To make me flip.
I don't run away.

Coming towards me with a snake on the tip
I don't run away
Until...They put it on me!
I run Away, Bye!

Kimber Meier, Grade 5
North Knox West Intermediate/Elementary School, IN

Losing a Friend

Have you ever lost a dear friend?
It's like your whole world would end.
You're afraid you won't ever meet a friend like that again,
Just remember, it's not the end.
It's like she vanished in the dry summer air,
Your soul could never bear.
Tear, tear, an out-flowing burst,
You can see in my eyes, it just hurts.
Watching her go,
It's very hard to know,
You won't ever see her again.

Anna Jaderholm, Grade 6
U S Grant Middle School, IL

Halloween

H appy and anxious to buy costumes
A nd to go trick-or-treating.
L ots of candy is passed out to the children who
L ove Halloween.
O n this special night, when it is beginning, kids go
W ild to get buckets of candy.
E veryone who passes out candy is
E ntertained by the scary and funny costumes.
N ever has any child hated Halloween.

Tarun Girn, Grade 4
Frank H Hammond Elementary School, IN

Bengal Cat

A flash of light
an agile figure in the shadows
the most exquisite in history
it ends purring.

A great jungle beast
a shrunken leopard cat
unstoppable in the face of danger
it ends purring.

Marbles glow in darkness
the midnight hunter
silent spots leap onto an unsuspecting meal
it ends purring.

Swiftness that never yields
a minisculed cheetah
a never hurried but always furry creature
it ends in a purrful catnap.

Angie Dauber, Grade 4
Highlands Elementary School, IL

Halloween

Halloween comes in handy
When you don't have any candy.
Some of my treats
Will go to Pete.

The rest was hurt
So it goes to Bert.
We trick-or-treat at night
Sometimes that gives me a fright.

After everything is dandy
Then we eat some candy.
I really love Halloween
Some costumes made me scream.

Puss in Boots
Has a lot of loot.
Mr. Bear has a lot of hair
He got extra loot, now that's not fair!

Amelia Bell, Grade 4
Coal City Intermediate School, IL

My Dog Dixie

I love her so much.
Always sleeps with me at night.
Found her in our driveway.
Plays with my other great dogs.
She loves me and I love her.
She is the best dog.
She is so so so so small.
I love my dog Dixie.

Riley Keister, Grade 5
Northern Heights Elementary School, IN

The Golden Shiny Trophy

A challenging game
With athletic players
Scoring goals — completing homework
Persistence and determination
Leading to many wins and fantastic grades

After the game
Team players pick me up
As I hold the golden, victorious trophy
That's a ticket to next season's challenge

6th grade

Ingrid Guevarra, Grade 5
Walker Elementary School, IL

Loud Noises in the Dark Night

Thunder, lightning, burning bright,
in your mind there's fear and fright.
Flashing clouds in the night,
from those hot zigzag lights.
Noises make you jump and shake,
like a leaf you start to quake.
Teeth chattering noises, lightning makes,
being brave your courage it takes.
Makes you shiver inside your bed,
brings an ache inside your head.
Over my house the mean cloud hovers,
I bury my head under my covers.

Emma Celaric, Grade 4
Copeland Manor Elementary School, IL

Winter

I walk outside into the cold,
A winter wonderland I behold.
The bare trees are now all white,
And the whole world is shining bright.
My ears and nose both turning numb,
I make a snow fort while I hum.
I make a snowman carrot and all,
I feel the cold snow as it falls,
I look at the paw prints in the snow,
I feel a pinch at my little toe,
But no matter how cold it will get,
The winter days I'll never forget.

Rachel Courtney, Grade 6
Christian Academy of Indiana, IN

My Preposition

With a halter in my hand
By the judge
At the fair
About to win
Among the others
With my cow by my side

Sadie Zumbrun, Grade 5
Northern Heights Elementary School, IN

Baseball

A swing, a miss.
Strike two.
I better get a hit
so I can stay with you.

Here's the pitch.
CRACK! A double.
I'm out of my slump,
no more trouble.

Here I am,
waiting to steal.
My dreams of the show,
are still real.

Cody Rogers, Grade 4
Coal City Intermediate School, IL

Time for Rhyme

Time for rhyme every day
At your house or down by the bay

Time for rhyme anytime anywhere
You may even feel some despair

If you want to rhyme every hour
You have serious rhyming power

Rhyme takes some time
But it is fine

At your house in your car
You can rhyme near and far

Lily Best, Grade 4
Coal City Intermediate School, IL

Winter

It's warm outside
But it's coming,
The wind is warm
Not like winter.
Why is it so cold around winter?
Why can't it be spring or fall that's cold?
Well that's ok
Cold is still good,
Right?
It must be.
People are all smiling around winter.
Next time you think of winter,
Don't think of cold,
Think of the good that comes with it!

Bella Costanzo, Grade 5
Hawthorne Elementary School, IL

A Splash into Summer
The summer sun had come today
The winter snow has gone away
The robin with its shiny breast
Has found a place to build her nest

The world again sings loud its song
The nights are warm and days are long
Summer is the time of joy
For every girl and happy boy
Jamie Strouts, Grade 6
Emmanuel-St Michael Lutheran School, IN

Piano
Fingers dancing lazily
A lonely melody
It's sweet
But sour
It's hot
But cold
Playing by the hour
Fingers dancing lazily
A lonely melody
Emma Johnston, Grade 4
Lincoln Elementary School, IL

The Season of Winter
When bundling coats with care
winter is approaching FAST!
playing in the winter snow,
and drinking hot cocoa

Enjoy it before it goes,
before you're slipping on ice in the road
soon it will be mush,
DON'T let winter rush!
Olivia Wilson, Grade 5
Grande Reserve Elementary School, IL

Furry Balls
What are those little balls
That I see down the hall
Look how they move
Look how they groove
Black and white
Orange with delight
They look like mittens
But they are only kittens
Sara Runyon, Grade 5
Dee Mack Intermediate School, IL

Spring
Spring is a great day.
The flowers are pretty and blue.
The flowers have color.
Naombi Givens, Grade 4
St Angela School, IL

Sounds Forever
Silent is the sound of me sleeping,
the sound of me working on this poem,
the sound of reading,

Loud is the big city,
at recess,
an action-packed movie,

Eternal is God in our hearts,
the Earth,
us learning every day.
Harley Zorn, Grade 4
Churubusco Elementary School, IN

Worm
I am an earthworm.
My favorite activity is to squirm.

I love to wiggle.
I also giggle.

I like to play under ground.
I hide under playgrounds.

I am always the color brown.
People never tell me to slow down.
Tyler Weishaupt, Grade 5
Dee Mack Intermediate School, IL

A Mini Little Minute
Tick-tock-tick-tock
a minute only has 60 seconds to live
tick-tock-tick-tock
1-2-3-4
a minute only has 60 seconds to do what
it wants before it fades and there is another
minute replacing its digits
to live its life
tick-tock-tick-tock
58-59-60
Done.
Sophie Friend, Grade 6
Stanley Clark School, IN

The Ocean
I wish that I could go to the ocean blue
and with a dolphin too!
Oh man, how I love the ocean.
Hey, how about you come along too?
There are fish, whales, and dolphins.
I love the ocean all the way through!
I wish that I could swim in the sea,
and I wish that the sting ray, sea horse,
and the manatee could all live with me.
Joe Sellett, Grade 4
St Matthew School, IL

Baseball
When I got on the field I felt so great
but I feel better when I step up to the plate

I hit the ball so far I can't see it
I heard a guy say I caught it in my mitt.

When I hit the ball so high
it looked like it was eaten by the sky.

After that day when we won the big game
I never felt so much fame.
Cameron Lander, Grade 4
Coal City Intermediate School, IL

The One and Only
I love him so much
I love him and he loves me!
Although he's in heaven now
We walk together
Together we walk through times
We love each other
I need things and he gives them!
Up in the air, he is there!
He hugged me a lot!
Video games was his thing!
The one and only
Rebekah Hollowell, Grade 5
Northern Heights Elementary School, IN

Food Fights
Food is flying,
Flies are fleeing,
Girls are crying,
Kids are hiding,
Boys are fighting,
Milk is spilling,
Our teachers are slipping,
Food fights are Fan-tast-ic,
But after the fight,
We're on the floor,
Cleaning up the fun of the food fight war.
Austin Martinez, Grade 5
Van Rensselaer Elementary School, IN

If I Were a Football
If I were a football,
I'd fly all day.
I would be on the ground.
But at the end I would lay.

If I were a football,
I would be like superman and fall.
I would be thrown super hard.
Nobody would catch me at all.
Hector Mata, Grade 5
Edison Elementary School, IL

Dance Class
The soft golden light welcomes me
Into the studio
Where many other dancers have with great effort
Learned to do jetés and pirouettes
On dainty pointe shoes
Or studied intricate tap routines
As we dance across the floor
It seems like we are delicate tiny snowflakes
As we are each individual but dance the steps with graceful care
We are petals floating from a pink rose in the gentle spring wind
Or the leaves on a maple tree floating to the ground
Then when show-time comes
We show all that we have to be proud of
Sophia Gerald, Grade 6
Bednarcik Jr High School, IL

I Am From
I am from crunchy Snickers,
From watching movies on cold nights.
(Hear the bed
calling your name)
I am from bad Chinese food.
From the Wedding Singer and adventure time!
I am from ring tones on the phone.
While we play with string foam
I am from going to movies with my mom!
and from cold dark nights
The wind calls my name
It is time to sleep,
Goodnight.
Raven Tolson, Grade 6
Knox Community Middle School, IN

Snowfall
The snow is coming.
Everyone is excited.
It's gonna be cold, get your winter clothes on.
The snow is coming.

Buy some shovels, there's gonna be a lot of snow.
We have to stay warm.
The snow is coming.

Don't get frostbite, so be careful.
You can make snow angels in the snow.
But when snow starts with the wind, get in the house.
The snow is coming.
Dennis Nezic, Grade 5
Walker Elementary School, IL

Clouds
Large clouds fill the sky
Unimaginably high
These cushions pass by.
Joel Gaudio, Grade 4
Frank H Hammond Elementary School, IN

Running Running
Running…running…the race has begun,
Running…running…the shot of the gun,
Running…running…the adrenaline rush,
Running…running…like your brain is mush,
Running…running…the strike of the foot,
Running…running…feel the earth underfoot,
Running…running…the wind in the air,
Running…running…you're half way there,
Running…running…step after step,
Running…running…add some pep,
Running…running…snap of a twig,
Running…running…emotions get big,
Running…running…we trample the ground,
Running…running…new energy is found,
Running…running…the finish in sight,
Running…running…we finish with might,
Running…running…is how we won,
Running…running…has just begun.
Brandon Bigus, Grade 6
Bednarcik Jr High School, IL

Stars
Stars are family members.
Watching you 24 hours, every day.
You may not notice, but they are there.
Twinkling, shining
D
O
W
N
There to pick you up when you
F
A
L
L
At night, they come out to tuck you in.
Smiling, laughing
The stars are there.
Don't worry if you can't find them in the daytime.
Stars are creatures of the night.
Grace Prendergast, Grade 5
Walker Elementary School, IL

Colors
Black is dull and lifeless, white is plain old blank.
This is why we need colors to lighten up our life.
Red for roses and flowers,
Orange for sun and fire,
Yellow for bees and honey,
Green for trees and plants,
Blue for sky and water,
Indigo for some birds and it's in a rainbow,
Violet for books and eggplants,
And more colors in between.
Julia McKenna, Grade 5
Good Shepherd Montessori School, IN

Hatred

hatred is bad
hatred destroys
hatred can trap you and make you hate
if we fight it, we can conquer anything
we can fight it
but it takes effort
we can take it head on
but it would take us
we need hope to fight it
hope is key
hope lays in friends
we all have friends
we can do it
we will

we will do anything
I will fight for good
no matter what happens
I will stick by my friends
for they have led me through
they have led me through
hatred

Reed Rouch, Grade 5
The Orchard School, IN

Where I'm From

I am from Taco Tuesdays, and
Wild Wing Wednesdays
I am from an old city
with cars that cover the streets
and people that fill the
stores. I am from Facebook and
Texting at late hours. I am
from the good times that make
me smile and bad times that
make me sob uncontrollably.
I am from experiences, the
good and the bad.
I am from the night skies shining
through my window at night.
I am from howling coyotes
howling at the night sky,
and I'm from the shining sun
providing light throughout
the world. I am from the
memories that run through
my mind.

Ashley Wilson, Grade 6
Knox Community Middle School, IN

Capture the Flag

Playing in the rain
Sliding down the mountain side
Running into trees

Ben Cooper, Grade 5
Stanley Clark School, IN

Halloween

H ow gracefully the leaves fall,
A nd the other things sure give a fright.
L ike the skeletons hanging around,
L ike the jack-o-lanterns eyeing you.
O r the awful gravestones,
W ith their cadavers not fully buried.
E vil bats all around,
E ntrancing witches staring you down.
N one of these things are too pleasing at all.

Luka Malovic, Grade 5
Central Elementary School, IL

Leaves in the Fall

Leaves fall.
Leaves are even in the hall.
Leaves fall all day long.
While raking, I whistle a song.

Leaves falling from way up tall,
The piles are not small.
Fall is a time for laughs and smiles,
Fall is never out of style.

Taiden Thomas, Grade 4
Chrisney Elementary School, IN

Meet a Jaguar

If I were a jaguar,
I would be fast.
My speed would be too much blast.
And I would never be last.

If I were a jaguar,
I would be long.
My color would be orange.
And I would never be wrong.

Maya Jimenez, Grade 5
Edison Elementary School, IL

Skateboarding

Skateboarding
Fast, Adrenaline-rush
Ramping, falling, speeding
Kick flips really rock.
Zoom!

Alan Minix, Grade 4
Van Rensselaer Elementary School, IN

Spring

S o wet
P retty flowers
R ains a lot
I ce cream
N othing better
G reat

Aerial Hope McCarty, Grade 4
Shoals Elementary School, IN

Hope the Hamster

Hope the hamster is a nerd.
Who is very, very fond of birds.
She lives in a cave
and is very brave.
She is sometimes cranky
and has a friend named, Frankie.
Hope has black eyes
and her favorite food is fries.
She has small feet
and tweets in her sleep.
She is very cute
and wants to play the flute.
Hope has big ears
and many fears.
She plays softball
in the fall.
That's everything about Hope the hamster.

Hope Benoit, Grade 4
Meadow Lane School, IL

Chocolate

Chocolate,
as sweet as delight
Rich and creamy,
when you bite
Chocolate,
as sweet as delight
Many kinds of delight…
Caramel
Toffee
White
But still more…
Milk
Macadamia Nut
and dark
I love chocolate!
Don't you?

Alina Fernandez, Grade 4
Lincoln Elementary School, IL

Cheeseburger vs Fries

I'm so glad that someone chose me to eat.
Same with me.
I'm so needing to meet him!
So am I!
I'm so excited!
Me too!
Here it comes!
And…
Chomp!
Oh boy!
Fries…it's dark in here!
I'm scared now, Cheeseburger!
Me too!

Haidyn Hinen, Grade 5
Northern Heights Elementary School, IN

Nature
I look outside and I see
A cute little bumblebee;

Then to my right,
A flying kite.

Ahead of me, I can see
A giant oak tree.

I close my eyes
And face the skies;

How wonderful it is
To be alive!
Caroline Elmer, Grade 6
Emmanuel-St Michael Lutheran School, IN

The Star, My Star
Shining brightly in the sky
Shining all day long
The star, my star
Is shining brightly all day long

It shines in the morning
It shines in the night
The star, my star
Is never out of sight

It dances and sings
and all other things
The star, my star
Is my only thing
Sarah Rohr, Grade 5
Manchester Intermediate School, IN

A Good Snake
There was a snake named Bob
Bob was very tall
When the snake went away, I was scared
Then Bob came back, and I had a ball

The snake really likes me
A snake is a great animal
This snake likes people
But he wished he was a mammal

Bob was good to me
He likes to play
He rattles his tail
He makes my day
Victor Badion, Grade 4
St Matthias/Transfiguration School, IL

My Fabulous Volleyball
My volleyball is red, white, and blue,
It is circular, and it bounces too.
It is as light as a feather;
It can keep on rolling right to the end.

The volleyball gets hit very hard.
It will leave a mark on your arm.
When you serve it travels far.
Just one tap, and it will move some more.

It spins in a spiral.
It can maybe go for a mile.
It's very soft and durable too.
Boom! It hits the floor!
Jacqueline Wojcik, Grade 6
Our Lady of Peace School, IL

Cats
I love lots of animals.
My favorite is a cat.
They are soft and cuddly.
They are known to eat rats.

I like them because they feel like silk.
Also, they are scared of bats.
Cats do not like water.
They also do not like being patted.

They are quite quiet.
Most do not chitchat.
When they have kitties, they are bitty.
Soon, they will need their own floor mat.
Kendra DeSimone, Grade 4
St Matthias/Transfiguration School, IL

Frigid
The frigid air.
My coat, hat, gloves, and scarf,
they all keep me warm.
A nice warm cup of hot cocoa
with marshmallows and whipped cream.
A snowflake lands on my nose,
another one lands on my eyelash.
"It's snowing!" I call out.
The cold snowflakes hit me over and over,
soon I am covered in snow,
and the ground is white.
The pine trees all white covered with snow.
Everything is so beautiful.
Frigid
Isabelle Fulton, Grade 5
Stanley Clark School, IN

I Am From
I am from Pepperoni pizza
and chocolate ice cream.
From steamy saucy spaghetti.
From "clean your room"
and "get off video games."
I am from TV and my remote.
From mowing lawns
and going camping in a camper.
I am not from gross cabbage
and disgusting green beans.
I am from my fluffy pillow for my head.
From going outside to play football.
I am from "Avenged Sevenfold"
and from "Eminem."
I am from "Don't touch my PlayStation 3,
my blankie
or my bed."
These are the things I want to remember.
Brady McCarty, Grade 6
Knox Community Middle School, IN

Music
Any kind of music
Is pleasing to the Lord
Through song
Through instruments
Any way
Any day
It's pleasing to the Lord

Music, music
Ringing, ringing
Throughout my mind
I hear it

I hear the melody
Along with the harmony
It's wonderful praises
To God, my Father
Grace McGuire, Grade 6
Christian Academy of Indiana, IN

Peaceful Relaxation
Silent is the wind blowing through my hair,
the tree leaves falling through air,
watching the clouds fly by me.

Loud is all the bird's singing,
the stream's flow gushing beside me,
all the squirrels bouncing through trees.

Eternal is all the trees in the forest,
the waves of a lake,
anything you dream of.
Deja Monroe, Grade 4
Churubusco Elementary School, IN

Cherished Item
You can take away my cheese.
You can take away my fishing hook.
But please don't take away my red rook.

I can do without pigs
I can do without a stick
But please don't take away my imaginary friend Rick.

I can live without my bones.
I can live without my ice rink.
But I can't live without my favorite green hat hero — Link.
Marie Estelle Corpuz, Grade 6
Sacred Heart School, IL

Gone
You never listen,
Never should have left me.
I can't hide it anymore,
I loved you,
and you always loved me.
I loved you for so long,
You never left my heart.
It's just the way you smiled,
That made my day…
Gone.
Just like you are.
Anna Smiley and Mackenzie Kirk, Grade 5
The Orchard School, IN

Saturday Morning
8 AM running 400 yards
Coaches yelling, hurry up don't stop running
Hitting heavy bags with force
Sweat all over my face and body
Trying to not let the quarterback get hit
And give the quarterback time to throw the ball
Very cold and tired
Muscles failing
Practice over at 10 AM
Can't wait to get back in bed
I am thankful for being an athlete this Saturday morning
Matthew Nummy, Grade 5
Walker Elementary School, IL

Ode to Quest
Ode to Quest, where we read lots of books,
Ode to Quest, where we hang our projects on hooks.
Thank you Mrs. Kristoff, for letting us have fun,
Thank you Mrs. Kristoff, now our book Gossamer is done.

Thank you all authors, for making books of all kinds,
Thank you Mrs. Kristoff, for all the great finds.
The Indian in the Cupboard, Gossamer, and Sadako, too,
Whenever I have Quest, I will never be blue.
Sarah Strubbe, Grade 4
Central Elementary School, IL

If…
If I were a color I'd be green
If I were a song I'd be "Grenade"
If I were a food I'd be chicken
If I were a car I'd be a Ferrari
If I were an animal I'd be a dog
If I were a place I'd be France
If I were a feeling I'd be mad
If I were a plant I'd be a rose
If I were a climate I'd be snow
If I were a musical instrument I'd be a guitar
If I were a shape I'd be a square
Isaiah Lewis, Grade 5
Henryville Elementary School, IN

If I Were
If I were a color I'd be blue
If I were a song I'd be "Days Go By"
If I were a food I'd be pizza
If I were a car I'd be a Dodge Ram
If I were an animal I'd be a blue whale
If I were a place I'd be The Bass Pro
If I were a feeling I'd be happy
If I were a plant I'd be a redwood tree
If I were a climate I'd be cool
If I were a musical instrument I'd be a drum or a tuba
If I were a shape I'd be a circle
Daniel Dabney, Grade 5
Henryville Elementary School, IN

Rose Bush
My thorns are as pokey as a briar patch.
I'm as pretty as a fern.
My buds are as soft as a rabbit's fur.
Long stems cover the ground like a roof covers a house.
Insects and bugs hide underneath me like small children.
I bloom as graceful as a swan.
My blooms are as pink as the night sky.
Bees softly land on me like a bird's feather.
I reach the sky like a bird in flight.
I sway in the wind like leaves during a storm.
I am a rose bush.
Amanda Roberson, Grade 6
Cloverdale Middle School, IN

If I Were Water
If I were water,
I would be clear.
People would drink me.
When you go in the pool I get stuck in your ear.

If I were water,
I would taste very good.
When something falls from the sky it's me.
I would make petrified wood.
Dahlia Mendoza, Grade 5
Edison Elementary School, IL

Fall

Towers of gold, silver, and bronze
Holding all life
on its shoulders
It is a creation of
Variety
It will shoot off in rockets of many kinds.
Parts of it disintegrating
While it's being
Replaced by the
Jewels of birth and
Imagination
The entire wonder
Happening only once
But it
Will soon come again.
Instead,
As a continuing
Mystery.

Ganesan Narayanan, Grade 5
Highlands Elementary School, IL

Thanksgiving

Do you smell that succulent turkey,
that's browning in the oven?
Do you enjoy apple laden stuffing,
with the nuts on the side?
Can you see fall colored vegetables,
displayed upon the table?
Do you like mashed potatoes,
with a river of gravy on them?
Do you like sweet potatoes,
with toasted fluffy marshmallows?
Can you smell that pumpkin pie,
baked with all the spices inside?
Do you like warm soft bread,
with melted butter upon it?
Do you feel the need for family,
gathering to share a feast?
Can you join me for Thanksgiving,
it would really be a treat?

Nathan Cibula, Grade 6
Home School, IL

Winter

Winter is cold,
It gets old.
Winter is fun,
All the snow weighs a ton.
Winter is freezing,
The wind is breezing.
Winter can be for coughin',
Winter is the name of a dolphin.
It stands to reason,
Winter is an unpredictable season.

Wesley Fleischmann, Grade 4
Chrisney Elementary School, IN

The Dark

The dark
is full of horrifying sounds.
But yet it's lifeless.
There's something watching you
and you see nothing.
Then the sound the dark doesn't make
fills your ears.

Dakota Pepper, Grade 5
Manchester Intermediate School, IN

Summer and Winter

Summer
Hot, sunny
Playing, splashing, swimming
Sun, breeze…clouds, wind
Sledding, skating, skiing
Cold, snowy
Winter

Nicole Biel, Grade 6
St John the Baptist Catholic School, IN

Bobcat

Bobcat
Hunt, wild
Running, hiding, hunting
Forest, desert, wildlife, mean
Pouncing, growing, eating
Predator, cute
Bobcat

Cory Strohmier, Grade 5
St Michael School, IN

Tony the T-Rex

This silly T-Rex eats exotic meats
for dinner along with beets.
After he eats, he watches TV
His favorite show is Glee.
While he was watching his mom showed up
And gave him a new pup!
What a wonderful day for this silly T-Rex.

Tony Boccia, Grade 4
Meadow Lane School, IL

Komodo Dragon

Komodo Dragon
Sneaky, aggressive
Running, eating, chewing
Cool, mean, fearless, black
Green, big
Awesome, scaly
Komodo dragon

Ethan Browning, Grade 5
St Michael School, IN

Deer

Deer,
Deer,
It's time to come near.
The salt lick is shining clear.
So lick it all up,
Till the sun rises up.
Salt licks are many,
Please do not leave any.
When the next day comes.
There will still be some.
In the sunbeams,
The salt lick will gleam.

Nevaeh Sims, Grade 4
Chrisney Elementary School, IN

Hannah

Sorrow filled my heart.
Tears flooded my eyes.
We had never been apart.
I thought their words were lies.
We rushed over to the vet,
I sat crying in the room.
That was the final time we met.
Then we left and I felt sadness: BOOM!
I will never meet her again,
But, I know that she's right next to me.
I won't see my dog now or then,
But my love for her is bigger than the sea.

Sophia Glabus, Grade 5
Hawthorne Elementary School, IL

The Lizard in the Blizzard

There was once a lizard named Kay
Who was caught in a blizzard one day.
She was fluffy and pink
And knew how to think
So she wished for a summer day.
The more that she wished
The snow turned to mist
And when it started to melt
Oh how happy she felt!
She was able to play
On a day warm as May
Oh my, what a wonderful day!

Elizabeth Delehanty, Grade 4
Meadow Lane School, IL

Buddy

Gold and bright,
His heart was full of light,
He loved me and filled me with glee,
He was super sweet,
No one could beat his adorable face,
I loved him and now he's gone.

Katherine Hart, Grade 6
Holy Family Catholic School, IL

Christmas

Your tree is up
you decorate the tree
you put the lights up on the roof
you make cookies
icicles are hanging
presents are wrapped
your house smells like Christmas
the stockings are hanging from the fireplace
the bells are ringing
the snow is falling to the ground
Santa is around the corner.

Kaylee Sparks, Grade 6
St Michael School, IN

Army

Army is strong
No Army is Army strong
The people in the service are my heroes
Army should be your hero, too
The Navy is always on guard
Don't forget the Air Force
The men and women are the bravest people in the world
They are respected by me and a lot of other people
Their battles are remembered forever
They give their lives for us
Army is Army strong

Luke Stirn, Grade 6
St Michael School, IN

If I Were A...

If I were a color I'd be blue.
If I were a song I'd be "Brighter Than the Stars."
If I were food I'd be pizza.
If I were a car I'd be a Cougar.
If I were an animal I'd be a German Shepherd dog.
If I were a place I'd be Florida.
If I were a feeling I'd be happy.
If I were a plant I'd be a rose.
If I were a climate I'd be a storm.
If I were a musical instrument I'd be a trombone.
If I were a shape I'd be a heart.

Haylee Smith, Grade 5
Henryville Elementary School, IN

Heights

Conquering my fear of heights was very hard.
But when I found out its reward,
I went to places that weren't too high.
There I found lots of things to spy.
After that, conquering my fear of heights was a breeze,
But the Willis Tower really made me freeze.
Heights are a fear most people have got.
But sometimes it can get you into a big knot.
The fear of heights should be a cannot.

Xavier S. Nuñez, Grade 5
Hawthorne Elementary School, IL

If I Were...

If I were a color I'd be red
If I were a song I'd be the "Grand Old Flag"
If I were a food I'd be Little Caesar's
If I were a car I'd be a Toyota
If I were an animal I'd be a hamster
If I were a place I'd be a store
If I were a feeling I'd be happy
If I were a plant I'd be a thorn plants
If I were a climate I'd be cool
If I were a musical instrument I'd be a clarinet
If I were a shape I'd be a square

Marc Thomas, Grade 5
Henryville Elementary School, IN

Halloween

Halloween, Halloween you're fun and sweet
Trick or treaters say "trick or treat"

For this holiday kids say "Boo"
Owls do too but they say, "Hoo hoo"

Jack-o-lanterns get light at night
And that's when they shine bright

Halloween, Halloween your colors orange and black
But the sun is rising but I know you'll be back

Sabrina Lee Dickinson, Grade 4
Summit Elementary School, IL

If

If I were a color I'd be blue
If I were a song I'd be "Through the Fire and Flames"
If I were a food I'd be pizza
If I were a car I'd be a Ferrari
If I were an animal I'd be a deer
If I were a place I'd be Ohio
If I were a feeling I'd be cool
If I were a plant I'd be a tree
If I were a climate I'd be hot
If I were an instrument I'd be a drum
If I were a shape I'd be a square

Blaine Lewis, Grade 5
Henryville Elementary School, IN

Gone with the Wind

You are there, you are not there.
All our tears fill the room,
Because you are gone forever,
But you will never leave our hearts,
You're there with us every step of the way,
Your laughter is still here, but you are sadly not,
We wish you were still here,
Please come, back.
Goodbye, farewell.

Haley Norris, Grade 5
Van Rensselaer Elementary School, IN

Dreams

They can be about anything
Magic unicorns,
Witches,
Or even talking dogs
With things like that they have to be interesting
They can be like a fairy tale
Or people trying to take over the school
They can be long and meaningful
Or they can be short and about a pig who likes cheese
They can even be nightmares
They can be about anything
But when you wake up in the morning
You think to yourself
What was that dream I had last night?
Then you realize that you forgot
But wait!
You suddenly remember it
Then you wonder why your subconscious mind is so crazy

Leo Q. Magid, Grade 5
The Orchard School, IN

Ocean

My family is like the ocean

My mother is like the water
She never stops, she keeps going on and on
She helps me with everything
But she irritates my dad of never stopping.

My grandmother is the coral.
She does the same things over again and she gets older
Isn't it almost time to do something different.

My father is the fish.
We only see him in the morning
Then he's gone.

My sister is the dolphin
All she wants to do is swim.

Trinidad Ruiz, Grade 6
Florence Nightingale Elementary School, IL

The Sun

The sun is a bright orange
like a tangerine
it is warm
like a blanket
but if you stay too long
you will burn like…
like a piece of toast
without the sun there would no light
if there was no light there would be no plants
with no plants there would be no oxygen
and no oxygen means we go byebye

Vincent Johnson, Grade 6
U S Grant Middle School, IL

Christmas Is Fun

Christmas is the best holiday of the year.
You can open presents and have some cheer.

You can play in the snow,
And watch the snow blow.

You can make snow angels or snowmen,
Christmas you want to make all of them.

Do you like Christmas? I do.
I also hope you like it too!

Arielle Detton, Grade 4
Summit Elementary School, IL

Halloween

Screams of terror and cries of fright,
Kids and candy fill the dark, cold, night.
Zombies and vampires I hope they don't bite.

Some dress cute and some dress scary,
Princesses, ladybugs, some are quite hairy.
I hope I don't bump into the scary cemetery.

Maybe you'll see Mickey Mouse,
But don't go in the haunted house.
When you get home be quiet like a mouse.

Valerie Schroeder, Grade 5
Dee Mack Intermediate School, IL

Birds of a Feather

Through night and day I hear sounds
through the world of birds,
colours shine on their wings and body light
as a feather they speak gently
and sing all day their hearts arc strong.
The Great Horned Owl flies and hunts through the night
the cardinal sings a song peacefully.
The humming bird has a gentle hum
all of the birds
fly, tweet, jump, run,
skip, flip, twirl, walk.

Michaela Gautsch, Grade 4
Copeland Manor Elementary School, IL

Jack

Small, quiet, funny, smart
Sibling of Matt and Maura
Lover of animals, video games, and creativity
Who feels bored when lonely
Who needs people to be happy
Who gives happiness to friends
Who fears guns and drugs
Who would like to see J.F.K. (John F. Kennedy)
Resident of Westchester

Jack Lyons, Grade 6
Divine Infant Jesus School, IL

Spring

Spring is a time for friends and flowers
You could talk of the wonders of spring for hours

Spring is like a painting, with God the painter
Spring really couldn't be much quainter

Spring is a time when both friendships and love strengthen
Many others and myself wish that springtime would lengthen

Peace and tranquility accompany this season
I think to make us happy was spring's purpose and reason

There are many happy things that occur during spring
And it brings the question, "What will the next season bring?"

Connor I. Loechner, Grade 6
Emmanuel-St Michael Lutheran School, IN

Hot Dog

My family is a hot dog.

My mom is the bun she holds all of us together.
She always cares for all of us.
She holds us all together and does everything she can for us.

My older brother is the Wiener. He is second in command
They can eat him without the bun on a stick.
He is always looking out for us.
If something happens to the bun he is there.

My younger sister is the mustard. She is the playful one.
She's the one that makes everyone happy and is such a bright color.

Adark Gonzalez, Grade 6
Florence Nightingale Elementary School, IL

Kyra

Kyra
Sibling of Quinton and Molcom
Lover of the paintbrush and microphone
Who feels loved and grateful
Who needs a nicer brother
Who gives people a good voice to listen to
Who fears tarantulas
Who would like to see the inside of a sea urchin
Resident of Illinois
Harrold

Kyra Harrold, Grade 6
Divine Infant Jesus School, IL

Brownies

Brownies
Chewy, moist
Melting, crumbling, sticking
Melts in your mouth
Sweets

Nicholas Rupnow, Grade 5
Washington Township Elementary School, IN

Talking to a Toddler When Someone Dies

He dies
Three year old has a good relationship with him
Say
He wanted to take a nap
He said he didn't want to wake up
We will put him in this special bed
We will put him in a special place
He will live in his own world

Shawn Margaret Erler, Grade 5
The Orchard School, IN

Cloud

I look up in the sky,
And see huge white puffballs floating by,
I reach out to touch them with my hand,
But they seem to slither away like a snake in the sand,
All I can do is watch them pass,
Then try to touch them but they seem to shatter like glass,
So I guess the dreamy things in the sky,
Will lay there forever to float silently by.

Nacoma Calandrelli, Grade 6
Alexandria Monroe Intermediate School, IN

Bullying

You think you're cool to bully me at school,
But the law and rules say you're not cool,
You laugh and laugh and make people stare,
All because I have different hair,
But that's okay,
I'm okay,
Because one day,
We'll all be treated the same way

Kaileigh Clifford, Grade 6
Alexandria Monroe Intermediate School, IN

Weird Stuff

What if lions ate only veggies?
What if pumpkins were homes?
What if Halloween and other holidays were every day?
What if cats swam?
What if bugs were nice?
What if BC meant "before comedy?"
What if people were made of plastic?
What if the Earth was flat?

Alyssa Whobrey, Grade 5
Henryville Elementary School, IN

Sunset

S ee the warm colors stretched across the sky.
U p high in the clouds, a kaleidoscope appears.
N ow, I gaze at the
S ignificant beauty of this picturesque scene.
E ven a group of white tailed deer pause and marvel at
T his wondrous masterpiece

Annie Ostojic, Grade 4
Frank H Hammond Elementary School, IN

Death

Death is an obstacle of life
It could happen with a knife
Death
You could die of old age
Or being trapped in a cage
Even on stage
Death
Don't be shoddy
It happens to everybody
Death
Now, don't throw a fit
You just have to accept it
It happens lickety-split
Death
It's like a timer your waiting for to go off
Or like a spaceship when your waiting for it to blast off
Death
It will happen to you
And everybody else too
Do not cry "boo hoo"
Death

Elena Coletta, Grade 5
Hawthorne Elementary School, IL

Volleyball

We come out of our home locker room.
All pumped up for our very first game.
The whole team is in their gold and maroon jerseys.
We and the other team all say our good lucks!
We get to our team bench and Angie gives,
Us a good way to win the game!
The referees say it's time to serve.
The ball bounces twice,
The server serves the ball.
It goes up and over the net!
The other team is setting it over.
MINE!
The players are going to get it,
And they got it over.
The other team let the ball hit the floor.
We won the game; the team and the crowd
Are so happy!
Angie is so proud of the whole team!
The game is finished.
We are so ready for the next game.
We are undefeated!

Lindsie Chaplin, Grade 6
Alexandria Monroe Intermediate School, IN

Britney Spears

It seems like it has been years,
Before I got to see my favorite singer Britney Spears.
She is the most talented I had ever seen,
Britney Spears is always nice and never mean.

Noelle Arrigo, Grade 5
Washington Township Elementary School, IN

Archie Comics

If there's a day you're feeling down,
Pull out a comic, it'll erase your frown.
It's so funny you'll laugh out loud,
They will surely cause a crowd.
Veronica has lots of money,
Betty is as sweet as honey.
Reggie is incredibly vain,
Dilton has a really big brain.
Archie is super clumsy,
Jughead is always hungry.
Archie comics rule!

Sophie Berberich, Grade 5
North Intermediate Center of Education, IL

Velociraptor

Hear the mighty dinosaur roar
'We want more war!'
The fearsome dino attacks with tremendous speed and power!
With endless soldier battalions!
This dinosaur is unbeatable!

This ferocious carnivore does not give his meat a chance to live!
With his team he will not quit,
But if he does he will throw a fit
Of fingers, he has three
I hope he does not devour me!

Owen Chilcoat, Grade 4
Highlands Elementary School, IL

From Everywhere

I am from steaming pizza, and rocky road ice cream,
from cacti and my pet cats, yes, all five!
Always hearing "Wake up Miss Sleeping Beauty!"
and clean your room!
Never wanting the gross ham and bean soup,
still been everywhere, from New York to California,
and everywhere in between
On my self my cat figurines,
from Florida, mostly handmade.
Precious moments sitting above my head at night
I am from, stop writing and clear the table!

Samantha Morgan, Grade 6
Knox Community Middle School, IN

Dog

Dog
Your companion
The friend you always wanted
Always there for you
Never without you
The day came for your dog
You hope to be together soon
The day came for you
When you got there your dog was waiting for you

Julia Phillips, Grade 5
The Orchard School, IN

Perfect

Nobody can be perfect,
It's a very well-known fact.
But if we could be perfect,
It would make a big impact.

There'd be no fights or quarrels,
It would all be worldwide peace.
If that could really happen,
Happiness would then increase.

People would be educated,
They would always know each answer.
We could always be real healthy,
And not get things like cancer.

We could live in harmony,
And no kid would be a brat.
But if we had no troubles,
What would be the fun in that?

Dalton Julian, Grade 5
North Knox West Intermediate/Elementary School, IN

The Best Trip Ever

We went on vacation
And it was the best,
We packed up the car
And headed out west.

We went to Mt. Rushmore
And the Badlands too,
We even saw Old Faithful
And boy did it spew.

We saw some elk
And also some bears,
And then we saw mule deer
Traveling in pairs.

We drove around
All day and night,
And finally saw a moose
Oh, what a sight!

Tyler Johnston, Grade 5
North Intermediate Center of Education, IL

Summer Wind

The cool breezes fly on a sweet, summery day.
I sit in content.
My back against the hard bark of the tree.
Even animals are happy.
Squirrels chatter cheerfully.
Deer prance in the meadow.
Birds fly from tree to tree.
Summer is the most wonderful time of the year.

Maxwell M. Imler, Grade 6
Emmanuel-St Michael Lutheran School, IN

I Am a 9/11 Helper

I am helpful and caring
I hear screams
I wonder who did this
I see (on TV) the towers collapsing
I want there to be many survivors
I am helpful and caring
I pretend none of this happened
I feel distraught
I touch the hands of the survivors
I worry for the lives of thousands
I cry for the loss of the towers
I am helpful and caring
I understand this was intentional
I say the ones who did this never should have
I dream we knew this would happen
I try to help many
I am helpful and caring

Ryan Henderson, Grade 5
Stratton Elementary School, IL

I Want to Be a Somebody...

I wanna make a difference somewhere here.
people call it home, so dear.
But I have seen so many things that haunt me.
Taunt me.
I don't want to just be a nobody.
I wanna make a difference to somebody.
Out here in the ocean blue.
Some don't even have a clue!
I don't want to be the nobody.
I wanna be the somebody!
So I will get out on the streets.
Say hi to every one I meet.
And make a difference to the orphan, widow, weary.
My eyes might get teary.
But I want to be a somebody
And eliminate poverty.

Laural Almquist, Grade 6
Galva Elementary School, IL

Restrooms

Flush, swish, swoop
People slamming, shutting doors, locking them up
Reading their books while using the restroom
Flush, swish, swoop
Unlocking the doors
People walking out
Faucet running
Water splattering
towels wiping hands
Open doors
People walking out
While the restroom is calling
"Come again, come again"

Kennedy Fierstos, Grade 5
Manchester Intermediate School, IN

I Am From

I am from rich and moist cake
on a hot summer day
I am from a very lazy body
on a rainy and gloomy day

I'm from Jerry and Joyce Fletcher,
and fresh apple pies
I'm from Topps Michael Jordan rookie cards.
I'm from cold and creamy ice cream
on a hot and sweaty day

I am from avoiding horrible green broccoli,
prison, and car crashes.

I'm from baseball on a cool summer day
I'm from basketball in a hot old gym
to football on a cool rainy day

I'm from my amazing black PS3
from being awesome at everything

I'm from all these great things.

Aaron Fletcher, Grade 6
Knox Community Middle School, IN

Heaven's Song

It creeps up slowly and you listen
Knowing it will happen
Listen to Heaven's song
It creeps up slowly upon you
Mad and crying you feel alone
Listen to Heaven's love song
Loved ones you lost
Talk softly to you
You remember the times you had
They will still be alive in your heart
Remember all the time you spent with them
Sadness and love combine into Heaven's sad love song

Abby Draper, Grade 5
The Orchard School, IN

Ode to My Dog

Ode to my dog, Chica,
How she cuddles with me in my bed
How she loves to go outside with me, and play fetch
How she begs with her puppy eyes
How she waits for me at the door
Telling me let's go outside
When I come home she goes wild
She makes smile
Anytime, anywhere
She's everything to me
I wouldn't give her up for anything in the world
My dog, Chica

Cielo Gomez, Grade 5
Walker Elementary School, IL

The Breeze

As I stand outside,
I feel the breeze blow.
Nothing will make it stop.
It seems to me
I should go inside,
But I love to feel the summer breeze.
As night falls,
The breeze gets very dull.
I feel just a little bit of the night breeze.
As I look up at the night sky,
All I see is the night stars.
I feel nothing,
But I know that the breeze is still there.

Abbey Dardeen, Grade 5
North Intermediate Center of Education, IL

My Evil Teddy Bear

I was sleeping last night
But, I woke up with a frightening fright
Oh, it was my closet, it started to shake
I opened the door with every fright in the world
I see my teddy bear with his ears all curled
My big fluffy teddy bear
Made my heart almost tear
Those black beady eyes
Tell me only lies
Oh why did Teddy Roosevelt make such a thing
I would rather massage the old king
But, I still love you so don't forget!
I knew you were the one when we met.

Laasya Poola, Grade 5
Ranch View Elementary School, IL

Fall

A rainbow of color
Falling from the heavens
When stepped on, they crack in agony
Suddenly the green of the land changes to beauty
Beasts from the underworld
Take treats from houses

The full moon comes
And canines howl
The darkness conquers all
And all the water stops.
And the world
Is in a cage of cold

Collin Sincaglia, Grade 4
Highlands Elementary School, IL

Snow

Snow falls in winter
Snowflakes are all different shapes
Flutter so slowly

Anthony Matejko, Grade 4
Frank H Hammond Elementary School, IN

Dreams

Dreams
What are they
Something you think
Something you do
Something you are
Magical
Mystical
Amazing
In your own world
Everything about you
Soaring
Walking on water
Like you can't fall
Unstoppable
Anything you want it to be
Anything you need it to be
People say they are just your thoughts
They are more than that
They are a power
Dreams
Thomas E. Fischer, Grade 5
The Orchard School, IN

King's Island

The day is hot
The park is full
I wish it was not
It would be better cool
The lines are long
The food cost is high
I wish I was wrong
But I can't tell a lie
We wait in line
And watch the time
I feel like it's time to dine
But the line still acts like a mime
Moving ever so slowly it will never end
This is the roller coaster I chose
As we come to a bend
The lines start to close
Now it's to me
I hop on and buckle in
The way is clearly up I see
The Diamondback was a definite win
Conrad Schaefer, Grade 6
Nancy Hanks Elementary School, IN

Nature

Mother Nature has
a wonderful feature
of creating flower blossoms
and when they bloom
they open up to reveal a sparkling center.
Madeleine Whirledge, Grade 5
Ranch View Elementary School, IL

Painting

I hear the swish swash
of the brush
gently hit the canvas
spreading the lavender
paint across the
rough canvas.

Swish swash
is the brush
spreading the
orange paint
across the canvas.

Swish swash
goes the brush
spreading the
golden yellow paint
across the canvas.

Silence is
the dried sunset
masterpiece.
Cora Barnett, Grade 5
Manchester Intermediate School, IN

Solitary

alone
all alone
I sit on my little brown steps
on my little brown house
all alone
I haven't seen anybody since…
well, I don't really know because
I'm alone
all alone
Emily Clark, Grade 5
Stanley Clark School, IN

Sun

A hovering flame,
Creating morning,
Moving sneakily,
Chasing the moon away,
Turning on the lights.

Great power,
Millions of miles away,
Crystal of brightness,
Light bulb lasting billions of years.

Perfect friend and enemy,
Brings hope and happiness,
Light and warmth,
Being tireless and energetic.
Mitchell Zhen, Grade 4
Highlands Elementary School, IL

Broken Heart

My broken heart.
Fragile and split.
I couldn't listen anymore.
The words so harsh.
They keep saying, "It'll be okay."
But it won't.
My broken heart.
Hurts so badly.
Tears streaming down my cheeks.
Why does he have to leave?
I don't want to let go.
My broken heart.
Makes me want to cry.
I love him so much.
He was the only one I trusted.
But soon he'll be gone.
That breaks my heart.
Emily Tauscher, Grade 5
The Orchard School, IN

Country Town

The tractors roar,
As I walk out the door.

The morning dew,
And the sky bright blue.

The wind is low,
Harvest is slow.

Empty fields,
Bring good yields.

It's way past noon,
But I see the harvest moon.

Then the dust settles down,
In this little country town.
Carl Schmidgall, Grade 5
Dee Mack Intermediate School, IL

Miranda Gutierrez

Miranda
Crazy, unique, weird, bubbly
Sibling of Antonio, Vanessa, and Mateo
Lover of music and sports
Who feels joyful when listening to music
Who needs love
Who gives hope
Who fears death
Who would like to see Mark Salling,
Naya Rivera, and New York City
Resident of Westchester, IL
Gutierrez
Miranda Gutierrez, Grade 6
Divine Infant Jesus School, IL

Marco Navarro

Marco
Cool, funny, awesome, smart
Brother of Juan
Lover of games
Who feels happy at cookouts
Who needs soda
Who gives to the homeless
Who fears snakes
Who would like to see Wisconsin
Resident of Westchester
Navarro
Marco Navarro, Grade 6
Divine Infant Jesus School, IL

Sid

Sid
funny, smart, careful, fun
lover of food
who feels happy when reading a good book
who needs water
who gives love to her family
who fears spiders
who would like to see Abby Wambach
play a full game of soccer in a chicken suit
resident of Westchester
Medjo Me Zengue
Sidonie Medjo Me Zengue, Grade 6
Divine Infant Jesus School, IL

Snow

Snow
Falling so gracefully
Like little notes
Sent from the angels
Pure white snow
Glistening on the ground
I wish it came every day
To greet me in the morning
To hush me to sleep at night
I dream I am in a world of snow
I just hope it will snow tomorrow!
Nolan Mccoy, Grade 5
The Orchard School, IN

Starry Night

The wind screams loudly
While the rain is pouring down
The clouds hide the moon
How dull it is now
It could have been beautiful
The clouds would go away
You see the stars out
And they would sing a new song
Goodnight and sleep tight
Taylor Goins, Grade 6
St Angela School, IL

Beyond the Skies*

An edge of the moon,
Glows down with grace;
His shining shadow,
Engulfed with white;
Oh so simply,
The sun reaches;
With golden fingers,
She grabs a hold;
Sparkling with glee,
Graceful and dear;
Shan't he say hello?
Or tint silver?

The moon wants to stay,
To greet his love;
Wake when dawn a-comes,
Greet with pillows;
Of swelling should be,
Clocks and beats;
Chiding North Star,
The Daughter of Day.
Maddie Pope, Grade 6
St John the Baptist Catholic School, IN
Dedicated to my grandparents

Bumble Bee

If I were a bumble bee,
I would sting.
I would eat pollen.
And I would fly around with my wings.

If I were a bumble bee,
I would make honey.
I would buzz.
I would be funny.
Darsé M. Sanchez, Grade 5
Edison Elementary School, IL

Alanna the Ant

When she was playing hide and seek
She saw a small pipe leak.
She tried to cover it up with tape
But all she found was a big brown cape.
then she went inside for lunch
And she mistakenly ate a whole bunch.
Soon, she had to go to sleep
That's when she heard something beep.
It was her pot of tea so she got up
and said "this is for me."
After that she went back to the pipe
And noticed that her tomatoes were ripe.
So she went and picked some
and then she started to hum.
She soon forgot all about the leak.
Alanna Clark, Grade 4
Meadow Lane School, IL

Sabotaged

This life just makes me fret
Am I being treated like a pet?
Someday I wish to be free
Life's not a cup of tea.

I'm stuck in a deep hole here
I don't see myself in the mirror.
Fear blocks my every step
I drown in my thoughts of death.

I'm such a helpless slave
I'm dirty, and without a shave.
The white men say I shouldn't be alive
They plan to sell me; I hope I survive.

Just when I think I'm at my worst
I hear the door open with a burst.
It's the rescuer, who says to me
"Come live in freedom for eternity!"
Lauren Selking, Grade 6
Emmanuel-St Michael Lutheran School, IN

The Jungle King

My snake's a survivor.
Black, brown, and brave.
As strong as an ox,
A rat he will crave.

My snake's a survivor,
Muscular and fierce.
Hiss, hiss, hiss
His bite will pierce.

My snake's a survivor.
Slithering like an eel,
Exploring the jungle,
Ravenous for a meal.

My snake's a survivor,
Shredding his rough skin.
His teeth are acute,
Like a sharp pin.
Lana Razma, Grade 6
Our Lady of Peace School, IL

Dirt

It's brown
It's flying in my face
Chunk by chunk
Piece by piece
I can hardly see anything
But it's okay because she's with me
She knows the course
Because she is my horse.
Emma Waugh, Grade 5
Northern Heights Elementary School, IN

The Big, Deadly Reptiles
Hiss hiss hiss,
goes the cobra.
If you're its prey,
than today's your last day.
Hiss hiss hiss

Snakes bite
and release
their venom,
Komodo dragons
kill prey
and eat 'em.

Lizards and snakes
are all alike,
you can find them
on a
rain forest hike.

Hiss hiss hiss,
goes the cobra.
Ethan Gabriola, Grade 6
Our Lady of Peace School, IL

Adventure in the Rain
The constant thrum of the first spring rain
on my window,
soothes me.
Its rhythmic tune,
luring and unchanging,
ravenously licking my windowpane,
punctuating the once still air.
I sway to its beat,
content and snug
under my plaid cotton quilt.
Misty winds carelessly caress my window.
And I can't help but sigh with contentment
until lightning begins
its threatening brawl with thunder.
When I must snap back into reality, and
heed the bright red digits
glaring out at me
from a blaring alarm clock.
And now I must take leave
to a new day and adventure
in the rain.
Sarina McCabe, Grade 6
Stanley Clark School, IN

Spoon
Spoon
Round, shiny
Scooping, washing, drying
Nice, device
Drew Crase, Grade 5
Forreston Grade School, IL

Suckers
One night when Susie was sleeping
Her suckers started a-leaping

Downstairs she went not noticing much
Her mom didn't know what to touch

Ten suckers stuck in her hair
Many to cut her head might go bare

Her clothes she couldn't get on
The process started at dawn

Eating breakfast was quite a chore
The stickiness bugged her more and more

Reaching the bus was quite a fuss
Too many kids wanting to discuss

Getting to school was very bad
Being teased made her very sad

Susie even forgot her lunch
So no potato chips to crunch

When home mom began to pull them out
It hurt so bad she began to pout

Next step was to shave her head
Instead she dyed her hair red
Kate Kaetzel, Grade 6
Nancy Hanks Elementary School, IN

I'm Late for School
I'm late, I'm late to go to school
I pull on my pants and
I put on my shoe
I brush my hair and I go down the stairs
I look in the mirror
Then I get my gear
So I run, I run, and I run to school
I grab my books, I grab a pen,
I have to be at school at ten!
Out the door, no bus in sight,
adding to my horrible plight!
Through the yard on my bike,
I look down and
Two flat tires, a broken chain.
Then I decide to run and
I'm the fool running 14 blocks to school
So so tired with a pounding chest,
when I get to school I'll rest!
One more block! I reach the door!
Then I realize and I say,
"Oh, my gosh, it's Saturday!"
Angelica Cervantes, Grade 5
Stanley Clark School, IN

A Forgotten Love on a Summer Day
Oh, how those days I miss,
We sat with the purple flowers,
In golden waves of wheat.
The perfume of fresh water,
And hearty maple leaves.
Milky clouds,
And warm blue skies,
And fields of joy and laughter.
The taste of candy,
And smooth, cold jam,
Smeared across berry-stained lips.
Dancing under stars,
And singing in the warmth.
Kissing under the trees,
Running amongst the bees,
And playing in the oceans.
The sun has memories,
A forgotten love on a summer day.
When the birds sang songs so sweet.
Oh, how those days I miss.
Isobel Bender, Grade 6
Frances W Parker School, IL

Punching Bag
A punching bag
Right in the middle
A target for them
Easy to hit
No power in him

Whacked and smacked
Bruised and bumped
I fall to the ground

I take the blow
Right in the face
Aching in pain
I roll off the ground
I jog to the huddle
For the next round

I'm smacked and whacked
A lot in a game
I play center, it's best for the team
Chris Wolfe, Grade 5
Walker Elementary School, IL

Dogs
I love dogs so much.
They protect me, love me
keep me safe.
I love them so much
Wait! Ha, I have a dog.
Who knew?
Ian Asklund, Grade 4
St Matthew School, IL

Winter Wonder World

Silent is the trees sleeping in the winter.
Silent is the frost melting.
Silent is the cold fluffy snow.

Loud is the frozen wind blowing the snow around.
Loud is the kids playing in the snow.
Loud is the animals running for shelter.

Eternal is the snow always falling.
Eternal is the ice that melts in the spring.
Eternal is the beautiful snow flakes.

Makiya Jackson, Grade 4
Churubusco Elementary School, IN

Cherished Item

You can take away my pillow
You can take away my bed
But please don't take away my precious head

I can do without my sister
I can do without my books
But I can't do without my very cool looks

I can live without my TV
I can live without my Game boy
But I can't live without my everlasting joy.

Chris Bauer, Grade 6
Sacred Heart School, IL

Fall

This is a time when all the leaves fall
And when we all throw around the old football.

We gather around to give thanks
For all the soldiers in their ranks.

We go around wishing snow
But when it comes we cry no, no, no.

This is my favorite time of all
Since life is calm in the fall.

Charlie McLain, Grade 6
Emmanuel-St Michael Lutheran School, IN

Raccoons

Silent is when a raccoon is asleep,
    when a raccoon is hiding,
    when a raccoon is running.
Loud is when a raccoon is rummaging through garbage,
    when a raccoon is stepping on leaves,
    when a raccoon is clicking its teeth.
Eternal is when the raccoons are scurrying on the trees,
    when raccoons heart is beating,
    when raccoons are stealing food.

Matthew Palmerton, Grade 4
Churubusco Elementary School, IN

Mother Nature

Once there was a mother bird
Who had two babies and was waiting for her third
Day by day, day and night
As she sat with her babies in the moonlight
By the sunrise the egg began to crack
As she watched for predators behind her back
The mother bird chirped with glee
As the baby bird was out of the egg and free
This mother, now, once alone
Has three babies of her own
She must feed them and keep them hydrated
But the time will come when their youth has faded
As much as she loves them, the mother knows
As they grow they will soon have to go
Go and find another place to have a home
This cycle will continue again and again
These birds will sing, sleep and roam!

Arianna Margaret Karnezis, Grade 6
Three Rivers School, IL

Mac

My family loved him like a brother.
We got him from a friend who had babies
Mac was not afraid of thunder
Mac liked my dad most, not us ladies.
MAC
His soft coat was as black as shiny coal
The poor baby rabbit he caught that day
It thought it would be safe deep in his hole
Never again would it go run and play
MAC
He ate homemade lasagna — we all laughed.
Long walks every day was his treat.
His water bowl looked sad when he left.
He was the nicest dog you'd ever meet.
MAC
As a pup he'd frolic in the white snow.
Best friends can leave, but memories don't go.

Annalise Soldano, Grade 5
Hawthorne Elementary School, IL

My Grandfather

Late at night my grandfather died.
I looked so bad because I was sad.
The birds won't sing,
Since you're not here with me.
Now, up all night crying a river,
I'm blue in the face, I might swim in my river.
Thinking of you is never hard to do.
If you're here or there, I will always care.
Things we do together, will last forever.
If you ever need me, just call for me, and I'll be right there.
No matter what me and you do,
I'll always love you.

Chyeann Canter, Grade 5
Van Rensselaer Elementary School, IN

Diversity
Diversity, diversity
What does it mean?
It means everything is different
Or so it seems.

Diversity, diversity
What's true about its name?
It's like snowflakes,
Whose shape is never the same.
Branden Osborn, Grade 5
Dee Mack Intermediate School, IL

If I Were a Baby
If I were a baby,
I would be chubby.
I am a ticklish baby.
My legs are very stubby.

If I were a baby,
I would be funny.
Sometimes I am sleepy.
Everyone says I'm as sweet as honey.
Jessica Marie Ciesla, Grade 5
Edison Elementary School, IL

Dog Breeds
Cute, courage, Chinese, Shar-Pei
Lazy, little Labradoodle
Pudgy, pretty Poodle
Cool, crazy Chihuahua
Pretty, petite Pit bull
Brown, bright Beagle
Big, beige Bulldog
Happy, Hershey Husky
Scary, stunning Shih tzu
Anna Padilla, Grade 5
Edison Elementary School, IL

Hunting
Hunting
Binoculars, camouflage
Walking, watching, aiming
Patiently waiting for deer.
Stalking
Blake Schultz, Grade 4
Van Rensselaer Elementary School, IN

The Hot Dog
Hungry people, lining up.
Off the grill, piping hot.
This sausage is named after a pup.
Don't worry, they're not real dogs
Off the hands, into the mouth
Good smothered in ketchup and mustard.
Jimmy Schatz, Grade 4
Ranch View Elementary School, IL

Friends
Friends are for everything
Jaylyn, Makinzi, Tali, Carter, Gavyn, and Hunter are some of my friends
They're always there for you no matter what
Even through the rough times
They cheer you up when you're feeling down
Friends are for everything

They hang out with you at recess
They sit with you at lunch
They help you with your homework
They text you every night
Friends are for everything

They help you tie your shoes
They invite you to your house
They paint your nails
They laugh at your jokes
Friends are for everything.
Holly Lanam, Grade 5
North Knox West Intermediate/Elementary School, IN

The Challenge of Many
From this numerous people suffer,
And it just keeps getting tougher
I believe that no one should have to sit down with an empty plate,
Because it feels like you are fighting for your life, it doesn't feel great.
Hunger…
People don't need much to eat, just something edible.
It is hard to believe that people just don't care, it's incredible.
The world around us is full of disillusion,
Instead I wish they would find a solution.
Hunger…
Some people may not survive,
But the ones who do suffer just to stay alive.
So many people, so many needs,
So many mouths, so many to feed.
Hunger…
If some people could donate a little money,
It would make everyone's lives a little more sunny.
Hunger.
Mary Brynn Rosenstein, Grade 5
Hawthorne Elementary School, IL

My Challenge
My mom is as beautiful as a solar eclipse
She takes all the light out of me
My dad is as kind as can be
And always there for me
That's why it's a challenge to see them leave
You see, they go on a lot of trips and sometimes without me.
When I see them go
It feels like I'm a cloud that just got squeezed
And all the rain fell out.
But, I know they'll come back and that'll be the happiest moment there'll be!
Artemis Siavelis, Grade 5
Hawthorne Elementary School, IL

Puppies

Puppies
Good pets to have
Are always on the move
Loving, caring, cute, and funny
Too cute

Drew Horne, Grade 5
Northern Heights Elementary School, IN

Animals

What if dogs walked like a human?
What if cats sat on their head?
What if sharks lived on land?
What if manatees could fly?
What if dragons had no teeth?

Joshua Otto, Grade 5
Henryville Elementary School, IN

Shining Lion/King

Shining lion
Powerful, wise
Ruling, hunting, providing
Strength, support, protective, mad
King

Jacob Jones, Grade 5
Henryville Elementary School, IN

Ice

Ice
Frigid, clear
Slipping, sliding, falling,
Frozen water, crystal clear,
Brrr!

Jasmine Widgery, Grade 4
Van Rensselaer Elementary School, IN

Floppy the Goldfish

Goldfish
Big, orange
Swimming, growing, eating
One that lives underwater
Pond

Alexander Cinkus, Grade 5
Edison Elementary School, IL

Hi!

Hi.
Pleasant, friendly
Greeting, astonishing, inviting
Short for hello.
Hola.

Katlyn Flachsenberger, Grade 4
Van Rensselaer Elementary School, IN

Prejudice Is War

Prejudice is inadequate facts,
Hatred of people of white and black.
Abuse and hate,
At any rate.

People have different thoughts for 9/11,
Some think it was hatred, jealousy, or to show that Earth's not heaven.
It was a terrible day when the Twin Towers fell,
And everyone knew it was definitely hell.

The 9/11 Help America Foundation helps people affected by that horrible day,
One thing you can do is to get people to work the same way.
It will save the world and every state,
Be a part of changing our fate!

Brandi Brooks and Taylor Byrd, Grade 6
Tri-West Middle School, IN

Where I'm From

I am from steaming hot melting pizza and avoiding rancid broccoli
I am from dreams of the future, from dreams in the past
Dreams of flying cars and horse-drawn carriages
I am from "get up, do your chores, clean your room, hurry up"

I'm from Disney World
and from hunting with deer all around
I'm from computer Xbox 360 to
Games and games everywhere I look

I am from fluffy puppy, lazy brother, working mom, and late night dad
I am from movies and books on shelves and shelves
series after series
I am from family recipes and amazing food.

Daniel Darda, Grade 6
Knox Community Middle School, IN

Basketball

He shoots, he scores! Around and around the ball goes and into the bucket it goes!
Coach claps. Then the other team gets the ball and Jordan steals it. He passes it to Armond.
He goes to the three point line and shoots and makes it!
We are four points away from winning
the game and Jordan shoots and makes it! Two seconds and then
the other team gets the ball. It gets stolen by Henry and then Coach calls a time out
with two points and one second left.
Coach tells me to chuck the ball down the court.
The time out is over. I get the ball and the ref says when I drop my hand
the clock will start ticking.
He drops his hand and I CHUCK it down the court to Evan.
He was guarded by four guys so I knew we were finished.
The game ended
proud and happy.

Nick Kaser, Grade 5
Stanley Clark School, IN

What is Caring
caring is to care for the needy
to help somebody that's hurt or bleeding
to be thankful for who you are
to not hurt anybody
to do good to every body

Dennis Wallace, Grade 5
Churubusco Elementary School, IN

Fairness Matters
Fairness is playing by the rules,
Sharing toys, games, and other tools,
Be open-minded, and listen to others,
Don't blame others carelessly.
That's fairness to me.

Chassy Gallmeier, Grade 5
Churubusco Elementary School, IN

Lion
Furious, muscular
Roaring, approaching, hunting
Snuggling with their cubs
Beast

Cody Walter, Grade 5
Van Rensselaer Elementary School, IN

Fireworks
They blow up in the sky
they are bright and shiny
they make a lot of noise
they come in different sizes, shapes, colors

Carlos Flores, Grade 6
Zapata Academy, IL

Travis
Travis
loves to skateboard
he is outside all day, it's hard to get him in
good grief

Travis Gerard, Grade 4
Warren Central Elementary School, IN

Abby
A wesome
B eyond cool
B asketball
Y oungster

Abby Orschell, Grade 5
St Michael School, IN

Tennis, Tennis
Tennis, tennis you're so cool.
Tennis, tennis you rule.
Tennis, tennis is a duel.
Tennis, tennis is better than school.

Maddie Marland, Grade 5
Near North Montessori School, IL

A Phenomenal Miracle
Rushing, hurrying, excited
Running, falling, all those things
Just there in time to hear his first cry and to see his beautiful face
Soft, cuddly, adorable
Warm, content, all of those things
Just happy he's here for us to be there with him for the rest of his life
Lovely smell, joy
Happy smile, all those things
Just cuddling him close, closer by the minute, never letting go
Kissing cheeks, fresh
Smiling face, all of those things
Just wishing I could be there for all time
But I know someday we'll dance and laugh
Wherever we may be
Aunt, sister, excited
Nephew, brother, all those things
Just glad he's in my arms, graciously
Holden

Sophia Shelby, Grade 5
Perry Central Elementary School, IN

The Arrival of Fall
It's cold outside yellow, green, brown, and orange leaves
The sun is hiding the sky is turning gray and white
I felt happy because fall is coming I hear echoes,
I could hear the wind whispering

Yelling everything is breezy the leafs are changing color
The trees are turning bare the flowers aren't beautiful anymore
The days are getting shorter the days are getting chilly

It's time to drink hot coffee mmm yummy the leaves fly in the air as
I say goodbye to summer the sun is hiding behind the gray and black
Clouds not much time till it would start getting cold
I can't wait till fall comes
It's time fall has just arrived I'm so happy

I love fall days get cold and shorter it's to make good things umm yummy
Fall is my season

Deisy Jimenez, Grade 6
Zapata Academy, IL

Angela Velasco
Angela
Shy, crazy, quiet
Sibling of Esperanza and Albert
Lover of nature, animals, music, and food
Who feels sad/mad when left out
Who needs friends
Who gives love
Who fears dark, dolls, clowns, mimes, height, spiders, and public speaking
Who would like to see the Grand Canyon
Resident of Hillside
Velasco

Angela Velasco, Grade 6
Divine Infant Jesus School, IL

I Am From

I'm from creamy chocolate chip cookie dough
and deep dark chocolate
I'm from the rich strawberry tree
You can say "I don't care," you can say brush your hair.
You can even say WAKE UP! or go to sleep.
I am from pictures in my head and posters on my wall.
I can say don't touch my rocks and DS.
I'm from Modern Warfare 3 and sunny sky in summer.
I am from Medieval times and Six Flags.
I'm from the long lost memories.

Alexander Thurman, Grade 6
Knox Community Middle School, IN

Summer Time!

The sun is out
The birds are flying about
The warning of Summer
Certainly no bummer
As warmth and happiness collide
With an ice cold drink at my side
White sandy beaches ahead
Is what I dream about in my head
With the animals on the run makes me wish
It was time for another season of Summer fun!

John Wagner, Grade 6
St Michael School, IN

Feelings

I sit on a shelf all alone
Kids read me, but never take in mind I have feeling too
Picture, mystery, fiction, history
Big or small, thick or thin I come in many sizes
Sometimes I get thrown on the ground
Sometimes I'm broke into pieces
It's no fair; I should be treated like a kid
I'm no piece of junk; I'm your resource in some cases
You learn from me, I'm like your second teacher
Treat me well and don't hurt me

Daniela Tavarez, Grade 6
The Skokie School, IL

Tree

You stand there as still as a rock.
With the grass beneath you.
And a stream as beautiful as a fair maiden nearby.
Your leaves as green as clover.
You sit with a picnic table beneath you.
Poison ivy as green as freshly cut grass running up your trunk.
You let off the scent of warm maple syrup.
Your leaves as soft as cotton.
With spider webs entangled in your limbs like a ball of yarn.
You wait there for the soil to be soaked by a spring shower.

Maddison Figg, Grade 6
Cloverdale Middle School, IN

School

My family is a school

My dad is the principal.
He is in charge of the school
He decides when to give detention;
and is always busy.

My mom is the vice principal.
She is in charge of the other stuff.
She makes sure she has
sent everything to the teachers.
She makes announcements that
the principal told her to say.

My older brother is the gym teacher.
He makes me athletic;
and is always helping me on my diet.

My little brother is the trouble maker.
He gets people and himself in trouble.
He gets detention.

My grandma is a social studies teacher.
She tells me about the past.

Oscar Gutierrez, Grade 6
Florence Nightingale Elementary School, IL

Packers Football

The football team Packers are undefeated.
This year they're wearing green and yellow.
I am hoping they go to the Super Bowl again.

The Packers are unleashed.
They're coming out of their cage to get some more.
The football team the Packers are undefeated.

Can they go to the Super Bowl?
Can they win the Super Bowl for the second time?
I am hoping they go to the Super Bowl again.

Brett Favre was on the Packers team.
Then he had to retire from football.
The football team the Packers are undefeated.

Then Aaron Rodgers came.
He has a good arm like Brett Favre.

He won the Super Bowl for the Packers.
That was a good year for the Packers.
The football team the Packers are undefeated.
I am hoping they win the Super Bowl again.

Cordell Cochran, Grade 5
Northern Heights Elementary School, IN

Manuel
Funny, Smart, Good and a Little Mean
Son of Sandra and Manuel
Who loves skating, comics and my family
Who gives love to my parents, shows happiness with my cousins and sadness when I make people mad
Who fears spiders, snakes and school
Who would like to see the Grand Canyon, the inside of a tornado and the under ground
Who lives in Chicago, IL Little Village

Manuel Ferreyra, Grade 6
Zapata Academy, IL

Nature
As I walk along the trail, I see trees as tall as mountains, and birds as loud as sirens.
The most beautiful thing I see is the flow of water, like a calming massage, and animals as curious as babies.
I see children as happy as a child on Christmas,
Leaves dropping like a knuckleball, and dogs as loud as whistles.
As the trail ends, squirrels are moving as fast as jets, and bunnies are hopping like a kid on a trampoline.
When the trail ends, friends surround me like nature does to everybody.

Tyce Jackson, Grade 6
Cloverdale Middle School, IN

What a Toad Sees
Through the toad's eyes, the world was as dangerous as defusing a bomb. Birds, snakes, and other creatures were as mean to it as an ogre. When the toad walked through the grass, it was as cautious as a butterfly. It travels from stone to stone as swiftly as a dragonfly. When camouflaged in the blossoms, it was invisible as a ghost. It leaps on a maple tree like a bird in flight. It stops, hearing the sound of leaves crunching as clear as day. It jumps into the water like a frog. Then a giant water snake sprang out of the water like a boy on a trampoline. The toad ran through the grass like a maniac. Being a toad, it leaped over some moss. The snake slipped and tumbled down the hill like an avalanche. That is what toad sees.

Abel Bates, Grade 6
Cloverdale Middle School, IN

Peace (Our World)
Peace is the quiet wind whistling through the air; the sound of happy children playing; the smell of a bunch of roses and no destruction. Peace is the words, "I love you." Peace is doves sitting quietly together on a ledge, the feeling of silky clothing, the warmth of heaven. Peace is when enemies did not exist, when no one decided to fight, when people are accepted for who they are, when you feel like nature is whispering to you.
Every morning you pick to be peaceful or mean. Every day you should pick to be peaceful because when you're peaceful it's like a contagious disease, but you want to catch it.

Madison Ohrt, Grade 5
Three Creeks Elementary School, IN

The Old Clock Still Ticks and Tocks
Through the hard long years there stood an old grandfather clock that would chime only horrid sorrowful notes. The king and the queen could not find a way to stop that old nonchalant grandfather clock. No matter how much effort and hope they put into it the townspeople could not touch the clock. All of a sudden a mighty rushing wind blew through the queen's palace and it sailed right toward the clock. The vibrations of the hammer hitting the bell eventually came to a slow stop. As the wind howled a sweet delicious note came from the grandfather clock. The world spun swiftly on the axle and all was well once again.

Caleb Williams, Grade 5
Arlington Elementary School, IN

Popolano's Food
Popolano's is the best! It's an Italian restaurant, which means it has wonderful things to eat like pizza and pasta, but their dessert is the best. They have cookie dough pizza. It has whipped cream on the top and ice cream in the middle, and the pizza tastes like vanilla with cookie dough inside. Their lunch is wonderful because they have squid with marinara sauce. Their cheese sticks are so cheesy that they won't let go.

Nathaniel Covington, Grade 5
Washington Township Elementary School, IN

Cherished Item
You can take away my money
You can take away my cooks
But please don't take away my wonderful books.

I can do without cats
I can do without Sam
But I can't do without my books about ham.

I can't live without my books
I can live without my frames
But I can't live without my amazing Hunger Games.
Annie Jones, Grade 6
Sacred Heart School, IL

Animals
Silent is a mouse snooping through everything,
Silent is a bird gliding through the air,
Silent is an empty room waiting to be opened,

Loud is a roar of a lion,
Loud is a jungle full of animals,
Loud is a crow in a corn field,

Eternal is the happiness you feel with a pet,
Eternal is the pain you feel when a pet dies,
Eternal is the memory of an animal.
Samuel Wood, Grade 4
Churubusco Elementary School, IN

Cats Change Our Lives!
Silent is Severus playing with a milk carton ring
Silent is Severus bolting through the house
Silent is Severus hugging me after a hard day of work

Loud is Severus and Hagrid rustling
Loud is Severus waiting for me at the door day after day
Loud is me reading Severus a good book as he falls asleep

Eternal is me and Severus together
Eternal is Severus being my favorite
Eternal is Severus in my heart
Fiona Nelson, Grade 4
Churubusco Elementary School, IN

Jodarius
Strong, funny, smart, handsome
Love of sports, music, video games
Who feels happy when helping people in need
Who needs love to live
Who give support to my friends and family
Who fears death
Who would like to meet Jesus Christ
Resident of Bellwood
Christy
Jodarius Christy, Grade 6
Divine Infant Jesus School, IL

Christmas Tree
My family is a Christmas tree.

My dad is the tree;
He's the one who supports us.
He also keeps us all together.

My mom is the star;
She is the head of the family.
She supports us and illuminates us.

My sister is the ornaments;
She's always everywhere.
She knows everything that happens.

My older sister is the lights;
She's very clever and full of ideas.
She helps us with everything and give us advice.

My dog is the present under the tree;
He is a very special part of the tree.
He is what everyone loves.
Aileen Rodriguez, Grade 6
Florence Nightingale Elementary School, IL

A Lost Memory
I was there on the beach
not knowing what was coming.
When I saw the first wave,
at the height of 33 feet,
I was paralyzed
from fear,
from thinking about
death, family, and memories.
I looked behind me
taking in everything that was about to happen to me
and then…it hit.
I was swept off my feet
and lurched forward.
I took a breath.
I couldn't hold it in anymore,
started to choke,
and that was the last thing I can remember.
They never found me.
I was just a memory
lost
forever.
Meagan Luck, Grade 6
Stanley Clark School, IN

Technology
Through new technology such as an MRI,
Can help doctors so people won't die,
Doctors do a lot of things for you,
Like fix a cut up with some surgical glue.
Ethan Martinez, Grade 5
Washington Township Elementary School, IN

Faith

When you feel like you're falling
And you just can't stop,
You should pray to God
For happier thoughts.

But if you still keep falling,
Have faith in God
For He will lift you up.
Shelby K. Hedges, Grade 6
Our Shepherd Lutheran School, IN

The Buck

I saw a buck yesterday
It was drinking in the bay.

Gulping slowly with a doe
The buck thought he had to go.

As I pulled out my bow
They ran off in the snow.
Tyger Clodfelter, Grade 6
West Salem Grade School, IL

Froggy, Froggy

Once there was a pretty frog.
Jumping, jumping through the fog.

Froggy, Froggy are you there?
I don't like it when you stare.

Sadly, you leap away.
Oh, but I wish you'd stay.
Maggie Hendricks, Grade 6
West Salem Grade School, IL

The Fall

Leaves falling everywhere,
Trees are really, really bare.
The grass is kind of green,
But it is right in-between,
Some grass is brown.
The leaves are on the ground.
I love the color of the leaves.
I think I'll go put on long-sleeves.
Nick Green, Grade 4
Chrisney Elementary School, IN

My Wonderful Day

The bird sings on trees
The wind whistles through the branches
The sun shines brightly
As the clouds smile so kindly
The kids play beach ball
As the sun sets for the day
Alexia Leggin, Grade 6
St Angela School, IL

Maybe Tomorrow

Maybe tomorrow
The sky will be blue
The sun will shine
Maybe tomorrow
Your dreams will come true
Maybe tomorrow
The tables
Will turn
Things will get better
Or for the worse
Maybe tomorrow
Will be better
Maybe it will
Be worse
Maybe tomorrow
You'll say goodbye
Or maybe tomorrow
The sun will shine
Corrine Hays, Grade 5
The Orchard School, IN

Christmas

Ho! Ho! Ho!
Snow! Snow! Snow!
See it snowing
The wind blowing
Christmas is coming
The elves are humming
What a great day to go
Play around in the snow
Santa's making a list
He's making sure that you're nice
Now he's loading his sleigh
And he's coming your way
Through the big black sky
With the stars rushing by
He lands on your roof
And the snow goes
Poof!
Then down your chimney he goes.
Gwen Fourman, Grade 6
Stanley Clark School, IN

The Double Rainbow

After a rain
And a dull gray sky
I saw a double rainbow
That stretched across the sea
It had many bright colors
That made me very excited
It made the dull gray sky run and hide
It made all dull colors go away
I saw a double rainbow
That stretched across the sea
Sydney Cheaney, Grade 5
The Orchard School, IN

Night of the Puffins

Puffins puffins peep peep peep
Oh puffins oh clowns of the sea
Come out come out
Come play with me
Puffins puffins peep peep peep
Cute little puffins burrow in the night
Stranded on the cliffs of height
Come on down for your first flight
Night of the puffins is soon to be here
Come down to the seashore
Watch me bobbing in the deep blue sea
Up and down
Up and down
Help to guide me before I get confused
I'll follow the city lights instead
Puffins puffins peep peep peep
Help me to follow the bright moonlight
Puffins puffins peep peep peep
Katrina Pietkiewicz, Grade 6
Three Rivers School, IL

I Have Two Toy Ducks

One is named Lucky
The other…Captain McQuakers
They both like to eat crackers

Lucky has four magnet hands and feet
His dancing…cannot be beat
He has funky, white hair
He loves to share
His special chair

Captain McQuakers is a rubber ducky
His flag he holds is kind of spunky
He went with me
To the state, Indiana

I love both of my duckies
I love them with care
I try to take them everywhere!
Aspen Johnson, Grade 4
Coal City Intermediate School, IL

The Thick Fog Day

The thick fog day,
Was a dead day,
A lifeless day,
When you get outside,
You think you're swimming, but you aren't,
You get thirsty,
You take a bite,
You take a swim,
That was the day,
When the fog was thick.
Wille Wallentine, Grade 5
The Orchard School, IN

Friends

F riendship never ends.
R ain doesn't stop us.
I am lucky to have friends that
E ncourage me.
N ever let them feel
D own or
S ad.

Brianne Moizuk, Grade 5
St Michael School, IN

Justyn

J ust quiet
U nusual
S uper funny
T errific
Y oung
N atural football lover

Justyn Rider, Grade 5
Forreston Grade School, IL

Veteran

What is a veteran?
They fight for our freedom
They risk their lives for us
They love our country
They are army strong
That's a veteran!

Coltin Rauch, Grade 6
Herrick Grade School, IL

Animals

I'm as fearless as a polar bear.
I am as gentle as a lamb.
I'm as fast as a cheetah.
I am as slow as a turtle.
I'm as loud as a roaring lion.
I am as quiet as a sleeping snow leopard.

Noah Schultz, Grade 5
Henryville Elementary School, IN

Basketball

Basketball is fun.
In basketball you have to run.
In basketball you play on courts.
In basketball you wear shorts.
I like to play basketball!
Basketball is fun for all!

Megan Keel, Grade 6
Holy Family Catholic School, IL

Friends

Always there for you
They will never leave your side
They are always there

Jacob Collier, Grade 5
Northern Heights Elementary School, IN

Roses

Petals whirl around
Like a fortune teller's large pendant on a chain
Raindrops little by little fall
To the damp ground
A sudden pinch from a thorn
Bursts into your palm
The wind blows
And echoes deep inside
Till it reaches the core
The scent of the rose reaches you
And you feel a wave of energy rise from your toes to your head
When you look into the rose
A feeling of great happiness and a gloomy feeling will come over you
You imagine a wedding decorated with white and pink roses everywhere you look
You also see a funeral held for one of your loved ones
When you touch, look, smell
The rose paints large pictures in your head
Each picture lasts
Each one different from the other

Caroline Rettig, Grade 5
The Orchard School, IN

Where I'm From

I am from my old rocking horse
From pampers diapers and my favorite blanket
I am from a brick ranch style home
And a bright yellow room
I am from a shady maple tree
Whose leaves hear my thoughts
I am from my homemade bench and my dress-up box
From Darlene Davis and Tim Davis
I am from a strong work ethic and the always on time family
And from the work hard then play family
From the never give up family
I am from always be thankful that you have food on your table
I am from Grandma Kleaving and Grandpa Kleaving
I am from my grandma's sugar cookies and my mom's zucchini bread
From my grandparents' 50th wedding anniversary
And from my great grandma's 80th birthday party
I remember playing hide and seek in the dark with my family
I am from those moments playing and celebrating and that's what makes me who I am

Claire Davis, Grade 5
Perry Central Elementary School, IN

Julio

funny happy nervous tired
son of Rosa and Julio
lover of video games scary movies and action movies
who feels happy after school nervous during school and mad at home
who gives money, clothes and food
who fears high places demons and ghosts
who would like to see Rome Moscow and Mexico
who lives in a yellow house on 26th street
Serrato

Julio Serrato, Grade 6
Zapata Academy, IL

Toy Chest

My family is a toy chest,
My father is the rocking horse,
That stays stored inside, reserved, quiet,
But willing to work with me to trigger my imagination,
My mother is the annoying, crying, baby doll,
She doesn't like to be ignored,
And she screams until her battery is dead,
My little brother is the monster truck,
Destroying everything in sight and within his reach,
But an entertaining toy despite the time of day,
My sister is my Spiderman walkie-talkie,
Always there to talk,
No matter what the season,
No matter how much time passes,
It will always be my favorite toy,
And the one I will never throw away,
Or sell at a yard sale.

Pablo Sanchez, Grade 6
Florence Nightingale Elementary School, IL

Where I'm From

I am from my old stuffed panda bear, Beary
from rubber boots and overalls.
I am from "let out the dog"
and cattle and bullfrogs at the porch.
I am from a swaying weeping willow tree
whose pale yellow bark and light green leaves I climb.
I am from rocking horses and porch swings
from the Harding's and the Etienne's.
I am from hiking and baking
and from playing outdoors,
from spending time with family.
I am from the Father and the Son and the Holy Spirit,
from cherry pies and cookies,
from fighting in the army,
and from pruning Christmas trees,
and from baby dolls.
I am from the moments when life is happy and feels never ending.

Alexandria Etienne, Grade 5
Perry Central Elementary School, IN

Crocodile

Like an old brown log
he lays basking in the sun
waiting in the early fog
for his meal to come
his dull bright eye slowly moves, a glimpse of what could be
his wrinkled flesh rests just above the lake
smiling with his pearly whites — that's all his prey will see
rearing up his knurled head he'll give his meal a shake
no one swims with this beast
no one wants to try
on and on he'll catch his feast
sleeping by and by

Emily Legg, Grade 6
Home School, IL

Garden

My family is a garden.

My mother is the most beautiful part of the garden;
she is the most beautiful red rose that brightens up the night,
when I see her I could really smile 'cause I am just a plain rock
that is always in a bad mood; but she loves my dad, and they
could not be separated for a moment.

My father is the shovel; he never surprises from me and
my sister, he is the one that helps us grow.

My oldest sister is a sunflower; she is always in a good
mood, she can't stop smiling, so her petals grow a brighter yellow.

My older sister is a carnation; she is so sensitive
she could start to cry over anything — her petals
are sensitive.

Julia Perez, Grade 6
Florence Nightingale Elementary School, IL

Cross Country Days

Like a flower without rain,
cross country gives me pain.

I was trying to get in shape,
now I'm only sore when I wake.

Daddy says soldier on,
but I just want to lay on the lawn.

Continue I will,
because I made a deal.

Finish the season,
for just one reason.

I will not quit,
just complain a bit.

Jenna Watters, Grade 6
Alexandria Monroe Intermediate School, IN

The Last Journal Entry: June 8th, 1897

The leaves flew windward as the wind rustled.
Our carriage bumped down the rocky, gravel path.
There was a feeling of simplicity in the air, and the
lake nearby sparkled in the sunset like
mercury. There was a family having a small archery
contest in the field by the road. They looked
so happy as I was restricted to stay in
my carriage. We slowly entered an orchard
oranges, grapes and prunes. As we approached the manor,
a small pennant was atop the great house. Suddenly,
the atmosphere turned gloomy as I saw a hearse. I saw
who was being carried…

Nick Kistler, Grade 6
Christian Academy of Indiana, IN

Treasure

Treasure
Shiny, light
Small, sink, throw
No more taxes forever.
Jewels

Shane Box, Grade 4
Van Rensselaer Elementary School, IN

Emma W.

Emma is one of my best friends
She is so nice and always there for me
I love her as my sister!
She is one of the funniest people I know
I love you!

Gracie Newton, Grade 5
Northern Heights Elementary School, IN

Snowflakes Falling

The tiny snowflakes fall to the ground
I see them fall from heaven above
In interest, I watch
One falls to the ground
And melts to water

Jackson Longenbaugh, Grade 5
Northern Heights Elementary School, IN

The Man with the Pan

There once was a talented man
Who loved to cook with his pan
He woke up one morning
All tired and groaning
To find his pan in his hand

Benjamin Fagan, Grade 6
West Salem Grade School, IL

Scary

Dark in the house
Everything is still
Frightened and scared
Go away
Boo! Got you!

Brianna Wright, Grade 5
Northern Heights Elementary School, IN

Austin

There once was a boy named Austin.
He always lived in Boston.
A big dog came.
The dog was tame.
Every day it lived with Austin.

Austin McWhirter, Grade 6
West Salem Grade School, IL

Winter

Winter is like a white sheet laying over the ground.
The Christmas tree lights up like a busy city.
You hear the crunch of snow under your feet.
You sit by the fire on a snowy day,
The crackle of the fire like branches snapping.
Snow falls down on houses to make them look like a perfect picture.
On Christmas Eve you can smell the fresh cookies just coming out of the oven.
You can smell the hot chocolate like candy on Halloween.
Winter is like a just shaken snow globe.

Anna Burnett, Grade 6
Bednarcik Jr High School, IL

What I Am From

I am from shopping at Wal-mart to "Turn the channel on the TV."
From Notre Dame blue to M&M green.
I am from toy cars and Jello, so sweet.
From Sports Center telling me, Colts win, also ND!
I am from Knox vs North Judson, sadly, we lost.
From very bad allergies, so we wait for frost.
All of these things wrapped up into one, will tell you where I am from.

Colin Kulpa, Grade 6
Knox Community Middle School, IN

The Right Choice

The sun shines high in the sky.
It's beautiful just like your big blue eyes.
Every time I think of your name it makes me want to jump up and sing.
The only wish I had was to tell you the truth.
I love you.

Hunter Emmanuel Carpenter, Grade 6
Emmanuel-St Michael Lutheran School, IN

Snakes

Cautiously creeping
Creating an eerie bubble
Making everything feel like
They're being watched

At times, a harmless vine
At others, an intravenous shot
Ready to use its wrath
And examine as everything unfolds

Time stands still when it watches you
Creating a wall from you
To the outside world
You are helpless

Mastering the art of illusion
Saddling the lessons of the hunt
Top of the class for everything

The ruler of the undergrowth.

Allen Chen, Grade 5
Highlands Elementary School, IL

Never Will Be

I am stuck incapable of rhyme
Seems like my brain is frozen in time

My pencil will never graze this page
If I wait too long I am going to age

I will not present my poem first
For mine will be certainly the worst

I am not having a good time
Trying to think of words that rhyme

It would be very helpful and nice
If someone in this classroom had advice

I think the gears in my head are dusty
So pooped that my eyes are getting crusty

I am not good at this kind of thing
I should be known as the bad poem king

Abigail Winkler, Grade 6
Nancy Hanks Elementary School, IN

Flying
What is flying?
Soaring high
Getting scared
Stuck at a terminal
Window seat
Flight attendant
Big jets, many buttons
That's flying!
Jarrett Sarver, Grade 6
Herrick Grade School, IL

Winter
Leaves dropping,
No one is stopping,
I can't get away,
From the cold, cold day.
The snow is piled high,
Up in the sky.
Why so cold today?
I want to go away.
Chloe Gideon, Grade 4
Chrisney Elementary School, IN

If I Were a Video Game Character
If I were a video game character,
It would be Mii,
I would play with the 3DS,
Or Mario Kart Wii.
If I were a video game character,
It would be Luma,
I would eat starbits,
And outrun a puma.
Matthew Gannon, Grade 5
Edison Elementary School, IL

Winter
I love winter,
I'm a very fast sprinter.
I love to play in the snow,
Sometimes inside with my yo-yo.
I sled down the hill,
It's quite a thrill.
I love to make a snowball,
I love to watch the snow fall.
Josie Keener, Grade 4
Chrisney Elementary School, IN

Winter and Summer
Snowy, freezing
Snowmen, skating, skiing
Snow, wind, ocean, beach
Swimming, biking, surfing
Sweating, sunny
Summer
Brianna King, Grade 5
Edison Elementary School, IL

Mrs. Simmons
She is really nice.
She is my favorite teacher.
she is so funny.
Energetic too.
She looks like she is thirty.
She is five foot seven.
She talks about her kids.
Her son is older than me.
It's fun in her class.
She gets a little angry.
She is very nice.
Brendan Roberts, Grade 5
Northern Heights Elementary School, IN

Kelly McGee
Kelly
Fun, playful, helpful, and kind
Sibling of Patrick, Emma, Sean, and Molly
Lover of music
Who feels happy with family
Who needs family
Who gives old clothes to the poor
Who fears guns
Who would like to see Taylor Swift
Resident of Westchester
McGee
Kelly McGee, Grade 6
Divine Infant Jesus School, IL

Popcorn
Pop-pop-pop goes the pop-pop-popcorn.
Popping away
Every day.
Never stops popping
Salty and buttery.
Oh, so yummy
Kernels inside them
Can't stop eating them
Light yellow
Dark yellow
So, so delicious.
Briley Spann, Grade 5
Manchester Intermediate School, IN

The Wild Horses
I restlessly stir in my seat,
Waiting for the end of the week,
For when I get to go to Aunt Lee's,
I'll see the wild horses running free.

I see them now!
I wonder how
The horses got to be,
In school with me!
Jacie Rae Grimm, Grade 5
Dee Mack Intermediate School, IL

Paralyzed
I cannot walk
I cannot talk
I sleep every night
But, my mind is awake
I can feel in my heart
Everything seems so empty
I have a heart
I have a soul
But, it has a huge hole
I am all alone but I fight strong
One day I will relive my pleasant times
But, now I do not remember when
I cannot love
I cannot cherish
There is no meaning of life
The only thing left to do is perish.
Rishi Modi, Grade 6
Bednarcik Jr High School, IL

Dogs
Great gray Great Dane
Real rotten Rottweilers
Puffy pink Poodles
Brilliant bad Border Collies
Dastardly dotted Dalmatian
Beautiful black Blood Hound
Brown brilliant Beagle
Lucky lovable Lab
Crazy chipper Chihuahua
BIG brown Bulldog
Happy HUGE Husky
Talkative tiny Terrier
Retrieving ridiculous Retriever
Cookie crazy Cocker Spaniel
Lazy lumpy Labradoodle
Crazy cute Chocolate Lab
Kierstyn Budz, Grade 5
Edison Elementary School, IL

Crazy Skiing
Crazy skiing is doing crazy
jumps and winning races.
Crazy skiing is black runs
and beating my dad.
Crazy skiing is doing flips in
the air and watching versus skiers.
Crazy skiing is Lindsay Vonn and
Bode Miller.
Crazy skiing is moguls and
being a ski patroller.
Skiing is hard and moguls
are harder, but doing crazy jumps
is even harder, but being a ski patroller
is the hardest out of all.
Bradley Larsen, Grade 4
Copeland Manor Elementary School, IL

The Night Hike

Hiking in the night,
very, very dark.
I'm waiting for something
to happen,
as I tiptoe silently.
I hear rustling and honking as I
go by,
all so silent, all so beautiful.
I want to stay a little longer,
but I can't just sit and stay.
I must go and leave the
beautiful woods behind.

Brady Luck, Grade 5
Stanley Clark School, IN

Dad

My dad loves me
He is the worker and
I am his helper
If I get tired of work
He will care for me
If I shut down he fixes
Me back up
If I fall down and break
He will pick me
Back up and he will do
Whatever it takes
For me

Michael Wirsing, Grade 5
Manchester Intermediate School, IN

Rain

I woke up this morning
And it was pouring,
The rain came down
And hit the ground,
The wind was rough,
But the trees were tough,
They did not come down
And hit the ground,
The rain got lighter
And the sun was brighter,
The wind stopped,
And the rain did not drop.

Chloe Christine Rooney, Grade 6
Our Shepherd Lutheran School, IN

Stars

bright yellow stars
floating in the air
look like they're dancing
in the big galaxy
that's where they live
bright yellow stars

Jadah Brubaker, Grade 5
Manchester Intermediate School, IN

Kites

1…2…3…Lift off
Flying high in the sky
Wind blowing in your hair,
how high will it fly?
As it floats by clouds of marshmallows,
so high in the air.
You wear your sunglasses and cap,
and hope that you can bear
the flash of sun in your eyes.
You now wonder of the sight of your kite.

Michelle Kee, Grade 4
Ranch View Elementary School, IL

Friends Are…

Everyone has friends
We talk to each other, English or Spanish
We play or go to each other's house
Friends are the best
We do homework
We have parties together
We have fun together
Friends love you
I love them too
Best friends forever

Alondra Castrejon-Hernandez, Grade 5
Walker Elementary School, IL

Icicle Cycle

I've always thought it's rather nice
That water freezes into ice
I'm also pleased that it is true
That ice melts back to water too
But even so I find it strange
The way that ice and water change
And how a single water drop
Can fathom when it's time to stop
Its downward drip and goes ahead
And starts an icicle instead

Georgie Rodriguez, Grade 5
Caledonia Elementary School, IL

The Freezing Day

The wind is blowing
I think it's snowing
I go outside
It is freezing
My mom is sneezing
The snow is bright
And it's really white
It looks like it's night
My coat is really tight
I wish it was summer.

Conrad Johnson, Grade 4
Lincoln Elementary School, IL

My Cat

Tiny soothes me
With her warm soft hair
As it rubs gently on my cold skin
When I pick her up.

Her lime green eyes glow
brighter than any shooting star
In the dark blue foggy sky

Her plump pink paw
Is like a bright pink raspberry
patting the ground with every step
"tap, tap, tap"

Her ink black fur
And her rich crystal white fur
Remind me of a wild black and white panda
roaming around

I can't see her and not notice
her solid pink nose
barking loudly whenever she has to sneeze.
Whey I think of you I think of a *key*
because you are the key to my heart.

Amiya Cullens, Grade 5
Walker Elementary School, IL

Finding Nemo

I was very sad and lonely
and filled with strong regret
for others had a dog,
or some other kind of pet.
I asked my mom and dad,
but "No" they'd always say,
I asked and asked and asked
until I got my way.

They took me to the shelter
to have a look around.
I looked at several dogs
and then at one last hound.

He was as playful as could be,
black from head to toe.
I loved him from the start
and his name was Nemo.

Now, I've had him several years
and he's been a lot of fun.
He's a perfect kind of friend
in the rain and in the sun.

Brayden Schilling, Grade 5
Northern Heights Elementary School, IN

Winning the Game of Football
Football is the coolest sport ever
You try to score and lose never
You try to score a touchdown
When you win, it's a prize like a crown
It's great to win, you feel like a king
You would just like to burst out and sing
Celebrating, with your touchdown dance
Hopping and jumping, with a prance
Running and jumping through the air
Dodging tackles without a care
Trying to get past the goal line
If I score, this great game is mine
Your team lines up in shotgun
You throw the ball and it's caught, you won!

Sean Hayes, Grade 5
Hawthorne Elementary School, IL

Snowflakes/Winter
They are all shapes and sizes, none the same.
When snowflakes land on trees they look shiny.
If you pack them, you will get a fun game.
Ever seen a snowflake? They are tiny.
When it snows, it looks like a big snowstorm.
Don't stay out too long or else you will freeze.
Wish it wasn't cold. I wish it was warm.
There is sometimes a cold, cold, cold, cold, breeze.
Most animals don't come out in the winter.
Snowflakes can fall fast or they can fall slow.
Don't touch a pine tree, you'll get a splinter.
It's hard to drive up our drive in snow.
Winter starts on a special day — 12/21
In the winter, you should always have fun.

Izzy Bishop, Grade 5
Northern Heights Elementary School, IN

Doing the Dishes
First of all it happens every day,
usually I get stiffed with no pay.
Plates, bowls, and also the cups,
sometimes I even catch the hiccups.
Bits of chicken and crumbs of bread,
getting all over my hands and my head.
My muscles always get so sore,
I can barely even open a door.
Putting away is the best of them all,
but it's bad when I bump the counter with my haul.
Once I get done I'm so very tired,
suddenly there's more, why'd I get hired?
Piles and piles are built up in the sink,
my dad always says, "Good luck!" with a wink.

Drew Diamente, Grade 5
Northern Heights Elementary School, IN

Leaves
Leaves
crunchy, colorful
falling, floating, swaying
I love the colors
Maple

Aidan Chism, Grade 4
Frank H Hammond Elementary School, IN

Strange
Strange things happen at the house of strange.
A green fog as thick as tomato soup lifts.
The green trees turn blue.
When blue jays fly in, they are never to fly out.
Cardinals fly in red and fly out black, this was the origin of crows.

Aisha DeSouza, Grade 4
St Matthew School, IL

Halloween
Scary, cold,
Walking, decorating, costuming,
All Hallows Eve, creepy, loving day, giving cards
Love, freezing
Valentine's Day

Mia Vargas, Grade 5
Edison Elementary School, IL

Animals
What if monkeys had wings?
What if buffalos had flowers for fur?
What if fish lived in trees?
What if ducks had no beaks?
What if chickens had sharp teeth and claws?

Madelyn McClendon, Grade 5
Henryville Elementary School, IN

Ghosts
Ghosts
creepy, mysterious
chilling, prowling, haunting
lurking in the shadows
Paranormal

Derek Sweitzer, Grade 5
Washington Township Elementary School, IN

The Nonflying Fly
There once was a fly.
Who would not fly.
He swallowed a frog,
While at the bog,
Now we know why he couldn't fly.

Justin Jayasinghe, Grade 5
Washington Township Elementary School, IN

A Story of Wonder

J.K. Rowling, an inventor of a book, a story full of wonder, character from good to crook.
A coward is Severus Snape, hidden like a turtle in his jet black cape.
Always runs when he's put to the test, but his head held high always better than the rest.
Then there's Hermione Granger, cleverest of the clever, very friendly, too, helped poor Neville find his toad Trevor.
At last the main character, resourceful like an otter, he's a heroic kind of wizard, but he's just plain old Harry Potter.

Karina D'Mello, Grade 5
Ranch View Elementary School, IL

Night of the Centipede

In the dim evening light, a centipede moves through the grass like a snake, as the cool night breeze blows the leaves like nothing else. The centipede finds a cricket as loud as a hyena on an old tree with as many branches as spots on a leopard. On the other side though, a huntsman, as big as an oak leaf, scurries as fast as the centipede up after the cricket. They meet on a branch as low as a goat, and as hungry as lions. They both want to eat. The centipede stands up and looks as scary as a dark, stormy night. The huntsman retreats as fast as a jumpy cat. Realizing it is dawn, the centipede creeps away as quiet as a mouse.

Aaron Gordon, Grade 6
Cloverdale Middle School, IN

Batman

Does every hero have this problem That the villain never dies? The villains always escape your traps. Have you heroes had very tricky villains. Like I have the villain Sub Zero, The Joker and Dr. Penguin. It is not fair. Superman has nobody I think. Green Arrow has nobody I think. Spiderman has Green Goblin. Captain America has nobody I think. And I have three villains to destroy. It is not fair!

Adrian Quiroz, Grade 6
Zapata Academy, IL

Car

My family is a car.

My mother is the radio; she sings
makes people happy tells the news

My father is the wheel; he spins
bumps into things lets us move

My brother is the windows; lets us see through it
lets us breath the air outside
goes up and down (always jumping)

My sister is the spare wheel;
there when dad leaves she is there then spins
never gets dizzy

My little brother is the gasoline;
we need him without him the car won't move

My older sister is the trunk;
put stuff in her we also need her

My little sister is the doors;
lock doors so no stranger comes in open and shut
lets people come in and out
push button for window (brother)

Jackie Contreras, Grade 6
Florence Nightingale Elementary School, IL

Do You Realize?

Do you realize
What you said?
You hurt someone's feelings
What about that?

Do you realize
That you are living life
Too fast?
You need to slow down.
Life won't last.

Do you realize
That what you have
Is great?
Always wanting more
Are you that greedy?

Do you realize
That you need to be
A good friend
To get one back?
If you don't do that they will leave you in the dust.

You have to realize the good things
In life to live it to its fullest.

Eilish Jasper, Grade 5
The Orchard School, IN

Kitty

K ind, fun, and sneaky
I s getting what he wants
T oo smart for cats or humans
T oo nice for words
Y et he is gone, he is still my fuzzy buddy
Spencer Koontz, Grade 5
Northern Heights Elementary School, IN

Clouds

Clouds
Puffy, dreamy
Snowing, drifting, pouring
Ravishing to look at
Water vapor.
Mercedes Airgood, Grade 4
Van Rensselaer Elementary School, IN

The Big Cat, Cheetah

Cheetah
Springy, speedy
Catching, eating, drinking
Sharp teeth that tear
Runners
Gabrielle Davis, Grade 5
Van Rensselaer Elementary School, IN

Jake

A cat named Jake
Bats at his ball
Cuddles with me
Does he love me?
Yes, he does!
Samantha Ball, Grade 5
Northern Heights Elementary School, IN

Chocolate Donut

Smells good,
Chocolate glazed,
I enjoy it very much,
It smells like a chocolate candy bar,
Try it.
Erick Delgadillo, Grade 5
Edison Elementary School, IL

Brother

Brother
Nice, interesting
Loving, caring, trusting
Protects me in danger.
Family
Hayley Kingman, Grade 4
Van Rensselaer Elementary School, IN

Ode to Books

I think books are great
I like to read them with the features of excitement
How would we survive without them
Ode to books whose words flow like a river, simply going into your mind
The pages turn like a hurricane going and blowing.
How the words can pierce or love you
Relate or show a point of view.
Ode to books in which so many love and care for
The books return the favor by telling their tales
They influence and are great
Oh how I love books
Ode to books who talk and give reaction to the confusing world
Show a whole different concept of life
Who grasp your heart and mind they can give you a thing to talk about.
This is why I am thankful for books.
Isaac Rubenstein, Grade 5
Walker Elementary School, IL

Cassidy's From

I am from monopoly and "You dork!"
playing soft ball and writing
I am from cheesy cheese pizza, dirt roads and twilight.

From Tennessee accents to peanut butter cookies with my cool aunt
to rocky road ice-cream and a big family.

I am from my autographed softball
to my small couch in my colorful room and my Wii
and my computer and country music
to my mom's catch phrase, "Clean your room" to me and my awesome sister
and juicy sweet pineapple or sweet chocolate chip cookies.

I am from all this and many more.
Trust me my family is a chore.
Cassidy Coldiron, Grade 6
Knox Community Middle School, IN

Prejudice Is Crime

Prejudice is judging people by their wealth, religion, or looks,
They steal dignity from others, like crooks.
Prejudice is bullying in the worst way,
Prejudice is still going on, even today.

At five AM Sunday morning, June 26, three white teens killed a black man,
One of the kids, Deryl Dedmond, got arrested as the leader of the clan.
They tortured him, and ran him over in a Ford F-250 pickup truck,
His uncle said he was a good boy who went corrupt.

The Emancipation Proclamation was passed by Abe Lincoln to free slaves,
It also stopped racism in many different ways.
Kids everywhere can stop prejudice today,
By speaking up because it matters what you say.
Ryan Starnes and Tyler Watson, Grade 6
Tri-West Middle School, IN

Acceptance

Horses frolic in the pasture
I slowly walk along the fence
The boundary to a different world
Timidly I approach the horse
He is a mighty beast
Muscles ripple under his skin
I know
There is no taming him
He stands alone, solitary and strong
Free will guides him
I slowly breathe
My breath plumes out
White cold
One more step
My hand rests against his nose
It's softer than a baby bird's down
He lets out a small snort of acceptance
We are one
Maximiliana Heller, Grade 5
Stanley Clark School, IN

Paces

Paces take me places
But they also take me to you

My heart beats for you
and you only

One day I may
want to walk away
But I will
come back to you

Paces for me are a foot

Step by step
foot by foot

I will walk back
to you
Caitlin Baker, Grade 5
Manchester Intermediate School, IN

Night Sky

Warm glow of the moonlight
On my face.

Palm trees dancing in the wind.

The stars like lights shining
Bright in the night sky.

I lay in the water and
Float away…
Olivia Carnagua, Grade 6
Our Shepherd Lutheran School, IN

Halloween Night

Halloween starts at night
So you can get a fright.

Halloween can be mean
So you might scream.

You can get lots of treats
But most people get sweets.

Halloween is a day
That you can play.
Sara Mendenhall, Grade 4
Summit Elementary School, IL

Farming

Work, work, out in the field.
Oh how I love to see a good yield.

Corn, corn, when will you grow?
That is what I'd like to know.

On, no, the tractor broke down,
Oh, oh, oh how I'll frown.

As I sit here and scratch my chin,
I realize it's time to turn in.
Jacob Henderson, Grade 5
Dee Mack Intermediate School, IL

Electricity

Where, oh where could we possibly be
If we did not have electricity?

We would have lamps that burn kerosene
And stoves that run on propane.

We'd warm our toes on open fires
And light our houses with candles

It's hard to imagine what life would be
If we didn't have electricity.
Henry Kraatz, Grade 4
St Matthew School, IL

Halloween

H ouses as scary as haunted barns
A lways love the crunchy candy corn!
L ove Halloween like you love your family.
L icorice is my favorite — as in red.
O wls loudly hoot!
W itches are attacking!
E ek — there's a ghost!
E at candy all night!
N ever enter a witch's house.
Aaron Arroyo, Grade 6
Three Rivers School, IL

Chicago Blackhawks

Black, red, and white are their colors
Soaring down the ice they go
Weaving in and out
One by one they juke them out
Skating towards the goal they go
Will they miss, will they score?
Shot after shot
Goal by goal
The game goes on
Till times up
They push hard and don't stop
Do they stop?
No they don't
Let's go Blackhawks
Watch out!!
Here they come
Alex Cate, Grade 5
The Orchard School, IN

Riverside

I can tell you where the river runs low
and the street lights glow.
This is Riverside.
With the winding roads
and the croaking toads.
The bridge that's green
and the magnificent Halloween.
The gas lamps are bright
with their beautiful light in the night.
Where the lacewings fly
and the wing goes by.
The birds tweet
while the deer eat.
Where I feel at home
and I'm never alone.
I truly love Riverside.
Jasper Epstein, Grade 5
Central Elementary School, IL

Me

Magical as an elf
Clumsy as a clown
Bad like a lion
Quizzical as a game show
Tall like a tree
Zippy like a mouse
Goofy like Goofy
Jumpy like a rabbit
Crazy as a puppy
Invincible as a super hero
Important as the president
Jolly like Santa
Friendly as a fish
Alert as an agent
Nico Spriggs, Grade 5
Edison Elementary School, IL

Troubles

Troubles can
Haunt you
But only if
You let them
It is your choice
If they are your
Friend or enemy
Build character
Or hurt it
Open or close
A door
Help or hurt you
Guide or mislead you
But then again
It is your choice
No one's but
Yours
Valerie Kraft, Grade 6
The Orchard School, IN

Skiing

The freshly plowed snow invites me.
Whoosh!
Whoosh!
Whoosh!
I rush down
the steep hill leaving
railroad tracks behind me.
Snowflakes attack my
unprotected nose.
I shift my hips side to side.
My pole twists as I turn away
from the trees.
I transfer my weight to the left
to form my hockey stop.
My cold fingers tingle.
I slide up on the chair lift planning
what slope will I ride next?
Shivani Patel, Grade 6
Stanley Clark School, IN

Sunshine

Sunshine
is like
when you eat your favorite food
It's like
when you bite into a sweet, sweet doughnut
It's like
when you meet your true love
Then the gleaming sun in your face,
makes me tingly inside.
Makes me think really happy thoughts
like, you can just lay on the grass and relax
That's sunshine.
Michael Wheaton, Grade 4
Lincoln Elementary School, IL

Fall Is Here

Leaves are falling from their trees,
Hibernating animals,
with the birds heading for warmth
Fall is here
making all the leaves fall.
The rakes being taken out from garages
and Halloween is just around the corner.
With all the different colors
and different smells
I know that fall is coming.
Erik Manzo, Grade 6
Zapata Academy, IL

Basketball

Basketball is fun
Basketball is cool
Basketball is awesome
Basketball is fantastic
I like being point guard
I like passing
I like scoring
I like getting steals
I love playing for St. Michael
I love basketball
Blake Jewell, Grade 6
St Michael School, IN

Cookie

soft, warm cookie dough
right from the oven
chocolate chips melted
upon the cookie

my first bite
mmmmm…
so good
crumbs fall onto my plate
all gone!
Carsyn Howard, Grade 5
Manchester Intermediate School, IN

Brookville

Brookville is the place to be
it gives us shelter, houses, and trees
there are so many different faces
there are many people in the town's spaces
you can run around in the grass
or go fishing at the lake to catch some bass
I could go down the Whitewater on a raft
or go to the library to make a craft
there is so much to see
Brookville is the place to be
Evan Apsley, Grade 6
St Michael School, IN

Pencil Sharpening

I was crazily sharpening my pencil
For two hours straight.
I got a blister,
Oh great!
Now my hand smells like a tree.
This is disgusting
Believe me.
I see a girl sharpening a pencil.
Don't sharpen for two hours long!
Daisy Rodriguez-Romero, Grade 4
Cossitt Avenue Elementary School, IL

Christmas

Christmas is time to share
Also it's time to care
It's time to get together
Also it's time to gather
Around and cheer
Make a snowman
Give it a beard
Don't forget to give gifts
To all your relatives
Cooper Girten, Grade 4
Summit Elementary School, IL

Ode to Flowers

Ode to flowers
And how they grow
From spring to the first snow
Makes the world feel beautiful
The touch of soft cotton
I pick them and put them in my home
All pretty colors and wonderful smells
Makes me feel swell
Ode to flowers and how pretty they are
Aaya Attiya, Grade 5
Walker Elementary School, IL

Butterflies

Flies high in the sky.
Clever and very playful.
Has unique colors.
Fragile and very simple.
Small lady bugs are its friends.
Abby Banet, Grade 5
Henryville Elementary School, IN

Balloons

In the clouds, drifting by,
To and fro in the sky.
Through the wind, rain, and snow,
In a balloon there you go.
Not on land, not in sea,
In the air floating free.
Mellissa Zhang, Grade 4
Ranch View Elementary School, IL

Beach

Get some sand between your toes,
To take away your woes,
Get a tan,
As red as a brick red van,
Get some water in your nose,
Feel the sting in your nose,
Get a surfboard,
Trying to surf forward.

Zach Kemp, Grade 4
Chrisney Elementary School, IN

Swimming

My heart is thumping.
Blood is pumping.
When I dive,
It's like everything is alive.
And when I swim,
Everything looks slim.
And now that I've won,
Everything is done.

Megan Bernacchi, Grade 4
St Matthew School, IL

The Ocean

The ocean.
Nothing but pure goodness.
The blueness.
The beautiful sand filled with
little rocks.
How wonderful is the beach? You may ask.
I can tell you.
It's nothing but pure goodness.

Amelia Najera, Grade 6
Zapata Academy, IL

Math and Reading

Math
Fun, easy
Adding, multiplying, subtracting
Ruler, calculator, book, workbook
Red, white, words, explained
Boring, hard
Reading

Citlaly Villegas, Grade 5
Edison Elementary School, IL

Monday

Monday
The cool breeze through my hair
The sun shines on my head
The bus comes down the street
When it is sunny,
I can't wait until I get to school
Monday is the best weekday!

Alexzandra Roberson, Grade 4
Lincoln Elementary School, IL

Words

All I hear is yelling
Screaming
What does it mean?
What words are they speaking?
Colors
Whites
These words fill my ears
But what do they mean?
What's happening?
My life has been turned upside down
Everything is just colors
Colors
Colors
Colors
And I am mixed up in it
Will it ever stop?
Will it ever stop?

Shachar Rosenblatt, Grade 5
Walker Elementary School, IL

Midnight Sky

I wait outside when it is dark,
feel the wind upon my heart,
I look up high to see the sky,
so beautiful and divine.

I see the fine stars up high,
making it bright in the sky.
The moon shining on my eyes,
making me smile in my mind.

Wish it would never end.
The sound of silent music is
all that I hear as I look up at the sky.
I see only dark, dark blue in the sky,
mom yells "Come in" but I just sigh,
look up at the sky one last time,
then I go inside.

Jaelyn Webb, Grade 5
Manchester Intermediate School, IN

The Wizard Roller Coaster

A roller coaster,
Aka principal's office,

Going down really fast,
Stomach aching,
I feel sick,
Feels like being punched several times,

When the ride is over,
I feel like crying,

But I don't!

Jorie L. Stephenson-Sterling, Grade 5
Walker Elementary School, IL

Cats in the Nighttime

Cats in the nighttime,
Their glowing eyes.
They match the city lights,
Without a surprise.
I see cats as thin, furry,
and cuddly animals.
Yikes! They are cute,
but sometimes not so cuddly.
I can use my five senses
to describe my cat. It's
easy you see. I can smell kitty litter
on his feet. I can taste his
fur when I rub him to my
face, and so on.
Also, I see a fur
ball of love and cuddles.
Zzzz…

Molly Bath, Grade 4
Copeland Manor Elementary School, IL

A Great Thanksgiving!

Pass the turkey,
Pass the yams.
Do I smell potatoes?
Pass the cranberries,
Pass the stuffing.
Do I hear potatoes hissing in the hot pot?
Pass the ham,
Pass the green beans.
Do I see potatoes hissing on a platter?
Pass the carrots,
Pass more turkey.
Do I feel potatoes on my plate?
It's lumpy and heavy.
Pass more yams.
I taste potatoes!
Pass the pecan pie.
That is how Thanksgiving goes.

Samuel Hurh, Grade 4
Copeland Manor Elementary School, IL

Santa Claus

Santa, Santa, beard so white
can't wait to see what you bring
on Christmas Eve Night.
Toys and goodies and candies galore
can't wait to see
what you have in store.

Santa, Santa, suit so red
you visit me while
I lay down my sleepy head.
Fast asleep with a smile
can't wait to play for a long, long while.

Keenan Diaz, Grade 5
Manchester Intermediate School, IN

Cupcake

Sweet, scrumptious icing
Delicious sprinkles on top
A great flavor! Yum!
Madison Bridges, Grade 5
Van Rensselaer Elementary School, IN

Winter Day

Trees are so nice now.
Today is a day with Mom.
I'll need a shovel.
Azariah Williams, Grade 4
St Angela School, IL

Winter

Winter is so cold
The snow is on the wet ground.
And we all need coats.
Samiyah Person, Grade 5
St Angela School, IL

Thanksgiving

Peace is found, A feast
To come, People having a
Great time, Three weeks end.
Lindsey Newland, Grade 6
Christian Academy of Indiana, IN

Weimaraner

Grey ones growing big
Grey beauties like running fast
Big ones like to run
Katrina Guardado, Grade 5
Edison Elementary School, IL

Black Hole

Life is like a black hole
It sucks my soul to its doom
It is gone for good
Shae Reiter, Grade 5
Edison Elementary School, IL

At the Coast

The sun is shining
Waves are crashing against shore
The palms are swaying
Haley Wanner, Grade 5
Central Elementary School, IL

Grasshopper

Its great life music
Comes from a small violin
That will work for life
Juan Pantoja, Grade 5
Van Rensselaer Elementary School, IN

My Complex Family

My family is a car,

My dad is the motor.
He makes sure that everything is working.
If it's not working he fixes it right away.
When my dad fixes something he shows us how to do it,
My dad tells me what to do and I do it, even when it involves dangerous tools

My mom is where the driver drives,
My mom oversees everything.
When my dad needs something she gets it for him.
When I and my brother fight, she splits us apart.
My mom decides how much money we can afford to spend each month.
My mom knows a lot of recipes, we eat something different each day.
My mom does most of the cleaning to try to keep the house tidy.

My brother is where the passenger sits.
My brother helps fix things around the house,
My brother helps my dad fix things.
My brother helps my mom clean the house.
My brother plays with me when we're bored; we mostly do everything together.
Emilio Reyes, Grade 6
Florence Nightingale Elementary School, IL

I'm From

I am from the leaves of fall
From the little pink cup and the brand new blue bike
I am from the so small house that I shared with my family of four at the time
And if I wished I could climb upon the gray shingled roof
I am from the willow tree
Whose branches hugged me
I am from blankets so soft and beds so warm
From Denise and Charlotte
I am from home cooking and great feast
And from never give uppers
From I'll always be there when you fall
I am from the best friends I could ever have
I am from Malones and Peters
From black wacky cake and mashed potatoes
From waddled around the fire at Grandpa and Grandma's house
And from Grandma Feast we ate
And the pink and red cherry dress
I am from those moments so great you cannot forget
And the so sad you wish you could forget but can't
Madelyn Peter, Grade 5
Perry Central Elementary School, IN

Shooting Stars

Shootings stars fly through the sky,
watching over the cold, cold Earth and flying past the hot, hot sun
while being a bubbling beauty of hot, blazing, boiling, shining gas.

SWISH! They go in the summer breeze, while people watch them, while they freeze.
They shine and shine very brightly while they watch over us when they fly.
Janis Wagner, Grade 6
Our Shepherd Lutheran School, IN

Grass
Earth's ground green and scratchy
Sways in the wind under blue skies
Grows and is cut down.
Jacob Nugent, Grade 5
Van Rensselaer Elementary School, IN

People
Many lives enforced
Size and colors different
All should go to school.
Jeffery Green, Grade 5
Van Rensselaer Elementary School, IN

Best Friend
My best friend lives near.
I play with him every day.
Four legs and a tail.
Hannah Redlin, Grade 4
Van Rensselaer Elementary School, IN

Snake
Slimy snake slithers.
Sprays venom at its prey's eyes
Ahh! RUN! It's coming!
Maddy Marchand, Grade 4
Van Rensselaer Elementary School, IN

My Dog Cooper
Muscular, huge, cute!
Hyper, smart, beautiful, and kind!
Strong, brindle, and chunky!
Hayly Manns, Grade 5
Van Rensselaer Elementary School, IN

Sin Cara
A masked high flyer
He was on Monday night Raw
A wrestling hero.
Adam Armstrong, Grade 4
Van Rensselaer Elementary School, IN

Dogs
Dogs are fun.
Moods happy, mad, and sad.
Cute and fluffy.
Max Herr, Grade 4
St Matthew School, IL

Whales
All the whales swim by.
All the birds fly high in the sky.
The whales swim by together.
Bronson Spivey, Grade 4
Warren Central Elementary School, IN

The Cold Fall
The cold, cold
Fall leaves falling from the trees.
I can feel the fall breeze on my face.
Raking all the leaves,
shaking the rake
trying to get the leaves to come off.
I hear noises from the crunchy leafs on the ground.
The colors I see are red, orange, yellow, brown hanging off of the trees.
Brr I'm shivering because I'm numb and cold.
The sun is shining, but it's still cold
I stand in the sunlight to stay warm.
It feels like I was frozen and had to defrost.
The birds fly south for the winter and animals store food.
There is a fog rolling in.
There is no sunshine.
The sky is all gray.
Not a single white cloud anymore today.
Shivani Shimko, Grade 5
Todd Academy, IN

Run!
Run, run away now from this horrible world
Run faster before it catches you and makes you think its menacing ways
Be careful.
Don't stop or you will be swallowed up by it
Please understand my ranting and raving
For it will help you ever so much
Don't think
For it will haunt you forever
It is sicker than the most horrible illness
For it will not rest until it has ripped your soul apart
It has no forgiveness or humanity
It hurts without meaning to
It kills by breathing
It is the monster every child fears
It is mankind
Savannah Mallon, Grade 5
Hawthorne Elementary School, IL

Prejudice Is an Offense
Prejudice is like a sin,
Destruction and devastation entering in.
Discrimination against people is one of the worst,
It's like a bubble full of hate about to burst.

It doesn't matter if they're part black or all white,
Discrimination to them isn't right.
Not including people could cause hate,
And everyone will start to debate.

Future generations can help show the way,
To get to a better day.
Children and even adults have to watch how they act and what they say,
Otherwise today will be a repeat of what happened yesterday.
Lexa Gilley and Mimi Evans, Grade 6
Tri-West Middle School, IN

Lauren Leopard

She's white spotted, wild, and free
She has a pink pet bunny
Green eyes, sweet, and black nose.
When a picture is taken, she strikes a pose.
She is a geek, she's purple and sparkly,
Her favorite singer is Gnarles Barkley.
She is as pretty as she is smart
Next to meat, her favorite food is pumpkin pie pop tarts!
She's darling, and bold, as well as brave.
She lives in a pink and sky-blue cave.
Lauren Leopard is the best leopard to know
Funny, sweet, and not at all shallow.

Lauren Henson, Grade 4
Meadow Lane School, IL

Leaf Pile

Leaves; red, yellow, green, and brown
They fall through the air and land softly
The roaring leaf blower scares the leaves away
Wind blowing the trees softly
The big leaf pile under the tree grows and grows
My dad pushing me on the swing
I fly through the air
Wind in my face
Then I let go
I land in the rough, crunchy leaves
I sink so low that no one can see my face
I find my way up the leaf pile

Kate Gunderson, Grade 5
The Orchard School, IN

Friends

They stick with you through thick and thin
They'll be with you until the end
They will never let you down
These are true friends
You won't be ignored by them
A true friend will not betray you
They'll never leave you alone
These are true friends
They're always understanding
True friends don't hold grudges
Always forgiving to your mistakes
These are true friends

Hannah Wesley, Grade 5
North Knox West Intermediate/Elementary School, IN

Popcorn

Popcorn so fresh and steamy.
The warm butter goes on top.
You smell it from a mile away.
When you get a piece your fingers get greasy.
You try for another.
POP goes a kernel.

Michael Funk, Grade 5
Washington Township Elementary School, IN

Hope!

Hope is what gets you out of bed on the morning of prom
and you haven't been asked yet.
Hope is what makes the caterpillar to a butterfly.
Hope doesn't hold a grudge, but greets you in every way.
Hope helps you stand up for yourself
Even when you're standing alone.
Hope doesn't hold up a mirror and judge on your appearance,
But it lets you know you're beautiful in every way.
Hope pushes you through all of life's problems.
Hope gives you courage that you never thought you had.
Hope makes you smile when you feel like crying.
It's hope that keeps the world moving even when you're frozen.
Hope is like the shoulder to cry on when you need it.
Hope is what keeps the sun and the moon rotating all the time.
Hope holds your head up when you feel like putting it down.
Hope gives you that spirit to go the extra mile and do something
You never thought possible.
Hope is something that you can give or take,
To have a good life with hope.
When you need something hope will be there.

Savannah Sobczak, Grade 6
Staunton Jr High School, IL

The First Snow

Today included an extraordinary sight.
It was the first snow of the season
Thursday, November 10th
On that day I witnessed snow. The first snow.
As it was falling almost too slowly,
I thought of all the Christmas tunes.
Humming, I almost cried
At its beautiful sight.
How can snowflakes be so simple
Yet so complicated
In every way imaginable
And so beautiful as well
They're like trees, almost
Come a long way to this point
To the ground below
To paper that used to be 50 feet tall
Each flake is like words on paper,
So simple but coming to the point
Of making the forms of one letter
It's so simple, but also complicated

Madison Galvez, Grade 6
Westmont Jr High School, IL

Race Horse

I see all of those horses in front of me
The crowd cheering, dirt flinging in front of me
I can just smell the horses and those riders
Ugh can I just get this bit and dirt out of my mouth
The sweat dripping down across my face
I can feel the riders' feet and that comfortable blanket

Trinity Brown, Grade 5
North Knox Intermediate School, IN

A White Hershey's

A white Hershey's,
is a burst of wind the milk so sweet.
melt in mouth chocolate,
chocolate so creamy.
how could anyone resist, the
flavor always uptight,
never gets boring.
it always keeps its same,
but new taste.
you never get old that's why,
I like to eat you in the day.
in the,
afternoon and at night in my eyes so bright.
you keep me satisfied and,
always happy.
I'll do anything if I get you,
my sweet, sweet white Hershey's
Hershey's cookies and creme
they'll have a sugar fene
your like a sugar machine, you come in all shapes and seasons
you also are a trick, and treat

Crystal Swire, Grade 6
U S Grant Middle School, IL

House

My family is a great big house.
My mom is the walls that keep the house stabilized
and sturdy.
My dad is the floor to the house, under everything and
always neutral.
My sister is the windows, she is always
transparent, you could see her "pane."
My niece is the door, you could open up new
things from her.
My grandma is the bricks, chipping away year after
year, waiting for her to be renewed.
My grandpa is the roof, always making us stay put
together and covering us.
My baby brother is a new flower from our garden, fresh
and beautiful.
My big sister is the fence protecting us from
danger.
My aunt is the stairs, always leading us to a new level,
each and ever single time.
My family makes up this big house, always leading to a surprise.
My family is big and we all represent each other.

Genesis Estrella, Grade 6
Florence Nightingale Elementary School, IL

Kobe Bryant

Kobe Bryant is the best,
He always finishes up his quest.
He gets an A+ in being a beast,
He's the most important and never the least.

Isaac Sum, Grade 5
Washington Township Elementary School, IN

If Buildings Were Up…and the Sky Was Down…

Lots of people would not frown,
If buildings were up and the sky was down,
If the ocean would take place of the sky,
To see a fish, you'd look up real high!
You'd dive off the ground, into the big vast blue,
Landing in space, you'd feel like you flew!
To take a break, heck, land on a cloud,
Feel so great, let out a "Whoop" real loud,
Roller skate with your cat on Saturn's rings,
Goin' so fast, just like you had wings,
Ride around on a comet's tail,
Always going so fast, you never feel like a snail,
When it's time for supper, "swim" back to your home,
Eating dinner on your ceiling and on the roof you'd roam,
Upside down instead of right side up, not right?
Because that's the dream I had last night!

Mallory S. Wolfe, Grade 5
North Knox West Intermediate/Elementary School, IN

Death

Death is a big time bomb,
Waiting to attack everything.
When it makes its move,
The best thing to do is rise against it.

When you have had enough,
That is the best time for you to forget about it.
Remember that no one can stop death from happening,
It is only a part of nature.

Never let Death control you,
In its own ways of making you sad.
So when life brings you down,
Get back up,
Dust yourself off,
Get back in the game of life.

Ben Airdo, Grade 5
Hawthorne Elementary School, IL

Santa's Wait !:)

Silent is the way we wait for Santa,
Silent is the way Santa eats sweet cookies,
Silent is when Santa puts presents under the tree,

Loud is the way the bells ring when he leaves,
Loud is the way Santa
Ho
Ho
Ho's,
Loud is the way we open the gifts,

Eternal is the way God spreads love,
Eternal is the way we have a birthday,
Eternal is the way we enjoy each other.

Sarah Lyons, Grade 4
Churubusco Elementary School, IN

Engagement*

It might not always be easy,
But it won't always be hard.
For if you remember the good, And not only the bad,
Not only will you be happy,
You truly will be glad.
When the skies are gray,
And you are feeling quite frightened,
Do not fret,
You shall be confided.
By the one you love,
Whom will not weep,
The one you care for,
The one is he,
The one you shall love
For your eternity.

Erin Hastings, Grade 6
Staunton Jr High School, IL
Dedicated to my brother, Brian, and his fiancée, Colleen.

Where I Am From

I am from Warsaw
from school and teacher
I am from texting my friends at night
(watching TV after school,
and before I go to bed)
I am from music from Usher,
the songs with Justin Bieber "Somebody To Love"
I'm from McDonald's smoothies and ice cream
I'm from the scar on my face from a doorknob
and the how many times I broke my arms
reset my arms two times, but they have healed
I am from Kristine and Andy Branch
good fresh cookies and milk
From the arm that broke to
the eye that got hit from a doorknob and got
27 stitches on my eye.

Cidney Fox, Grade 6
Knox Community Middle School, IN

Shiver, Shiver, Shiver

As wind whips up
trees shiver
shiver, shiver, shiver
a weary day
trees hope spring will come eventually
shiver, shiver, shiver
trees are exhausted from swaying
back and forth, back and forth
air is crisp and chilly
trees try to coil together to keep warm even though they are bare
shiver, shiver, shiver
as day grows to night the frost tickles the trees
as it tries to find a way to nestle somewhere nearby
shiver, shiver, shiver

Sarah Downs, Grade 6
Stanley Clark School, IN

Library

My family is like a library.

My little brother is like a fiction book.
He always makes everything fun.
He has a vivid imagination. He is kids' favorite.
My mom is the realistic fiction book.
She always tells the truth, but sometimes makes it up.
But there are always accidents.

My dad is a nonfiction book.
He is always correct.
When you have a question he always has an answer.

My big brother is like a novel.
You won't know what might happen next.
And always has a twisting end.

Alejandra Morales, Grade 6
Florence Nightingale Elementary School, IL

Waiting

As I sweep the ocean floor,
The ocean bed,
I wait for a fish to swim in my door.
I shall eat it for dinner.

As I sweep the ocean floor,
The ocean bed,
I wait for a squid to swim in.
I shall eat it for dessert.

As I sweep the ocean floor,
The ocean bed,
I also sweep up dreams and wishes that did not come true.
I see mine,
A dream and a wish,
For a dinner of a yummy fish!

Victoria Kindratenko, Grade 5
Stratton Elementary School, IL

Prejudice Is a Dark Room with No Flashlight

Prejudice is when someone hates another's face,
Because of religion, color, or race.
It can be a wrong impression,
A misunderstanding or misconception.

In Indiana, skinheads are causing trouble,
It makes some minorities want to stay in their own little bubble.
Skinheads do weird things like shave their heads,
Their white power beliefs against other races may spread.

So far there aren't any groups to stop a skinhead,
But we can try to stop the skinhead spread.
Don't make the only anti-group the police,
Join them to make skinhead ideas and power cease.

Nathan Walton and Austin Dickson, Grade 6
Tri-West Middle School, IN

My Grandpa

How I miss you so!
Then Grandpa, why did you go?
My tears fall slowly.

When I picture all
The memories we had
Then, the tragic day came,
And I stayed strong just for you,
Now my guardian angel.

How I remember
Up above the high clouds,
My guardian angel
Faith Lang, Grade 5
Northern Heights Elementary School, IN

Hum, Hum, Hum!

Hum, hum hum!
My dog is home!
Hurry, hurry, my dog is hungry
I open the door, my dog is on the floor.
I go to the kitchen,
I give him some chicken.
Then he ran to my room
Kaboom!!!
He got hit by a broom!
Then he stood back
And his tail he wagged,
Then he looked me in the eye
As he was saying goodbye.
Alex Cardos, Grade 4
St Matthias/Transfiguration School, IL

The Big One

I walk into the rustling leafy woods
I climb the dewy wet ladder
I sit there
I load my gun and wait and wait and wait
Then I see it
It's there
A monster rack
I know it's a monster buck
I get really nervous
My hands start to sweat
I get ready to shoot.
BOOM!
Yes, I got it!
Hunter Miller, Grade 5
Manchester Intermediate School, IN

Summer Time

It is summer time.
I am going to the pool.
The weather is nice.
Shanell Pigram, Grade 4
St Angela School, IL

O Hairbrush!

O hairbrush!
How you untangle
My messy hair
In the morning
In the night.

O hairbrush!
When you make
My hair into a
Braid that is French
Or regular.

O hairbrush!
When you help
A barber
Make my hair even
To cut it perfectly,
Or when I sing into
You for the fun of it.

O hairbrush!
Thank you
A bunch!
Clara Valentine, Grade 6
Our Shepherd Lutheran School, IN

Bats

They embark
for the
hunt

Under the
sparkly, glimmering
moon

They
catch numerous
insects

They track
them with
echolocation

The sun
rises over the
horizon

Soaring back
the bats will roost
until next hunt
Matteus Webb, Grade 5
Stanley Clark School, IN

1.21 Jigowatts!

Science, oh science
All sorts of science
Electricity, plants
Motion, magnetism
All sorts
1.21 Jigowatts of electricity
or 1.21 milliwatts
It's endless
Ah, science
So much fun
Really nice
It's wonderful
Science, oh science.
Casey Wright, Grade 4
Copeland Manor Elementary School, IL

Iron Wolf Days

Once there was a ride,
It was a fast ride.
Upside down hoops,
and lots of other loops.
Wind in your face,
Blowing in your hair too.
Having tons of fun,
While screaming too.
What a good ride,
It once was a ride,
No one can go on it anymore.
It's gone forever now.
No more Iron Wolf anymore.
Maeve Rattin, Grade 4
Copeland Manor Elementary School, IL

Bobby Grimes

Bobby
Athletic, cool, fun, strong
Sibling of Maeve, Gillian Grimes
Lover of sports
Who feels happy
Who needs food
Who gives happiness
Who fears drugs
Who would like to meet Hunter Pence,
Larry Fitzgerald, Evan Turner, Derrick Rose,
Ray Lewis, and Deven Hester
Resident of Westchester
Grimes
Robert Grimes, Grade 6
Divine Infant Jesus School, IL

Winter

Crunch, crunch, crunch, you hear
White snowflakes cover the blue sky
Slowly drifting down
Jane Cox, Grade 5
Van Rensselaer Elementary School, IN

Life
In the daylight the sun is bright
As the butterflies fly time goes by

When the animals roar
the birds will soar

While the parents are working
the kids are improving

While the earth is movin'
that is when life is grovin'

In the nighttime
it is dream time

The children are sleeping
the puppies are dreaming

When the daylight comes
the kids start to run

The buses are zooming
the flowers are blooming

I hear the music playing
in the beautiful church I see people praying

I am thankful for my family and friends
I wish I had much longer weekends
Ashley Carpenter, Grade 6
Three Rivers School, IL

For Now
Rain droplets brush the window
pitter-patter
pitter-patter
Looking through the
rain-spattered window,
I can see
bare trees shiver
uncontrollably in the
chilly, whipping air;
a gloom-filled gray sky with
no clouds but
somehow
it's still raining
pitter-patter
pitter-patter
Maybe soon the rain will cease,
and a rainbow may appear,
but the rain still falls
pitter-patter
pitter-patter
for now
Ari Kirsch, Grade 6
Stanley Clark School, IN

Beagles
They like to run,
In the sun.
They will play,
And they will stay.
They like rabbits,
And they have habits.
All the dogs,
Jump over logs.
They have big noses,
They like hoses.
Some are big,
Some like to dig.
Some are small,
They play with a toy ball.
A lot of the drool,
Beagles rule!
Ashlee Rice, Grade 4
Chrisney Elementary School, IN

Stuck
Have you ever felt like you're stuck
Like there is nowhere you can go
Like you are trapped in a box
A box of sorrow and regret
Do you ever feel like
You can't get out
Alone or alive
You think
You're worthless
You think nobody
Cares about your life
You are important and
Your friends know that
You can't go on this trip alone
Take your friends with you
And you will never get lost
Kevin Morton, Grade 5
The Orchard School, IN

Different Dimensions
Come on take me to another dimension,
a world that could take my attention.
Different from ours,
different from yours.

A world that fills each one of our desires,
Where there are no liars.
Where I can feel safe,
and recognize each face.

For once in my life,
let me go in yours.
Let me get through your pages,
and read you once more.
Roxana Arroyo, Grade 6
Zapata Academy, IL

I'm From
I'm from juicy tender steak,
from extra cheesy macaroni, and
Kentucky fried chicken
I am from the rose bushes in the garden
I am from the gossipers and dramas
and stand up straight, and no phones
at the table
I'm from Amy and Shane's
Tuesday taco night.
From the grandpa who lost
a limb in the war.
Under my bed a box
over flowing memories.
Paige Hilt, Grade 6
Knox Community Middle School, IN

If the World Were Perfect
If the world were perfect
Nothing would be the same
I wouldn't have to go to school
If the world were perfect
We wouldn't have wars or fights
And lonely boys or girls
If the world were perfect
People wouldn't die
No one would get hurt
If the world were perfect
Most important
Everybody would be loved
If the world were perfect
Violet Worth, Grade 5
The Orchard School, IN

This Is Mine
This is my cat,
He is fat and black.
If you don't watch out,
He will attack.

This is my cat,
He sleeps all day.
He's not very good
At keeping mice away.

This is my cat,
He doesn't listen when I call
Instead he plays all day in the fall.
Nikki Lehmann, Grade 5
Forreston Grade School, IL

Rabbit
Hop, hop, hop, hop, hop
Dark brown leaping on the ground
Looking for a home
Jacob Parrish, Grade 4
Van Rensselaer Elementary School, IN

Happy
My mom is cooking.
My brother is happy too.
Spring is coming soon.
Jared Florent, Grade 4
St Angela School, IL

Summer
The summer has passed.
We have a month of summer.
The summer is hot.
Kimberly Halwenge, Grade 4
St Angela School, IL

Fall, Fall, Fall
The fall is here now.
The people play outside now
It is cold outside.
Jazmin Brown, Grade 4
St Angela School, IL

Spring
Spring is a cold month
Spring is a rainy season
Flowers come in spring
Kamyrn Little, Grade 4
St Angela School, IL

Ocean
Clear water shining
Gently lapping the moist shore
Sun reflects the waves
Claire Hurley, Grade 5
Van Rensselaer Elementary School, IN

Leaves
The leaves are falling
The leaves are changing colors
Leaves are different
Ashanti McFarland, Grade 4
St Angela School, IL

A Basketball
Bounces up and down
Dribble down the court with it
A bright orange sphere.
Ilene Marzke, Grade 5
Van Rensselaer Elementary School, IN

A Great Season
The birds are chirping
The flowers are blooming
The sun is shining.
Dasanti Peterson, Grade 5
St Angela School, IL

Halloween
H aHaHa! The witch goes flying in the sky.
A ll adults always bob for apples.
L aughter out in the neighborhood and some screams.
L aughing at the houses that are teepeed; it looks like snow!
O h my gosh! The kids are screaming and running from scary teenagers.
W hack! The ball is hit out of the field and the ghost catches it.
E asy candy to get from neighborhood people.
E eee! The kids got a stomach cramp from eating candy.
N o, Ghost. Halloween is over and go back to your grave.
Jerad Price, Grade 6
Three Rivers School, IL

Halloween
H aving candy stuck in your teeth is not very swell.
A dventuring into the woods to this house that is as scary as Frankenstein.
L urking in the shadows was a huge, huggable cat.
L ollipop, licorice, lime, oh my!
O uch! Something bit me! It was a hissing witch — ahhhhhhh!
W ith wandering eyes I'm looking for the houses with the most candy.
E volving creatures come crawling to the cemetery,
E ventually going back to the dark side.
N ever see those ghosts again until next Halloween.
Wiley Boen, Grade 6
Three Rivers School, IL

Fall
red orange and yellow
a wondersome time
joy never leaves your heart
a red feather flutters to the ground
jumping into a golden pool
the crisp wind blows wildly around and makes the feathers take flight
soon the feathers will be covered in pillows of cotton candy
red orange and yellow what wonderful colors
tomorrow the world will be new all over again
Allison Kautz, Grade 4
Highlands Elementary School, IL

Sun Sun Sun
Sun Sun Sun
You're always on the run you make it easier to have lots of fun.
You make things bright to give us lots of light so it's not as dark as night.
You light up the sky to help birds fly.
Sun Sun Sun
We're sad when you go but we always know you will be back I know that for a fact!!!
Dayton Marcum, Grade 6
U S Grant Middle School, IL

Christmas
Santa and his elves how sweet they can be, I know this because we put up a Christmas tree.
He checks his list not once but twice, If you want a present this is my advice.
My stocking is filled with goodies for me, maybe I will get a game for my Wii.
I wait and I wait waiting for you, you know what I want a new pair of shoes.
Santa and his elves how sweet you can be, please, please, please bring the presents to me.
Courtney Hall and Lauren Howard, Grade 5
Grande Reserve Elementary School, IL

Colors
Where can you find all of the colors?
Maybe in the sea with all the peachy pink corals,
Or maybe green valleys with all the bright flowers?
How about a clock that counts all the hours?
What if it was a rainbow or two?
What about the fish?
They might qualify.
What about all sorts of pie?
Do any of these have all the colors or more?
I don't know,
So how about the floor?
Magdalen Barnes, Grade 4
St Matthew School, IL

Niagara Falls
People in AWE watching the rapids
Falling gracefully, but dangerously over the rocks.

The natural wonder surprises
So people gasp loudly.

Viewing these remarkable rapids
People shiver from the frigid water spraying.

The majestic beauty is known to be
Famous, colorful, and amazing!
Rowan Hannah, Grade 6
Alexandria Monroe Intermediate School, IN

Cherished Item
You can take away my school.
You can take away my car.
But please don't take away my awesome candy bar.

I can do without tea.
I can do without hens.
But I can't do without my very best friends.

I can live without my book
I can live without my house.
But I can't live without my really cute mouse.
Althea Belen, Grade 6
Sacred Heart School, IL

Snowflake
S ometimes melts on your hand.
N ever stays too long, and
O n the ground it slowly drops
W hen the weather gets cold.
F un is its purpose,
L aughing and playing
A ll day long in it.
K ids make snowmen with it.
E veryone is cold because of the weather it brings.
Maria Lutas, Grade 4
Frank H Hammond Elementary School, IN

A Computer
My family is a computer

My dad is the internet,
he gives me whatever I need and want.

My mom is the hard drive,
she doesn't look like she
remembers anything,
but once you ask her something
she has the mind of an elephant

My brother is the monitor,
he thinks he is the head of the pack
and shows us new things,
but he is just sitting there looking
pretty most of the time.

My sister is the mouse,
she is capable of moving,
but not unless someone
moves or touches her first

My other sister is the keyboard,
once you touch her she reacts fast
and she is ticklish and squeamish.
Michelle Garcia, Grade 6
Florence Nightingale Elementary School, IL

My Favorite Season
The season passing by
Kids enjoying last minute playing

The buzzing of bees buzz, buzz, buzz
The tweets of some birds tweet, tweet, tweet
The swooshing of leaves swoosh, swoosh, swoosh.

The smell of sweet flowers
The smell of red tomatoes
The smell of damp air
The smell of hot chocolate when at home.

The touch of soft and crunchy leaves
The touch of hard cement
The touch of dried up dead grass
The touch of soft round tomatoes.

The sight of bees taking out pollen
The sight of birds migrating south in a V sign
The sight of colorful leaves

The taste of cold air
The taste of delicious Halloween candy
The taste of warm hot chocolate
The taste of marvelous pumpkin pie.
Adrian Medina, Grade 6
Zapata Academy, IL

Basketball Practice
It's 7:30 pm
A coach yells "2 laps around the gym!"
Shooting free throws "oops" I miss
Darn I have to run again
Running plays over and over
Building defense to be the best
Coach always yells
"Don't let the other team score"
Sweating a lot and out of breath
Muscles weak
Body sore
Even though I go through all of this hard work
I am still thankful for being athletic
9:00 pm
Practice is over!

Nia Williams, Grade 5
Walker Elementary School, IL

The Ocean
The waves crash against the shore
Revealing the sand's beautiful treasures
White foam explodes onto the beach
Children laugh and splash
The mist spraying them like a squirt of nature's perfume
Hundreds of creatures roam the ocean's floor
Adventuring to where no human has ever gone before
The warm sunshine overwhelms souls and bodies
Kissing them with a ray of light
Skin tinting to a golden brown shade
The sand and the ocean touch
Meeting again and again like old friends
The turquoises and periwinkles tie-dye the water
These colors going on and on for miles
The ocean

Grace Whittington, Grade 6
Bednarcik Jr High School, IL

Hole in the Wall
Hole, hole in the wall
Big and round you are
At night I get a
Fright, spiders, rats
And all those arachnids
Circle, circle in the wall
You are thirty inches tall
Dark and scary
Staring right at me
I wake up at night
Wondering
If something pounces on me
I wake up at night
Knowing it's just a
Hole in the wall

Jared Oary, Grade 6
Alexandria Monroe Intermediate School, IN

Soccer
Soccer, soccer, soccer!!!
Soccer is just about fun and good stuff like that,
Soccer to some people is just plain stupid,
But, soccer is a big part of my life,
I have been playing since I was three,
One day I hope to go to Brazil,
And last, but not least, people that are so competitive,
They forget all about the reason they are on the field.

Drew Rentschler, Grade 5
Van Rensselaer Elementary School, IN

Mouse/Rat
Mouse
small, gray
running, walking, eating
fat, playful/mean, large
chasing, diving, teasing
ugly, weird
Rat

Emma Hawkins, Grade 5
Washington Township Elementary School, IN

Spiders
Spiders are scary.
They are really hairy!
They will creep;
They crawl.
They are in the wall,
big and fat.
I would really like to step on them all!

Rachelle Nelson, Grade 6
Alexandria Monroe Intermediate School, IN

Softball
Softball
fun, exciting
throwing, catching, batting
girlie, tiring, sweaty, joyful
entertaining, running, amusing
playful, awesome
Basketball

Katelyn Majda, Grade 5
Washington Township Elementary School, IN

Ice Cream
As cold as a deep freeze
It drips from your hand
You are trying to eat faster
and faster
Then you get down to the cone
and get a
brain freeze!

Peyton Abbott, Grade 6
Alexandria Monroe Intermediate School, IN

My King

He is the
Savior, the King,
the Light, and the
only route
to Heaven.
He died on the cross to forgive us of our sins.
He was the only person to never commit a sin.
He never
gave in to
temptation,
and He was
the only
person to be
resurrected
from the
dead. He is
the one and only
Son of God.
He is Jesus.
He is my King.

Grant Adams, Grade 5
Stanley Clark School, IN

The Ocean

My mother is the sand
the sand is really warm and cozy
just like her and you could go with her
and have fun.

My dad is the ocean
when he is happy he is calm
but when he's mad he makes big waves
and makes a big mess when he is
asleep he is frozen just like
the winter weather.

My little brother is a dolphin
he never stops playing and he is cute
and every day he grows.

My brother is a crab
he is always pinching me and
stopping me from doing things and
he is really slow when he is running

Gabriela Meza, Grade 6
Florence Nightingale Elementary School, IL

Christmas Cookies

Christmas cookies are fun to bake
They're really something I like to make
At Christmas time you're preparing the food
For me it's hard not to be in a good mood
The house is pretty with lights everywhere
And you can stay in your pajamas all day if you dare.

Frances Hendrickson, Grade 4
St Matthew School, IL

Sky

Sky, so high
How I wish I could fly
The sky so blue
What should I do?
Clouds so white
A perfect day to fly a kite
How the clouds puff
Getting up there will be tough
A rain drop lands on my hand
As noticeable as a step on the sand
I can see myself in the sky so, so, clear
Just almost like a new mirror
As it happens, a light breeze
It makes the wind chimes clink like keys
Bang goes the thunder, clash goes the lightning
How it is so very frightening
As it comes crashing down, chips of hail
I guess that's how the sky sends mail
All the birds with wings, how lucky they are
That could be my wish for the next shooting star

Ainsley Reynolds, Grade 4
Grande Reserve Elementary School, IL

I Am Bio

I am a dog lover and a care taker.
I wonder when I get my boxer puppy.
I hear barking as it echoes through the wind.
I see her running around in the yard.
I want to feel her lying next to me.
I am a dog lover and a care taker.

I pretend that we go on adventures together.
I feel the wind blowing on me and her.
I touch her cotton ball-soft fur.
I worry that she might run away while I'm at school.
I cry because she could get really sick.
I am a dog lover and a care taker.

I understand she's a good dog.
I say she's faster than a bird.
I dream that she'll be happier than ever.
I try to give her as much exercise as I can.
I hope that she will never run away.
I am a dog lover and a care taker.

Kayla Billow, Grade 5
Perry Central Elementary School, IN

Halloween/Christmas

Halloween
Dark, spooky
Costume, candy, joy, laugh
Wrapping, singing, eating
Presents, trees
Christmas

Maddisyn Sickles, Grade 5
Washington Township Elementary School, IN

The Life of an Apple Tree

I am a seed inserted into the ground.
My fellow seeds, planted beside me, strive for a downpour of wonderful, cool rain.
Me, I'm just content to be here, waiting to experience life ahead of me.
Two years pass, and I am the only surviving seed of my kind in this whole yard.
Right now, I am only a small sapling, but I will grow into a wonderful, powerful, full-grown tree.
Sometimes rabbits and rodents nip at me and my roots, trying to find a small bit of nourishment.
Someone puts a small wire fence around me, defending my precious roots.
For now, I am protected.
Until Jack Frost comes, I am happy and proud of my crimson and golden leaves.
They fall to the ground in brown and discarded crumpled piles.
He grinds me, pounds me, and freezes me whole.
Hundreds of years pass.
I am a matured tree, eager to lend my fruit to others in need of a cool, juicy treat.
Next winter, Jack takes my strength forever.
My last shriveled fruit falls, and I slumber in peace for centuries to come.
My advice for humans: Spend your life wisely. It goes too fast.

Makennah Koos, Grade 6
Bednarcik Jr High School, IL

The Somber Song of the Forgetful One

The surprise came down with a thud, hard as steel, though in real life, light as paper.
The pain came in several layers — disgrace, disappointment, despair!
A whispered voice came in, with its "I don't remember that assignment" and its "that was never due."
The chill came in as a dark sweater was pulled up over the face,
And it looked as if night had come into the dark world of woes and worries.
The worries came in with a colder chill each time.
The Woman that gave birth to the child wouldn't be pleased.
She would, in fact, be enraged, irritated, and aggravated.
The Man would be disappointed. Lightly disappointed.
Just like the light disappointment the child felt from the slip of paper that spiraled around, creating a whirlwind of a mess.
This would become a vicious circle, a very vicious cycle,
Seeing that vicious events had led up to this long-coming climax.
The child would relax soon after the end of this tornado, and the bow would come in,
Its many dazzling colors help to reflect on that little mishap, symbolizing another chance,
How it hadn't forgotten, and He will never forget.
I know that I, the Observer, will never forget.

Kealoha Ogunseitan, Grade 6
Frances Xavier Warde School, IL

The Brook

The gentle water flows steadily.
Leaves fall off the trees and float down the brook like tiny boats sailing to their destination.
Butterflies dance through the air above the brook like graceful ballerinas.
Baby chipmunks scurry around, playing games like happy puppies when they meet someone new.
Berries as red as roses cover the brook's banks.
Moss covers the brook's rocks, like a light snowfall covers the ground.
A mother deer and her fawn frolic through the tall grass like joyful children playing games.
Tulips sway in the breeze near the brook like swings swinging back and forth.
A maple tree towers above the brook like a skyscraper does a city.
Birds sing beautifully in the treetops above the brook like a choir during a performance.
The brook is as beautiful as the heavens.
I flow by all of these things each day and I will continue to for as long as I live.

Hannah Nichols, Grade 6
Cloverdale Middle School, IN

Fascinating
A personality, fascinating
A soccer game, fascinating
LIFE, it all fascinates me.
That book that I read,
the picture I saw!
Fascinating.
A science experiment, bubbling over.
A squirrel trapped in a bird feeder.
A movie with a giant monster.
Fascinating.
It's just a word.
Grace Beutter, Grade 5
Stanley Clark School, IN

My Dog Rusty
I have a dog named Rusty,
When he gets wet he smells musty.
He will drink water,
It will get on the floor,
And we will let him out the door.
I love taking him on walks,
And we will also talk.
I like to throw squeaky toys,
When he picks them up he makes a noise,
I love Rusty around,
He's the best dog in town.
Samantha Miller, Grade 4
St. Matthew School, IL

Seasons
Spring cries with rain full of joy
like a little kid with a toy.

Summer shines with blankets of the sun
making children have more fun.

Autumn falls with leaves so full of glee
in a pile to play with me.

Winter snows with the cold chill air
making people fill with joy everywhere.
Cassie Westfall, Grade 5
Allen J. Warren Elementary School, IN

Dogs
If I were a dog,
I would be loud.
I would be fast.
I would make my owners proud.

If I were a dog,
I would be light.
I would chase mailmen.
I would be white.
Zachary Contreras, Grade 5
Edison Elementary School, IL

Crystals
Crystals are glittery
bright and gold
They glimmer and shimmer
and sparkle gold

When you hold
a crystal
it shines bright

Crystals are glittery
bold and bright
Madison Cook, Grade 5
Manchester Intermediate School, IN

Clock
Click clock
As the minutes tick tock
And the hours go by
And the minutes go by
All you hear is
Click
Clock
All day long
While people go by
Looking at the clock
While they walk by.
Dawson Arndt, Grade 4
Van Rensselaer Elementary School, IN

Silence
Silence is when
the whole world stops,
The wind sleeps,
The clock doesn't go tick-tock,
When the birds don't sing,
When the plants don't grow,
Even the rooster does not crow,
When the leaves don't dance on the trees,
When nothing moves,
People breathe softly,
That is silence.
Lilja Carden, Grade 6
Clarendon Hills Middle School, IL

Colors
Colors, colors, all around,
Colors, colors, up and down.
Colors, colors, up the wall,
Colors, colors, down they fall.
Colors, colors, near and far,
Colors, colors, have some fun,
Colors, colors, the day is done.
Colors, colors, now go away
Colors, colors, come again another day.
Megan Kaefring, Grade 4
St Matthew School, IL

Colors
Orange is the color of my basketball
White is not in the rainbow at all!

Yellow is the color of the sun
Gold is the color of my gun!

Brown is the color of the leaves in fall
Tan is the color of my friend, Paul.

Blue is the color of the sky
Red is the color that says want to buy?

Pink is the color of love
Purple is the color of my winter glove!

What are colors to you?
Katrina Stevens, Grade 5
Forreston Grade School, IL

Winter
With fields of white
Animals hide with fright
For snow is coming down hard.

No more birds chirping
No more frogs croaking
The bears build up their lard.

When darkness appears
Nothing is near
Except for the cold white snow.

When the birds give the sign
Everything is fine
Now it is time to go.
Daniel Siemer, Grade 6
St Michael School, IN

Dogs
I don't want a frog
I really want a dog
They say they're man's best friend
And not as boring as a log.

They are really nice
They are really loyal
Some are big, maybe small
I think they should be royal

Sure, there are some downsides
They don't catch mice
Hey, what's that on the floor?
I don't think that is spice
I think I'll get a cat instead.
Daniel Castellanos, Grade 4
St Matthias/Transfiguration School, IL

Winter

Winter is wonderful, don't you think so
My favorite part, is about all the snow

Christmas is neat
With all its sweet treats
And presents so sleek
I just want a peek

It's getting late
And I can't wait
To just play and play
Snowball fights all day

Winter is falling
And spring is rising
The snow is melting
And the trees are drying

I am sad because winter is leaving
But it isn't bad because we're still gleaming
About all those good times
And those nice rhymes
When winter was still here
And I was still there
Riley Mooneyham, Grade 5
Dee Mack Intermediate School, IL

School

School is fun
school is neat,
if you do something good,
you will get a treat.

In gym you run,
so so much fun.
Your heart will be pounding,
if you are astounding.

Next is music,
you get to sing and dance.
If your class is good,
you'll get to do the prance.

And then there is art,
where you will get to color.
If you get into trouble,
your day will get duller.

Math is so much fun,
that is, unless you are a bum.
And that's all I have to say,
I hope you have a very nice day.
Emily Spreitzer, Grade 4
Coal City Intermediate School, IL

White on Black

All the colors dance in a rainbow,
laughing, singing, full of color.
Two stand out.
One stands to the side,
one stands in the middle.

White remains silent and serene
amidst the blanket of wholesome joy.
Her innocence and purity
seem not to belong.

Black is forever restless,
looking for attention.
His naughtiness and humor
are accepted by all.

Outcast on accepted,
accepted on Outcast.
White on Black,
Black on White.

'Tis the way of our world.
Maya Bhagat, Grade 6
Bednarcik Jr High School, IL

Between the Spaces

In the remote places
between the spaces
time stops.
But we don't live in those
in between spaces,
our world is not remote,
and time does not stop
therefore we shall
go on with our lives.
Austin Welch, Grade 5
Stanley Clark School, IN

All About Me

C is for caring
H is for hyper
E is for excitable
Y is for young
E is for entertaining
N is for nosy
N is for nice
E is for enthusiastic

S is for sweet
E is for eager
A is for awesome
T is for talented
O is for outgoing
N is for neat
Cheyenne Seaton, Grade 6
Herrick Grade School, IL

My Heart Aches for Snow

My heart aches for snow
Not chilling winds
Not harsh rains
Snow, just snow

I want snow and only snow
To prance in and play in.
To have snowball fights
Build snowmen
Snow, just snow
Genna Long, Grade 6
Stanley Clark School, IN

Diversity

Diversity means…
We are not the same
Everyone is different
They think we are lame

We can be different
Everyone can get along
If we just try to help
We can be strong
Alec Reed, Grade 5
Dee Mack Intermediate School, IL

Fall

Fall is coming,
The wind will be ear-numbing.
Fall is very near,
School is out, we have fun, and we cheer!

Leaves fall everywhere,
Even in my hair.
In fall I can run,
Fall is fun fun fun!
Trevor Scott Osborne, Grade 4
Chrisney Elementary School, IN

Sharks

Sharks
Blue, orange
Sneaking, killing, fighting
Always ready for blood
Predators
Jordan Adams, Grade 5
Van Rensselaer Elementary School, IN

Home Sweet Home

Home
Fun place
Quiet, peaceful, happy
Wakes me up smiling
Residence
Corina Bailey, Grade 6
Our Shepherd Lutheran School, IN

Tallon Orion Bolander

T rue and responsible
A lways on the go
L ikes ice cream
L ikes candy
O nly Tallon there is
N o one can beat me at games

O rion is my name
R ain I like to be in
I sometimes make a lie
O n time sometimes
N o one hates me

B ones I like to search for
O n my mind is video games
L ittle guy I am
A s I'm at school
N o like money
D resses properly on Sunday
E very time I climb, I get better
R unner I am

Tallon Orion Bolander, Grade 5
North Knox West Intermediate/Elementary School, IN

Christmas

On Christmas day, I'll get a lot of toys
Some kids don't 'cause they make a lot of noise.
Most toys people get are really, really small.
But the toys I get are bigger, like a ball.
I hope I'll get a big board game.
The games my friends get me are very, very lame.
Maybe I'll get a better present.
I could get a ringed-neck pheasant.
I am not allowed to get a trampoline,
At least until I'm finally thirteen.
I can't wait to see the decorations and lights,
And see all the colorful sights.
I can't wait to sit by the fire,
And listen to my dad play his lyre.
I'll get my dad a really good gift.
I'll get him a big barbell to weight lift.
I'll get my mom a lot of treats.
You won't believe how much she eats.
I bet you're wondering what I got my brother.
Nothing, he can share with my mother.
I can't wait for Christmas day, even though it's only May.

Luke Bunting, Grade 5
North Intermediate Center of Education, IL

Playing Outside in Winter Snow

I love to play,
Outside all day,
In the snow,
Where the wind will blow.

Alisha Lemmon, Grade 5
Washington Township Elementary School, IN

My Little Seed

I had a little seed
The kind of little seed
Is a flower that I know,
But all I could think of is how much it would grow
It would sprout out of my little pot
And into the air
Little would it be,
Green here and there.

Water I would feed it,
And maybe a worm
And sunlight would it need,
And inside something will churn.

A day or so later,
A bud will pop,
More water and sunlight,
And some more roots will drop.

After a couple days more,
The bud will fly open,
It will release colors,
Like magic unspoken.

Sarah Chung, Grade 6
Judah Christian School, IL

Miracle

Nature is truly a miracle.
I wonder about how nature helps us,
how it helps the world,
how it works.
How tiny seeds grow to be lovely trees.
How trees help us breathe.
How flowers get their beautiful colors.
How nature gives living creatures a place to live.
I don't know the answers,
But, I know
nature is
a miracle.

Miriam Haque, Grade 6
Stanley Clark School, IN

A Can of Coke

My family is like a can of coke.
My mother is like the sweet taste of the coke
because she is sweet.
My dad is like the hard metal container
because sometimes I fight with him and he is like the metal.
My sister is the red letters on the can
because sometimes she helps me read.
My brother is like the gas that makes it fizzy
because he sometimes gives me trouble.
I am like the fizz and bubbles
because I like to laugh.

Miguel Serrano, Grade 6
Florence Nightingale Elementary School, IL

Cupcakes

Soft, delicious, fluffy, and fun
A different flavor for everyone

A delightful treat
with frosting so sweet

Please take a seat
It's time to eat!
Lexi Bucciarelli, Grade 6
Three Rivers School, IL

No Drugs

N icotine
O dor smell

D angerous
R isking lives
U gly
G ross
S ick
Morgan Burr, Grade 5
Dee Mack Intermediate School, IL

Air!

Air is everywhere.
Nothing can compare.
The world should take care.
Preserve our precious air. Beware!
Cars pollute the air.
So spare some air,
And walk everywhere.
Now that's being fair.
Jon Peterson, Grade 5
Dee Mack Intermediate School, IL

Fall

Fall is coming,
People are humming,
Malls are closing,
Dudes are dozing,
Birds are calling,
Leaves are falling,
Doors are closing,
Fall is coming.
Jayden Harris, Grade 4
Chrisney Elementary School, IN

Peace

When you
Meditate, you
Calm yourself through
thought, making you less stressed, it's
hard,
Not easy.
Scott Milenkovic, Grade 5
Edison Elementary School, IL

I Saw a Witch!

I saw a witch!
I saw a witch!

Making children stew,
I hope she doesn't take me too!

I saw a witch!
I saw a witch!
Hannah Burgett, Grade 5
Forreston Grade School, IL

Best Friend

What is a best friend?
A person who cares
Someone to talk to
A trustworthy person
A good playmate
Someone to back you up
A good influence
That's a best friend!
Tia Howell, Grade 6
Herrick Grade School, IL

The Sky Is Blue

The grass is green
Just like the outdoors,
when you go out
You see everything that one
And only one person
Can make in seven days.
And that name is
Jesus.
Mason Moore, Grade 5
Van Rensselaer Elementary School, IN

Love

What's love?
Passion
Stick with it to the end
Devotion
Caring strongly
Believing
Admiring
That's love!
Katie Smith, Grade 6
Herrick Grade School, IL

The Midnight Flower

The flower as black as night
Gives an eerie glow
Whilst the moon shines bright
At midnight the flower blooms
Then the petals one by one whither away
Into the abyss that is the night
Will Sorek, Grade 6
Bednarcik Jr High School, IL

Doctor Fudge

Don't have a grudge
Against Doctor Fudge.
He'll make you better
Instantly.

Take a bite
And it might
Be the perfect remedy…
CHOCOLATE!!!

Cures a headache,
Cures a cough.
Just take a nibble to feel better
And if it works write him a letter.

Thank you
Doctor Fudge!!!
Katherine Krupicka, Grade 5
Meadow Glens Elementary School, IL

Kittens

Every night before I go to bed
I like to check on my kittens
So when I lay down my head
I know they are as snug as mittens

When I get up in the morning
I go downstairs I look out the door
I see the kittens snoring
I want to lay some more

Kittens are playful and fun
They need love and care
Kittens play in the sun
You need to brush their hair

Training and discipline they will need
So that their owners they will heed
Korynne Elliott, Grade 4
Coal City Intermediate School, IL

Water

It runs through streams
It lies in salt water oceans
It keeps us clean
It can be used in lotions
It quenches our thirst
It can fit in a purse
It is always on the run
It can weigh all kinds of tons
It keeps us very healthy
It is good use for the wealthy
It helps the poor
It helps me and many more
Chelsea Hawthorne, Grade 6
U S Grant Middle School, IL

Clouds
Clouds cover the sun
Look like fuzzy cottonballs
Fluffy, white, pretty
Caleb McKeever, Grade 4
Frank H Hammond Elementary School, IN

Snow
Snowflakes falling down
Slowly from the azure sky
Winter is coming
Stephanie Niemiec, Grade 4
Frank H Hammond Elementary School, IN

Animal
It is black and white
They can be found at the zoo
Now guess what it is
Jalyn Roach, Grade 5
North Knox West Intermediate/Elementary School, IN

Pond
Life is like a pond.
You jump to one lily pad,
And you never know.
Savannah Owens, Grade 6
Alexandria Monroe Intermediate School, IN

Tom Hanks
Has accounts in 50 banks,
His earnings took a jump,
When he said "Call me Forrest Gump."
Stephanie Hartman, Grade 5
Washington Township Elementary School, IN

Colors
Silver are the stars shining in the sky
Gold is the medal soldiers get when they die

Black is the color of eyelashes
White is the bone you see in my gashes

Gray is the rainy clouds up above
Orange is the fruit of which I love

Red was my hair when I was born
Yellow is the tip of candy corn

Green is the ground where I play
Blue is the sky on a sunny day

Purple are grapes hanging on trees
Pink is the color of my knees

What are colors to you?
Katie Erdmann, Grade 5
Forreston Grade School, IL

Ten Little Worms
Ten little worms sitting on a branch
One got stuck in a vine, now there are nine

Nine little worms sitting on a branch
One got a date, now there are eight

Eight little worms sitting on a branch
One went to heaven, now there are seven

Seven little worms sitting on a branch
One fell on sticks, now there are six

Six little worms sitting on a branch
One took a dive, now there are five

Five little worms sitting on a branch
One hit the floor, now there are four

Four little worms sitting on a branch
One climbed a tree, now there are three

Three little worms sitting on a branch
One got stuck in a shoe, now there are two

Two little worms sitting on a branch
One got stung, now there is one

One little worm sitting on a branch
He baked in the sun, now there are none
Austyn Krawiecki, Grade 6
Holy Family Catholic School, IL

Where I'm From
I'm from camping,
from steaming Alfredo and soccer,
I'm from the four-wheeling, and
from the mud pits,

I'm from the old teddy bears,
from the constant nagging,
I'm from "Go clean your room,"
to "Try your best."
I am from learning twenty verses,
and from living an eternal life,

I'm from trophies,
from long, cheesy potato soup,
I'm from hating my dog's bites,
to loving shopping,

I am from looking in the closet,
to see all the memories flow back,
I'm from not remembering everything,
from the tree's leaves that fall.
Haley Bailey, Grade 6
Knox Community Middle School, IN

Prejudice Is Injustice

Prejudice is unfair as it makes judgments known,
Those with conscience will never condone.
Prejudice is an opinion that is not fair,
Those that support it must beware.

Prejudice is all around us and not hard to find,
Anyone can find it even the common mind.
I look at all the people and what do I see,
All the different colors, this effects even me.

Acknowledging our faults is the first step, we know,
Knowing this fault will help us grow.
As I go through life day to day,
"I will avoid prejudice," is what I say.
Dawson Ash and Eli Brown, Grade 6
Tri-West Middle School, IN

Snowy

Snowy
So soft with her lush hair.
A high energetic miniature schnauzer.
Always ready to play with anyone.
Sniffing around, trying to find treasure.
Will take any chance to lick you to death.
She is a very bad pet peeve.
Only a year old, but so small.
Got a collar with a rabies shot tag.
Can eat all of her food in a minute.
Pretty brown eyes and a short tail.
Loves to run around and jump everywhere.
Always falls for the funniest pranks.
Glad she is a man's best friend.
Zach Beltz, Grade 6
Alexandria Monroe Intermediate School, IN

Prejudice Is Inequality

There are blacks and there are whites,
Prejudice is when we take their rights.
Just because they're a different race,
Doesn't mean that they are a disgrace.

In the year 2008, ABC news,
Revealed some of their researched clues,
That Barack Obama's past church priest,
Said all blacks should be treated the least.

The job of the American-Arab Anti-Discrimination Committee,
Is to see that all people, black or white, are treated with equality.
When it comes to discrimination,
It takes everyone's participation.
Alex King and Derek Wagner, Grade 6
Tri-West Middle School, IN

Prejudice Is a Scar

Prejudice is a scar across your face,
You feel like you are a mere disgrace.
This technique is spreading across the nation,
In many forms of discrimination.

In 2010, at the McDonald's restaurant,
Timothy was hurt from getting a taunt.
He had an intellectual disability.
A 90,000 dollar fine was paid; should have been a felony.

Timothy thought he lost his rights, but he got them back,
Thanks to the Americans With Disabilities Act.
Now that McDonald's has paid their fee,
We give thanks to this kind of help from sea to shining sea!
Lexi Bell, Grade 6
Tri-West Middle School, IN

Prejudice Is a Preconceived Opinion

Why do we have to mess with rights?
Not everything is black and white.
There are going to be times we don't agree,
I don't understand why we all just can't be.

Osama bin Laden, the cause of 9/11,
Killing innocent Americans, such a rebellion.
The Twin Towers once stood proud and high,
But Osama caused them to fall from the sky.

Don't judge someone because of their grade,
Their looks, their disability, or their shade.
That is what the Kids Club promotes,
"World Peace, World Love" is its quote.
Maya Sears, Grade 6
Tri-West Middle School, IN

Prejudice Is an Opinion

Prejudice is a state of mind,
It can be against your kind.
These are people with strong opinions,
About living in divided dominions.

A few years ago in the Boston division,
An obese girl named Heather applied for a position.
There was a mean comment, a bad look, a stare,
She never got the job due to the affair.

The National Association to Advance Fat Acceptance takes a stand,
Since 1969 has met much demand.
A civil rights program for the nation,
Helping overweight people fight discrimination.
Bri Butler, Grade 6
Tri-West Middle School, IN

The Moon

Darkness falls, day turns to night.
The moon turns on its bright night-light.

The light shines down for all to see,
Not just for you and me.

It casts a shadow, more beautiful than the sun,
For everyone to see when day is done.

When I first saw the moon with my very own eyes,
I was amazed by its great size.

The moon is so big and round,
Yet it can change its shape without a sound.

The moon can take a different shape.
Now, it looks like a round, white grape.

The moon is a clock, working the night away.
It keeps the time until the break of day.

Sunlight comes, way too soon.
And I have to say, "Good day moon."

Jaclyn Heigert, Grade 5
Dee Mack Intermediate School, IL

Where My Memories Are

I am from playing sports,
and from shopping on the weekends,
to trying on new clothes.
I am from going to Alabama,
to regretting coming home.
I am from reading my books,
to passing the test.

I am from doing projects, and to getting an A.
I am from making crafts,
to giving them to my friends.
I am from loving Fettuccini Alfredo, to hating fish.
I am from watching movies at home,
to going to the movie theaters.

I am from working hard,
to earning rewards.
I am from playing Just Dance,
to dancing on my own.
I am from slurping Dr. Pepper,
to gobbling up cheesy pizza.
I am from helping in the kitchen,
to making daily memories.

Natalie Banks, Grade 6
Knox Community Middle School, IN

The Little Child

There once was a little child
And yes, he was a boy
He cried every day
All because of a toy!

His parents said "NO!"
And all he did was whine
They couldn't take it
And he said "THAT TOY IS MINE!"

They told him no all the time
But he never really cared
He yelled and screamed
So then they bought him the bear!

Destany York, Grade 5
North Knox West Intermediate/Elementary School, IN

Christmas Tree

My family is a Christmas tree.
My mom is the star because,
she is the one, who watches,
over us and takes care of us,
My sister is the snowflake.
because she loves to be,
in the snow and covered in it.
My brother is Santa Claus
because when he goes outside
he has a lot of sweaters and a red coat.
My big brother is the reindeer,
because he walks,
almost a mile to his high school and he loves,
to discover new thing.

Christian Morales, Grade 6
Florence Nightingale Elementary School, IL

Lauren

Lauren is short, but has the biggest heart.
She's funny, smart, and my very best friend.
She's great at music, and she loves art.
She'll be there to the very, very end.
Her hair is short, and her eyes are bright blue.
She has a cute cat, that hisses and purrs.
When we met, I gave her really good clues,
That I wanted to be best friends with her.
She has four bunnies, Blitz is my favorite.
I like to spend the night at her cool house.
She wants the American Girl Doll Kit.
At night, we creep through the house like a mouse.
Even if my tears are just a'pourin',
She'll be there for me, I love you Lauren.

Kati Jones, Grade 5
Northern Heights Elementary School, IN

Grass

The soft grass is like
A brush with millions of
Bristles that is all green.
Daniel Pollock, Grade 5
Central Elementary School, IL

Winter Fun

Big, white sheets of snow
Makes you want to go and jump
So much fun — yee haw!
Xavier Amsler, Grade 4
Van Rensselaer Elementary School, IN

Ice Cream

Tasty, delicious,
So sweet, different flavors,
Scoop, lick, bite…Yummy!
Ariana Sol Gonzalez, Grade 5
Edison Elementary School, IL

Birds

Birds fly around trees
They play in nests happily
Hanging on a branch.
Samuel Blankenship, Grade 4
Van Rensselaer Elementary School, IN

The Rain

The rain goes drip, drip
Then a rainbow comes to shine
Oh, what a beautiful day.
Camden Chapman, Grade 4
Van Rensselaer Elementary School, IN

My Friend

She enjoys ice cream
She is good at dribbling
She is my best friend
Lesly Sanchez, Grade 5
Edison Elementary School, IL

Ice Cream

Ice cream is melting
Ice cream is cold and yummy
Do you love ice cream?
Imani Monique Gennell, Grade 5
Edison Elementary School, IL

Summer

Summer is so hot.
Summer is the time for pools.
Summer means no school.
Abby May, Grade 5
Henryville Elementary School, IN

I Know…

I know a soft azure blue riverbank
Where lilacs bathe and bubbles burst.
I know a chipped wooden canopy
Whose voice resonates from a far-off cluster of stars.
I know the lushest blossoming flower garden
Sprinkled with starry delphinium and rosy orchids.
I know a hectic math room on test day
Where every student tries to conquer with grades.
I know a bright, firework-blasted holiday
When Americans sit, and stare at temporary indigo stars.
I know the loudest heavy metal concert
That rattles every time the strings unfittingly clash.
I know a silent religious shrine
Where the presences of gods and offerings stay at rest.
I know a cave with turquoise pools
Light, echoing drips of water, the world still and seemingly frozen
I know a nation where there is no war;
A safe place to hide while the world falls to flames.
I know a house where no one lives
Water trickling and wind crawling in through narrow cracks of brick
I know a world where time never stops, beyond every human's grasp.
Sarah Kim, Grade 5
Avery Coonley School, IL

Reaching Heaven

We knew you had been climbing the stairs of heaven for a while,
Then came the day when we heard the news that you had finally reached heaven.
Though I hoped that you would get better,
And come downstairs.
But as long as you are happy,
I will be strong, and be happy for you.
Know that I miss you
And that I write this for you,
As a reminder that I love you, and always will.
Though I dearly miss your presence on earth,
I am so glad you are comfortable.
Your last words were "I love you"
I love you too.
Avalon Husain, Grade 5
The Orchard School, IN

The World

Wind blows like a fan.
Plants grow like a little girl on her first day of school.
The water whispers to the creek as it rolls on like a soccer ball.
A bee buzzes on a daffodil as lazy as a lion basking in the sun.
The zebra grass flows as graceful as a ballerina lost in her music.
The Penn Oaks and Tulip Poplars sway in the sky like a plane sailing smoothly.
Ivy wraps around the rails of a bridge like a boa constricting its prey.
The tulips are as smooth as buttermilk.
The dandelions are growing rapidly and are as pesky as flies on a hot summer day.
Wild berries grow as wild as a panther in the woods.
Clovers are as green as a hosta leaf.
This is the way the world is in my vision.
Hannah Long, Grade 6
Cloverdale Middle School, IN

The Biggest Snow Fall Ever

It's the biggest snow fall ever.
It's Christmas, it's snowing everywhere,
the shovels are out, the plows are out.
The news reporter is saying
a foot of snow this week!
School's out, school's out. Hipporhay!
Everyone is happy.
I went outside.
It smelled really snowy.
I walked, I saw a big plow getting all the snow.
I felt the snow – it was so cold I fell over.
I heard the snow plowing everywhere.
I did not taste the snow.
That was the best week.

Joey Bissing, Grade 4
Copeland Manor Elementary School, IL

Fall

The sound of sneezing fills the air
as germs battle their way through the body
the nut-thieves stocking up
preparing for the worst
the monster of darkness overpowering the ball of light
just as it seems it will be dark for eternity
the ball of light subdued the horrible creature
airplanes plummeting down
all the color of the Grand Canyon
screams of protests ring in the air
as the master decides their fate
everything looking dull
as the season of despair strikes its final blow,
putting all life into hibernation.

Allen Gu, Grade 4
Highlands Elementary School, IL

Grandma's House

The smell of cookies baking, the old creaky floor,
the sweet caring lady that answers the door,
she's the one that you love,
you're the one she's proud of
and you walk into your Grandma's house,
she gives you some cookies and turns on the TV,
you say, "Grandma, why do your eyes roll back
when you're laughing at me?"
She says because you're so funny
and because you're so cute
now it's time for a nap and puts the TV on mute,
you lay down in bed
and think in your head,
"I love Grandma's house!"

Alexis Quemeneur, Grade 5
Hadley Middle School, IL

A Tiger Doing Zumba

Have you seen a tiger do Zumba?
The tiger gained a lot of weight.
That is why the tiger joined the class.
The teacher thought that he was great.

The tiger's name was Wyatt
He had to run to the gym
because he didn't have a car.
So now he wears a 24 slim.

Now there is not a Zumba teacher
because Mrs. Zipper Wyatt ate.
So then the YMCA had to find a new one.
They hired Wyatt because they thought he was great.

Katie Jo Kixmiller, Grade 5
North Knox West Intermediate/Elementary School, IN

Bad Habits

Bad habits are hard to stop
Without them it would be easy to be at the top
If I put my mind to it
I know that I can do it
Be strong
And to stop it won't take long
If I put my mind to it
I know that I can do it
Bad habits seem like devils coming from below
But God has a plan for us that we really don't know
If I put my mind to it
I know that I can do it
When a habit is stopped it feels like 100 pounds being lifted away
I hope we can all stop our bad habits one day

Maggie Mathews, Grade 5
Hawthorne Elementary School, IL

Dreams

Everybody has at least one,
Some people have a ton.
You'll think mine is funny,
I want to earn tons of money.
Maybe Bob wants to be a ping pong pro,
No one will ever know.
Some people's dreams are about soccer,
Or maybe to have an awesome locker.
My dog's is to have a giant bone,
My friend's is to have a cell phone.
Maybe you want to learn how to sew,
Or maybe you want to meet an Eskimo.
Maybe there's a hand you want to lend,
Well I guess this is the end!

Ali Ross, Grade 5
North Intermediate Center of Education, IL

The Outstanding Five

My teachers are a team of five.
They really make learning come alive.

I go to room 21 for math.
Where Mrs. Kanipe sends you down the right path.

Mrs. Fleetwood is my homeroom teacher.
She is so nice I think I'll keep her.

Mr. Jansen is the only guy.
He can tell you the square root of pi.

I have Mrs. Merritt for reading.
She is very good at leading.

Mrs. Richison teaches us about the past.
I know this knowledge will always last.

Now you know the outstanding five.
Maybe one of them could teach me to drive.
Andrew Webb, Grade 5
North Intermediate Center of Education, IL

The Perfect Person

She hops on the bus, with a twinkle in her eye;
Everyone smiles, and wants her by their side.
She walks into school, a flower in her hair;
Beautiful face, it's hard not to stare.
She walks the hallways, with perfect balance;
Everyone thinks she lives in a palace.
Outfits are to die for, especially the shoes;
In any game, she will never lose.
Her nails are a perfect shade of pink with flowers;
Trust me, she's got magical powers.
Makeup is brilliant, not too much, just right;
If you mess with her friends, she'll put up a good fight.
The smartest one in the class, might I say;
Helps tutor kids throughout the day.
Beautiful, funny, and very bright;
If there's a spider, she's out of sight.
She's also helpful, if I might add too;
And who would have guessed, her favorite color's blue.
Who is this perfect person, filled with glee?
Don't be silly! It's none other than me!
Haley Flamion, Grade 6
Nancy Hanks Elementary School, IN

Summer

Summer, summer, here it comes.
I'm so glad let's have some fun.
We play and play at the park.
We play and play until it gets dark.
It is time to go home, say goodnight.
I'll see you tomorrow — don't let the bugs bite.
Kelsie Floyd, Grade 5
Van Rensselaer Elementary School, IN

Boating

When going boating it takes forever
Getting dressed and putting things together

After you reach the lake, you have to sit and wait
Until the driver comes to speed up the rate

Faster we go, the cooler the breeze, I freeze
"Can we tube now," I ask my mom, "Please?"

She says "Fine, just for a little while."
We tube and scream for what seems like a mile

Not getting one drop of the water on me
Suddenly we hit a huge wave and my knee

We fall off the tube and make a big splash
Underwater the splash sounded like a crash

I came back up and gasped for fresh air
Suddenly I realized my bottom was bare

I looked behind us and they were a blur
I swam to get them and there they were

I put them on immediately
My parents say it happens commonly

I got back on the boat and we rode back
We rode home listening to the soundtrack
Claire Brinkman, Grade 6
Nancy Hanks Elementary School, IN

Rain

Standing on wet mulch
Damp and humid;
Air was musty
Wasn't raining
It was obvious it had lately
Trees were dripping
Leaves sagging, Rain on their surface
I entered the woods
Thick fog covering the ground
Very peaceful
Tree bark was sodden
Quiet. I wondered,
"Can it get more quiet than this?"
Then CRACK, thunder was set free.
One raindrop, then two
Kids were screaming and shouting
They ran to enter building.
I was quiet, Observing rain.
I found it interesting we left
It stared to pour
It was miraculous how fast it started to pour
Bonnie Bostic, Grade 5
The Orchard School, IN

Monsters

S omething's rattling in the closet!
T oo scared to see!
U nder the bed I hear thumps!
V icious little creatures, I think in my head!
And wait…Ahhhh! A monster!
Cameron Hall, Grade 5
Northern Heights Elementary School, IN

Phil

There once was a fellow named Phil
Who found a one hundred dollar bill
He then began to gloat
As the bill started to float
Away from the fellow named Phil
Terri Legg, Grade 6
West Salem Grade School, IL

Dragon

Dragon
Different, mysterious
Flies at night
So very very mysterious
Mystery
Stephanie Fluty, Grade 6
West Salem Grade School, IL

Parrots

Parrots.
Noisy birdies.
Always squawking around.
Smart, noisy, always mimicking.
So loud.
Maggie Balding, Grade 6
West Salem Grade School, IL

Soul

Soul
Clear, harmless
Controlling, moving, roaming
Always in the body.
Pneuma
Kellie Mullikin, Grade 4
Van Rensselaer Elementary School, IN

Milo

Orange tabby
Small, fuzzy
Loving, playing, sleeping
Chubby and very cute
Milo
Lanie Elder, Grade 6
Herrick Grade School, IL

A Beloved Community

As a community we have to go by Dr. King's dream,
We love, care, and protect one another.
As a collective community we work together as a team,
Children are able to play with one another, no matter the skin color!

In a community there are no challenges we face,
Thanks for Dr. King the black community has changed.
We are peaceful and loving and getting all along as a race,
As a community we have changed and rearranged!

A community means to me a special bond,
We all come together as one to help someone in need.
If there is trouble, someone in the community will respond,
As a community, by reliving Dr. King's dream, we will succeed!

A community means to me one big family,
We care for each other in need, help, and concern.
If it weren't for Dr. King, we wouldn't be together, he gave us the capability,
From his dream, we have gotten along and learned.

Martin Luther King's vision for a beloved community means no discrimination,
People of all races will live up to his dream and keep it alive.
In the past, the blacks and whites didn't get along as one nation,
Thanks to Dr. King all the races came together as one and we will strive!
Alanta' Story, Grade 6
Whistler Elementary School, IL

I Am From

I am from spicy hot wings
and creepy Ghost Adventures, and
from "Get up!" and "Clean your room!"
I am from steaming beef and noodles
to watching TV with my father,
or waking up early on Christmas day and opening presents.

I am from a zebra print bedspread and pink walls,
from going ice fishing as soon as we see ice.
from tubing in the hot summer,
and Christmas lights in the freezing winter.
I'm from juicy steak right off the grill
then jumping in my pool.
From summers spent at my great grandmother's lake
from making people laugh and brightening their day.

I'm from jumping on my trampoline or playing soccer with my sister.
I am from playing the French horn,
or having fun in band.
I am from big family parties, talking and playing games, and
From the fireplace downstairs.
I am from laying in bed staring into space
and falling asleep, dreaming about the good times that I have.
Rylee Hart, Grade 6
Knox Community Middle School, IN

Winter

Winter is my favorite season of all
Opening presents both big and small

Getting a break from school
Helps our minds to cool

Christmas reminds us of Jesus' birth
He came that night to save the Earth

Staying up late and waiting for a New Year
So much celebration you can barely hear

Sledding down a tall hill
Makes us scream from the thrill

Decorating a Christmas tree
Will make you scream with glee

After winter comes spring, summer, then fall
What is your favorite season of all?

Jackson Wright, Grade 6
Emmanuel-St Michael Lutheran School, IN

My Phenomenal Future

I am an athlete and I am smart
I wonder if I can be a star someday
I hear rain falling from the sky and down into a puddle, drip, drip
I see a future for my brother and myself
I want to be better at caring and helping people
I am Devyn McSheridan

I pretend the world is perfect
I feel refreshed and happiness all around me
I touch the animals all around the world
I worry about my family
I cry when I think of my cousin that died
I am Devyn McSheridan

I understand that I can't always have my way
I say that there should be peace on Earth
I dream that everyone makes great choices in life
I try to stick with what I do
I hope the people I care about are safe today and every day
I am Devyn McSheridan

Devyn McSheridan, Grade 6
St Matthias/Transfiguration School, IL

Wonderful Christmas Time

I absolutely adore Christmas.
The glossy white snow covers up the mucky brown mud;
the aroma of chocolate chip cookies floating in the air.
They are absolutely divine at Christmas time.
It's the time you spend with wonderful, loving family.
Christmas is phenomenal!

Jacklyn Lukes, Grade 5
Washington Township Elementary School, IN

The Cay

The wind is silent. The
water is still. It's peaceful
the sand makes not even the
slightest sound as I walk across
the beach. Then the wind starts
to pick up and the sea makes a
sound like a child throwing a
tantrum. A wave pulls me
into the water while another
pushes me under. As I fight
my way back to shore I think
about how something that was
so serene can turn into
the Devil's mouth so quickly
I will never understand
As I trudge out of the
water the wind dies down
and the sea becomes again
like smooth blue glass.

Tabitha Allen, Grade 6
Todd Academy Inc., IN

The Boy and the Giant

A boy in a field stands calling his sheep,
Always and ever watching, their safety to keep.
The lions and wolves come to take one as prey,
But he fights them off, by his sheep he will stay.

In another place, a giant warrior stands tall,
A fighter from birth, and stranger than all.
His voice rings out loudly, "Now send me your best,"
I'll finish them off, like I have done to the rest.

Finding himself on that same battlefield,
Five stones and a sling the boy has to wield.
As the giant mocks his God, waving a sword,
The boy declares the battle belongs to the LORD!

The stone that he chooses to twirl around,
Brings the warrior crashing down.
The battles is won, the Lord triumphs again,
The shepherd boy will soon, be leading God's men.

Daniel Hein, Grade 6
Emmanuel-St Michael Lutheran School, IN

Christmas

On Christmas morning presents fill the tree.
We all run to the tree so we can see.
We all get up in the morning here.
So we can shout our Christmas cheers.
Then we all go home to sit by the fire.
Everybody says they are tired.
So we all celebrate Christmas with family and friends.
We go visit family and friends I hope Christmas never ends.

Eric Kindle, Grade 4
Summit Elementary School, IL

My BFF

My BFF is a special friend
She's everywhere
In everything with me
She has everything I have
My BFF is like family
My BFF is always there for me
She is my best friend forever
Abigail Leon, Grade 6
Zapata Academy, IL

Moon Light Sky

Moon is like a sun from the dark side
War is coming at midnight
See the light on the black blanket sky
The sides are getting ready
Practice makes perfect as they say
People are wondering
Who is going to win?
Thea Vogelsburg, Grade 5
Walker Elementary School, IL

What Is Responsibility?

Responsibility is
Keeping track of your stuff
Don't be a messy person
Don't lose anything
Do your homework
Do chores
That is responsibility
Nathan Konger, Grade 5
Churubusco Elementary School, IN

My Dog Bella

Black and white,
Furry and bright,
She wags her tail with all her might.

Small and fluffy,
Soft and puffy,
She is sure a lovely delight.
Kayla Bridick, Grade 6
Holy Family Catholic School, IL

Brandie

B ig, fat, lovable dog
R otten little brat
A wonderful gift
N ever forgotten
D elivered to Heaven's gates on December 8
I will love her always
E very second was precious
RJ Craft, Grade 5
Northern Heights Elementary School, IN

Colors of the Rainbow

White is the color of snow
Yellow is like a bow.

Orange is like the fruit
Red is like my boot.

Pink is like my eraser
Gray is like my chaser.

Green as in grass
Clear is the color of glass.
Paige Chamberlin, Grade 5
Forreston Grade School, IL

Facing the Earth

The rain falls down hard
I run to find shelter, none
I holler and cry
No help anywhere
Why does this have to happen?
Why me, why now?
Why can't I fight my sadness?
Now I feel like a disgrace
Anger management
Yeah right, never heard of it
Why does this happen?
Fiona Gavin, Grade 5
Northern Heights Elementary School, IN

Grass

Does grass get tired of
getting stepped on all the time?

Do they ever want to
get big and tall?

Do they want to go
to school and learn?

Would they want family
and friends?
Natalie Sciutto, Grade 5
Forreston Grade School, IL

Halloween Night

I got some jellybeans for Halloween.
For Halloween I was a queen.
People have some jack-o-lanterns to show.
Some jack-o-lanterns have an eerie glow.

I saw someone that was the same as me.
I also saw an odd queen bee.
Many people say "trick or treat,"
Just like that person wearing a sheet.
Kennedie Brown, Grade 5
Dee Mack Intermediate School, IL

Bobcat

Bobcat
Strong, sneaky
Pouncing, eating, striking
Growling, howling, killing rabbits
Ferocious, teeth, spots
Mean, lean
Bobcat
Chris Flaspohler, Grade 5
St Michael School, IN

Summer

S izzling hot days!
U mbrellas no more!
M ore time to play!
M ore time to explore!
E xcited about cooling!
R ainbows are often!
Snow is melting all around!
Carson Smalley, Grade 5
Dee Mack Intermediate School, IL

Raindrop

Raindrop
Wet, blue
Cooling, shining, sweating
Absorbent, little or big, harsh, colorful
Falling, dropping, amusing
Colors, cold
Raindrops
Grant Halcomb, Grade 5
St Michael School, IN

Dog

Dog
fuzzy, cute
jumping, rolling, licking
food, water, fur, bones
running, wagging, sleeping
sweet, friendly
Dog
Maggie Marshall, Grade 5
St Michael School, IN

Christmas

Join the holiday teams
The jingle bells ring
You would listen to doorbells ring
Look up in the sky to see the stars cling
You could hear the angels sing
Sometimes you could hear ovens bing
On Christmas pictures we say bling
Kartecia White, Grade 4
Summit Elementary School, IL

Racing Water Park

Once at the water park
the water was rather fast.
It was so fast I didn't think
I would last.
I went down that water slide
and I barely cried.
The next slide seemed to just
be completely downhill.
This is making me start to think
about my will.
So the next time you go to the
water park bring a life preserver.
Because once you go down
that slide there won't
be a server.

George Harvey, Grade 4
Copeland Manor Elementary School, IL

Invention Box

It's a box full of mysteries,
From spirals to springs
And feathers to fluff.

It's a box, an unknown world,
From brick to blocks
And plastic to paper.

It's a box filled with colors,
From pink to purple
And green to gray.

It's a box I can make creations out of,
From gadgets to gizmos
And paint to play dough.

Aila Haffner, Grade 6
Our Lady of Peace School, IL

Something

It was my first time,
I strummed it,
I plucked it,
Nothing.
It sounded like a sour chime,
I tried a flick,
Even a stick,
Nothing.
I heard it strumming in my mind,
I grabbed my pick,
I strummed it quick,
Something.
My guitar sang a song,
So no matter what,
Don't ever give up.

Samantha Kao, Grade 5
Hawthorne Elementary School, IL

Fall

Large snowflakes
falling on the floor
to make a pile
of wonder
and beauty
the world will change
the ground is a rainbow
of shape
tiny to huge
it will develop
it will change
and framed
at the finish line
the whiteness will come
to bring away life
until the finale comes again

Max Levitt, Grade 5
Highlands Elementary School, IL

When You Smile

When you smile
I smile, too
When you giggle
I giggle, too
When you say, "I love you"
I do the same
Nobody loves you the way I do

And when you dance
No one else can
And when you cry
The beavers build dams
So never cry
It makes me sad
No one can love you
The way I can

Sydney Andreano, Grade 6
Three Rivers School, IL

My Sweet Love

Violets are blue,
Roses are red,
Without your sweet love,
I am a spout with no hole.
Your love, I know, cannot be leased,
But my love for you will never be ceased.
To you I'll always be true,
So long as the seas are blue,
Forever, is that too long?
My love for you will only grow strong.
Every day with you feels like Valentine's,
Is it too much to ask, will you be mine?
If you shall ever walk away,
My heart will never stray.

Spencer Neal, Grade 6
Holy Family Catholic School, IL

Life

Life is rough and hard
Life is just going up and down
Just like on a roller coaster.

Life, life

You keep me so busy…
Math journal pages,
spelling sorts and
social studies research.
I don't want so much
HOMEWORK!

Life, life

I don't want to be swept
Back and forth —
Back and forth —
Between mom's and grandma's.

I have a hard time with life
On a roller coaster
Day after day, after day…
Life is rough!

Kevaughn Heslop, Grade 5
Walker Elementary School, IL

Family

I love my family so,
We are always on the go.
We always have a fun time,
That's why we know how to rhyme.

We all like arts and crafts,
And we all like ginger snaps.
Carter is my brother,
And Jayme is my mother.

Devyn is my lil' sis,
She always sends me a kiss.
Patrick is my dad,
When he is around I am always glad.

My dog's name is Piper,
She is very hyper.
Gizmo is my other dog.
He doesn't lay around like a log.

Well that is the end,
My family replaces 1 million friends.
We all love one another,
I even love my little brother.

Kierstyn Krouse, Grade 5
Northern Heights Elementary School, IN

Wildlife Abuse

The wildlife is astonishing.
The way ecosystems work and change.
How species' numbers have a range.
The rabbits hop,
The people chop,
And the animals are hurt.

Ryan Deany, Grade 5
Dee Mack Intermediate School, IL

Syerra the Seal

After swimming, she ate a core.
The core had given her a sore.
She went to get something to drink
And slipped on a puddle of ink.
She lost balance and did a flip
Then she decided to take a dip.

Syerra Rios, Grade 4
Meadow Lane School, IL

A Gift

Life is a gift.
Life is an amazing thing,
Life is lovely,
And God is our King,
He gives us hope.

Alexis Galvan, Grade 4
Van Rensselaer Elementary School, IN

With You

The grass is green and the sky is blue
And all I want to do is be with you
With the wind blowing
And the clouds so white
I might want to see you tonight!

Stefanie Delaney, Grade 6
Three Rivers School, IL

Dog

Dog
Midnight black, adorable
Bulldozing, bamboozling, lightning fast
As nice as icing
Swaybee

Samantha Williams, Grade 5
Van Rensselaer Elementary School, IN

Crocodile

Crocodile
Rough, scary
Biting, scratching, chomping
Hunting in the swamp
Alligator

Mark McNeal, Grade 4
Van Rensselaer Elementary School, IN

One of Those Moments

Have you ever had one of those moments
When you think back and say
"I wish I had done that then" or
"I wish I still could"
But those moments are gone and never shall return.
I know how you feel,
I wish those moments would come back,
But I don't think they would.
So here's my lesson for everyone that reads this:
Always DO what you love before you can't.
Don't just put it off till tomorrow.
If a day doesn't go by without thinking about something then…DO IT!

Kanna Smiley, Grade 5
The Orchard School, IN

A Rainy Day

Yesterday I went outside and found out it was raining.
I stood outside in amazement for how hard it was pouring.
So I ran farther out and I looked at the weather vane.

The rain was pouring down so hard right here in Maine.
The rain fell so hard I couldn't hear my own self talking.
The rain hitting my head so hard was giving me a migraine.

The rain was now slowing down and flowing down the drain.
I stayed outside to jump in the puddles when I took a fall.
My mom called me in and saw the stain I didn't know how I'd explain.
HELP!

Jessica Carithers, Grade 5
Dee Mack Intermediate School, IL

Autumn

Autumn is like a vacation from the other main seasons of the year
Where leaves fall down like snowflakes in the sky
Apple orchards are in the distance
The smell of caramel apples and cinnamon candles in the air like a holiday shop
Hear the sound of a soccer ball hitting the net
Like a breeze from the wind
Haystacks and scarecrows as décor
Rows of pumpkins like an audience at a fashion show
And pumpkin spice coffee
Inside every store window

Ally Bentel, Grade 6
Bednarcik Jr High School, IL

Blue Jay Brighten My Day

When the wind blows I hear something in the air.
But then it stops.
When it starts again I feel kind of scared.
Then I look out the window and feel my spirits brighten when I see a beautiful Blue Jay.
I am so happy.
I run outside to feel the breeze.
After a while I get sad when the Blue Jay leaves me.
I will always remember you Blue Jay.

Jack Peterson, Grade 5
St Rita Catholic School, IL

I Am a Tree

I am a tree, my bark is as smooth as glass.
I sit under the sky as the sun, hotter than fire, bakes me like a cake.
I watch as a spider scurries by the ivy as fast as a bullet.
I look beside me where my friend was, but all I saw was a tree stump as round as a circle, laying there quietly.
There in front of me, was a creek that trickled like the sound of a running sink.
Above me my leaves are rustling like sandpaper rubbing together.
All around me birds are chirping like whistles on a morning day.
The owls hoot like a ghost saying boo.
The crickets chirp like the morning sound of a mockingbird.
All of these sounds make up the forest song. It is the only thing that keeps me company in this forest,
as lonely as a boy without a Gameboy.

Jason Miller, Grade 6
Cloverdale Middle School, IN

Ode to Recess

Children run around like maniacs,
we play, we yell, we have fun
the ball goes through the net with a swish after a shot as we run around blocking each other's
the football is passed around with tackling and jumping
and cheering after a touchdown
the girls and boys play tag, chasing each other and running away, laughing
the equipment, monkey bars and the slide tunnel as we climb up and slide down
children playing soccer, kicking around on the wet slipper, and muddy, hot field as the sun shines bright after a spring rain.
RRRRRIIIIINNNNNGGGGG!!!…Ooops it's time to go in!
Recess over!!!

Cameron Hagaman, Grade 5
Walker Elementary School, IL

Winter Is Everywhere!

The white snow glistens everywhere, shining like small diamonds on the ground.
I take a look at the winter wonderland in front of me, and watch as tiny speckles fall from the sky.
I lift my foot, and it slowly crushes the snow beneath it, just like a giant would.
I begin to feel as if I'm walking on a cloud, everything light and fluffy.
Inhaling deeply, the aroma of freshly baked peanut brittle
And grandma's homemade chocolate chip cookies surround me.
Christmas lights shine everywhere, like traffic lights in New York City.
"Jingle Bells," "Winter Wonderland," "Santa Claus is Coming to Town,"
They all blare through windows of homes, just like your alarm clock with no off button.
This is winter, and even when it can seem too cold and dreadful, this is the season I love!

Emily Schultz, Grade 6
Bednarcik Jr High School, IL

Halloween

H owling from the wolves as they creep up in the night, waiting to strike.
A t last it's the night to play as people put our their hay and candy.
L ots and lots of candy for the scariest and funniest costumes around the block.
L oading your bag with different types of candy.
O ptimistic — don't be too optimistic about getting the candy you want.
W e will go house to house around the block to get the best candy around.
E scape, entering this jail cell is extraordinarily confusing, as I explore the jail cell, expecting a way out!
E verything is like a black room outside.
N oooo! Halloween is almost over — you must get every house!

Collin McUmber, Grade 6
Three Rivers School, IL

Josh Lehman

J ust the only boy in the family
O n the A and B honor roll
S o smart
H ides very well

L ooks good
E asy to beat on soaker
H ome a lot
M ost important player on basketball
A hard thrower
N eat handwriting

Josh Lehman, Grade 5
North Knox West Intermediate/Elementary School, IN

Morning

As I lay in bed awake
Mom is yelling GET OUT OF BED
I go down and eat my breakfast
Another day goes on
I head back up and brush my hair and teeth
I 'm yelling downstairs DO YOU KNOW WHERE MY HOMEWORK IS?
Found it I shove it into my backpack and grab my bag
Another day goes on
Run out to the bus
Yelling STOP as it was driving off
It stopped finally and we got on

Bethany Keasling, Grade 5
North Knox West Intermediate/Elementary School, IN

I Am Thankful for Dance

I like to move my feet.
When I dance, I dance to the funky beat.
I get excited when I hear music.
I have talent and I will use it.
I want to show you how I groove.
I want to show you how I move.
Shake your shoulders,
Sway your hips,
Turn around, do a flip.
Then you repeat the moves and you have a creation.
Now you are a dancing sensation.

Sadahri Wright, Grade 5
Walker Elementary School, IL

Candy

Candy
tasty, sugary
tempting, chewing, craving
delicious, gushy
creamy, healthy
slurping, sipping, guzzling
liquid, favorite
Milk

Stefanie Wood, Grade 5
Washington Township Elementary School, IN

Car

My life is a car

My dad is the engine that
starts the car;
He can be the fastest and
can be the slowest.

My mom is the steering wheel
she helps my dad drive through
his life, even if she irritates him.

My older sister is like the
front lights that let the
car see. She always helps
me and looks out for me.

My younger sister is like
the seats, she is always
there to talk if you need her.

My little sister is the lights
inside when you turn her on
she has a smile and hugs you,
and when you turn her off she
is still smiling.

Ana Garcia, Grade 6
Florence Nightingale Elementary School, IL

Vacation

One day in my summer break
I went on vacation to Tennessee
But instead I said goodness sake!
I thought we were going the other way,
The other way is Maine
Also with the possibility of driving all day.

Having to get some gas,
We stopped so my dog (Buddy) could play.
Then I felt like I had a free pass,
When I saw a baseball field in the distance
My family went over and played awhile
Back on the road we went, in an orderly style
It felt like we only went 1 mile
Until we finally got there.

I couldn't believe we were staying here
So I fell into a stare.
We went swimming, played baseball, threw a football
And had a ball in a 2 days' time,
Then we had to go home on the tiring ride.

I couldn't wait for the next time,
It was fun, I had a blast!

Sam Pinckert, Grade 6
Nancy Hanks Elementary School, IN

My Animal Is a Horse

My favorite animal is a horse.
My horse's name is Rose.
I train her every single day.
She has a sensitive nose.

My horse is so cute.
She is black and gray.
My family loves her.
I play with her all day.

She makes a wonderful noise.
My brothers and sisters ride her all afternoon.
She runs so fast and free.
At night, she stares at the moon.

Jadzia Augustin, Grade 4
St Matthias School, IL

School

I wake up at 7:00 A.M.
I then get ready to go to school.
There we have to play by the rules.
It's fun talking to my friends.
I hope it never ends.

We get packed with homework.
I work till my hand hurts.
When someone gets in trouble everyone smirks.

This is the place I go to learn.
My grades are what I've earned.
So I go and stay.
I do it every day.

Luke Grant, Grade 5
Northern Heights Elementary School, IN

Snow

I always like the snow,
because it has a white glow.
I like having a snowball fight,
and the forts we build get great height.

I built a snowman big and tall,
it looks just like the one outside the mall.
A red beanie hat and a carrot nose,
sticks for arms and all it's missing are its toes.

I sled on the snow, and slide down the hill,
I slid so far I ended up at Goodwill.
The snow was like ice, and had such a glare,
I slid by my brother, just missing him by a hair.

Carson Forrester, Grade 5
Northern Heights Elementary School, IN

Leaves

Leaves
colorful, vibrant
falling, blowing, drifting
sad, seeing them fall
Maple

Jack Landmesser, Grade 4
Frank H Hammond Elementary School, IN

Hugs and Cuddles

According to me…
Hugs and cuddles are…
Beyond the best warmth that you could get.
Around you are arms bearing warmth and love.
Then you smile and you just can't let go!

Mariah Schaefer, Grade 5
Northern Heights Elementary School, IN

Jed

There once was a man named Jed,
"I can do anything," he said.
So he jumped off a tree,
And broke his knee,
And wound up in the hospital bed.

Skyler LaPrad, Grade 5
Washington Township Elementary School, IN

Sam's Shopping

There once was a guy named Sam,
Who went out to buy some ham.
But when he got there,
Oh no, he despaired,
All he found was a big leg of lamb.

Everett Mitchell, Grade 5
Washington Township Elementary School, IN

Blake

My best friend is Blake.
He is as skinny as a rake.
His mom's name is Heather.
Her hair looks like a feather.
Blake loves Dale Hollow Lake!

Austin Paddock, Grade 6
Alexandria-Monroe Intermediate School, IN

Battle

Some people call it war.
Since near the beginning of man it has raged.
Will there ever be world peace.
Some things like a gun fired, or a ship engaged.

Charles Kirgan, Grade 5
North Knox West Intermediate/Elementary School, IN

Shiloh

Out of the about 30 pets I've had
a praying mantis, some fish, a ladybug, a katydid,
my favorite one is Shiloh, my dog.
She knows how to play rough
if you get her hyper.
She is the most energetic creature
I've ever had.
If she sees a dog,
a cat,
a squirrel,
a rabbit,
a deer,
anything at all,
she goes wild
Shiloh is my favorite pet,
my favorite out of the 30 I've had.
Siddharth Das, Grade 5
Stanley Clark School, IN

Car

My family is a car.

My father is the wheels.
He keeps my family going.

My mother is the engine.
She is the heart of the family.

My little sister is the radio.
She never stops talking.

My older sister is the steering wheel.
She's the one that leads us to the right directions.

My other older sister is the seat belt.
She always keeps me safe.
Ruperto Morales, Grade 6
Florence Nightingale Elementary School, IL

Blue

Blue,
The color of the beautiful ocean's waves
Water
The crystal clear liquid that looks so blue
Zircon
The blue gem that sparkles in the silver moonlight
Sky
What we look up at and see clouds in
Rainbow
The blue streak in the rainbow that is so hard to see
Flower
The beautiful deep blue petals that have rain drops on them
Earth
The blue oceans rest on what can become more peaceful
Anjali Mirmira, Grade 5
The Orchard School, IN

Christmas Tree

My family is a Christmas tree.

My mother is the star on the top;
her light is bright which shines at night.
When they see her at first sight they think she's quite nice.
My brother is a candy cane,
he is very sweet, but dangerous at the teeth.
My sister is a bow,
very stylish, she hates to be ugly,
but loves to glow.
My other sister is an ornament,
she is plain, but she is the most important part in the tree.
My dad is the tree,
he is the main part because he holds us all together,
also he runs the family,
he's the one who makes us a family.
Guadalupe Tolentino, Grade 6
Florence Nightingale Elementary School, IL

It's Never too Late

The wind blows beneath the tree
In the pretty, autumn glow
Where it will end up or go
Only my Maker knows
God our Heavenly father
Has come to set us free
He died for us so we could be
With Him eternally
It is never too late or too early
For all of us to say,
"Jesus, please forgive me,
For all my sinful ways"
No matter how many times you have fallen short
Or maybe gotten lost,
He paid every single bit
All upon the cross
Reagan Shourds, Grade 6
Christian Academy of Indiana, IN

Prejudice Is Evil Dictatorship

Prejudice is the hatred some people share,
It can be found anywhere.
Prejudice is why some people fight,
Over something as simple as another's religious right.

Prejudice is an unfavorable thought,
Many people hated what the Catholics taught.
In 2007, New York Times called them beasts,
Even today the prejudice has not ceased.

There are two easy ways to make this stop,
These things will put you and others on top.
Be yourself and kind to others,
Treat them as if they were your sisters and brothers.
Lauren Duckett, Eli Schabel, and Lucas Engels, Grade 6
Tri-West Middle School, IN

Haze

H appy every day
A wesome
Z estful I am full of zest
E xciting all the time

Haze Kidd, Grade 5
St Michael School, IN

Friend

Friend
Kind, adoring
Always cheering me on.
Kinzey

Kaya Schrum, Grade 4
Van Rensselaer Elementary School, IN

Ice Cream

Who invented ice cream
A genius it would seem
To create such a scrumptious dream
Of yummy, delicious ice cream!

Lily Pan, Grade 5
Ranch View Elementary School, IL

The Great Catch

He caught the ball
He looked like a doll
He went to fetch
He made the catch

Brayden Souerdike, Grade 4
Shoals Elementary School, IN

Ode to Grandma Nelson

I remember you all the time.
I wish I could have known you longer.
I miss you so much.
I see you in my dreams all the time.

McKayla Nelson, Grade 5
Northern Heights Elementary School, IN

Florida

The sand on my feet
The warmth of the sun
Under the sparkling reef
I go on the beach to have some fun

Alivia Pease, Grade 5
Northern Heights Elementary School, IN

I Am from the Sun and Moon

I am from the sun so bright.
I make the stars shine at night.
I like to make the stars have a fight,
and have a star concert at night.

Abi Tolson, Grade 6
Knox Community Middle School, IN

A Different Perspective

Sometimes you wonder
Where, when, and how
When you're sitting in your bed
After your parents say goodnight
You think and think and think
You think into a deep space
A reality of yourself that you are not entirely aware of
You think about who you are
What's your purpose
Where you come from
With your whole life in one balance
Then you go to the top of a building
You jump
You're falling and see your whole life like a home theater
And right when you're about to splat
You wake up
And you're grasping to the side of your bed
And you think some more
Your brain falling into a different cosmos
You mull over the fact of everything small is a version of something big
Then you fall asleep

Carl Meyer, Grade 5
The Orchard School, IN

Fall

A million lives children and adults alike
Released into a world to live on the world
A war inside itself replaying the lives old and new
The final ballroom dance before the giants come to take away their lives
The battle ground is set
Weapons among the forces of nature
Some dance perfectly and some slip but the moment they fear is upon
Them
The bombs fall and come to contact with the dance floor
They dig themselves into the blocks of
Ice
In years to
Come
He will grow new lives for those who have
Fallen
But two forces battle on the south and the north the U.S. and Great Britain and the Rebels
Duking it out and all of a sudden
A bang a slice a death
Then a blanket of nothingness falls
And there is and another
Fall of the rainbow

Nathan Hu, Grade 5
Highlands Elementary School, IL

I Love You the Bluest

I love you the bluest,
I love you the color of waterfalls when it slides off and hits the rocks,
I love you the color of the sky and when it has clouds in it,
The blue of blueberries, the blue bugs over the pond, the blue square on the American flag.

Letitia VanWienen, Grade 5
Van Rensselaer Elementary School, IN

Ribbons of Pink

It is a horrible disease
That longs for a cure
One day that cure will come
But today is not that day

Like spring after winter
The frost will go away
Shoots will find their way through the dirt
But until then we can only hope

Hope until that day comes
Where no one will have to go through
What my mom did
But for now it is crowned with a ribbon
That is like a flower in winter
A surprise to everyone
Ashley Tyburski, Grade 6
Bednarcik Jr High School, IL

My Dog

My dog likes to have fun
He likes to jump
He likes to bark
He likes to bump

My dog likes to eat
He eats so much
Like bones, and treats
Meats and sweets
He likes to eat lunch.

My dog is a boxer
He is always sleepy
He likes to be loved
I love him deeply
He's my best friend.
Isaac Navar, Grade 4
St Matthias/Transfiguration School, IL

Colors, Colors, Colors

Green is the color of the grass.
Clear is the color of pretty glass.

Blue is the color of the water.
Gray is the color of a fly swatter.

Black is the color of the night.
White is the color of an overbite.

Red is the color of my blood.
Brown is the color of yucky mud.

Yellow is the color of the shiny sun.
Tan is the color of a hot dog bun.
Jackie Ludwig, Grade 5
Forreston Grade School, IL

Inventors

People so great,
And at an alarming rate,
They make amazing things,
What're their names?
Don't you know,
People so great,
Who make terrific things,
Have one and only one name,
That name is Inventors!
Nancy Liu, Grade 5
Ranch View Elementary School, IL

New Year's Day

It is so fun on New Year's Day
I will watch fireworks in every way
We all wait till the sun goes down
The fireworks go off and we yell a sound

I always have so much fun
Then I wait and sit in the sun
I never have anything bad to say
On this fun and exciting New Year's Day
Samantha Whitehead, Grade 4
Summit Elementary School, IL

Things

The world is full of things
Quite amazing things in fact
I never get them right in tact
Sometimes they're big
Sometimes they're small
But sometimes they end up with all
The world is full of amazing things
Ice cream soda, cherry dream
The world is full of wonderful things
Madison Wilkeson, Grade 5
Good Shepherd Montessori School, IN

Summer Breeze

It rises with the heat
It's faster than a beat.
Swooshing with pleasant sound,
Twirling, not earthbound.
In the land of ultimate freedom.
Alex Nagel, Grade 4
McKenzie Elementary School, IL

Lady Rox Games

W is for whatever you never say
O ffense but not always
L ost but that is ok
V iolence basketball is
E rror dang we lost
S trong you will become
Abbi Haviland, Grade 4
Shoals Elementary School, IN

Santa's Sleigh Ride

Merry Christmas! Merry Christmas!
Merry Christmas to all!
Bring joy and laughter to your family.
Bring joy when you sing carols,
Have fun in the snow with friends.
Say hi to aunts and uncles
don't forget your cousins!
Be sure to wear footies when
you go to bed 'cause
your toes will be chilly!
Don't forget Santa or Saint
Nicholas you might call.
Sleighs soaring through the midnight sky
Santa saying, "Ho, ho, ho!"
Merry Christmas! Merry Christmas!
Rachel Bond, Grade 4
Copeland Manor Elementary School, IL

5th Grade Teachers

Mrs. Simmon's class is super great.
Just hope I don't end up late.
Spelling and writing is in this class.
At recess we play on the grass.

Mr. Geiger teaches math.
He's teaching us the path.
He taught us to add decimals.
Science is what he teaches
And we learned about new animals.

Mrs. Bretzman teaches us reading.
They give us bandages when we're bleeding.
She also teaches social studies.
We go to class to see our buddies.
Colin Temple, Grade 5
Northern Heights Elementary School, IN

Birds

Soaring up high,
Swooping down low
Whoosh, whoosh, whoosh

Pecking on the ground,
Bathing in the fountain
Splash, splash, splash

Nesting in the trees
Singing a sweet tune
Tweet, tweet, tweet

No matter the color or size
I love them all big or small!
Birds, Birds, Birds!
Ashlyn Longanecker, Grade 5
Manchester Intermediate School, IN

The Truth

Nature is a signal,
for everyone to see,
How much the One who made it,
loves you and loves me.
The puffy white clouds,
the dark miraculous sky,
shows how much that He can do,
with just a blink of His eye.
The words of His mouth have spoken,
us into life,
that we might live for His glory,
and see the true light.
Though we are weak and small,
an insignificant man,
we serve a greater purpose,
to show who's the Shepherd and the Lamb.
The Greater One above us,
knows what path to take,
though the path is narrow,
it leads to no fiery lake.

Hannah Powell, Grade 6
Christian Academy of Indiana, IN

Cycle of Friendship

Friends are fun
They care for you
But when they leave
You're sad
They move away
Leave
Or just go to camp
For a little
You will cry
Then get over it
You'll find someone new
And ask them, "Wanna be my friend?"
They'll say, "Yes!"
You'll get older
And move away yourself
They'll be sad
Live their life
And find a new best friend
But when your time comes
Your cycle of friendship ends

Katelin Ballou, Grade 6
Holy Family Catholic School, IL

Tom

Happy birthday Tom!
All twelve candles are ready
Please blow them out, Tom!

Tommy Longo, Grade 5
Forreston Grade School, IL

Rose

Scarlet like the sun
Smell of beauty in the air
Elegant and smooth.

Leah Harvey, Grade 5
Van Rensselaer Elementary School, IN

Puppy

Puppy
Jumping, running, licking
House, cage, outside, school
Sniffing, playing, barking
Friendly, cuddly
Puppy

Karen Kahles, Grade 5
St Michael School, IN

Just Think

Just think
If no one died
We would be crammed
And squished
Just think
If we were all the same
There would be no difference between you and me
We would be just plain; we would be boring
Just think
If the world didn't have people,
The world would be an empty place
No you
No me

Kate Seger, Grade 5
The Orchard School, IN

Index